China Ethnic Statistical Yearbook 2020

Rongxing Guo

China Ethnic Statistical Yearbook 2020

palgrave
macmillan

Rongxing Guo
Capital University of Economics and Business
Beijing, China

ISBN 978-3-030-49023-2 ISBN 978-3-030-49024-9 (eBook)
https://doi.org/10.1007/978-3-030-49024-9

Cover illustration: ZUMA Press, Inc. / Alamy Stock Photo

This Palgrave Macmillan imprint is published by the registered company Springer Nature Switzerland AG.
The registered company address is: Gewerbestrasse 11, 6330 Cham, Switzerland

Preface

The objective of this book is to collect and estimate a set of data on the socioeconomic situations of China's 56 ethnic groups.

Although the majority of China's population is of the Han nationality (which accounts for more than 90% of China's population), the non-Han ethnic groups have a population of more than 100 million. China has officially identified, except for other unknown ethnic groups and foreigners with Chinese citizenship, 55 ethnic minorities. In addition, ethnic minorities vary greatly in size. With a population of more than 15 million, the Zhuang are the largest ethnic minority, and the Lhoba, with a population of only about three thousand, the smallest.

China's ethnic diversity has resulted in a special socioeconomic landscape for China itself. However, till present, a complete socioeconomic picture of China's ethnic groups—especially of its smallest ethnic minorities—still remains unclear. How different have been China's ethnic groups in every sphere of daily life and economic development during China's fast transition period? In order to answer these questions, we need a detailed and comparable set of data for each of China's ethnic groups.

There has not been any official statement of China's socioeconomic development from a multi-ethnic dimension. The only official data released can be found in *China Ethnic Statistical Yearbook* (released by the State Ethnic Affairs Commission of the People's Republic of China since 1994). However, as the above Yearbook has only reported the socioeconomic statistics for the minority-based autonomous areas, a complete set of China's multi-ethnic data cannot be derived from it. For instance, only five provincial level minority-based autonomous regions (i.e., Inner Mongolia, Tibet, the Zhuang-based Guangxi, the Hui-based Ningxia, and the Uygur-based Xinjiang) and 30 ethnic minority autonomous divisions at prefecture-level and 120 ethnic minority autonomous divisions at county-level—all of the latter cover China's 16 provinces, three autonomous regions and one municipality directly under the central government—are included in this Yearbook. The entire minority-based autonomous areas, however, account for only less than a half of their total population of the ethnic minorities (see Appendix C for details). This means that the Han Chinese has now become the majority of many, if not all of the above minority-based autonomous areas. In addition, still quite a few of non-Han minority people are found in the Han-based administrative areas (see Appendix B for details)—the breakdowns of their socioeconomic data have never been mentioned in China's existing statistical reports.

Another reason why the data of an ethnic minority autonomous area should not represent as those of that ethnic people stems from two facts in China: first, there usually exist two or more ethnic peoples in each ethnic minority autonomous area; second, each ethnic group is usually included geographically in at least two administrative divisions (provinces, prefectures, counties and others). For instance, according to the composition of population, the Mongol people have now become a true minority in Inner Mongolia, hometown of the ethnic Mongols, as a result of the large-scale Han immigration during the twentieth century.

Organization of This Book

This book sets out to present, in an easy-to-use format, a broad collection of social and economic indicators on China's 56 ethnic groups. It is a resource book that profiles the general social and economic situations for each of these ethnic groups.

In this book, data are presented on an ethnic group-by-ethnic group basis, and the ethnic groups are ordered alphabetically, from the Achang to the Zhuang. Though most of the data are as of 2018—the latest year when our research was conducted, we have also provided some historical data for a few of indicators and have spent the past years developing these data sets and indicators for analysis. This is intended to help readers to conduct time-series comparisons and analyses.

This book is organized as follows.

This book focuses on the following topics: population growth and structural changes (Chap. 1); economic growth and expenditure (Chap. 2); employment and income distribution (Chap. 3); living conditions and the means of livelihood (Chap. 4); agricultural production and other rural activities (Chap. 5); education, science and technological progress (Chap. 6); health care and social security (Chap. 7); and entertainment and other cultural activities (Chap. 8).

There are four appendices in this book. Appendix A presents a short introduction to each of China's 56 ethnic groups. Appendix B provides ethnic populations of 31 provinces, autonomous regions and municipalities and of China as a whole, which are derived from China's two recent national population censuses (2000 and 2010). In Appendix C the administrative and demographic statistics of the minority-based administrative divisions at different levels (including autonomous regions as the first-class administrative divisions; cities, prefectures and autonomous prefectures as the second-class administrative divisions; and cities, counties, autonomous counties and banners (*Qi*) as the third-class administrative divisions) are presented. Appendix D provides selected indicators on the social and economic development of ethnic minority autonomous areas. At last, in Appendix E, using the multiethnic statistical data, we provide an in-depth quantitative analysis of the Chinese spatial economy.

At the end of this book, some notes on the data as well as the main statistical indicators are provided.

Lake Yanqi, Huairou, Beijing
Springer 2020

Rongxing Guo

A List of 56 Ethnic Groups in China

Name	Chinese name	Name in Pinyin	Other name(s)	Population share (%)
Achang	阿昌族	Āchāng Zú		0.0030
Bai	白族	Bái Zú		0.1451
Baonan	保安族	Bǎo'ān Zú	Bao'an, Bonan	0.0015
Blang	布朗族	Bùlǎng Zú	Bulang	0.0090
Bouyei	布依族	Bùyī Zú	Buyi, Buoyei, Buoyi	0.2153
Dai	傣族	Dǎi Zú		0.0946
Daur	达斡尔族	Dáwò'ěr Zú		0.0099
Deang	德昂族	Dé'áng Zú	Benglong	0.0015
Derung	独龙族	Dúlóng Zú	Drung, Dulong	0.0005
Dong	侗族	Dòng Zú		0.2161
Dongxiang	东乡族	Dōngxiāng Zú		0.0466
Ewenki	鄂温克族	Èwēnkè Zú		0.0023
Gaoshan	高山族	Gāoshān Zú	Taiwan aborigines	0.0003
Gelao	仡佬族	Gēlǎo Zú	Gelo	0.0413
Han	汉族	Hàn Zú		91.6474
Hani	哈尼族	Hāní Zú	Akha	0.1246
Hezhen	赫哲族	Hèzhé Zú	Hezhe	0.0004
Hui	回族	Huí Zú		0.7943
Jing	京族	Jīng Zú	Gin	0.0021
Jingpo	景颇族	Jǐngpō Zú		0.0111
Jino	基诺族	Jīnuò Zú	Juno	0.0017
Kazak	哈萨克族	Hāsàkè Zú	Kazakh	0.1097
Kirgiz	柯尔克孜族	Kē'ěrkèzī Zú		0.0140

(*continued*)

(continued)

Name	Chinese name	Name in Pinyin	Other name(s)	Population share (%)
Korean	朝鲜族	Cháoxiǎn Zú		0.1374
Lahu	拉祜族	Lāhù Zú		0.0365
Lhoba	珞巴族	Luòbā Zú	Luoba	0.0003
Li	黎族	Lí Zú		0.1098
Lisu	傈僳族	Lìsù Zú		0.0527
Manchu	满族	Mǎn Zú	Man	0.7794
Maonan	毛南族	Máonán Zú		0.0076
Miao	苗族	Miáo Zú	Hmong, Xiong, Hmu	0.7072
Monba	门巴族	Ménbā Zú	Menba	0.0008
Mongol	蒙古族	Měnggǔ Zú	Mongolian	0.4488
Mulao	仫佬族	Mùlǎo Zú	Mulam	0.0162
Naxi	纳西族	Nàxī Zú	Nakhi	0.0245
Nu	怒族	Nù Zú		0.0028
Oroqen	鄂伦春族	Èlúnchūn Zú	Oroqin	0.0006
Pumi	普米族	Pǔmǐ Zú	Primi	0.0032
Qiang	羌族	Qiāng Zú		0.0232
Russian	俄罗斯族	Éluósī Zú		0.0012
Salar	撒拉族	Sālā Zú		0.0098
She	畲族	Shē Zú	Shanha	0.0532
Shui	水族	Shuǐ Zú		0.0309
Tajik	塔吉克族	Tǎjíkè Zú		0.0038
Tatar	塔塔尔族	Tǎtǎ'ěr Zú	Dada	0.0003
Tibetan	藏族	Zàng Zú	Zang	0.4713
Tu	土族	Tǔ Zú	Monguor	0.0217
Tujia	土家族	Tǔjiā Zú		0.6268
Uyghur	维吾尔族	Wéiwú'ěr Zú	Uigur	0.7555
Uzbek	乌孜别克族	Wūzībiékè Zú	Ozbek	0.0008
Va	佤族	Wǎ Zú	Wa	0.0322
Xibe	锡伯族	Xībó Zú	Sibe	0.0143
Yao	瑶族	Yáo Zú		0.2098
Yi	彝族	Yí Zú		0.6538
Yugur	裕固族	Yùgù Zú	Yugu	0.0011
Zhuang	壮族	Zhuàng Zú		1.2700

Notes: (1) Population shares are based on the Sixth National Populaiton Census of the People's Republic of China that was conducted on November 1, 2010. (2) See Appendix A for a historical and geographical description of each of the 56 ethnic groups

Maps

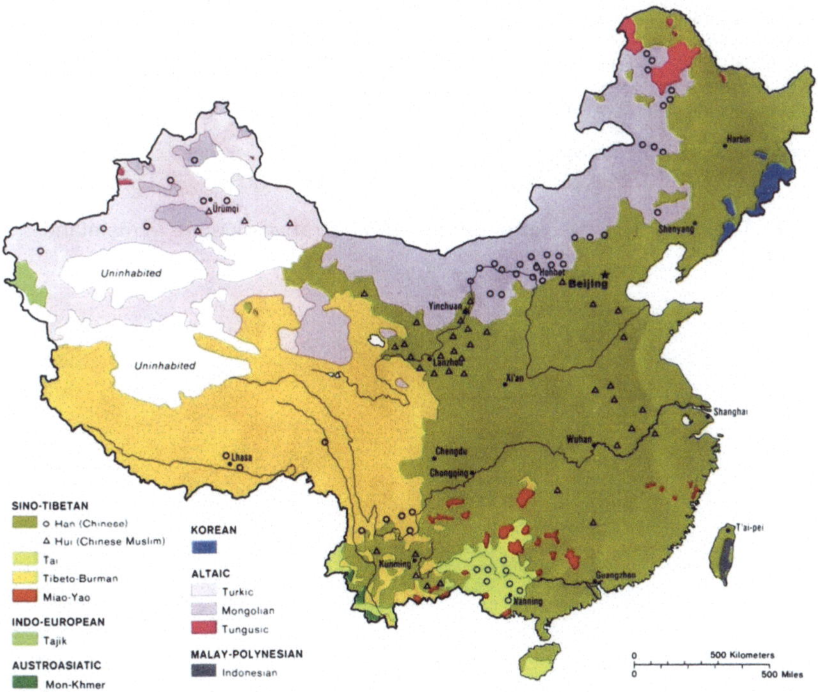

Map 1 The spatial distribution of China's ethno-linguistic groups. *Source*: Courtesy of the University of Texas Libraries, University of Texas at Austin

Map 2 The minority-based autonomous administrative divisions in mainland China

Acknowledgments

It is a challenging task for us to prepare the statistical data that cover various fields of all ethnic groups in China. The major obstacle is that China has not established any ethnically-oriented statistical reporting or surveying system. During the process when this research was conducted, we have received generous help from the following organizations:

- Association of Power Generation Enterprises of China (APGE)
- China Mobile Corp. Ltd.
- China Telecom Corp. Ltd.
- China Unicom Corp. Ltd.
- Department of Financial Management, Ministry of Culture (MOC)
- Department of Financial Management, State Administration of Broadcasting, Film and Television (SABFT)
- Department of Financial Management, General Administration of Press and Publication (GAPP)
- Department of Planning and Development, Ministry of Education (MOE)
- Department of Population and Employment Statistics of the National Bureau of Statistics (NBS)
- Department of Urban Socio-economic Survey, National Bureau of Statistics (NBS)
- Finance Department, General Administration of Sport (GAS)

- Information Center, Ministry of Health (MOH)
- Inspection and Quarantine and State Intellectual Property Office (IQSIPO)
- Ministry of Health (MOH)
- Rural Socio-economic Survey Organization, National Bureau of Statistics (NBS)
- State Administration for Industry and Commerce (SAIC)
- General Administration of Press and Publication (GAPP)

This book has also benefited from the skilful assistance from many individuals. They are (in alphabetical order by family name): Ba Yunhong, Bian Lihua, Chang Wenli, Cui Ruchun, Deng Weiping, Ding Yong, Du Weiqun, Du Yan, Guan Xiaojing, Guo Dong, Guo Dong, Guo Dong, Hao Shenglong, Hou Rui, Ju Chuanling, Li Jiao, Li Junbo, Li Suoqiang, Liang Erwei, Liu Huiping, Long Ling, Lu Shan, Luan Jinhui, Luo Weihua Fan Xiaoyu, Qian Chunlin, Que Xiaoqing, Sheng Laiyun, Shi Faqi, Shi Yihua, Song Shaoying, Tan Xiaomei, Tang Ping, Wan Zhongbing, Wang Ping, Wang Qi, Wang Yixuan, Wu You, Xiao Li, Xu Lan, Yan Xianpu, Yang Hongjun, Ye Liqi, Yin Yi, Yu Hongwen, Zhang Huiying, Zhang Lei, Zhang Peng, Zhang Xin, Zhang Yanhua, Zhong Shouyang, and Zhu Hong

Last but not least, we are grateful to various anonymous reviewers whose comments and suggestions have helped us refine many parts of this research. However, all views and errors in this book certainly are those of the respective authors only and not necessarily those of the book's editors and of the organizations and individuals who provided the original data.

Notes on the Text

The ethnic groups and their socioeconomic indicators reported in this book are only based on the geographical scope of mainland China. National-level data in this book do not include those of Hong Kong or Macau. The classification of ethnic groups is based on China's official criteria, which sometimes may not satisfy academia. For example, the Pumi are also called Mongolians or Naxi, depending on where they live; and most of the Yao on Hainan island are now classified as Miao.

Unless stated otherwise, all data reported in this book are as of 2018 and indicators in monetary values are measured at current prices, while their time-series indices are calculated at constant prices. The data on a selected set of social and economic indicators of China's 56 ethnic groups for 2005, 2010, 2011 and 2014 can be found in *China's Ethnic Minorities—Social and Economic Indicators* (Routledge, London, 2013), *China's Multicultural Economies—Social and Economic Indicators* (Springer, New York, 2013), *Multicultural China—A Statistical Yearbook* (Springer, Berlin, 2015), and *China Ethnic Statistical Yearbook 2016* (Springer, Berlin, 2017), respectively. In addition, the following notes are also of usefulness for those who want to apply the data reported in this book:

1. Data have been adjusted for all those Han majority who changed to ethnic minority (shaoshu minzu) status in the 1980s.
2. Unless states otherwise, all data reported in this book are compiled and estimated based on the regional and local data gathered from a variety of sources. (Details about the estimation methodology can be found in *China's Multicultural Economies—Social and Economic Indicators* (Springer, New York, 2013, pp. 165–8); or *China's Ethnic Minorities—Social and Economic Indicators* (Routledge, London, 2013, pp. 208–10).
3. Data may be overestimated if an ethnic group is mainly located in geographically remote and economically poor areas (since geographically remote areas usually have less attractions to statistical officers who either had little professional ethics or wanted to reduce the costs of data collection).
4. Statistical discrepancies due to rounding are not adjusted in the book.
5. Blank space indicates that the figure is not large enough to be measured with the smallest unit in the table, or data are unknown or are not available.
6. Due to reasons that are beyond our control, estimation errors may exist in the indicators reported in the book.

While the definitions of some of the terms and statistical indicators that have been used in this book are consistent with those that have adopted by various international organizations (including the International Monetary Fund and the World Bank), many others are only defined with Chinese characteristics. The explanations of all the terms shown in the following are mainly based on the official definitions provided by the National Bureau of Statistics of China.[1]

Average Real Wage refers to the average wage of employed persons after removing the effects of the price changes.

Average Wage refers to the average per capita wage in money terms during a certain period of time for employed persons. It shows the general level of wage income of staff and worker during a certain period of time, one major indicator to reflect the wage level.

[1] More details are available in Chinese at http://www.stats.gov.cn/tjsj/zbjs/, accessed on 2016-08-18.

Average Wage Index refers to the ratio of average wage of employed persons the reference period to that at the base period, which reflects the relative increasing or decreasing level of real wage of employed persons at the different period.

Birth Rate (or Crude Birth Rate) refers to the ratio of the number of births to the average population (or mid-period population) during a certain period of time (usually a year), expressed in ‰. Birth rate in the chapter refers to annual birth rate. Number of births refers to live births, i.e. when a baby has breathed or showed any vital phenomena regardless of the length of pregnancy. Annual average population is the average of the number of population at the beginning of the year and that at the end of the year. Sometimes it is substituted by the mid-year population.

Budgetary Fund for Education refers to education funding that is planned to be allocated to various schools and education institutions by central and local financial departments at various levels within the reference year, which is within the State budgetary expenditure, including: appropriated funds for education, for science and research, for capital construction and others.

Business Volume of Post and Telecommunications refers to the total amount of postal and telecommunication services, expressed in value terms, provided by the post and telecommunications departments for society. This indicator reflects the overall results of development of postal and telecommunication services. It can be classified as postal services and telecommunication services. Business volume of post and telecommunications is the sum of each service in kind multiplying with its correspondent unit price (constant price).

Cash Income refers to income received by rural households and their members in the form of cash during the reference period. It is classified, by source of income, into income from wages and salaries, cash income from household operations, income from properties and income from transfers.

Certified Grade Athletes refer to those who are awarded the title of athletes through assessment. The titles rank from high to low as: international level athletes, national level athletes, first grade athletes, second grade athletes and third grade athletes.

Children Dependency Ratio also called children dependency coefficient, refers to the ratio of the children population to the working-age population, expressed in %. It describes the number of children population that every 100 people at working ages will take care of.

Consumer Price Index reflect the trend and degree of changes in prices of consumer goods and services purchased by urban and rural households during a given period. China's nation-wide consumer price indices are obtained by combining the consumer price indices of both urban and rural households. The Indices enable the observation and analysis of the degree of impact of the changes in the prices of retailed goods and services on the actual living expenses of urban and rural residents.

Consumption Expenditure of Urban Households in Cash refers to total cash expenditure of households for consumption in daily life, including expenditure on the eight categories of food; clothing; housing; household appliances; transport and communications; education, cultural and recreational activities and medical care.

Cotton Output refers to cotton production in the whole country including cotton planted in spring and in autumn. Output is measured as the weight of ginned cotton. Ceiba is not included.

Currency refers to currency that is in circulation in the market, including local and foreign currencies.

Death Rate (or Crude Death Rate) refers to the ratio of the number of deaths to the average population (or mid-period population) during a certain period of time (usually a year), expressed in ‰. Death rate refers to annual death rate.

Designs refer to the aesthetics and industrially applicable new designs for the shape, pattern and color of the product, or their combinations. This indicator reflects the appearance design achievements with independent intellectual property.

Disposable Income refers to the actual income at the disposal of members of the households which can be used for final consumption, other non-compulsory expenditure and savings. This equals to total income minus income tax, personal contribution to social security and subsidy for keeping diaries in being a sample household.

Electricity Consumption per Unit of GDP refers to the electricity consumption per unit of Gross Domestic Product (GDP) in the same reference period.

Employed Persons refer to persons aged 16 and over who are engaged in gainful employment and thus receive remuneration payment or earn business income. This indicator reflects the actual utilization of total labor force during a certain period of time and is often used for the research on China's economic situation and national power.

Energy Consumption per Unit of GDP refers to the energy consumption per unit of Gross Domestic Product (GDP) in the same reference period.

Energy Consumption per Unit of Industrial Value-added refers to the energy consumption per unit of industrial value-added in a country or region in the same reference period.

Expenditure of basic pension insurance program refer to payment made on pensions and funeral subsidies to those retired and resigned people covered in pension insurance programs according to related national policies on scope and standard of expenditure.

Final Consumption Expenditure refers to the total expenditure of resident units for purchases of goods and services from both the domestic economic territory and abroad to meet the needs of material, cultural and spiritual life. It does not include the expenditure of non-resident units on consumption in the economic territory of the country. The final consumption expenditure is broken down into household consumption expenditure and government consumption expenditure.

Floating population is a terminology used to describe a group of people who reside in a given population for a certain amount of time and for various reasons, but are not generally considered part of the official census count.

Government Appropriation for Education refers to State budgetary fund for education, taxes and fees collected by governments at all levels that are used for education purpose, education fund for enterprise-run schools, income from school-run enterprises, work-study program and social services that are used for education purpose.

Government Consumption Expenditure refers to the consumption expenditure spent for the provision of public services provided by the government to the whole country and the net expenditure on the goods and services provided by the government to households free of charge or at reduced prices. The former equals to the output value of the government services minus the value of operating income obtained by the government departments. The latter equals to the market value of the goods and services provided by the government free of charge or at reduced prices to the households minus the value received by the government from the households.

Government Expenditure refers to the distribution and use of the funds which the government finance has raised, so as to meet the needs of economic construction and various undertakings. Government expenditure is divided into central government expenditure and local government expenditure according to the different functions of the governments played in economic and social activities.

Government Revenue refers to income for the government finance through participating in the distribution of social products. The government revenue includes the following main items: (1) various tax revenues including domestic value added tax (VAT), domestic consumption tax, VAT and consumption tax from imports, VAT and consumption tax rebate for exports, business tax, corporate income tax, individual income tax, resource tax, city maintenance and construction tax, house property tax, stamp tax, urban land use tax, land appreciation tax, tax on vehicles and boat operation, ship tonnage tax, vehicle purchase tax, tariffs, farm land occupation tax, deed tax, and tobacco tax, etc.; and (2) non-tax revenue, including special program receipts, charge of administrative and institutional units, penalty receipts and others non-tax receipts.

Grain Output refers to the total output in the whole country including grains produced by state farms, collective units, rural households, as well as by farms affiliated to industrial and mining enterprises and other production units. Grain includes rice, wheat, corn, sorghum, millet and other miscellaneous grains as well as tubers and beans. Output of beans refers to dry beans without pods. The output of tubers (sweet potatoes and potatoes, not including taros and cassava) are converted into that of grain at the ratio of 5:1. Tubers supplied as vegetables (such as potatoes) in cities and suburbs are calculated as fresh vegetables and their output is not included in the output of grain. Output of all other grains refers to husked grain.

Gross Dependency Ratio refers to the ratio of non-working-age population to the working-age population, expressed in %. Describing in general the number of non-working-age population that every 100 people at working ages will take care of, this indicator reflects the basic relation between population and economic development from the demographic perspective. The gross dependency ratio is the sum of **Children Dependency Ratio** and **Old Dependency Ratio**.

Gross Domestic Product (GDP) refers to the final products at market prices produced by all resident units in a country during a certain period of time. Gross domestic product is expressed in three different perspectives, namely value, income, and products respectively. GDP in its value perspective refers to the balance of total value of all goods and services produced by all resident units during a certain period of time, minus the total value of input of goods and services of the nature of non-fixed assets; in other words, it is the sum of the value-added of all resident units. GDP from the perspective of income includes the primary income created by all resident units and distributed to resident and non-resident units. GDP from the perspective of products refers to the value of all goods and services for final demand by all resident units plus the net exports of goods and services during a given period of time. In the practice of national accounting, gross domestic product is calculated from three approaches, namely production approach, income approach and expenditure approach, which reflect gross domestic product and its composition from different angles.

Gross Output Value of Agriculture, Forestry, Animal Husbandry and Fishery refers to the total value of products of agriculture, forestry, animal husbandry and fishery, and total value of services in support of agriculture, forestry, animal husbandry and fishery activities. It reflects the total scale and results of agricultural production during a given period. The gross output value is obtained by multiplying the output of each product or by-product by its price, resulting in the output value of each single item. For a small number of products, annual output of which is not available or difficult to get due to the long production (growing) process involved, the output value is estimated through an indirect approach. The sum of output values of all products of agriculture, forestry, animal husbandry and fishery and services in support to those industries is then equal to the gross output value of agriculture.

Hospitals include general hospitals, hospitals specialized in traditional Chinese medicine, hospitals of integrated traditional Chinese and western medicine, nationalities hospitals, specialized hospitals and nursing hospitals.

Households refer to resident individuals or groups of resident individuals who share common living facilities, pool together entire or part of their income and properties for their common disposal, and share their housing, food and other consumer goods and services. All households together make up the sector of households.

Household Consumption Expenditure refers to the total expenditure of resident households on the final consumption of goods and services. In addition to the consumption of goods and services bought by the households directly with money, the household consumption expenditure also includes expenditure on goods and services obtained by the households in other ways, i.e. the so-called imputed consumption expenditure, which includes the following: (a) the goods and services provided to households by employers in the form of payment in kind and transfer in kind; (b) goods and services produced and consumed by the households themselves, in which the services refer to the owner-occupied housing and services offered by paid family employees; (c) financial intermediate services provided by financial institution.

Income from Household Operations refers to income by the rural households as units of production and operation. Operations by rural households are classified according to their economic activities namely agriculture, forestry, animal husbandry, fishery, manufacturing, construction, transportation, post and telecommunications, wholesale, retail and catering, social service, culture, education, health, and other household operations.

Income from Properties refers to the income received as returns by owners of financial assets or tangible non-productive assets by providing capitals or tangible non-productive assets to other institutional units.

Income from Transfers refers to the receipt by rural households and their members of goods, services, capital or rights of assets without giving or repaying accordingly, excluding capital provided to them for the formation of fixed assets. In general, it refers to all income received by rural households through redistribution.

Income from Wages and Salaries refers to income from labor earned by the members of rural households employed by other units or individuals.

Internet Users refer to the number of Chinese citizens aged 6 and over who use the Internet in the past six months.

Inventions refer to new technical proposals to the products or methods or their modifications. This is universal core indicator reflecting the technologies with independent intellectual property.

Investment in Fixed Asset refers to the urban investment in fixed assets under the previous statistical coverage plus project investments by rural enterprises and institutions.

Length of Highways refers to the actual length of highways at the end of reference period. It covers public roads running vehicles among cities, city and rural areas, township (villages), highways passing through streets at small cities and towns, length of bridges and tunnels, width of ferry piers. It does not include the length of streets in cities, dead end highways, the length of streets built for agricultural (forest) production and inside factories (mines). It can only be calculated with the actual mileage having been completed, checked and accepted or put into operation. If two or more highways go the same section of the way, the length of the section is only calculated for once.

Length of Railways in Operation refers to the total length of the trunk line for passenger and freight transportation in full operation or temporary operation.

Licensed Assistant Doctors refer to the medical workers who have obtained the licenses of qualified assistant doctors and are employed in medical treatment, disease prevention or healthcare institutions, excluding the licensed assistant doctors engaged in management job. The classification of licensed assistant doctors is clinician, Chinese medicine, dentist and public health.

Licensed Doctors refer to the medical workers who have obtained the licenses of qualified doctors and are employed in medical treatment, disease prevention or healthcare institutions, excluding the licensed doctors engaged in management job. The licensed doctors are divided into 4 categories: clinician, Chinese medicine physicians, dentist and public health physicians.

Life expectancy is the expected (in the statistical sense) number of years of life remaining at a given age. It is important to note that life expectancy is an average. In countries with high infant mortality rates, life expectancy at birth is highly sensitive to the rate of death in the first few years of life. For example, in a hypothetical stationary population in which half the population dies before the age of five, but everybody else dies at exactly 70 years old, the life expectancy at age zero will be about 37 years.

Medical and Health Care Institutions refer to the units which have been qualified the Certification of Health Care Institution by the administration of public health, or qualified the Certification of Corporate Unit by the civil affairs, administration for industry and commerce, commission office for public sector reform, and engaging in medical care, disease prevention and control, health supervision and inspection, medicine research and on-job training, etc., including: hospitals, health care institutions at grass-root level, specialized public health institutions, and other medical and health care institutions.

Natural Growth Rate of Population refers to the ratio of natural increase in population (number of births minus number of deaths) in a certain period of time (usually a year) to the average population (or mid-period population) of the same period, expressed in ‰.

Net Enrolment Ratio of Primary Schools refers to the proportion of school age children enrolled at schools to the total number of school age children both in and outside schools (including retarded children, but excluding blind, deaf and mute children).

Net Income of Rural Households refers to the total income of rural households from all sources minus all corresponding expenses (including household operation expenses, taxes and fees-depreciation of fixed assets for production, and gifts to rural relatives). Net income is mainly used as input for reinvestment in production and as consumption expenditure of the year, and also used for savings and non-compulsory expenses of various forms. "Per capita net income of farmers" is the level of net income averaged by population, reflecting the average income level of rural population in a given area.

New Rural Cooperative Medical System is proposed by the central government to finance farmers who face high medical costs for severe diseases or injuries. It is a multi-channel fundraising system composed by the government, collectives and individuals. Under this system, each farmer pays 20 yuan to join in the fund while the governments contribute 80 yuan (in 2008, this amount has increased to 120 yuan in 2010, 200 yuan in 2011, and 240 yuan in 2012) for each participant. By the end of 2009, about 833 million rural residents had joined in the system, accounting for more than 90 percent of the rural population.

Old Dependency Ratio also called old dependency coefficient, refers to the ratio of the elderly population to the working-age population, expressed in %. It describes the number of the elderly population that every 100 people at working ages will take care of. Old dependency ratio is one of the indicators reflecting the social implication of population aging from the economic perspective.

Output of Oil-bearing Crops refers to the total production of oil-bearing crops of various kinds, including peanuts (dry, in shell), rapeseeds, sesame, sunflower seeds, flax seeds, and other oil-bearing crops. Soybeans, oil-bearing woody plants, and wild oil-bearing crops are not included.

Patent is an abbreviation for the patent right and refers to the exclusive right of ownership by the inventors or designers for the creation or inventions, given from the patent offices after due process of assessment and approval in accordance with the Patent Law of the People's Republic of China. This indicator reflects the achievements in science and technology and in design with independent intellectual property. Patents are granted for three types—"**Inventions**", "**Utility Models**" and "**Designs**".

Price Index for Means of Agricultural Production reflects the trend and degree of changes in the prices of the means of agricultural production during a given period. Compilation of these indices helps to understand the price changes of material input in agricultural production and facilitate the compilation of national accounts. Before 1994, price indices for means of agricultural production were a sub-category in the retail price indices for commodities, and it has been compiled separately since 1994.

Primary Industry refers to agriculture, forestry, animal husbandry and fishery industries.

Private Enterprises refer to enterprises which have been registered at the departments of industrial and commercial administration for which the business operation are situated at a county town (i.e. a town where the county government is located), or at urban areas with administrative hierarchy higher than a county town.

Producer Price Index reflects the trend and degree of changes in producers' prices during a given period. These indices depict the change in the level and structure of producer prices for products of the country and meet the needs of national accounts statistics. The producer price index for a given product is calculated as the geometrical mean of individual indices for all surveyed units which sell such product, and the indices for a product category is obtained as the weighted mean of price indices for all products in the category.

Radio Coverage of Population refers to the percentage of population, which can receive central, provincial, city, prefecture, and county radio programs relayed by wireless, cable, satellite and other technical means, in the surveying area, to national total population.

Registered Unemployed Persons in Urban Areas refer to the persons with non-agricultural household registration at certain working ages (16 years old to retirement age), who are capable of working, unemployed and willing to work, and have been registered at the local employment service agencies to apply for a job.

Registered Unemployment Rate in Urban Areas refers to the ratio of the number of the registered unemployed persons to the sum of the number of persons employed in various units (minus the employed rural labor force, re-employed retirees, and Hong Kong, Macau, Taiwan or foreign employees), laid-off staff and workers in urban units, owners of private enterprises in urban areas, owners of self-employed individuals in urban areas, employees of private enterprises in urban areas, employee of self-employed individuals in urban areas, and the registered unemployed persons in urban areas.

Regular Institutions of Higher Education refer to educational establishments set up according to the government evaluation and approval procedures, recruiting graduates from senior secondary schools as the main target by the national matriculation test. They include full-time universities, colleges, institutions of higher professional education, institutions of higher vocational education, institutions of higher vocational education and others (non-university tertiary, branch schools and undergraduate classes).

Retail Price Index reflects the trend and degree of change in retail prices of commodities during a given period. The change in retail prices of commodities is related to government revenue, the equilibrium of market supply and demand, and the ratio of consumption to accumulation. Therefore, the retail price indices are useful from an oblique perspective for observing and analyzing the changes of the above economic activities.

Revenue of the basic pension insurance program refers to payments made by employers and individuals participating in the pension insurance program in accordance with the basis and proportion stipulated in State regulations, and income from other sources that become source of pension insurance fund, including the premium paid by employers and staff and workers, interest income, subsidies from higher level agencies, income as transfer from subordinate agencies, transferred income, government financial subsidies and other income.

Rural Households refer to usual resident households in rural areas. Usual resident households in rural areas are households residing on a long term basis(for more than one year) in the areas under the administration of township governments (not including county towns), and in the areas under the administration of villages in county towns. Households residing in the current addresses for over one year with their household registration in other places are still considered as resident households of the locality. For households with their household registration in one place but all members of the households having moved away to make a living in another place for over one year, they will not be included in the rural households of the area where they are registered, irrespective of whether they still keep their contracted land.

Rural Population refers to population other than **Urban Population**.

Rural Residents Entitled to Minimum Living Allowances refers to those receiving the minimum living allowances from the local government or community in the rural areas where this allowances system is in place as of the end of the reference period.

Secondary Industry refers to mining and quarrying, manufacturing, production and supply of electricity, water and gas, and construction.

Self-Employed Individuals in Urban Areas refer to persons who hold the certificates of residence in urban areas or have resided in the urban areas for a long time and have been registered at the departments of industrial and commercial administration and approved to be engaged in individual industrial or commercial business, including self-employed persons as well as helpers and hired laborers who work in individual households.

Television Coverage of Population refers to the percentage of population, which can receive central, provincial, city, prefecture, and county television programs relayed by wireless, cable, satellite and other technical means, in the surveying area, to national total population.

Tertiary Industry refers to all other economic activities not included in the primary or secondary industries.

Three Strata of Industry Classification of economic activities into three strata of industry is a common practice in the world, although the grouping varies to some extent from country to country. In China economic activities are categorized into the three strata of primary, secondary and tertiary industries. See more details under the separate entries of "**Primary Industry**", "**Secondary Industry**", and "**Tertiary Industry**"

Total Disposable Income Total income from primary distribution is re-distributed through current transfer, resulting in the total disposable income of various institutional sectors. The sum of total disposable income of all institutional sectors makes up the total national disposable income.

Total Expenditure of Urban Households refers to all actual expenditure of households except expenditure on lending. It includes cash expenditure; property expenditure, transfer expenditure, social insurance expenditure and expenditure on house purchasing or house building.

Total Income of Urban Households refers to the sum of wage, net business income, income from properties, and income from transfers of members of the households. Income from selling of properties and income from borrowing are not included.

Total Population refers to the total number of people alive at a certain point of time within a given area. The annual statistics on total population is taken at midnight of 31 December, not including residents in Taiwan, Hong Kong and Macau and Chinese citizens residing abroad.

Total Wage Bill It is revised according to the "Provision of Composition of Total Wages" (Order No.1 by National Bureau of Statistics on January 1,1990), total wage bill refers to the total remuneration payment to all employed persons in various units during the reporting period (by quarter or by year), including hourly-paid wages, piece-rate wages, bonuses, allowance and subsidies, overtime wages and wages paid under special circumstances. It equals to the sum of total wages of employed staff and workers, dispatch labors and other employed persons. Total wage bill is pre-tax wages, including the room charges, utility bills, housing funds and social insurance paid or withheld by employee's units. Total wage bill, whether or not included in cost, whether or not paid in money or in kind, shall be included in the calculation of total wage.

Urban Population refers to all people residing in cities and towns. Before 2005 urban population does not include **Floating Population**. Since then, part of the latter is also included in urban population. See more details under the entry "**Usual Resident Population**".

Urban Residents Entitled to Minimum Living Allowances refers to those whose average family income is below a minimum local standard by the end of the reporting period, including both the employed and unemployed, laid off and retired, and those jobless people without stable residence or valid IDs.

Usual Resident Population refers to persons staying at home regularly or for over 6 months during a year and integrated with the household economically and in terms of living. Members of the household staying away from the household for over 6 months but keeping a close economic relation with the household by sending the majority of income to the household are regarded as usual resident of the household. Government staff and workers or retirees living as close members of the household are also considered as usual resident. However, servicemen, students of secondary technical schools or schools of higher education and persons with stable jobs and residence outside the household (excluding those visiting relatives or seeking medical service) are not included as resident population of the household.

Utility Models refer to the practical and new technical proposals on the shape and structure of the product or the combination of both. This indicator reflects the condition of technological results with certain technical content.

Contents

List of Figures

List of Tables

1

Population Growth and Structural Change

Data in this chapter are prepared by the Department of Population and Employment Statistics of the National Bureau of Statistics. In Table 1.1 figures for the years of 2000 and 2010 are the census year estimates; and the rest of the figures covered in those tables are estimates from the annual national sample survey on population changes and data for selected years have been revised according to the census results. In Table 1.2 data are estimates from the national sample survey on population changes. In Table 1.3 data are calculated by using the results of the 2000 and 2010 censuses.

The statistical surveys on population, which are conducted by Department of Population and Employment Statistics of the NBS, are as follows: The national population censuses are conducted in the years ending with 0; the 1 percent nation-wide population sample surveys are conducted in the years ending with 5; and the sample surveys on population changes are conducted in the rest of the years which cover about 1 per thousand of the total population of the country.

The sample survey on population change takes the whole nation as the population and each province, autonomous Ethnic group or municipality as sub-populations, and the stratified multi-stage systematic

R. Guo, *China Ethnic Statistical Yearbook 2020*,
https://doi.org/10.1007/978-3-030-49024-9_1

probability proportional to size (PPS) cluster sampling scheme is used. The PPS is a sampling procedure under which the probability of a unit being selected is proportional to the size of the ultimate unit, giving larger clusters a greater probability of selection and smaller clusters a lower probability. It is most useful when the sampling units vary considerably in size because it assures that those in larger sites have the same probability of getting into the sample as those in smaller sites, and vice verse.

Table 1.1 Population at year-end (10,000 persons)

Ethnic group	2000	2006	2007	2008	2009	2010	2012	2018
National total	126,743	131,448	132,129	132,802	133,450	134,091	135,404	139,538
Achang	3.4	3.6	3.6	3.6	3.7	3.9	3.7	3.9
Bai	187.7	195.6	196.5	197.4	198.2	199.4	201.6	209.0
Baonan	1.7	1.7	1.7	1.7	1.7	1.7	1.7	1.8
Blang	9.2	9.7	9.8	9.8	9.9	10.0	10.1	10.5
Buyi	315.8	311.4	307.0	304.3	299.8	295.3	296.0	306.1
Dai	116.1	122.6	123.4	124.2	125.0	125.8	127.4	132.1
Daur	13.6	13.9	13.9	14.0	14.1	14.1	14.2	14.4
Deang	1.8	1.9	1.9	1.9	1.9	1.9	2.0	2.1
Derung	0.7	0.8	0.8	0.8	0.8	0.8	0.8	0.8
Dong	312.1	306.9	304.9	304.2	302.3	300.4	302.3	313.8
Dongxiang	51.5	52.7	52.8	53.0	53.2	53.4	53.8	55.7
Ewenki	3.1	3.2	3.2	3.2	3.2	3.2	3.3	3.3
Gaoshan	0.5	0.5	0.5	0.5	0.5	0.5	0.5	0.5
Gelao	61.6	60.7	59.8	59.3	58.4	57.5	57.6	59.5
Han	115,190.4	118,425.7	119,210.6	120,150.2	121,075.9	122,156.0	123,423.8	127,768.8
Hani	144.2	152.3	153.4	154.4	155.3	156.4	158.3	164.1
Hezhe	0.5	0.5	0.5	0.5	0.5	0.5	0.5	0.5
Hui	997.5	1045.1	1053.2	1062.9	1071.7	1083.2	1100.2	1151.6
Jing	2.4	2.4	2.4	2.5	2.5	2.4	2.4	2.5
Jingpo	13.2	14.0	14.1	14.2	14.3	14.4	14.5	15.1
Jino	2.1	2.2	2.2	2.2	2.3	2.3	2.3	2.4
Kazak	125.3	138.8	141.9	144.3	146.2	148.0	151.2	168.4
Kirgiz	16.1	17.8	18.2	18.5	18.8	19.0	19.4	21.6
Korean	194.6	197.9	198.6	199.1	199.8	200.9	201.6	199.5

(continued)

Table 1.1 (continued)

Lahu	45.4	48.0	48.3	48.6	48.9	49.3	49.9	51.7
Lhoba	0.3	0.3	0.3	0.3	0.3	0.3	0.3	0.4
Li	130.3	137.6	138.9	140.3	141.8	142.4	145.3	152.9
Lisu	63.6	67.1	67.5	67.9	68.3	68.8	69.6	72.2
Manchu	1075.6	1102.4	1109.3	1115.2	1122.2	1136.8	1145.1	1151.2
Maonan	11.5	11.4	11.5	11.5	11.6	11.1	11.2	11.8
Miao	929.7	922.4	917.7	916.3	912.0	909.2	915.9	950.5
Monba	0.9	1.0	1.0	1.0	1.0	1.0	1.0	1.2
Mongol	590.5	603.6	607.2	611.1	614.7	619.1	623.9	635.5
Mulao	22.4	22.2	22.4	22.6	22.7	21.7	22.0	23.1
Naxi	30.9	32.6	32.8	33.1	33.3	33.5	33.9	35.1
Nu	2.9	3.0	3.1	3.1	3.1	3.1	3.2	3.3
Oroqen	0.8	0.9	0.9	0.9	0.9	0.9	0.9	0.9
Pumi	3.4	3.6	3.6	3.6	3.6	3.6	3.7	3.8
Qiang	31.0	30.4	30.2	30.3	30.5	30.0	30.1	31.1
Russian	1.6	1.7	1.7	1.7	1.8	1.8	1.8	2.0
Salar	11.1	11.7	11.8	11.8	11.9	12.0	12.2	12.9
She	71.8	75.8	76.5	77.1	77.7	78.7	79.6	83.4
Shui	43.3	42.7	42.1	41.8	41.2	40.5	40.6	42.0
Tajik	4.1	4.5	4.6	4.7	4.8	4.8	4.9	5.5
Tatar	0.5	0.5	0.6	0.6	0.6	0.6	0.6	0.7
Tibetan	547.7	576.9	581.1	586.6	592.9	595.9	605.6	652.0
Tu	25.5	26.9	27.1	27.2	27.3	27.6	28.0	29.4
Tujia	801.9	792.2	791.6	793.4	793.9	800.8	809.1	839.4

Uygur	841.4	932.4	952.8	969.2	981.7	993.8	1015.4	1130.6
Uzbek	1.2	1.4	1.4	1.4	1.4	1.5	1.5	1.7
Va	39.7	41.9	42.2	42.5	42.7	43.0	43.6	45.2
Xibe	19.0	19.7	19.8	20.0	20.1	20.3	20.5	20.9
Yao	279.3	278.8	281.2	283.7	286.0	280.4	284.3	298.2
Yi	784.9	806.4	807.5	810.2	813.2	811.7	819.1	848.1
Yugur	1.4	1.4	1.4	1.4	1.4	1.4	1.4	1.5
Zhuang	1738.0	1740.3	1758.6	1776.6	1792.1	1715.6	1741.9	1831.8

Notes: Data of 2000 and 2010 are the census year estimates; the rest are the estimates from the annual national sample survey on population changes. Since 2005, all data are of usual resident population

Table 1.2 Total population, birth rate, death rate, and natural growth rate

Ethnic group	Total population (year-end) (10,000 persons)	Urban population (%)	Rural population (%)	Birth rate (‰)	Death rate (‰)	Natural growth rate (‰)
National total	139,538	59.58	40.42	10.94	7.13	3.81
Achang	3.87	47.97	52.03	13.18	6.32	6.86
Bai	209.01	48.63	51.37	13.16	6.42	6.73
Baonan	1.76	48.12	51.88	11.19	6.56	4.63
Blang	10.47	48.03	51.97	13.17	6.33	6.84
Buyi	306.05	48.11	51.89	13.81	6.80	7.00
Dai	132.08	47.96	52.04	13.17	6.32	6.84
Daur	14.40	61.52	38.48	7.72	6.15	1.57
Deang	2.05	47.88	52.12	13.18	6.32	6.86
Derung	0.84	50.46	49.54	12.63	6.34	6.29
Dong	313.76	51.31	48.69	13.30	6.77	6.53
Dongxiang	55.70	48.15	51.85	11.06	6.41	4.64
Ewenki	3.32	62.65	37.35	8.24	6.02	2.22
Gaoshan	0.50	58.48	41.52	11.44	6.44	5.00
Gelao	59.53	48.01	51.99	13.85	6.81	7.03
Han	127,768.75	60.11	39.89	11.20	6.40	4.80
Hani	164.13	47.95	52.05	13.17	6.32	6.85
Hezhe	0.49	60.55	39.45	6.48	6.61	−0.13
Hui	1151.57	56.44	43.56	11.68	6.15	5.54
Jing	2.53	50.78	49.22	13.98	5.99	7.99
Jingpo	15.07	47.97	52.03	13.18	6.32	6.86
Jino	2.38	47.95	52.05	13.17	6.32	6.84
Kazak	168.35	50.92	49.08	10.69	4.57	6.12
Kirgiz	21.61	51.04	48.96	10.64	4.59	6.06
Korean	199.53	60.08	39.92	6.76	6.48	0.29
Lahu	51.71	47.97	52.03	13.17	6.33	6.85
Lhoba	0.38	33.60	66.40	14.89	4.74	10.15
Li	152.91	58.60	41.40	14.42	6.04	8.37
Lisu	72.15	48.08	51.92	13.11	6.34	6.77
Manchu	1151.21	63.93	36.07	7.65	6.86	0.79
Maonan	11.75	49.79	50.21	14.01	6.21	7.81

(*continued*)

Table 1.2 (continued)

Ethnic group	Total population (year-end) (10,000 persons)	Urban population (%)	Rural population (%)	Birth rate (‰)	Death rate (‰)	Natural growth rate (‰)
Miao	950.50	51.64	48.36	13.13	6.79	6.34
Monba	1.17	32.78	67.22	14.98	4.66	10.32
Mongol	635.53	62.22	37.78	8.49	6.16	2.33
Mulao	23.12	50.55	49.45	14.01	6.06	7.95
Naxi	35.14	48.04	51.96	13.11	6.33	6.78
Nu	3.29	47.85	52.15	13.19	6.30	6.89
Oroqen	0.88	61.63	38.37	7.32	6.34	0.99
Pumi	3.83	48.03	51.97	13.15	6.32	6.83
Qiang	31.07	52.37	47.63	11.07	7.00	4.07
Russian	1.95	56.18	43.82	9.80	5.20	4.61
Salar	12.86	53.71	46.29	13.76	6.23	7.53
She	83.43	64.44	35.56	12.69	6.02	6.68
Shui	42.02	48.06	51.94	13.82	6.78	7.04
Tajik	5.49	51.23	48.77	10.71	4.63	6.08
Tatar	0.65	51.37	48.63	10.70	4.71	5.99
Tibetan	651.99	42.88	57.12	13.62	5.71	7.91
Tu	29.41	53.99	46.01	13.69	6.26	7.43
Tujia	839.41	57.78	42.22	12.09	7.03	5.06
Uygur	1130.58	50.97	49.03	10.69	4.57	6.12
Uzbek	1.66	51.15	48.85	10.72	4.59	6.13
Va	45.17	48.21	51.79	13.15	6.34	6.81
Xibe	20.88	64.25	35.75	7.34	6.75	0.59
Yao	298.19	53.23	46.77	13.41	6.19	7.22
Yi	848.12	49.16	50.84	12.66	6.57	6.09
Yugur	1.46	48.18	51.82	11.09	6.58	4.50
Zhuang	1831.77	50.91	49.09	13.98	5.94	8.03

Notes: Data in the table are estimates from the 2018 National Sample Survey on Population Changes. The national total population was adjusted on the basis of sampling errors and survey errors. Similar adjustments were not made to regional figures. The military personnel were included in the national total population, but were not included in the population by ethnic group

Table 1.3 Population life expectancy

Ethnic group	Life expectancy in 2000	Male	Female	Life expectancy in 2010	Male	Female
National total	71.40	69.63	73.33	74.83	72.38	77.37
Achang	65.57	64.31	66.98	69.62	67.13	72.51
Bai	66.03	64.72	67.50	70.18	67.68	73.07
Baonan	67.43	66.67	68.30	72.16	70.50	74.02
Blang	65.60	64.34	67.01	69.64	67.16	72.53
Buyi	66.22	64.77	67.85	71.27	68.61	74.27
Dai	65.58	64.32	67.00	69.63	67.14	72.52
Daur	70.74	69.02	72.77	74.95	72.55	77.75
Deang	65.53	64.28	66.93	69.58	67.09	72.47
Derung	66.73	65.37	68.25	70.70	68.24	73.55
Dong	68.24	66.65	70.04	72.83	70.19	75.84
Dongxiang	67.47	66.69	68.38	72.24	70.56	74.15
Ewenki	70.25	68.61	72.21	74.67	72.27	77.49
Gaoshan	71.58	69.73	73.58	75.07	72.55	77.92
Gelao	66.16	64.72	67.79	71.24	68.58	74.25
Han	71.89	70.05	73.89	75.34	72.98	77.99
Hani	65.56	64.30	66.97	69.60	67.12	72.50
Hezhe	72.38	70.44	74.62	75.97	73.55	78.74
Hui	69.97	68.44	71.66	73.65	71.49	76.09
Jing	71.04	68.89	73.42	74.90	71.65	78.73
Jingpo	65.57	64.31	66.98	69.62	67.13	72.51
Jino	65.56	64.30	66.97	69.60	67.12	72.50
Kazak	67.42	65.99	69.14	72.35	70.31	74.86
Kirgiz	67.47	66.03	69.21	72.39	70.34	74.91
Korean	72.97	71.17	74.99	76.18	74.00	78.60
Lahu	65.58	64.32	66.99	69.62	67.14	72.51
Lhoba	64.89	63.06	66.69	68.72	66.83	70.69
Li	72.59	70.37	74.90	76.06	72.98	79.72
Lisu	65.73	64.45	67.16	69.76	67.27	72.65
Manchu	72.89	71.07	74.92	75.99	73.73	78.50
Maonan	69.76	67.78	71.97	73.96	70.83	77.60

(*continued*)

Table 1.3 (continued)

Ethnic group	Life expectancy in 2000	Male	Female	Life expectancy in 2010	Male	Female
Miao	68.01	66.45	69.76	72.52	69.92	75.48
Monba	64.78	62.93	66.57	68.56	66.70	70.48
Mongol	70.48	68.84	72.41	74.67	72.32	77.41
Mulao	70.62	68.51	72.96	74.60	71.39	78.37
Naxi	65.72	64.44	67.16	69.75	67.27	72.64
Nu	65.62	64.34	67.04	69.65	67.18	72.53
Oroqen	71.34	69.55	73.44	75.33	72.92	78.13
Pumi	65.62	64.36	67.03	69.66	67.17	72.55
Qiang	71.17	69.23	73.36	74.73	72.23	77.57
Russian	68.75	67.23	70.56	73.41	71.24	76.02
Salar	66.34	64.95	67.92	70.40	68.56	72.50
She	72.27	70.27	74.49	75.80	73.40	78.58
Shui	66.31	64.85	67.96	71.32	68.64	74.35
Tajik	67.57	66.12	69.31	72.45	70.40	74.98
Tatar	67.61	66.19	69.32	72.49	70.45	74.98
Tibetan	66.67	64.98	68.43	70.52	68.52	72.71
Tu	66.60	65.19	68.19	70.63	68.76	72.77
Tujia	70.22	68.53	72.12	74.35	71.93	77.11
Uygur	67.44	66.01	69.17	72.37	70.32	74.88
Uzbek	67.51	66.07	69.25	72.42	70.37	74.94
Va	65.73	64.45	67.15	69.75	67.27	72.64
Xibe	72.12	70.37	74.10	75.58	73.36	78.08
Yao	70.78	68.79	72.98	74.65	71.70	78.09
Yi	67.18	65.71	68.83	71.21	68.70	74.10
Yugur	67.56	66.81	68.40	72.29	70.63	74.15
Zhuang	70.95	68.79	73.33	74.76	71.53	78.57

Note: Data in this table are calculated according to the 2000 and 2010 National Population Censuses

Table 1.4 Household, population, and sex ratio

Ethnic group	Number of households (household)	Family household	Collective household	Population (person)	Male	Female	Sex ratio (female = 100)
National total	378,643	371,225	7419	1,144,648	585,299	559,349	104.64
Achang	9	9	0	32	16	15	107.63
Bai	508	503	7	1713	887	826	107.37
Baonan	4	4	0	14	7	7	103.68
Blang	25	25	0	86	44	41	107.60
Buyi	766	779	5	2507	1309	1198	109.27
Dai	320	314	4	1082	561	521	107.60
Daur	44	41	0	118	60	58	103.58
Deang	5	5	0	17	9	8	107.64
Derung	2	2	0	7	4	3	106.90
Dong	776	794	9	2570	1328	1242	107.03
Dongxiang	132	137	2	457	232	225	103.23
Ewenki	10	9	0	27	14	13	104.20
Gaoshan	1	1	0	4	2	2	104.61
Gelao	149	152	1	488	255	233	109.37
Han	340,591	327,467	7065	1,047,261	535,514	511,745	104.49
Hani	397	390	5	1345	697	648	107.63
Hezhe	2	1	0	4	2	2	102.90
Hui	2969	2822	48	9438	4780	4658	102.75
Jing	6	6	0	21	11	10	108.42
Jingpo	36	36	1	123	64	59	107.65
Jino	6	6	0	20	10	9	107.63
Kazak	442	394	2	1379	689	690	99.78
Kirgiz	57	51	0	177	88	89	99.81
Korean	614	578	3	1636	827	809	102.19
Lahu	125	123	2	424	220	204	107.61
Lhoba	1	1	0	3	2	2	99.56

Li	334	316	15	1254	642	612	104.97
Lisu	175	172	2	591	306	285	107.36
Manchu	3458	3213	27	9439	4752	4687	101.38
Maonan	28	28	0	96	50	46	108.80
Miao	2368	2409	27	7787	4018	3769	106.67
Monba	2	2	0	10	5	5	99.21
Mongol	1924	1770	15	5211	2652	2560	103.59
Mulao	56	55	0	189	99	91	108.72
Naxi	85	84	1	288	149	139	107.35
Nu	8	8	0	27	14	13	107.48
Oroqen	3	3	0	7	4	4	103.48
Pumi	9	9	0	31	16	15	107.57
Qiang	86	83	1	255	127	128	98.80
Russian	5	5	0	16	8	8	101.58
Salar	32	30	1	105	55	51	107.40
She	228	215	7	684	356	328	108.35
Shui	105	107	1	344	180	165	109.23
Tajik	14	13	0	45	22	23	99.94
Tatar	2	2	0	5	3	3	100.10
Tibetan	1519	1405	27	5342	2689	2653	101.44
Tu	72	68	2	241	125	116	107.63
Tujia	2143	2194	44	6878	3510	3368	104.30
Uygur	2968	2649	14	9262	4626	4636	99.79
Uzbek	4	4	0	14	7	7	99.91
Va	110	107	1	370	192	178	107.49
Xibe	63	58	0	171	86	85	100.58
Yao	718	714	11	2443	1265	1179	107.21
Yi	2137	2096	25	6950	3567	3383	105.37
Yugur	3	4	0	12	6	6	103.60
Zhuang	4376	4292	83	15,007	7816	7190	108.67

Notes: Data in this table are obtained from the 2018 National Sample Survey on Population Changes. The sampling fraction is 0.820‰

Table 1.5 Household size and population by gender

Ethnic group	Family household population (person)	Male	Female	Collective household population (person)	Male	Female	Average family size (person/household)
National total	1,113,633	566,631	547,002	31,015	18,668	12,347	3.00
Achang	31	16	15	1	1	0	3.30
Bai	1672	858	814	41	29	12	3.29
Baonan	14	7	7	0	0	0	3.41
Blang	84	43	41	2	2	1	3.30
Buyi	2486	1295	1191	21	14	7	3.25
Dai	1055	541	514	27	20	7	3.30
Daur	117	59	58	1	1	0	2.64
Deang	16	8	8	0	0	0	3.30
Derung	7	3	3	0	0	0	3.22
Dong	2529	1307	1222	41	21	20	3.26
Dongxiang	447	226	221	9	6	3	3.39
Ewenki	27	14	13	0	0	0	2.63
Gaoshan	4	2	2	0	0	0	3.10
Gelao	484	252	232	4	3	1	3.25
Han	1,018,020	517,838	500,179	29,241	17,674	11,568	3.02
Hani	1311	672	639	34	25	9	3.30
Hezhe	4	2	2	0	0	0	2.63
Hui	9216	4676	4540	223	105	118	3.13
Jing	20	11	10	0	0	0	3.38
Jingpo	120	62	59	3	2	1	3.30
Jino	19	10	9	0	0	0	3.30
Kazak	1370	683	687	9	5	3	3.10
Kirgiz	176	88	88	1	1	0	3.09
Korean	1623	820	803	13	7	7	2.65
Lahu	413	212	201	11	8	3	3.30

Lhoba	3	2	2	0	0	0	3.79
Li	1191	627	564	62	15	47	3.57
Lisu	577	295	281	15	11	4	3.29
Manchu	9298	4706	4592	141	46	95	2.70
Maonan	95	49	46	1	1	1	3.35
Miao	7652	3943	3709	135	74	60	3.24
Monba	9	5	5	0	0	0	3.81
Mongol	5143	2605	2538	68	46	22	2.68
Mulao	187	97	90	3	2	1	3.36
Naxi	281	144	137	7	5	2	3.29
Nu	26	13	13	1	1	0	3.30
Oroqen	7	4	4	0	0	0	2.62
Pumi	31	16	15	1	1	0	3.29
Qiang	250	125	126	4	2	2	2.91
Russian	16	8	8	0	0	0	2.92
Salar	103	53	50	3	2	1	3.26
She	660	341	320	23	15	9	2.93
Shui	341	178	164	3	2	1	3.26
Tajik	45	22	22	0	0	0	3.10
Tatar	5	3	3	0	0	0	3.11
Tibetan	5237	2625	2612	105	64	41	3.46
Tu	235	121	114	6	4	2	3.26
Tujia	6673	3397	3277	204	113	91	3.12
Uygur	9203	4590	4613	60	36	24	3.10
Uzbek	14	7	7	0	0	0	3.10
Va	361	185	176	9	7	2	3.29
Xibe	169	85	84	2	1	2	2.67
Yao	2385	1232	1153	58	32	26	3.33
Yi	6804	3467	3337	146	100	46	3.19
Yugur	12	6	6	0	0	0	3.41
Zhuang	14,741	7658	7083	265	158	108	3.38

Notes: Data in this table are obtained from the 2018 National Sample Survey on Population Changes. The sampling fraction is 0.820‰

Table 1.6 Population residing in the townships, towns and street communities by sex (person)

Ethnic group	With permanent household registration			With permanent household registration elsewhere having been away from that places for more than 6 months.		
	Sub-total	Male	Female	Sub-total	Male	Female
National total	902,280	460,014	442,266	235,999	122,062	113,937
Achang	27	14	13	4	2	2
Bai	1463	756	707	243	127	116
Baonan	13	6	6	2	1	1
Blang	74	38	36	12	6	6
Buyi	2113	1113	1000	380	189	191
Dai	929	480	449	149	79	70
Daur	89	45	44	29	15	14
Deang	14	7	7	2	1	1
Derung	6	3	3	1	1	1
Dong	2148	1120	1028	409	201	207
Dongxiang	394	199	194	61	31	30
Ewenki	19	10	10	8	4	4
Gaoshan	3	2	2	1	0	0
Gelao	411	217	194	74	37	37
Han	822,463	419,050	403,412	218,953	113,493	105,458
Hani	1155	596	559	185	99	87
Hezhe	3	2	2	1	0	0
Hui	7571	3850	3721	1826	910	916
Jing	18	9	9	3	1	1
Jingpo	106	55	51	17	9	8
Jino	17	9	8	3	1	1
Kazak	1109	553	556	262	133	130
Kirgiz	142	71	71	34	17	17
Korean	1257	642	615	356	173	182
Lahu	364	188	176	58	31	27
Lhoba	3	1	1	0	0	0
Li	959	511	448	284	125	159
Lisu	507	262	245	82	44	39
Manchu	7492	3818	3675	1886	903	983

(*continued*)

Table 1.6 (continued)

Ethnic group	With permanent household registration			With permanent household registration elsewhere having been away from that places for more than 6 months.		
	Sub-total	Male	Female	Sub-total	Male	Female
Maonan	83	43	39	13	7	6
Miao	6471	3367	3104	1277	632	645
Monba	9	4	4	1	0	0
Mongol	3800	1938	1863	1389	703	686
Mulao	162	85	78	26	13	13
Naxi	247	127	119	40	21	19
Nu	23	12	11	4	2	2
Oroqen	6	3	3	2	1	1
Pumi	27	14	13	4	2	2
Qiang	203	102	101	51	24	27
Russian	12	6	6	4	2	2
Salar	83	43	40	22	12	10
She	478	244	234	197	107	90
Shui	291	153	138	51	26	26
Tajik	36	18	18	9	4	4
Tatar	4	2	2	1	1	1
Tibetan	4624	2313	2311	701	367	333
Tu	189	97	92	51	27	24
Tujia	5483	2820	2663	1363	674	689
Uygur	7447	3712	3735	1762	891	871
Uzbek	11	5	5	3	1	1
Va	318	164	154	51	27	24
Xibe	135	68	67	35	17	18
Yao	2038	1058	981	391	200	190
Yi	5848	3007	2841	1075	547	528
Yugur	10	5	5	2	1	1
Zhuang	12,850	6702	6148	2060	1071	988

Notes: Data in this table are obtained from the 2018 National Sample Survey on Population Changes. The sampling fraction is 0.820‰

Table 1.7 Age composition and dependency ratio of population

Ethnic group	Population (person)	Aged 0–14	Aged 15–64	Aged 65 and over	Gross dependency ratio (%)	Children dependency ratio	Old dependency ratio
National total	1,144,648	192,963	815,039	136,645	40.44	23.68	16.77
Achang	32	6	23	3	38.29	24.99	13.29
Bai	1713	317	1225	171	40.10	26.04	14.06
Baonan	14	3	10	2	40.58	25.08	15.50
Blang	86	16	62	8	38.32	24.99	13.33
Buyi	2507	549	1674	283	49.91	32.95	16.97
Dai	1082	196	783	104	38.31	24.98	13.33
Daur	118	15	90	13	30.73	16.82	13.90
Deang	17	3	12	2	38.26	25.00	13.27
Derung	7	1	5	1	38.52	24.53	13.99
Dong	2570	538	1736	296	48.31	31.22	17.10
Dongxiang	457	84	324	49	40.84	25.58	15.26
Ewenki	27	4	21	3	30.41	17.16	13.25
Gaoshan	4	1	3	0	41.69	25.47	16.21
Gelao	488	107	325	55	50.16	33.17	17.00
Han	1,047,261	174,591	746,267	126,401	40.95	23.75	17.19
Hani	1345	243	973	129	38.28	24.98	13.30
Hezhe	4	0	3	0	30.55	14.63	15.92
Hui	9438	1727	6724	987	40.87	25.92	14.95
Jing	21	4	14	2	46.28	31.53	14.75
Jingpo	123	22	89	12	38.31	25.01	13.30
Jino	20	4	14	2	38.26	24.97	13.29
Kazak	1379	312	969	99	42.41	32.18	10.21
Kirgiz	177	40	124	13	42.28	32.01	10.26
Korean	1636	195	1235	206	32.58	15.83	16.76
Lahu	424	77	306	41	38.32	25.00	13.32
Lhoba	3	1	2	0	41.39	32.60	8.78

Li	1254	242	908	105	38.31	26.70	11.61
Lisu	591	107	427	58	38.50	24.95	13.55
Manchu	9439	1184	6981	1273	35.37	17.04	18.33
Maonan	96	21	65	10	47.67	32.29	15.38
Miao	7787	1581	5311	895	46.98	30.02	16.97
Monba	10	2	7	1	41.17	32.64	8.53
Mongol	5211	715	3942	555	32.31	18.14	14.17
Mulao	189	41	129	19	46.89	31.89	15.00
Naxi	288	52	208	28	38.48	24.97	13.51
Nu	27	5	19	3	38.36	25.10	13.26
Oroqen	7	1	6	1	30.48	15.82	14.66
Pumi	31	6	23	3	38.31	24.97	13.34
Qiang	255	42	175	38	45.61	23.88	21.72
Russian	16	3	12	1	37.77	26.06	11.71
Salar	105	20	77	8	37.85	26.73	11.12
She	684	114	498	72	37.51	23.09	14.42
Shui	344	75	230	39	49.76	32.91	16.86
Tajik	45	10	32	3	42.38	31.93	10.44
Tatar	5	1	4	0	42.15	31.49	10.65
Tibetan	5342	1104	3786	453	41.35	28.75	12.60
Tu	241	46	175	20	37.95	26.46	11.49
Tujia	6878	1257	4759	862	44.69	26.52	18.17
Uygur	9262	2093	6505	665	42.41	32.16	10.23
Uzbek	14	3	10	1	42.34	32.05	10.29
Va	370	67	267	36	38.48	25.02	13.46
Xibe	171	23	127	22	35.06	17.36	17.70
Yao	2443	500	1686	256	45.22	29.87	15.35
Yi	6950	1255	4920	775	41.63	25.59	16.05
Yugur	12	2	9	1	40.58	24.87	15.72
Zhuang	15,007	3200	10,315	1492	45.66	31.15	14.51

Notes: Data in this table are obtained from the 2018 National Sample Survey on Population Changes. The sampling fraction is 0.820‰

Table 1.8 Population by marital status (I)

Ethnic group	Population aged 15 and over	Male	Female	Never married	Male	Female
National total	951,684	481,358	470,326	172,875	103,409	69,466
Achang	26	13	13	5	4	2
Bai	1396	718	678	289	186	103
Baonan	12	6	6	2	1	1
Blang	70	36	34	15	10	5
Buyi	1958	1009	949	415	256	159
Dai	887	457	430	185	120	65
Daur	103	52	51	16	10	6
Deang	14	7	7	3	2	1
Derung	6	3	3	1	1	0
Dong	2032	1036	996	413	255	158
Dongxiang	373	188	186	74	45	29
Ewenki	24	12	12	4	2	1
Gaoshan	3	2	2	1	0	0
Gelao	380	196	184	81	50	31
Han	872,670	441,343	431,327	157,232	93,928	63,302
Hani	1102	568	534	230	149	81
Hezhe	4	2	2	1	0	0
Hui	7712	3863	3849	1460	839	621
Jing	16	8	8	4	2	1
Jingpo	101	52	49	21	14	7
Jino	16	8	8	3	2	1
Kazak	1067	528	540	208	123	84
Kirgiz	137	68	69	27	16	11
Korean	1441	724	717	211	123	88
Lahu	347	179	168	72	47	25
Lhoba	2	1	1	1	0	0
Li	1012	509	503	281	151	130
Lisu	485	250	235	101	65	36
Manchu	8254	4128	4126	1296	731	565
Maonan	75	39	36	17	10	6
Miao	6206	3162	3044	1256	776	480
Monba	7	4	4	2	1	1
Mongol	4497	2279	2218	725	436	288
Mulao	148	77	72	33	21	12
Naxi	236	122	114	49	32	17
Nu	22	11	11	5	3	2
Oroqen	6	3	3	1	1	0
Pumi	26	13	12	5	3	2
Qiang	213	105	108	37	21	16
Russian	13	6	6	2	1	1

(*continued*)

Table 1.8 (continued)

Ethnic group	Population aged 15 and over	Male	Female	Never married	Male	Female
Salar	85	44	41	17	10	6
She	570	293	277	98	62	37
Shui	269	139	130	57	35	22
Tajik	35	17	18	7	4	3
Tatar	4	2	2	1	0	0
Tibetan	4238	2112	2125	991	568	423
Tu	195	101	94	38	24	15
Tujia	5620	2830	2790	1083	662	421
Uygur	7170	3543	3627	1394	828	566
Uzbek	11	5	5	2	1	1
Va	303	156	147	63	41	22
Xibe	149	74	74	25	14	11
Yao	1943	996	947	414	260	155
Yi	5695	2900	2796	1139	716	423
Yugur	10	5	5	2	1	1
Zhuang	11,807	6106	5701	2659	1679	980

Notes: Data in this table are obtained from the 2018 National Sample Survey on Population Changes. The sampling fraction is 0.820‰

Table 1.9 Population by marital status (II)

Ethnic group	First married (1)	Male	Female	Re-married (2)	Male	Female
National total	705,367	352,315	353,052	14,647	7005	7642
Achang	18	9	9	0	0	0
Bai	992	491	502	23	12	11
Baonan	9	4	4	0	0	0
Blang	50	25	25	1	1	1
Buyi	1361	681	680	36	18	18
Dai	630	312	319	15	8	7
Daur	78	39	39	2	1	1
Deang	10	5	5	0	0	0
Derung	4	2	2	0	0	0
Dong	1440	714	726	34	17	17
Dongxiang	268	132	137	6	3	3
Ewenki	18	9	9	0	0	0
Gaoshan	2	1	1	0	0	0
Gelao	264	132	132	7	4	3

(continued)

Table 1.9 (continued)

Ethnic group	First married (1)	Male	Female	Re-married (2)	Male	Female
Han	648,563	324,104	324,466	13,107	6237	6870
Hani	783	388	396	18	9	9
Hezhe	3	1	1	0	0	0
Hui	5653	2816	2837	139	69	70
Jing	11	6	6	0	0	0
Jingpo	72	36	36	2	1	1
Jino	11	6	6	0	0	0
Kazak	769	374	395	50	26	24
Kirgiz	99	48	51	6	3	3
Korean	1090	549	541	26	12	13
Lahu	247	122	125	6	3	3
Lhoba	2	1	1	0	0	0
Li	677	341	335	9	5	4
Lisu	345	171	174	8	4	4
Manchu	6206	3118	3088	145	69	76
Maonan	52	26	26	1	1	1
Miao	4409	2184	2225	108	54	54
Monba	5	2	2	0	0	0
Mongol	3435	1719	1716	90	41	49
Mulao	103	52	52	2	1	1
Naxi	168	83	85	4	2	2
Nu	16	8	8	0	0	0
Oroqen	5	2	2	0	0	0
Pumi	18	9	9	0	0	0
Qiang	156	76	80	4	2	2
Russian	10	5	5	0	0	0
Salar	61	31	30	2	1	1
She	431	218	213	8	4	4
Shui	187	93	93	5	2	2
Tajik	25	12	13	2	1	1
Tatar	3	1	2	0	0	0
Tibetan	2870	1425	1444	55	27	29
Tu	139	71	68	4	2	2
Tujia	4067	1999	2068	100	48	51
Uygur	5167	2514	2653	335	174	161
Uzbek	8	4	4	0	0	0
Va	216	107	109	5	3	2
Xibe	109	55	55	3	2	2
Yao	1377	685	692	25	12	13
Yi	4070	2008	2063	100	50	50
Yugur	7	3	4	0	0	0
Zhuang	8240	4122	4119	142	71	71

Notes: (1) Data are obtained from the 2018 National Sample Survey on Population Changes. The sampling fraction is 0.820‰. (2) Data are obtained from the 2012 National Sample Survey on Population Changes. The sampling fraction is 0.831‰

Table 1.10 Population by marital status (III)

Ethnic group	Divorced	Male	Female	Widowed	Male	Female
National total	20,082	11,095	8986	53,360	14,538	38,821
Achang	1	0	0	1	0	1
Bai	33	18	15	82	23	59
Baonan	0	0	0	1	0	1
Blang	2	1	1	4	1	3
Buyi	56	36	21	125	36	89
Dai	20	11	9	51	14	37
Daur	3	2	1	5	1	4
Deang	0	0	0	1	0	1
Derung	0	0	0	0	0	0
Dong	51	31	20	128	36	92
Dongxiang	7	4	3	23	6	17
Ewenki	1	0	0	1	0	1
Gaoshan	0	0	0	0	0	0
Gelao	11	7	4	24	7	17
Han	18,034	9989	8045	48,835	13,323	35,515
Hani	25	14	12	63	18	46
Hezhe	0	0	0	0	0	0
Hui	185	98	87	413	109	304
Jing	0	0	0	1	0	1
Jingpo	2	1	1	6	2	4
Jino	0	0	0	1	0	1
Kazak	39	18	21	51	12	39
Kirgiz	5	2	3	7	2	5
Korean	57	30	27	84	23	61
Lahu	8	4	4	20	6	14
Lhoba	0	0	0	0	0	0
Li	12	7	5	42	10	32
Lisu	11	6	5	28	8	20
Manchu	282	149	132	470	130	341
Maonan	1	1	1	5	1	3
Miao	157	94	63	384	108	276
Monba	0	0	0	0	0	0
Mongol	119	66	53	218	57	161
Mulao	3	2	1	9	2	7
Naxi	5	3	2	14	4	10
Nu	1	0	0	1	0	1
Oroqen	0	0	0	0	0	0
Pumi	1	0	0	1	0	1
Qiang	6	3	3	14	4	10
Russian	0	0	0	1	0	0
Salar	3	2	1	5	1	4

(continued)

Table 1.10 (continued)

Ethnic group	Divorced	Male	Female	Widowed	Male	Female
She	11	6	5	30	7	23
Shui	8	5	3	17	5	12
Tajik	1	1	1	2	0	1
Tatar	0	0	0	0	0	0
Tibetan	118	49	69	259	69	190
Tu	7	3	3	11	3	8
Tujia	131	74	57	339	95	244
Uygur	265	121	143	344	80	264
Uzbek	0	0	0	1	0	0
Va	7	4	3	17	5	13
Xibe	6	3	3	8	2	6
Yao	35	21	15	116	31	85
Yi	140	78	62	346	97	249
Yugur	0	0	0	1	0	0
Zhuang	192	117	75	716	188	528

Notes: Data in this table are obtained from the 2018 National Sample Survey on Population Changes. The sampling fraction is 0.820‰

Table 1.11 Population by educational attainment (person) (I)

Ethnic group	Population aged 6 and over	Male	Female	No schooling	Male	Female
National total	1,064,195	542,369	521,826	57,483	16,481	41,001
Achang	29	15	14	2	1	2
Bai	1580	816	764	126	40	86
Baonan	13	7	7	1	0	1
Blang	79	41	38	6	2	4
Buyi	2278	1184	1094	220	60	160
Dai	1000	517	483	82	26	55
Daur	112	57	55	5	2	3
Deang	15	8	7	1	0	1
Derung	6	3	3	0	0	0
Dong	2347	1207	1140	166	46	119
Dongxiang	421	213	208	40	12	28
Ewenki	26	13	13	1	0	1
Gaoshan	4	2	2	0	0	0
Gelao	443	230	212	43	12	31
Han	974,453	496,620	477,832	51,553	14,560	37,000
Hani	1243	643	600	101	33	69

(continued)

Table 1.11 (continued)

Ethnic group	Population aged 6 and over	Male	Female	No schooling	Male	Female
Hezhe	4	2	2	0	0	0
Hui	8712	4397	4315	622	191	431
Jing	19	10	9	1	0	1
Jingpo	114	59	55	9	3	6
Jino	18	9	9	1	0	1
Kazak	1244	621	623	57	24	33
Kirgiz	160	80	80	7	3	4
Korean	1566	790	776	49	15	34
Lahu	392	203	189	32	10	22
Lhoba	3	1	1	1	0	1
Li	1154	586	568	51	15	37
Lisu	547	282	264	45	14	30
Manchu	8984	4518	4466	275	91	184
Maonan	88	45	42	5	1	4
Miao	7131	3664	3467	519	148	371
Monba	9	4	4	3	1	2
Mongol	4917	2502	2416	242	82	160
Mulao	172	90	83	8	3	6
Naxi	266	138	129	22	7	15
Nu	25	13	12	2	1	1
Oroqen	7	4	3	0	0	0
Pumi	29	15	14	2	1	2
Qiang	238	118	120	18	5	13
Russian	15	7	7	1	0	0
Salar	97	50	47	11	4	7
She	632	327	305	40	10	30
Shui	313	163	150	30	8	22
Tajik	41	20	20	2	1	1
Tatar	5	2	2	0	0	0
Tibetan	4875	2446	2430	1018	376	642
Tu	221	114	107	25	8	17
Tujia	6356	3230	3126	335	96	239
Uygur	8355	4168	4187	380	159	220
Uzbek	12	6	6	1	0	0
Va	342	177	165	28	9	19
Xibe	162	81	81	5	2	3
Yao	2236	1153	1082	97	30	66
Yi	6430	3291	3139	525	160	365
Yugur	11	6	5	1	0	1
Zhuang	13,683	7107	6576	608	195	413

Notes: Data in this table are obtained from the 2018 National Sample Survey on Population Changes. The sampling fraction is 0.820‰

Table 1.12 Population by educational attainment (person) (II)

Ethnic group	Primary school	Male	Female	Junior secondary school	Male	Female
National total	268,951	127,947	141,004	401,864	216,604	185,260
Achang	10	5	5	10	6	4
Bai	549	271	278	539	305	234
Baonan	4	2	2	4	2	2
Blang	28	14	14	27	15	12
Buyi	781	403	378	780	449	331
Dai	357	176	181	339	193	146
Daur	26	12	14	43	23	20
Deang	6	3	3	5	3	2
Derung	2	1	1	2	1	1
Dong	718	358	360	856	472	384
Dongxiang	132	64	68	127	70	57
Ewenki	6	3	3	9	5	4
Gaoshan	1	0	0	1	1	1
Gelao	152	79	74	152	87	64
Han	243,132	115,346	127,780	369,033	198,750	170,283
Hani	443	219	225	421	240	181
Hezhe	1	0	0	2	1	1
Hui	2367	1148	1220	3026	1647	1379
Jing	5	3	3	8	4	4
Jingpo	41	20	21	39	22	17
Jino	6	3	3	6	3	3
Kazak	358	175	183	420	216	204
Kirgiz	46	22	23	54	28	26
Korean	358	169	189	655	345	310
Lahu	140	69	71	133	76	57
Lhoba	1	1	0	1	0	0
Li	215	102	113	486	263	223
Lisu	194	96	99	185	105	80
Manchu	1855	869	986	3829	2004	1825
Maonan	26	13	14	36	20	16
Miao	2244	1119	1125	2531	1400	1131
Monba	3	2	1	2	1	1
Mongol	1132	534	598	1822	979	843
Mulao	50	24	26	73	40	33
Naxi	95	47	48	90	51	39
Nu	9	4	4	8	5	4
Oroqen	2	1	1	3	1	1
Pumi	10	5	5	10	6	4

(continued)

Table 1.12 (continued)

Ethnic group	Primary school	Male	Female	Junior secondary school	Male	Female
Qiang	78	39	39	76	41	36
Russian	4	2	2	5	3	2
Salar	32	16	16	27	16	12
She	174	82	92	230	131	99
Shui	107	55	52	108	62	46
Tajik	12	6	6	14	7	7
Tatar	1	1	1	2	1	1
Tibetan	1652	856	795	1187	665	522
Tu	73	36	37	64	37	27
Tujia	1754	847	907	2244	1190	1054
Uygur	2403	1176	1227	2822	1449	1373
Uzbek	4	2	2	4	2	2
Va	121	60	62	116	66	50
Xibe	34	16	18	68	35	33
Yao	621	294	327	917	499	419
Yi	2236	1109	1127	2151	1209	942
Yugur	3	2	2	3	2	1
Zhuang	3944	1866	2078	5869	3242	2626

Notes: Data in this table are obtained from the 2018 National Sample Survey on Population Changes. The sampling fraction is 0.820‰

Table 1.13 Population by educational attainment (person) (III)

Ethnic group	Regular senior secondary schools	Male	Female	College students	Male	Female
National total	138,751	77,363	61,388	78,481	41,065	37,416
Achang	2	1	1	2	1	1
Bai	141	83	57	90	48	43
Baonan	2	1	1	1	1	0
Blang	7	4	3	5	2	2
Buyi	205	115	89	112	58	54
Dai	82	49	33	57	30	26
Daur	14	8	7	11	6	5
Deang	1	1	1	1	0	0
Derung	1	0	0	0	0	0
Dong	278	157	121	132	66	65
Dongxiang	50	29	21	31	16	15

(continued)

Table 1.13 (continued)

Ethnic group	Regular senior secondary schools	Male	Female	College students	Male	Female
Ewenki	3	2	2	3	1	1
Gaoshan	0	0	0	0	0	0
Gelao	40	22	17	22	11	10
Han	128,740	71,870	56,867	72,264	37,869	34,400
Hani	102	61	41	71	38	33
Hezhe	1	0	0	0	0	0
Hui	1038	550	489	682	349	333
Jing	2	1	1	1	0	0
Jingpo	9	6	4	6	3	3
Jino	1	1	1	1	1	0
Kazak	129	66	63	133	66	67
Kirgiz	17	9	8	17	8	9
Korean	218	114	104	108	55	52
Lahu	32	19	13	22	12	10
Lhoba	0	0	0	0	0	0
Li	141	85	56	87	46	41
Lisu	45	27	18	31	17	15
Manchu	1198	614	583	710	368	342
Maonan	9	5	4	4	2	2
Miao	808	456	352	415	212	203
Monba	1	0	0	0	0	0
Mongol	621	328	293	481	253	228
Mulao	18	11	8	8	4	4
Naxi	22	13	9	15	8	7
Nu	2	1	1	1	1	1
Oroqen	1	0	0	1	0	0
Pumi	2	1	1	2	1	1
Qiang	25	13	12	17	8	9
Russian	2	1	1	2	1	1
Salar	9	5	4	7	4	3
She	73	43	30	43	22	20
Shui	28	16	12	15	8	7
Tajik	4	2	2	4	2	2
Tatar	1	0	0	1	0	0
Tibetan	379	209	169	262	137	125
Tu	21	12	9	16	9	7
Tujia	919	500	419	450	230	220
Uygur	867	446	421	891	443	449
Uzbek	1	1	1	1	1	1
Va	28	17	11	20	10	9

(*continued*)

Table 1.13 (continued)

Ethnic group	Regular senior secondary schools	Male	Female	College students	Male	Female
Xibe	21	10	10	14	7	7
Yao	285	164	121	126	64	62
Yi	571	328	243	386	199	187
Yugur	1	1	1	1	0	0
Zhuang	1484	853	630	672	353	320

Notes: Data in this table are obtained from the 2018 National Sample Survey on Population Changes. The sampling fraction is 0.820‰

Table 1.14 Illiterate population aged 15 and over by sex

Ethnic group	Population aged 15 and over (person)	Male	Female	Percentage of illiterate population to total aged 15 and over (%)	Male	Female
National total	951,685	481,358	470,327	4.94	2.42	7.52
Achang	26	13	13	8.11	4.71	11.72
Bai	1396	718	678	7.93	4.48	11.58
Baonan	12	6	6	10.12	5.39	14.94
Blang	70	36	34	8.10	4.71	11.71
Buyi	1958	1009	949	9.68	4.58	15.09
Dai	887	457	430	8.11	4.71	11.72
Daur	103	52	51	3.76	2.19	5.38
Deang	14	7	7	8.12	4.73	11.74
Derung	6	3	3	7.43	4.25	10.78
Dong	2032	1036	996	6.95	3.28	10.80
Dongxiang	373	188	186	9.61	5.16	14.13
Ewenki	24	12	12	4.33	2.48	6.24
Gaoshan	3	2	2	4.76	2.31	7.27
Gelao	380	196	184	9.74	4.59	15.20
Han	872,670	441,343	431,327	4.94	2.39	7.54
Hani	1102	568	534	8.11	4.72	11.73
Hezhe	4	2	2	2.59	1.49	3.71
Hui	7712	3863	3849	6.83	3.77	9.91
Jing	16	8	8	3.54	1.55	5.64
Jingpo	101	52	49	8.11	4.71	11.72
Jino	16	8	8	8.11	4.72	11.72

(continued)

Table 1.14 (continued)

Ethnic group	Population aged 15 and over (person)	Male	Female	Percentage of illiterate population to total aged 15 and over (%)	Male	Female
Kazak	1067	528	540	3.70	2.77	4.61
Kirgiz	137	68	69	3.67	2.75	4.58
Korean	1441	724	717	2.68	1.47	3.90
Lahu	347	179	168	8.10	4.71	11.71
Lhoba	2	1	1	32.52	24.06	40.72
Li	1012	509	503	4.24	2.06	6.46
Lisu	485	250	235	8.09	4.69	11.70
Manchu	8254	4128	4126	2.50	1.42	3.60
Maonan	75	39	36	5.17	2.33	8.17
Miao	6206	3162	3044	7.17	3.51	11.02
Monba	7	4	4	33.75	25.04	42.17
Mongol	4497	2279	2218	4.25	2.43	6.13
Mulao	148	77	72	4.12	1.82	6.57
Naxi	236	122	114	8.19	4.77	11.82
Nu	22	11	11	8.46	5.00	12.14
Oroqen	6	3	3	3.44	1.97	4.94
Pumi	26	13	12	8.10	4.71	11.71
Qiang	213	105	108	7.47	3.88	10.94
Russian	13	6	6	4.05	2.68	5.42
Salar	85	44	41	9.97	5.58	14.66
She	570	293	277	6.01	2.42	9.80
Shui	269	139	130	9.50	4.50	14.81
Tajik	35	17	18	3.72	2.74	4.68
Tatar	4	2	2	3.96	2.84	5.07
Tibetan	4238	2112	2125	20.68	14.39	26.90
Tu	195	101	94	9.82	5.44	14.50
Tujia	5620	2830	2790	4.97	2.42	7.59
Uygur	7170	3543	3627	3.69	2.76	4.60
Uzbek	11	5	5	3.69	2.75	4.62
Va	303	156	147	8.05	4.67	11.65
Xibe	149	74	74	2.15	1.41	2.89
Yao	1943	996	947	3.61	1.69	5.62
Yi	5695	2900	2796	8.11	4.47	11.89
Yugur	10	5	5	10.07	5.34	14.89
Zhuang	11,807	6106	5701	3.55	1.60	5.62

Notes: Illiterate population in this table refers to the population aged 15 and over who are unable or have difficulty in reading. Data in this table are obtained from the 2018 National Sample Survey on Population Changes. The sampling fraction is 0.820‰

Table 1.15 Family households by size (household)

Ethnic group	Number of family households	One person	Two persons	Three persons	Four persons	Five persons
National total	371,225	61,961	105,040	86,851	61,107	31,873
Achang	9	1	2	2	2	1
Bai	508	68	113	113	107	59
Baonan	4	0	1	1	1	0
Blang	25	3	6	6	5	3
Buyi	766	121	183	157	153	82
Dai	320	42	70	71	68	38
Daur	44	7	16	14	5	2
Deang	5	1	1	1	1	1
Derung	2	0	0	0	0	0
Dong	776	118	185	168	153	82
Dongxiang	132	15	32	30	26	15
Ewenki	10	1	4	3	1	0
Gaoshan	1	0	0	0	0	0
Gelao	149	24	35	30	30	16
Han	340,591	57,267	97,157	79,549	55,547	28,986
Hani	397	52	87	89	85	47
Hezhe	2	0	1	0	0	0
Hui	2969	422	796	717	545	271
Jing	6	1	1	1	1	1
Jingpo	36	5	8	8	8	4
Jino	6	1	1	1	1	1
Kazak	442	60	107	113	93	43
Kirgiz	57	8	14	15	12	5
Korean	614	101	223	174	67	33
Lahu	125	16	27	28	27	15
Lhoba	1	0	0	0	0	0
Li	334	45	66	69	78	41
Lisu	175	23	39	39	37	21
Manchu	3458	595	1199	954	414	192
Maonan	28	5	6	6	6	3
Miao	2368	361	568	517	463	250
Monba	2	0	0	1	0	0
Mongol	1924	288	655	591	256	87
Mulao	56	9	12	12	11	6
Naxi	85	11	19	19	18	10
Nu	8	1	2	2	2	1
Oroqen	3	0	1	1	0	0
Pumi	9	1	2	2	2	1

(continued)

Table 1.15 (continued)

Ethnic group	Number of family households	One person	Two persons	Three persons	Four persons	Five persons
Qiang	86	16	25	20	13	8
Russian	5	1	2	2	1	0
Salar	32	5	7	7	6	3
She	228	47	62	46	36	20
Shui	105	16	25	22	21	11
Tajik	14	2	4	4	3	1
Tatar	2	0	0	0	0	0
Tibetan	1519	244	320	343	270	156
Tu	72	13	17	16	13	7
Tujia	2143	342	556	501	380	206
Uygur	2968	405	719	758	627	285
Uzbek	4	1	1	1	1	0
Va	110	14	24	25	23	13
Xibe	63	11	21	18	8	4
Yao	718	114	157	155	142	79
Yi	2137	316	513	475	414	236
Yugur	3	0	1	1	1	0
Zhuang	4376	708	905	916	883	503

Notes: Data in this table are obtained from the 2018 National Sample Survey on Population Changes. The sampling fraction is 0.820‰

2

Macroeconomic Growth and Structural Change

Data on Gross Domestic Product (GDP) are computed by the Department of National Accounts of the National Bureau of Statistics (NBS) based on different approaches in the light of the different features of various sectors, various expenditure structures and different data sources. GDP is a measurement of value which changes depending on changes of price and production. GDP at constant prices converts the gross domestic product based on the current price into a value based on the price of the base period. When adjusted for price changes, the values of two different periods can be compared to reflect changes of both products and production activities.

GDP is a measurement of value which changes depending on changes of price and production. GDP at constant prices converts the gross domestic product based on the current price into a value based on the price of the base period. When adjusted for price changes, the values of two different periods can be compared to reflect changes of both products and production activities. GDP index is derived from the constant-price GDPs of the two periods. As economy grows, changes will take place in the price structures of various industries, and the base period for the measurement of constant-price GDP thus needs to be adjusted every

R. Guo, *China Ethnic Statistical Yearbook 2020*,
https://doi.org/10.1007/978-3-030-49024-9_2

few years in order to better reflect the impact of price change on the economy. Since China started GDP calculation, eight constant-price base periods have been used, i.e., 1952, 1957, 1970, 1980, 1990, 2000, 2005, 2010 and 2015 and the current base period is 2015. That is to say, the 2016 GDP is calculated on the basis of the 2015 prices. As the calculation of constant-price GDP is based on different base periods, the constant-price GDP data in this yearbook shall also be announced in accordance with various periods.

The coefficient for the conversion of electric power into standard coal equivalent (SCE) is calculated on the basis of the heat value equivalent. One kilowatt is equal to 0.1229 kg SCE.

Data on investments in fixed assets by individuals in rural areas are provided by the Department of Rural Social and Economic Survey of the NBS through its rural social and economic survey. Other data on investments in fixed assets are from surveys conducted by the Department of Investment and Construction Statistics of the NBS. All data on investments in fixed assets are collected by the system of reporting form with complete enumeration, except data on individual investments in fixed assets in rural areas, which are collected through sample surveys.

Data for compilation of the consumer price indices and the retail price indices in China are collected by the Department of Urban Social and Economic Survey, NBS and the Department of Rural Social and Economic Survey, NBS through a combination of sample surveys and surveys of key units. Areas distributed in different economic regions are selected as the sample areas and representative commodities are selected as the sample commodities. Regular surveys are conducted to collect data on their market prices. Population parameters are inferred on the basis of the sample data. At present, 500 cities and counties of all provinces, autonomous regions and municipalities directly under the central government have been selected for this purpose.

Table 2.1 Gross domestic product (GDP), 2007–2011 (100 million yuan) and per capita GDP (yuan)

Ethnic group	2008	2009	2010	2011	2012	2018	Per capita GDP
Achang	4.63	5.02	5.88	7.23	8.37	14.49	37,546.23
Bai	256.09	279.08	328.64	403.89	467.16	820.34	39,375.24
Baonan	2.21	2.36	2.88	3.51	3.95	5.83	32,820.97
Blang	12.57	13.63	15.97	19.63	22.73	39.36	37,694.94
Buyi	328.12	359.96	424.15	522.56	621.04	1302.81	42,442.15
Dai	157.72	171.03	200.36	246.41	285.32	494.31	37,528.36
Daur	41.73	46.43	55.80	68.27	75.30	86.48	59,606.11
Deang	2.43	2.63	3.08	3.79	4.39	7.61	37,320.05
Derung	1.21	1.32	1.56	1.90	2.17	3.55	42,206.90
Dong	426.63	473.67	570.32	698.58	802.72	1481.30	46,940.78
Dongxiang	71.02	75.41	92.46	112.62	126.94	189.33	33,581.20
Ewenki	10.77	12.25	14.68	18.00	19.89	22.23	66,530.35
Gaoshan	1.16	1.28	1.53	1.82	2.02	3.16	61,576.82
Gelao	62.69	68.79	81.00	99.89	119.01	252.09	42,233.82
Han	312,399.25	342,370.85	409,254.77	487,614.46	538,440.14	855,860.52	65,598.97
Hani	196.01	212.52	248.91	306.12	354.47	614.06	37,516.91
Hezhe	1.15	1.20	1.45	1.75	1.91	2.39	47,463.63
Hui	2347.98	2565.61	3107.43	3753.42	4188.98	6458.47	54,776.63
Jing	3.72	4.11	5.04	6.16	6.86	10.87	42,959.05
Jingpo	18.01	19.53	22.87	28.12	32.56	56.40	37,527.39
Jino	2.84	3.08	3.61	4.44	5.14	8.90	37,457.47
Kazak	283.34	289.77	368.29	447.69	508.28	826.03	49,473.72
Kirgiz	36.52	37.36	47.46	57.68	65.46	106.10	49,500.42
Korean	505.18	559.76	669.40	810.85	906.34	1128.15	55,597.71

(continued)

Table 2.1 (continued)

Ethnic group	2008	2009	2010	2011	2012	2018	Per capita GDP
Lahu	61.86	67.08	78.57	96.61	111.85	193.69	37,571.44
Lhoba	0.47	0.53	0.61	0.73	0.84	1.72	45,100.21
Li	245.09	269.64	335.65	409.92	464.26	790.06	51,783.80
Lisu	86.84	94.25	110.53	135.90	157.24	271.91	37,837.57
Manchu	3253.69	3588.50	4314.31	5193.93	5764.78	6703.11	57,122.45
Maonan	15.81	17.43	21.25	26.03	29.36	49.63	42,241.15
Miao	1286.87	1426.44	1711.74	2103.11	2422.42	4469.33	46,943.49
Monba	1.45	1.61	1.86	2.21	2.54	5.22	45,083.94
Mongol	1961.51	2222.38	2667.95	3264.06	3616.68	4113.66	64,529.68
Mulao	33.45	36.86	45.09	55.03	61.47	99.87	43,088.13
Naxi	42.40	46.02	53.97	66.34	76.74	132.92	37,931.56
Nu	3.98	4.31	5.05	6.21	7.18	12.45	37,972.48
Oroqen	2.45	2.70	3.24	3.95	4.35	5.05	56,769.58
Pumi	4.61	4.99	5.85	7.20	8.33	14.40	37,708.71
Qiang	47.28	53.05	64.40	78.76	89.38	152.28	49,071.17
Russian	4.46	4.83	5.93	7.22	8.07	11.19	58,071.24
Salar	21.41	22.73	28.31	34.90	39.52	60.02	46,438.60
She	232.64	256.91	309.30	366.47	404.51	706.61	84,432.94
Shui	45.01	49.41	58.33	71.93	85.37	177.52	42,207.42
Tajik	9.34	9.57	12.14	14.75	16.73	27.16	49,871.78
Tatar	1.12	1.15	1.45	1.76	2.00	3.24	49,899.76
Tibetan	882.52	970.76	1159.74	1407.97	1608.95	2895.42	44,706.57
Tu	49.76	53.00	65.68	80.75	91.23	139.47	47,184.97
Tujia	1445.91	1628.15	1982.60	2439.72	2768.89	4877.61	58,151.57
Uygur	1907.30	1951.30	2479.29	3013.36	3420.74	5558.84	49,587.93
Uzbek	2.83	2.90	3.68	4.47	5.07	8.24	49,903.65

Va	55.20	59.88	70.16	86.13	99.54	171.76	38,147.52
Xibe	57.78	63.43	77.28	93.16	104.20	118.54	56,738.54
Yao	489.01	540.19	656.86	797.30	887.26	1439.20	47,936.51
Yi	1069.81	1173.81	1391.52	1708.99	1971.47	3463.79	41,179.16
Yugur	1.84	1.97	2.40	2.91	3.28	4.83	32,817.15
Zhuang	2738.99	3015.27	3688.57	4495.62	4997.31	7916.68	43,094.72

Table 2.2 Gross domestic product—indices (preceding year = 100)

Ethnic group	2008	2009	2010	2011	2012	2018
Achang	110.61	112.10	112.31	113.68	112.93	108.88
Bai	110.92	112.14	112.53	113.74	112.85	108.81
Baonan	110.28	110.23	111.91	112.54	112.51	106.34
Blang	110.63	112.11	112.33	113.68	112.93	108.87
Buyi	111.30	111.42	112.81	114.83	113.41	109.01
Dai	110.61	112.11	112.32	113.69	112.93	108.88
Daur	115.28	114.49	113.97	113.43	110.95	105.18
Deang	110.61	112.10	112.31	113.69	112.95	108.89
Derung	111.04	112.14	112.64	113.55	112.56	108.43
Dong	112.23	112.32	113.50	113.90	112.44	108.38
Dongxiang	110.23	110.07	111.70	112.47	112.48	106.29
Ewenki	116.95	116.13	114.70	113.98	111.26	105.30
Gaoshan	112.38	112.08	113.35	112.30	110.72	107.15
Gelao	111.31	111.41	112.81	114.88	113.45	109.03
Han	112.17	111.97	113.43	112.32	110.70	107.08
Hani	110.62	112.10	112.31	113.68	112.94	108.88
Hezhe	112.00	111.55	112.77	112.30	110.12	104.90
Hui	112.02	111.32	112.97	112.42	111.40	106.90
Jing	112.66	113.67	114.08	112.38	111.30	106.94
Jingpo	110.62	112.09	112.31	113.68	112.93	108.88
Jino	110.62	112.11	112.32	113.69	112.94	108.88
Kazak	111.00	108.11	110.61	112.00	111.96	106.10
Kirgiz	111.02	108.15	110.63	112.00	111.94	106.09
Korean	114.56	113.00	113.57	113.14	111.14	104.84
Lahu	110.62	112.10	112.31	113.68	112.93	108.88
Lhoba	110.29	112.32	112.38	112.74	111.78	108.94
Li	110.37	111.68	115.81	112.13	109.34	105.97
Lisu	110.62	112.16	112.39	113.72	112.92	108.85
Manchu	112.91	112.44	113.55	112.21	109.95	105.71
Maonan	112.32	113.10	113.76	113.06	111.89	107.47
Miao	112.07	112.37	113.54	114.12	112.63	108.36
Monba	110.16	112.36	112.34	112.67	111.73	109.00
Mongol	116.18	115.33	114.49	113.70	111.16	105.56
Mulao	112.52	113.42	113.95	112.61	111.49	107.12
Naxi	110.62	112.16	112.39	113.71	112.91	108.85
Nu	110.62	112.10	112.32	113.65	112.89	108.86
Oroqen	114.48	113.86	113.73	113.13	110.67	105.10
Pumi	110.63	112.11	112.33	113.68	112.92	108.86
Qiang	111.01	114.45	115.07	114.97	112.54	107.99
Russian	113.28	111.31	112.26	112.72	111.62	105.87
Salar	112.99	110.09	114.69	113.30	112.24	107.06

(*continued*)

Table 2.2 (continued)

Ethnic group	2008	2009	2010	2011	2012	2018
She	112.10	111.41	113.30	111.61	110.55	108.03
Shui	111.34	111.51	112.84	114.77	113.37	108.96
Tajik	111.05	108.25	110.73	112.03	111.93	106.13
Tatar	111.01	108.35	110.76	112.02	111.92	106.13
Tibetan	111.03	112.24	113.53	113.40	112.13	108.20
Tu	112.88	110.23	114.61	113.26	112.17	107.11
Tujia	113.28	113.32	114.70	114.02	112.00	107.68
Uygur	111.01	108.13	110.62	112.00	111.95	106.11
Uzbek	111.02	108.18	110.66	111.99	111.92	106.12
Va	110.66	112.11	112.34	113.65	112.88	108.83
Xibe	112.93	112.11	113.42	112.20	110.11	105.74
Yao	112.71	113.33	114.01	112.40	111.17	107.26
Yi	110.80	112.68	113.13	114.18	112.88	108.65
Yugur	110.20	110.29	111.84	112.50	112.49	106.31
Zhuang	112.54	113.59	113.99	112.32	111.27	106.95

Table 2.3 Gross domestic product (GDP) by three strata of industry (100 million yuan)

Ethnic group	GDP	Primary industry	Secondary industry	Tertiary industry
Achang	14.49	2.00	5.64	6.84
Bai	820.34	108.43	319.86	392.05
Baonan	5.83	0.65	2.04	3.14
Blang	39.36	5.41	15.35	18.60
Buyi	1302.81	180.94	508.86	613.01
Dai	494.31	68.27	192.41	233.64
Daur	86.48	10.17	30.84	45.46
Deang	7.61	1.06	2.96	3.59
Derung	3.55	0.43	1.40	1.73
Dong	1481.30	171.47	585.86	723.97
Dongxiang	189.33	22.02	66.88	100.43
Ewenki	22.23	2.27	8.51	11.45
Gaoshan	3.16	0.24	1.28	1.63
Gelao	252.09	35.32	98.28	118.49
Han	855,860.52	58,189.23	353,116.68	444,554.61
Hani	614.06	84.81	239.20	290.05
Hezhe	2.39	0.36	0.65	1.39
Hui	6458.47	515.64	2597.50	3345.34
Jing	10.87	1.53	4.32	5.03

(continued)

Table 2.3 (continued)

Ethnic group	GDP	Primary industry	Secondary industry	Tertiary industry
Jingpo	56.40	7.79	21.96	26.65
Jino	8.90	1.23	3.46	4.21
Kazak	826.03	114.35	333.09	378.59
Kirgiz	106.10	14.71	42.69	48.70
Korean	1128.15	100.34	431.51	596.30
Lahu	193.69	26.71	75.54	91.44
Lhoba	1.72	0.15	0.73	0.84
Li	790.06	159.54	186.08	444.44
Lisu	271.91	37.31	105.89	128.72
Manchu	6703.11	555.36	2546.02	3601.73
Maonan	49.63	7.09	19.62	22.93
Miao	4469.33	515.78	1761.99	2191.56
Monba	5.22	0.44	2.19	2.60
Mongol	4113.66	399.18	1610.64	2103.83
Mulao	99.87	13.87	39.58	46.41
Naxi	132.92	18.12	51.66	63.14
Nu	12.45	1.69	4.87	5.90
Oroqen	5.05	0.62	1.71	2.72
Pumi	14.40	1.98	5.61	6.81
Qiang	152.28	16.46	57.40	78.42
Russian	11.19	1.28	4.35	5.56
Salar	60.02	5.70	25.41	28.91
She	706.61	41.76	321.33	343.53
Shui	177.52	24.93	69.38	83.21
Tajik	27.16	3.70	10.95	12.51
Tatar	3.24	0.43	1.29	1.52
Tibetan	2895.42	276.52	1190.71	1428.19
Tu	139.47	12.89	59.13	67.45
Tujia	4877.61	428.36	1999.24	2450.01
Uygur	5558.84	767.55	2241.92	2549.38
Uzbek	8.24	1.12	3.31	3.80
Va	171.76	23.30	67.16	81.30
Xibe	118.54	10.97	45.94	61.63
Yao	1439.20	160.47	574.15	704.58
Yi	3463.79	448.03	1335.88	1679.88
Yugur	4.83	0.53	1.65	2.65
Zhuang	7916.68	1088.80	3144.42	3683.47

Table 2.4 Gross domestic product of tertiary industry (100 million yuan)

Ethnic group	Industry	Construction	Transport, storage and post	Wholesale and retail trade	Hotels and catering services	Financial intermediation	Real estate
Achang	2.82	0.78	0.21	0.84	0.27	0.44	0.20
Bai	160.97	40.77	15.47	45.35	14.53	23.63	11.69
Baonan	1.48	0.37	0.22	0.27	0.09	0.14	0.10
Blang	7.68	2.11	0.56	2.29	0.72	1.20	0.55
Buyi	208.05	41.41	57.68	48.52	22.95	33.63	17.63
Dai	96.16	26.57	6.99	28.72	9.08	15.03	6.88
Daur	34.27	4.89	4.95	6.86	1.99	2.66	2.15
Deang	1.47	0.41	0.11	0.44	0.14	0.23	0.10
Derung	0.81	0.18	0.07	0.21	0.06	0.11	0.06
Dong	304.62	51.45	54.72	65.22	23.16	34.37	24.27
Dongxiang	46.93	11.70	6.98	8.64	2.92	4.57	3.30
Ewenki	9.48	1.31	1.43	1.80	0.54	0.68	0.52
Gaoshan	0.86	0.13	0.10	0.18	0.05	0.11	0.09
Gelao	39.53	7.87	11.34	9.21	4.46	6.45	3.35
Han	234,639.84	32,775.95	25,563.97	51,826.23	11,578.60	28,694.87	23,422.48
Hani	119.37	33.03	8.68	35.79	11.28	18.65	8.54
Hezhe	0.73	0.11	0.09	0.19	0.05	0.08	0.08
Hui	1707.83	329.30	234.31	344.68	84.74	240.25	151.84
Jing	2.76	0.50	0.33	0.53	0.19	0.31	0.26
Jingpo	10.97	3.03	0.81	3.28	1.04	1.71	0.79
Jino	1.73	0.48	0.13	0.52	0.16	0.27	0.12
Kazak	192.95	42.74	24.24	28.97	7.36	24.45	13.20

(*continued*)

Table 2.4 (continued)

Ethnic group	Industry	Construction	Transport, storage and post	Wholesale and retail trade	Hotels and catering services	Financial intermediation	Real estate
Kirgiz	24.87	5.49	3.12	3.76	0.96	3.14	1.71
Korean	402.51	57.41	39.23	81.25	19.26	29.38	26.95
Lahu	37.77	10.41	2.75	11.28	3.56	5.87	2.70
Lhoba	0.10	0.20	0.03	0.05	0.03	0.04	0.03
Li	88.88	45.22	22.24	48.49	16.01	21.46	37.75
Lisu	53.60	14.55	3.91	15.63	4.97	8.26	3.81
Manchu	2572.13	358.55	322.96	515.48	115.21	247.67	229.78
Maonan	11.44	2.10	1.72	2.26	0.88	1.37	1.06
Miao	910.82	168.13	151.69	199.88	69.29	115.28	76.53
Monba	0.28	0.62	0.10	0.17	0.08	0.13	0.08
Mongol	1716.01	241.02	248.60	320.44	92.16	127.07	100.65
Mulao	24.58	4.36	3.21	4.80	1.75	2.85	2.35
Naxi	25.99	7.14	1.91	7.62	2.42	4.07	1.88
Nu	2.41	0.68	0.18	0.72	0.23	0.38	0.18
Oroqen	1.92	0.27	0.27	0.41	0.11	0.16	0.14
Pumi	2.82	0.77	0.21	0.84	0.26	0.44	0.20
Qiang	39.39	6.65	2.70	5.11	2.32	4.90	2.67
Russian	3.41	0.59	0.48	0.62	0.17	0.36	0.23
Salar	18.07	4.00	1.57	2.37	0.50	1.78	0.74
She	176.02	29.20	19.91	37.28	7.65	24.18	21.13
Shui	28.68	5.78	7.76	6.66	3.14	4.56	2.42
Tajik	6.38	1.39	0.80	0.98	0.25	0.81	0.45
Tatar	0.76	0.17	0.10	0.12	0.03	0.10	0.05
Tibetan	476.34	259.88	59.44	98.49	40.65	75.67	42.02

Tu	41.71	8.94	3.69	5.77	1.25	4.11	1.89
Tujia	1154.07	186.64	140.53	222.18	62.26	127.95	97.35
Uygur	1299.46	287.13	163.13	195.68	49.59	164.73	89.12
Uzbek	1.92	0.42	0.24	0.30	0.07	0.25	0.14
Va	34.04	9.15	2.53	10.06	3.13	5.20	2.46
Xibe	46.58	7.00	5.36	8.88	2.02	4.39	4.14
Yao	362.98	58.00	41.19	75.22	22.58	36.97	33.43
Yi	728.41	167.35	64.39	167.06	60.12	105.20	51.57
Yugur	1.20	0.30	0.18	0.23	0.08	0.12	0.09
Zhuang	2017.91	360.13	231.29	399.80	138.45	228.42	195.19

Note: All data are as of 2012

Table 2.5 Composition of gross domestic product (GDP) (%)

Ethnic group	Primary industry	Secondary industry	Tertiary industry
Achang	13.91	38.92	47.17
Bai	13.52	38.99	47.48
Baonan	11.18	34.53	54.30
Blang	13.87	38.95	47.18
Buyi	14.30	38.96	46.73
Dai	13.90	38.92	47.18
Daur	12.84	34.50	52.68
Deang	13.93	38.92	47.15
Derung	12.88	39.23	47.89
Dong	12.38	39.39	48.22
Dongxiang	11.44	34.69	53.86
Ewenki	10.71	38.01	51.29
Gaoshan	9.23	41.67	49.10
Gelao	14.37	38.93	46.70
Han	8.17	41.63	50.20
Hani	13.90	38.94	47.16
Hezhe	16.65	26.81	56.60
Hui	9.31	41.11	49.57
Jing	14.45	39.68	45.88
Jingpo	13.90	38.94	47.17
Jino	13.90	38.92	47.17
Kazak	13.85	40.28	45.81
Kirgiz	13.89	40.15	45.90
Korean	9.78	38.24	52.00
Lahu	13.88	38.96	47.16
Lhoba	8.93	42.35	48.73
Li	20.22	23.70	56.09
Lisu	13.81	38.91	47.27
Manchu	9.15	38.99	51.86
Maonan	14.57	39.47	45.97
Miao	12.32	39.28	48.39
Monba	8.72	42.28	48.99
Mongol	9.96	39.39	50.65
Mulao	14.42	39.61	45.98
Naxi	13.79	38.90	47.31
Nu	13.76	39.02	47.21
Oroqen	13.74	32.42	53.87
Pumi	13.86	38.94	47.20
Qiang	10.87	37.71	51.37
Russian	12.09	39.50	48.37

(continued)

Table 2.5 (continued)

Ethnic group	Primary industry	Secondary industry	Tertiary industry
Salar	9.69	42.18	48.13
She	6.53	45.46	48.02
Shui	14.38	38.98	46.64
Tajik	13.68	40.28	45.98
Tatar	13.52	39.90	46.53
Tibetan	9.71	40.78	49.50
Tu	9.60	42.01	48.39
Tujia	9.30	40.82	49.86
Uygur	13.83	40.30	45.81
Uzbek	13.77	40.23	45.95
Va	13.76	39.02	47.22
Xibe	9.54	38.97	51.47
Yao	12.21	39.73	48.06
Yi	13.12	38.60	48.27
Yugur	11.15	34.20	54.65
Zhuang	14.34	39.65	46.02

Table 2.6 Indices of gross domestic product (GDP) (preceding year = 100)

Ethnic group	GDP	Primary sector	Secondary sector	Tertiary sector
Achang	108.88	106.26	111.23	107.61
Bai	108.81	106.10	110.74	107.92
Baonan	106.34	104.96	104.00	108.32
Blang	108.87	106.25	111.21	107.62
Buyi	109.01	106.75	109.39	109.42
Dai	108.88	106.26	111.23	107.62
Daur	105.18	103.37	104.09	106.28
Deang	108.89	106.28	111.26	107.61
Derung	108.43	105.69	110.16	107.66
Dong	108.38	105.56	108.12	109.35
Dongxiang	106.29	104.96	103.89	108.35
Ewenki	105.30	103.21	104.85	106.12
Gaoshan	107.15	103.47	106.47	108.43
Gelao	109.03	106.80	109.39	109.46
Han	107.08	103.14	106.24	108.45
Hani	108.88	106.27	111.25	107.61
Hezhe	104.90	103.47	102.59	106.49
Hui	106.90	103.77	106.22	108.00
Jing	106.94	105.53	104.72	109.31
Jingpo	108.88	106.27	111.23	107.61

(continued)

Table 2.6 (continued)

Ethnic group	GDP	Primary sector	Secondary sector	Tertiary sector
Jino	108.88	106.27	111.24	107.61
Kazak	106.10	104.70	104.20	108.00
Kirgiz	106.09	104.68	104.19	107.98
Korean	104.84	102.47	104.12	105.78
Lahu	108.88	106.26	111.23	107.61
Lhoba	108.94	103.47	116.51	104.51
Li	105.97	104.03	105.03	106.94
Lisu	108.85	106.19	111.13	107.66
Manchu	105.71	102.91	105.71	106.26
Maonan	107.47	105.94	105.86	109.40
Miao	108.36	105.60	108.34	109.13
Monba	109.00	103.30	116.91	104.32
Mongol	105.56	103.22	105.38	106.23
Mulao	107.12	105.69	105.09	109.36
Naxi	108.85	106.17	111.16	107.65
Nu	108.86	106.19	111.28	107.57
Oroqen	105.10	103.35	103.72	106.30
Pumi	108.86	106.23	111.20	107.61
Qiang	107.99	103.61	107.49	109.39
Russian	105.87	103.95	104.60	107.30
Salar	107.06	104.52	107.21	107.12
She	108.03	103.33	107.97	108.73
Shui	108.96	106.74	109.28	109.41
Tajik	106.13	104.65	104.25	108.02
Tatar	106.13	104.62	104.25	108.00
Tibetan	108.20	103.86	111.81	106.39
Tu	107.11	104.54	107.24	107.22
Tujia	107.68	104.09	106.71	109.38
Uygur	106.11	104.69	104.21	108.00
Uzbek	106.12	104.67	104.23	108.00
Va	108.83	106.19	111.11	107.63
Xibe	105.74	103.36	106.40	105.61
Yao	107.26	104.98	105.80	109.08
Yi	108.65	105.59	110.00	108.31
Yugur	106.31	104.94	103.89	108.37
Zhuang	106.95	105.57	104.89	109.20

Table 2.7 Government expenditure in selected sectors (100 million yuan)

Ethnic group	Expenditure for public security	Expenditure for education	Expenditure for science and technology	Expenditure for culture, sport and media	Expenditure for social safety and employment effort	Expenditure for medical and health care
Achang	0.27	0.54	0.03	0.05	0.35	0.21
Bai	15.81	28.92	1.50	2.66	18.30	11.39
Baonan	0.16	0.26	0.01	0.04	0.21	0.10
Blang	0.74	1.46	0.07	0.13	0.95	0.58
Buyi	35.76	42.59	2.62	4.24	20.25	17.02
Dai	9.26	18.45	0.91	1.70	11.99	7.29
Daur	1.62	2.39	0.17	0.38	2.15	0.89
Deang	0.14	0.29	0.01	0.03	0.19	0.11
Derung	0.06	0.12	0.01	0.01	0.08	0.05
Dong	31.64	40.94	2.69	3.64	21.42	16.00
Dongxiang	5.13	8.21	0.40	1.12	6.13	3.17
Ewenki	0.42	0.57	0.04	0.11	0.54	0.22
Gaoshan	0.04	0.07	0.01	0.01	0.04	0.03
Gelao	7.02	8.28	0.51	0.82	3.91	3.31
Han	10,470.34	18,324.42	2107.25	1861.73	10,823.93	6498.01
Hani	11.52	22.94	1.13	2.11	14.90	9.06
Hezhe	0.04	0.07	0.01	0.01	0.06	0.02
Hui	107.60	190.56	17.70	23.22	138.30	70.85
Jing	0.20	0.31	0.02	0.02	0.15	0.13
Jingpo	1.06	2.11	0.10	0.19	1.37	0.83
Jino	0.17	0.33	0.02	0.03	0.22	0.13
Kazak	20.54	32.07	2.24	4.62	15.44	9.88
Kirgiz	2.63	4.11	0.29	0.59	1.99	1.27

(*continued*)

Table 2.7 (continued)

Ethnic group	Expenditure for public security	Expenditure for education	Expenditure for science and technology	Expenditure for culture, sport and media	Expenditure for social safety and employment effort	Expenditure for medical and health care
Korean	18.14	32.68	2.68	3.48	24.22	11.08
Lahu	3.63	7.22	0.36	0.66	4.69	2.85
Lhoba	0.16	0.10	0.01	0.03	0.07	0.04
Li	16.16	25.75	1.96	3.19	17.01	9.72
Lisu	5.05	10.04	0.50	0.93	6.53	3.97
Manchu	111.58	182.55	21.75	20.47	154.77	58.14
Maonan	1.05	1.47	0.10	0.12	0.70	0.62
Miao	92.25	127.23	8.03	11.45	71.47	49.49
Monba	0.49	0.32	0.02	0.08	0.22	0.12
Mongol	78.51	108.95	8.33	18.70	100.89	41.39
Mulao	1.94	2.85	0.21	0.23	1.36	1.20
Naxi	2.52	4.92	0.25	0.46	3.20	1.95
Nu	0.25	0.47	0.02	0.05	0.30	0.18
Oroqen	0.09	0.14	0.01	0.02	0.13	0.05
Pumi	0.27	0.54	0.03	0.05	0.35	0.21
Qiang	2.08	3.72	0.23	0.45	2.54	1.58
Russian	0.24	0.36	0.03	0.06	0.23	0.12
Salar	1.70	3.42	0.15	0.39	3.46	1.20
She	6.66	12.01	1.36	1.08	4.81	4.11
Shui	4.85	5.82	0.36	0.58	2.78	2.33
Tajik	0.66	1.04	0.07	0.15	0.50	0.32
Tatar	0.08	0.12	0.01	0.02	0.06	0.04
Tibetan	172.40	151.39	7.80	29.77	118.95	57.42
Tu	3.76	7.55	0.35	0.85	7.57	2.67

Tujia	72.95	109.40	7.60	8.85	71.83	40.34
Uygur	137.87	215.22	15.07	30.96	103.62	66.31
Uzbek	0.20	0.32	0.02	0.05	0.15	0.10
Va	3.17	6.30	0.32	0.58	4.09	2.48
Xibe	2.33	3.60	0.43	0.43	3.04	1.05
Yao	23.55	36.48	2.81	2.86	19.34	14.60
Yi	63.05	114.09	6.06	11.36	72.83	45.95
Yugur	0.13	0.21	0.01	0.03	0.17	0.08
Zhuang	143.12	223.75	16.92	17.86	110.08	94.29

Note: All data are as of 2012

Table 2.8 Final consumption expenditure (100 million yuan)

Ethnic group	Final consumption expenditures	Household consumption	Rural household	Urban household	Government consumption
Achang	5.09	3.66	1.30	2.36	1.42
Bai	275.21	199.44	69.03	130.41	75.77
Baonan	2.30	1.50	0.49	1.01	0.81
Blang	13.79	9.94	3.52	6.41	3.86
Buyi	352.33	259.68	85.87	173.82	92.65
Dai	173.57	125.09	44.44	80.65	48.48
Daur	32.61	19.87	4.17	15.69	12.74
Deang	2.68	1.93	0.69	1.24	0.75
Derung	1.21	0.87	0.28	0.59	0.34
Dong	411.50	307.93	93.18	214.75	103.57
Dongxiang	74.09	47.52	15.35	32.16	26.57
Ewenki	8.06	4.92	0.98	3.94	3.14
Gaoshan	0.93	0.67	0.16	0.51	0.26
Gelao	67.83	50.05	16.55	33.50	17.79
Han	250,440.59	180,659.64	41,477.50	139,182.14	69,780.96
Hani	215.70	155.41	55.20	100.20	60.29
Hezhe	0.99	0.62	0.14	0.48	0.37
Hui	2067.48	1368.98	339.02	1029.95	698.51
Jing	3.44	2.58	0.74	1.84	0.86
Jingpo	19.80	14.27	5.06	9.20	5.53
Jino	3.13	2.25	0.80	1.45	0.88
Kazak	288.63	160.63	45.74	114.89	127.99
Kirgiz	37.12	20.68	5.88	14.80	16.44
Korean	397.59	270.79	62.53	208.26	126.80
Lahu	67.96	48.97	17.40	31.57	18.99
Lhoba	0.52	0.21	0.08	0.12	0.32
Li	226.43	153.95	42.66	111.28	72.48
Lisu	94.99	68.53	24.37	44.15	26.46
Manchu	2467.47	1779.81	344.59	1435.22	687.67
Maonan	15.14	11.34	3.37	7.97	3.80
Miao	1263.72	938.50	284.59	653.91	325.22
Monba	1.61	0.63	0.25	0.38	0.98
Mongol	1475.43	933.44	188.88	744.56	541.99
Mulao	31.16	23.42	6.69	16.72	7.75
Naxi	46.42	33.40	11.84	21.56	13.02
Nu	4.35	3.11	1.10	2.01	1.24
Oroqen	1.95	1.20	0.25	0.95	0.75
Pumi	5.05	3.64	1.29	2.35	1.41
Qiang	44.67	34.00	12.07	21.93	10.68

(*continued*)

Table 2.8 (continued)

Ethnic group	Final consumption expenditures	Household consumption	Rural household	Urban household	Government consumption
Russian	3.92	2.30	0.54	1.76	1.62
Salar	21.05	12.50	3.89	8.61	8.55
She	178.11	135.47	32.32	103.14	42.64
Shui	48.33	35.58	11.81	23.76	12.75
Tajik	9.44	5.30	1.50	3.81	4.14
Tatar	1.13	0.64	0.18	0.46	0.49
Tibetan	922.34	487.40	179.72	307.69	434.93
Tu	48.27	29.37	8.94	20.42	18.90
Tujia	1309.53	968.74	251.93	716.81	340.79
Uygur	1940.48	1081.13	307.33	773.80	859.35
Uzbek	2.87	1.61	0.45	1.15	1.26
Va	59.86	43.14	15.19	27.94	16.72
Xibe	45.45	32.97	6.18	26.79	12.48
Yao	440.87	334.12	90.36	243.77	106.74
Yi	1124.56	824.60	291.48	533.12	299.95
Yugur	1.91	1.25	0.40	0.85	0.66
Zhuang	2532.49	1904.42	537.81	1366.61	628.07

Note: All data are as of 2012

Table 2.9 Composition of final consumption expenditure

	Final consumption expenditures = 100		Household consumption expenditures = 100	
Ethnic group	Household consumption	Government consumption	Rural household	Urban household
Achang	72.04	27.96	35.62	64.38
Bai	72.51	27.49	34.93	65.07
Baonan	65.34	34.66	32.89	67.11
Blang	72.05	27.95	35.57	64.43
Buyi	73.68	26.32	33.78	66.22
Dai	72.07	27.93	35.64	64.36
Daur	61.01	38.99	21.62	78.38
Deang	72.02	27.98	35.69	64.31
Derung	71.85	28.15	33.36	66.64
Dong	74.62	25.38	31.51	68.49
Dongxiang	64.83	35.17	32.58	67.42
Ewenki	61.11	38.89	20.22	79.78

(continued)

Table 2.9 (continued)

Ethnic group	Final consumption expenditures = 100		Household consumption expenditures = 100	
	Household consumption	Government consumption	Rural household	Urban household
Gaoshan	72.70	27.30	26.55	73.45
Gelao	73.72	26.28	33.79	66.21
Han	72.49	27.51	25.79	74.21
Hani	72.05	27.95	35.64	64.36
Hezhe	62.40	37.60	23.84	76.16
Hui	67.26	32.74	27.50	72.50
Jing	75.05	24.95	29.20	70.80
Jingpo	72.06	27.94	35.61	64.39
Jino	72.05	27.95	35.64	64.36
Kazak	55.67	44.33	28.50	71.50
Kirgiz	55.71	44.29	28.44	71.56
Korean	68.14	31.86	24.29	75.71
Lahu	72.05	27.95	35.62	64.38
Lhoba	39.25	60.75	43.17	56.83
Li	68.04	31.96	27.94	72.06
Lisu	72.16	27.84	35.64	64.36
Manchu	72.59	27.41	21.05	78.95
Maonan	74.80	25.20	30.42	69.58
Miao	74.16	25.84	31.50	68.50
Monba	37.83	62.17	43.78	56.22
Mongol	63.78	36.22	20.96	79.04
Mulao	75.07	24.93	29.43	70.57
Naxi	72.01	27.99	35.65	64.35
Nu	71.54	28.46	35.67	64.33
Oroqen	61.83	38.17	22.00	78.00
Pumi	72.03	27.97	35.58	64.42
Qiang	76.17	23.83	35.65	64.35
Russian	58.49	41.51	25.00	75.00
Salar	59.68	40.32	31.54	68.46
She	75.99	24.01	25.02	74.98
Shui	73.66	26.34	33.75	66.25
Tajik	56.24	43.76	28.38	71.62
Tatar	56.57	43.43	28.41	71.59
Tibetan	53.73	46.27	38.64	61.36
Tu	60.94	39.06	31.26	68.74
Tujia	73.98	26.02	26.98	73.02

(*continued*)

Table 2.9 (continued)

	Final consumption expenditures = 100		Household consumption expenditures = 100	
Ethnic group	Household consumption	Government consumption	Rural household	Urban household
Uygur	55.72	44.28	28.48	71.52
Uzbek	55.97	44.03	28.39	71.61
Va	72.07	27.93	35.43	64.57
Xibe	72.59	27.41	19.71	80.29
Yao	75.53	24.47	28.57	71.43
Yi	73.38	26.62	35.45	64.55
Yugur	65.71	34.29	32.78	67.22
Zhuang	75.09	24.91	29.07	70.93

Note: All data are as of 2012

Table 2.10 Household consumption expenditure

Ethnic group	Level (yuan) All households	Rural household	Urban household	Urban/rural consumption ratio (rural household = 1)	Index (preceding year = 100) All households	Rural household	Urban household
Achang	9843.24	5673.00	16,564.31	2.92	113.65	114.41	108.83
Bai	9897.72	5630.36	16,608.66	2.97	112.86	113.83	108.26
Baonan	8714.72	4668.42	15,156.00	3.26	112.07	113.20	108.89
Blang	9863.60	5680.78	16,581.53	2.92	113.65	114.42	108.83
Buyi	8726.97	4641.07	15,739.60	3.43	109.26	110.95	105.59
Dai	9843.71	5676.24	16,560.30	2.92	113.66	114.42	108.82
Daur	13,930.26	6858.88	19,297.33	2.81	109.80	111.53	108.16
Deang	9806.92	5655.51	16,532.71	2.92	113.68	114.43	108.85
Derung	10,660.66	5958.55	17,158.93	2.90	113.00	114.12	108.58
Dong	10,093.30	5348.17	16,836.10	3.22	109.31	110.94	105.83
Dongxiang	8812.59	4675.89	15,334.53	3.28	112.25	113.18	109.28
Ewenki	15,005.67	7071.59	20,875.61	2.96	111.03	113.16	109.11
Gaoshan	13,515.55	7179.41	19,301.51	2.80	109.76	111.58	106.86
Gelao	8652.03	4576.91	15,687.57	3.45	109.20	110.89	105.53
Han	14,294.22	7629.66	19,882.28	2.70	110.03	112.32	107.09
Hani	9841.37	5673.14	16,563.32	2.92	113.66	114.41	108.84
Hezhe	12,286.46	6733.09	16,394.65	2.45	106.47	107.40	105.38
Hui	12,220.45	6431.28	18,106.47	2.90	111.02	113.75	107.86
Jing	10,712.94	5481.60	17,558.33	3.22	110.31	109.72	107.47
Jingpo	9841.53	5667.08	16,565.15	2.93	113.64	114.40	108.82
Jino	9835.57	5668.55	16,554.39	2.92	113.67	114.42	108.83
Kazak	10,679.91	5413.29	17,442.45	3.22	115.84	116.18	114.79
Kirgiz	10,703.16	5429.63	17,439.22	3.21	115.75	116.09	114.71
Korean	13,300.83	7245.41	17,866.85	2.47	109.57	109.51	109.06
Lahu	9844.07	5673.57	16,566.60	2.92	113.65	114.41	108.83
Lhoba	6054.42	3449.39	13,512.79	4.07	108.74	107.72	109.35

Li	10,631.02	5983.70	15,208.41	2.55	109.28	111.75	106.96
Lisu	9877.69	5714.41	16,560.38	2.91	113.62	114.49	108.74
Manchu	15,430.81	7735.09	20,496.61	2.67	109.49	112.41	107.07
Maonan	10,074.39	5165.00	17,028.39	3.31	109.95	109.89	106.91
Miao	10,193.22	5405.64	16,866.95	3.19	109.98	111.88	106.23
Monba	5982.47	3425.63	13,463.69	4.10	108.66	107.50	109.42
Mongol	14,947.76	7143.17	20,799.08	2.93	111.28	113.61	109.12
Mulao	10,590.72	5380.06	17,505.79	3.27	110.09	109.66	107.22
Naxi	9881.93	5713.04	16,565.31	2.91	113.59	114.44	108.75
Nu	9836.57	5669.01	16,559.15	2.94	113.55	114.29	108.82
Oroqen	13,627.22	6892.52	18,614.22	2.70	108.71	110.27	107.18
Pumi	9867.18	5687.86	16,575.28	2.92	113.64	114.41	108.82
Qiang	11,309.97	7139.75	16,689.95	2.34	112.16	116.82	105.91
Russian	12,775.87	6280.05	19,117.44	3.10	113.79	114.93	112.32
Salar	10,215.24	5956.17	15,235.76	2.59	114.74	119.83	110.49
She	16,857.94	9859.00	21,900.29	2.29	107.36	110.28	105.06
Shui	8726.88	4644.52	15,742.57	3.42	109.38	110.97	105.71
Tajik	10,781.93	5467.97	17,504.93	3.21	115.64	116.05	114.54
Tatar	10,851.19	5514.24	17,531.17	3.20	115.45	115.88	114.27
Tibetan	8206.21	4885.65	14,584.59	3.28	111.17	112.97	108.79
Tu	10,461.11	6030.30	15,556.50	2.61	114.34	119.21	110.13
Tujia	11,941.48	6147.19	17,993.14	2.98	109.82	113.24	106.08
Uygur	10,702.34	5425.06	17,460.81	3.22	115.82	116.16	114.77
Uzbek	10,785.02	5464.26	17,525.13	3.22	115.72	116.07	114.65
Va	9928.33	5706.58	16,638.56	2.92	113.59	114.41	108.79
Xibe	16,213.41	7916.95	21,539.57	2.76	111.16	114.09	108.91
Yao	11,663.36	5932.79	18,366.79	3.11	110.09	110.25	107.12
Yi	10,103.17	5953.45	16,486.26	2.82	112.75	114.69	107.65
Yugur	8775.68	4676.20	15,241.60	3.28	111.88	112.89	108.73
Zhuang	10,907.23	5530.63	17,790.00	3.22	110.46	109.78	107.60

Note: All data are as of 2012

Table 2.11 Total investment in fixed assets by status of registration (100 million yuan)

Ethnic group	Total	State-owned firms	Private firms	Self-employed individuals	Others
Achang	6.32	2.30	1.20	0.29	0.17
Bai	348.93	124.70	66.58	15.58	9.54
Baonan	3.58	1.57	0.54	0.10	0.23
Blang	17.16	6.23	3.27	0.78	0.46
Buyi	498.77	188.43	70.10	18.62	6.48
Dai	215.58	78.51	40.87	9.82	5.75
Daur	55.21	17.85	8.77	1.11	1.44
Deang	3.33	1.22	0.63	0.15	0.09
Derung	1.61	0.54	0.33	0.06	0.05
Dong	577.16	184.93	116.96	24.48	17.92
Dongxiang	113.39	49.03	17.43	3.47	6.77
Ewenki	14.64	4.71	2.20	0.22	0.31
Gaoshan	1.34	0.31	0.34	0.04	0.06
Gelao	95.99	36.62	13.11	3.58	1.17
Han	339,610.03	81,203.21	85,002.48	10,501.36	14,673.87
Hani	267.92	97.54	50.93	12.21	7.11
Hezhe	1.32	0.40	0.26	0.05	0.06
Hui	3162.55	921.35	775.67	102.27	110.72
Jing	5.05	1.24	1.43	0.29	0.24
Jingpo	24.59	8.95	4.66	1.12	0.65
Jino	3.89	1.42	0.74	0.18	0.10
Kazak	416.82	169.39	65.06	21.60	6.00
Kirgiz	53.59	21.73	8.39	2.77	0.78
Korean	693.96	159.12	163.86	23.22	32.78
Lahu	84.55	30.70	16.10	3.85	2.27
Lhoba	0.77	0.47	0.06	0.04	0.06
Li	347.17	88.65	36.06	13.79	9.63
Lisu	118.76	42.95	22.55	5.36	3.28
Manchu	4573.67	948.69	1437.81	103.31	162.81
Maonan	22.16	6.08	5.60	1.19	0.91
Miao	1770.27	587.31	348.88	70.68	50.54
Monba	2.30	1.45	0.15	0.11	0.20
Mongol	2735.51	828.37	495.47	45.73	64.66
Mulao	44.97	11.46	12.19	2.51	2.06
Naxi	57.85	21.06	10.89	2.61	1.60
Nu	5.42	1.99	1.02	0.25	0.15
Oroqen	3.14	0.99	0.53	0.07	0.10
Pumi	6.29	2.28	1.20	0.29	0.17
Qiang	63.64	20.00	10.56	2.14	3.57

(continued)

Table 2.11 (continued)

Ethnic group	Total	State-owned firms	Private firms	Self-employed individuals	Others
Russian	6.12	2.20	0.96	0.20	0.11
Salar	38.27	17.46	4.38	1.51	1.13
She	240.41	64.01	57.53	6.93	6.19
Shui	68.82	25.69	10.16	2.63	0.99
Tajik	13.62	5.48	2.16	0.70	0.21
Tatar	1.61	0.65	0.25	0.08	0.03
Tibetan	1443.21	737.44	147.92	59.38	89.87
Tu	85.68	38.43	10.21	3.32	2.61
Tujia	1920.21	562.88	454.12	66.10	75.21
Uygur	2800.83	1136.21	438.28	145.04	40.44
Uzbek	4.12	1.66	0.65	0.21	0.06
Va	74.84	26.78	14.40	3.38	2.10
Xibe	88.11	20.08	28.39	2.09	2.71
Yao	585.54	150.63	154.92	30.87	27.21
Yi	1474.28	517.03	261.91	60.67	50.35
Yugur	2.92	1.26	0.45	0.08	0.19
Zhuang	3588.69	885.28	1004.30	205.63	172.90

Note: All data are as of 2012

Table 2.12 Indicators of energy consumption

	Energy consumption per 10,000 yuan of GDP (equivalent value)		Energy consumption per 10,000 yuan of Industrial value-added change	Electricity consumption per 10,000 yuan of GDP change
Ethnic group	Index (ton of SCE/10,000 yuan)	Change (±%)	Above designated size, equivalent weight (±%)	(±%)
Achang	1.16	−3.21	−9.86	5.40
Bai	1.19	−3.29	−9.56	4.09
Baonan	1.43	−1.72	−1.14	2.66
Blang	1.16	−3.22	−9.85	5.37
Buyi	1.67	−3.50	−7.94	−1.51
Dai	1.16	−3.23	−9.88	5.37
Daur	1.27	−2.50	−4.22	1.61
Deang	1.16	−3.21	−9.88	5.44
Derung	1.15	−3.18	−8.96	4.35

(continued)

Table 2.12 (continued)

Ethnic group	Energy consumption per 10,000 yuan of GDP (equivalent value) Index (ton of SCE/10,000 yuan)	Change (±%)	Energy consumption per 10,000 yuan of Industrial value-added change Above designated size, equivalent weight (±%)	Electricity consumption per 10,000 yuan of GDP change (±%)
Dong	1.33	−3.55	−7.84	−1.67
Dongxiang	1.43	−1.40	−0.63	3.52
Ewenki	1.35	−2.63	−4.53	3.31
Gaoshan	0.94	−3.24	−5.97	0.18
Gelao	1.68	−3.51	−7.94	−1.63
Han	0.92	−3.49	−6.27	−0.45
Hani	1.16	−3.22	−9.89	5.41
Hezhe	1.03	−3.45	−5.27	−3.93
Hui	1.42	−0.07	−0.06	5.43
Jing	0.83	−3.32	−6.15	−0.15
Jingpo	1.16	−3.22	−9.87	5.38
Jino	1.16	−3.23	−9.88	5.40
Kazak	1.63	6.92	9.22	14.63
Kirgiz	1.62	6.83	9.09	14.47
Korean	0.97	−3.57	−4.76	−3.68
Lahu	1.16	−3.23	−9.88	5.39
Lhoba	0.11	−0.20	−0.41	0.08
Li	0.74	4.70	11.32	3.62
Lisu	1.16	−3.25	−9.82	5.20
Manchu	1.11	−3.49	−5.56	−2.36
Maonan	1.06	−3.40	−6.65	−0.70
Miao	1.31	−3.47	−7.83	−0.84
Monba	0.05	−0.17	−0.30	−0.04
Mongol	1.33	−2.38	−4.25	2.85
Mulao	0.92	−3.39	−6.36	−0.50
Naxi	1.15	−3.24	−9.78	5.17
Nu	1.14	−3.17	−9.68	5.28
Oroqen	1.19	−3.08	−4.94	−0.34
Pumi	1.16	−3.22	−9.84	5.35
Qiang	1.00	−4.20	−7.74	−1.83
Russian	1.48	2.81	3.19	9.61
Salar	1.96	7.77	7.98	5.93
She	0.70	−3.25	−2.78	1.84
Shui	1.64	−3.49	−7.93	−1.38

(continued)

Table 2.12 (continued)

Ethnic group	Energy consumption per 10,000 yuan of GDP (equivalent value) Index (ton of SCE/10,000 yuan)	Change (±%)	Energy consumption per 10,000 yuan of Industrial value-added change Above designated size, equivalent weight (±%)	Electricity consumption per 10,000 yuan of GDP change (±%)
Tajik	1.61	6.58	8.72	14.12
Tatar	1.59	6.19	8.20	13.56
Tibetan	0.80	0.59	−0.35	1.12
Tu	1.89	6.82	6.80	5.30
Tujia	1.05	−3.68	−7.26	−2.41
Uygur	1.63	6.89	9.18	14.59
Uzbek	1.61	6.75	8.97	14.36
Va	1.15	−3.23	−9.82	5.26
Xibe	1.19	−1.51	−2.49	0.23
Yao	0.85	−3.45	−6.97	−0.45
Yi	1.17	−3.53	−9.08	2.62
Yugur	1.41	−2.19	−1.67	2.38
Zhuang	0.82	−3.34	−6.31	0.09

Notes: GDP (gross domestic product) and industrial value-added are at 2010 constant prices. SCE denotes standard coal equivalent. All data are as of 2012

Table 2.13 Consumer price indices and retail price indices (preceding year = 100)

	Consumer price index			Retail price index		
Ethnic group	General	Urban household	Rural household	General	Urban household	Rural household
National average	101.91	101.91	100.66	101.56	101.54	100.58
Achang	101.58	101.65	101.40	101.51	101.46	101.78
Bai	101.63	101.70	101.31	101.59	101.57	101.60
Baonan	102.06	101.94	102.21	101.65	101.78	101.08
Blang	101.58	101.65	101.14	101.51	101.46	101.52
Buyi	101.77	101.96	101.26	101.83	101.95	101.13
Dai	101.58	101.65	101.35	101.51	101.46	101.73
Daur	101.90	101.88	100.85	101.40	101.34	100.76
Deang	101.58	101.65	101.40	101.51	101.45	101.78
Derung	101.67	101.73	99.20	101.55	101.50	99.47

(continued)

Table 2.13 (continued)

Ethnic group	Consumer price index General	Consumer price index Urban household	Consumer price index Rural household	Retail price index General	Retail price index Urban household	Retail price index Rural household
Dong	101.89	102.01	101.45	101.93	102.00	101.33
Dongxiang	102.05	101.92	102.25	101.58	101.70	101.13
Ewenki	101.86	101.83	100.89	101.56	101.52	100.79
Gaoshan	102.12	102.16	96.36	102.00	101.99	96.43
Gelao	101.76	101.96	101.11	101.84	101.95	100.97
Han	102.10	102.11	96.02	101.91	101.89	96.02
Hani	101.58	101.65	101.35	101.51	101.46	101.73
Hezhe	102.00	102.02	99.40	101.21	101.11	99.38
Hui	102.17	102.13	97.31	102.05	102.03	97.34
Jing	102.28	102.35	101.88	101.65	101.64	101.43
Jingpo	101.58	101.65	101.41	101.51	101.46	101.78
Jino	101.58	101.65	101.22	101.51	101.46	101.60
Kazak	102.03	101.85	102.35	100.88	100.78	101.94
Kirgiz	102.03	101.85	102.35	100.89	100.79	101.95
Korean	102.13	102.11	100.17	101.97	101.91	100.38
Lahu	101.58	101.65	101.34	101.51	101.46	101.72
Lhoba	101.74	101.39	101.06	101.52	101.35	101.32
Li	102.43	102.41	102.42	102.48	102.53	102.10
Lisu	101.59	101.65	101.42	101.51	101.46	101.77
Manchu	102.35	102.39	99.07	101.66	101.63	98.78
Maonan	102.15	102.26	101.85	101.70	101.73	101.47
Miao	101.84	101.95	95.78	101.83	101.89	95.73
Monba	101.72	101.35	100.77	101.51	101.33	101.04
Mongol	101.96	101.95	100.88	101.62	101.58	100.74
Mulao	102.24	102.33	101.85	101.68	101.69	101.42
Naxi	101.59	101.65	101.28	101.50	101.45	101.63
Nu	101.59	101.65	101.39	101.51	101.46	101.76
Oroqen	101.93	101.93	100.56	101.37	101.30	100.49
Pumi	101.59	101.65	101.37	101.51	101.46	101.74
Qiang	101.74	101.75	101.51	101.39	101.40	101.14
Russian	101.98	101.86	99.83	101.20	101.12	99.56
Salar	102.46	102.44	102.00	102.01	101.95	101.93
She	101.82	101.83	101.53	101.65	101.65	101.43
Shui	101.78	101.97	101.36	101.82	101.93	101.22
Tajik	102.03	101.86	101.76	100.91	100.82	101.36
Tatar	102.03	101.87	101.29	100.95	100.86	100.87
Tibetan	101.91	101.73	101.97	101.61	101.52	101.93
Tu	102.42	102.41	102.02	102.02	101.97	101.93
Tujia	101.94	101.98	83.53	101.70	101.72	83.45

(*continued*)

Table 2.13 (continued)

Ethnic group	Consumer price index			Retail price index		
	General	Urban household	Rural household	General	Urban household	Rural household
Uygur	102.03	101.85	102.31	100.89	100.79	101.90
Uzbek	102.03	101.86	102.10	100.90	100.80	101.70
Va	101.60	101.66	101.06	101.52	101.47	101.43
Xibe	102.35	102.38	100.97	101.35	101.33	100.40
Yao	102.15	102.20	101.93	101.84	101.84	101.69
Yi	101.65	101.71	101.41	101.51	101.50	101.52
Yugur	102.05	101.93	101.82	101.65	101.79	100.66
Zhuang	102.26	102.33	102.01	101.65	101.64	101.60

3

Employment and Income Distribution

Data on basic conditions of employment, total wage bills of staff and workers are collected and compiled through *The Reporting Form System on Labor Statistics*, *The Sample Survey System on Labor Force*, and *The System of Rural Social and Economic Surveys* by the Department of Population and Employment Statistics, the NBS. *The Reporting Form System on Labor Statistics* covers corporate units (does not include township enterprises, private units or self-employed individuals). The scope of survey and estimate of *The Sample Survey System on Labor Force* are the whole country. The scope of statistics in the chapter is the population aged 16 and over of the whole country. *The System of Rural Social and Economic Surveys* covers all rural areas below township level in China.

Data on the number of registered unemployed persons in urban areas are collected through *The Reporting Form System on Training and Employment Statistics,* which provided by the Ministry of Human Resources and Social Security. *The Reporting Form System* covers all agencies and units providing employment services. Data on the number of employed persons in private enterprises and self-employed individuals are provided by the State Administration for Industry and Commerce.

R. Guo, *China Ethnic Statistical Yearbook 2020*,
https://doi.org/10.1007/978-3-030-49024-9_3

The scope of statistics on private enterprises and self-employed individuals covers the whole country.

A complete reporting form system from lower-level statistical bureaus to higher level statistical bureaus is used in the labor statistics. *The Sample Survey on Labor Force* is conducted by using sampling methods. Statistics on training, employment, private enterprises and self-employed individuals are collected and compiled on basis of administrative registering records.

Table 3.1 Number of employed persons in urban units at year-end (10,000 persons) (I)

Ethnic group	Total	Agriculture, forestry, animal husbandry and fishery	Mining	Manufacturing	Production and distribution of electricity, gas and water
National total	17,258.2	192.6	414.4	4178.3	369.2
Achang	0.34	0.00	0.01	0.05	0.01
Bai	18.56	0.18	0.49	2.75	0.46
Baonan	0.17	0.00	0.01	0.02	0.01
Blang	0.93	0.01	0.02	0.14	0.02
Buyi	27.02	0.08	0.93	3.16	0.77
Dai	11.74	0.13	0.31	1.74	0.28
Daur	1.59	0.14	0.08	0.19	0.07
Deang	0.18	0.00	0.00	0.03	0.00
Derung	0.08	0.00	0.00	0.01	0.00
Dong	27.43	0.13	0.63	4.13	0.74
Dongxiang	5.44	0.10	0.20	0.64	0.25
Ewenki	0.37	0.03	0.02	0.05	0.02
Gaoshan	0.06	0.00	0.00	0.01	0.00
Gelao	5.24	0.01	0.18	0.60	0.15
Han	16,057.36	168.02	379.16	3995.69	334.14
Hani	14.59	0.16	0.39	2.17	0.35
Hezhe	0.06	0.01	0.00	0.01	0.00
Hui	132.10	1.94	5.41	22.17	4.17
Jing	0.21	0.00	0.00	0.03	0.01
Jingpo	1.34	0.01	0.04	0.20	0.03
Jino	0.21	0.00	0.01	0.03	0.01
Kazak	20.67	0.69	0.99	2.20	0.65

(*continued*)

Table 3.1 (continued)

Ethnic group	Total	Agriculture, forestry, animal husbandry and fishery	Mining	Manufacturing	Production and distribution of electricity, gas and water
Kirgiz	2.65	0.09	0.13	0.28	0.08
Korean	22.23	1.26	0.87	4.11	0.74
Lahu	4.60	0.05	0.12	0.69	0.11
Lhoba	0.04	0.00	0.00	0.00	0.00
Li	16.27	0.62	0.09	1.27	0.36
Lisu	6.41	0.07	0.17	0.95	0.16
Manchu	130.69	5.30	5.03	24.29	4.05
Maonan	0.97	0.01	0.02	0.13	0.03
Miao	85.94	0.45	2.02	13.04	2.23
Monba	0.13	0.00	0.00	0.00	0.00
Mongol	70.22	3.89	3.20	9.93	3.08
Mulao	1.93	0.02	0.02	0.29	0.05
Naxi	3.14	0.03	0.08	0.46	0.08
Nu	0.29	0.00	0.01	0.04	0.01
Oroqen	0.10	0.01	0.01	0.01	0.00
Pumi	0.34	0.00	0.01	0.05	0.01
Qiang	2.93	0.01	0.05	0.48	0.08
Russian	0.24	0.01	0.01	0.03	0.01
Salar	1.35	0.03	0.06	0.19	0.05
She	13.62	0.05	0.04	4.00	0.21
Shui	3.68	0.01	0.12	0.42	0.10
Tajik	0.67	0.02	0.03	0.07	0.02
Tatar	0.08	0.00	0.00	0.01	0.00
Tibetan	67.09	0.62	1.57	5.77	2.34
Tu	3.11	0.06	0.14	0.48	0.11
Tujia	84.76	0.55	1.09	16.46	1.94
Uygur	138.86	4.62	6.66	14.88	4.35
Uzbek	0.21	0.01	0.01	0.02	0.01
Va	4.04	0.04	0.11	0.61	0.10
Xibe	2.49	0.10	0.11	0.46	0.08
Yao	26.52	0.26	0.24	5.33	0.64
Yi	76.35	0.61	1.93	11.36	1.97
Yugur	0.14	0.00	0.00	0.02	0.01
Zhuang	153.83	2.11	1.35	25.39	3.83

Table 3.2 Number of employed persons in urban units at year-end (10,000 persons) (II)

Ethnic group	Construction	Transport, storage and post	Information transmission, computer service and software	Wholesale and retail trades	Hotels and catering services
National total	2710.9	819.0	424.3	823.3	269.8
Achang	0.06	0.01	0.00	0.02	0.01
Bai	3.18	0.75	0.23	0.98	0.32
Baonan	0.02	0.01	0.00	0.00	0.00
Blang	0.16	0.04	0.01	0.05	0.02
Buyi	4.02	1.05	0.33	1.07	0.25
Dai	2.03	0.47	0.14	0.65	0.22
Daur	0.09	0.11	0.03	0.06	0.02
Deang	0.03	0.01	0.00	0.01	0.00
Derung	0.01	0.00	0.00	0.00	0.00
Dong	4.47	1.12	0.37	1.08	0.29
Dongxiang	0.71	0.32	0.06	0.16	0.06
Ewenki	0.02	0.03	0.01	0.01	0.00
Gaoshan	0.01	0.00	0.00	0.00	0.00
Gelao	0.77	0.20	0.06	0.21	0.05
Han	2559.20	757.81	403.03	774.78	254.05
Hani	2.52	0.59	0.17	0.81	0.27
Hezhe	0.00	0.00	0.00	0.00	0.00
Hui	14.40	7.31	3.24	5.94	1.85
Jing	0.04	0.01	0.00	0.01	0.00
Jingpo	0.23	0.05	0.02	0.07	0.03
Jino	0.04	0.01	0.00	0.01	0.00
Kazak	1.48	1.13	0.22	0.59	0.16
Kirgiz	0.19	0.14	0.03	0.08	0.02
Korean	1.55	1.29	0.58	0.98	0.25
Lahu	0.80	0.18	0.05	0.25	0.09
Lhoba	0.00	0.00	0.00	0.00	0.00
Li	1.01	1.22	0.36	0.89	0.95
Lisu	1.11	0.26	0.08	0.35	0.12
Manchu	9.67	8.13	4.14	5.93	1.77

(*continued*)

Table 3.2 (continued)

Ethnic group	Construction	Transport, storage and post	Information transmission, computer service and software	Wholesale and retail trades	Hotels and catering services
Maonan	0.16	0.04	0.01	0.03	0.01
Miao	14.45	3.62	1.17	3.65	1.06
Monba	0.01	0.00	0.00	0.00	0.00
Mongol	4.44	4.83	1.50	2.48	0.85
Mulao	0.32	0.09	0.03	0.07	0.02
Naxi	0.54	0.13	0.04	0.17	0.06
Nu	0.05	0.01	0.00	0.02	0.01
Oroqen	0.01	0.01	0.00	0.00	0.00
Pumi	0.06	0.01	0.00	0.02	0.01
Qiang	0.60	0.14	0.07	0.10	0.04
Russian	0.02	0.01	0.00	0.01	0.00
Salar	0.13	0.10	0.02	0.05	0.01
She	3.52	0.46	0.26	0.56	0.20
Shui	0.55	0.14	0.04	0.14	0.03
Tajik	0.05	0.04	0.01	0.02	0.01
Tatar	0.01	0.00	0.00	0.00	0.00
Tibetan	6.72	2.94	1.00	1.97	0.80
Tu	0.32	0.21	0.05	0.11	0.03
Tujia	16.07	4.04	1.37	3.96	1.09
Uygur	9.95	7.58	1.46	4.00	1.05
Uzbek	0.01	0.01	0.00	0.01	0.00
Va	0.70	0.16	0.05	0.22	0.08
Xibe	0.18	0.16	0.06	0.10	0.03
Yao	4.27	1.20	0.43	1.04	0.37
Yi	13.64	3.22	1.16	3.69	1.23
Yugur	0.02	0.01	0.00	0.00	0.00
Zhuang	25.29	7.32	2.25	5.58	2.01

Table 3.3 Number of employed persons in urban units at year-end (10,000 persons) (III)

Ethnic group	Financial intermediation	Real estate	Leasing and business services	Scientific research, technical services, and geological prospecting	Management of water conservancy, environment and public facilities
National total	699.3	466.0	529.5	411.5	260.6
Achang	0.01	0.01	0.01	0.01	0.01
Bai	0.50	0.59	0.52	0.43	0.31
Baonan	0.01	0.00	0.00	0.00	0.00
Blang	0.02	0.03	0.03	0.02	0.02
Buyi	0.79	0.76	0.67	0.59	0.44
Dai	0.29	0.38	0.34	0.27	0.20
Daur	0.08	0.03	0.04	0.04	0.04
Deang	0.00	0.01	0.01	0.00	0.00
Derung	0.00	0.00	0.00	0.00	0.00
Dong	1.00	0.72	0.66	0.58	0.44
Dongxiang	0.17	0.10	0.09	0.14	0.13
Ewenki	0.02	0.01	0.01	0.01	0.01
Gaoshan	0.00	0.00	0.00	0.00	0.00
Gelao	0.15	0.15	0.13	0.11	0.09
Han	652.28	436.17	495.32	382.93	238.21
Hani	0.36	0.47	0.42	0.34	0.24
Hezhe	0.00	0.00	0.00	0.00	0.00
Hui	5.97	3.39	4.27	3.96	2.62
Jing	0.01	0.00	0.01	0.00	0.00
Jingpo	0.03	0.04	0.04	0.03	0.02
Jino	0.01	0.01	0.01	0.00	0.00
Kazak	0.65	0.35	0.68	0.44	0.40
Kirgiz	0.08	0.04	0.09	0.06	0.05
Korean	1.14	0.51	0.66	0.63	0.53
Lahu	0.11	0.15	0.13	0.11	0.08
Lhoba	0.00	0.00	0.00	0.00	0.00
Li	0.80	1.36	0.34	0.33	0.58
Lisu	0.16	0.21	0.18	0.15	0.11
Manchu	7.52	3.18	4.25	3.98	2.74

(*continued*)

Table 3.3 (continued)

Ethnic group	Financial intermediation	Real estate	Leasing and business services	Scientific research, technical services, and geological prospecting	Management of water conservancy, environment and public facilities
Maonan	0.04	0.02	0.03	0.02	0.02
Miao	2.97	2.46	2.20	1.86	1.38
Monba	0.00	0.00	0.00	0.00	0.00
Mongol	3.66	1.44	1.62	1.65	1.86
Mulao	0.07	0.04	0.06	0.04	0.03
Naxi	0.08	0.10	0.09	0.07	0.05
Nu	0.01	0.01	0.01	0.01	0.00
Oroqen	0.01	0.00	0.00	0.00	0.00
Pumi	0.01	0.01	0.01	0.01	0.01
Qiang	0.12	0.08	0.07	0.08	0.04
Russian	0.01	0.00	0.01	0.01	0.01
Salar	0.05	0.02	0.02	0.05	0.02
She	0.46	0.33	0.37	0.19	0.13
Shui	0.11	0.10	0.09	0.08	0.06
Tajik	0.02	0.01	0.02	0.01	0.01
Tatar	0.00	0.00	0.00	0.00	0.00
Tibetan	2.18	0.90	1.24	1.78	1.07
Tu	0.11	0.05	0.04	0.10	0.06
Tujia	3.17	2.39	2.16	1.88	1.33
Uygur	4.35	2.36	4.57	2.96	2.70
Uzbek	0.01	0.00	0.01	0.00	0.00
Va	0.10	0.13	0.12	0.09	0.07
Xibe	0.13	0.05	0.07	0.06	0.05
Yao	1.05	0.68	0.77	0.52	0.42
Yi	2.28	2.36	2.07	1.82	1.24
Yugur	0.00	0.00	0.00	0.00	0.00
Zhuang	5.91	3.57	4.81	2.92	2.67

Table 3.4 Number of employed persons in urban units at year-end (10,000 persons) (IV)

Ethnic group	Services to households and other services	Education	Health, social securities and social welfare	Culture, sports and entertainment	Public management and social organization
National total	77.4	1735.6	912.4	146.6	1817.5
Achang	0.00	0.05	0.05	0.00	0.05
Bai	0.10	2.64	2.64	0.16	2.74
Baonan	0.00	0.02	0.02	0.00	0.03
Blang	0.01	0.13	0.13	0.01	0.13
Buyi	0.13	4.64	4.64	0.21	5.24
Dai	0.07	1.66	1.66	0.10	1.68
Daur	0.01	0.19	0.19	0.02	0.25
Deang	0.00	0.03	0.03	0.00	0.03
Derung	0.00	0.01	0.01	0.00	0.01
Dong	0.11	4.15	4.15	0.23	4.64
Dongxiang	0.01	0.79	0.79	0.06	1.09
Ewenki	0.00	0.04	0.04	0.00	0.06
Gaoshan	0.00	0.01	0.01	0.00	0.01
Gelao	0.02	0.91	0.91	0.04	1.03
Han	72.70	1573.02	1573.02	134.83	1612.93
Hani	0.08	2.06	2.06	0.13	2.09
Hezhe	0.00	0.01	0.01	0.00	0.01
Hui	0.55	15.67	15.67	1.50	19.71
Jing	0.00	0.03	0.03	0.00	0.03
Jingpo	0.01	0.19	0.19	0.01	0.19
Jino	0.00	0.03	0.03	0.00	0.03
Kazak	0.04	3.12	3.12	0.18	5.37
Kirgiz	0.01	0.40	0.40	0.02	0.69
Korean	0.18	2.53	2.53	0.26	2.75
Lahu	0.03	0.65	0.65	0.04	0.66
Lhoba	0.00	0.01	0.01	0.00	0.02
Li	0.07	2.15	2.15	0.22	2.57
Lisu	0.04	0.90	0.90	0.06	0.92
Manchu	0.94	13.98	13.98	1.39	16.43
Maonan	0.00	0.16	0.16	0.01	0.16
Miao	0.36	12.63	12.63	0.72	13.83

(continued)

Table 3.4 (continued)

Ethnic group	Services to households and other services	Education	Health, social securities and social welfare	Culture, sports and entertainment	Public management and social organization
Monba	0.00	0.02	0.02	0.00	0.05
Mongol	0.27	8.47	8.47	0.80	11.77
Mulao	0.00	0.30	0.30	0.02	0.29
Naxi	0.02	0.44	0.44	0.03	0.45
Nu	0.00	0.04	0.04	0.00	0.04
Oroqen	0.00	0.01	0.01	0.00	0.01
Pumi	0.00	0.05	0.05	0.00	0.05
Qiang	0.01	0.36	0.36	0.02	0.38
Russian	0.00	0.03	0.03	0.00	0.05
Salar	0.00	0.17	0.17	0.02	0.27
She	0.05	1.12	1.12	0.09	1.04
Shui	0.02	0.63	0.63	0.03	0.71
Tajik	0.00	0.10	0.10	0.01	0.17
Tatar	0.00	0.01	0.01	0.00	0.02
Tibetan	0.06	9.93	9.93	1.15	21.05
Tu	0.00	0.38	0.38	0.04	0.60
Tujia	0.29	10.13	10.13	0.76	10.62
Uygur	0.26	20.92	20.92	1.21	36.01
Uzbek	0.00	0.03	0.03	0.00	0.05
Va	0.02	0.57	0.57	0.04	0.57
Xibe	0.01	0.27	0.27	0.02	0.39
Yao	0.08	3.56	3.56	0.22	3.52
Yi	0.36	10.67	10.67	0.63	11.08
Yugur	0.00	0.02	0.02	0.00	0.03
Zhuang	0.38	23.37	23.37	1.24	21.55

Table 3.5 Number of engaged persons in private enterprises and self-employed individuals at year-end (10,000 persons) (I)

Ethnic group	Total	Manufacturing	Construction	Transport, storage and post
National total	37,413.0	5775.8	1765.4	963.7
Achang	0.68	0.07	0.04	0.01
Bai	37.33	3.57	1.86	0.48
Baonan	0.32	0.02	0.02	0.00
Blang	1.86	0.18	0.10	0.02
Buyi	63.45	5.33	2.44	0.62
Dai	23.32	2.27	1.25	0.31
Daur	2.85	0.24	0.11	0.12
Deang	0.36	0.03	0.02	0.00
Derung	0.16	0.02	0.01	0.00
Dong	60.63	5.41	2.03	0.97
Dongxiang	9.94	0.79	0.74	0.09
Ewenki	0.76	0.07	0.03	0.03
Gaoshan	0.13	0.02	0.01	0.00
Gelao	12.33	0.99	0.47	0.12
Han	34,974.21	5530.12	1647.58	773.40
Hani	29.03	2.84	1.55	0.38
Hezhe	0.08	0.01	0.00	0.00
Hui	243.24	26.87	11.87	0.01
Jing	0.49	0.05	0.02	0.68
Jingpo	2.67	0.26	0.14	0.01
Jino	0.42	0.04	0.02	0.03
Kazak	27.71	2.88	1.00	1.62
Kirgiz	3.55	0.37	0.13	0.39
Korean	49.26	4.76	2.66	0.11
Lahu	9.15	0.90	0.49	0.01
Lhoba	0.12	0.01	0.02	0.00
Li	36.02	1.44	2.78	1.59
Lisu	12.67	1.24	0.67	0.18
Manchu	252.12	37.31	12.01	0.03
Maonan	2.30	0.20	0.08	0.00
Miao	194.17	17.25	7.33	0.32
Monba	0.36	0.02	0.07	893.50
Mongol	145.13	14.35	6.28	0.49
Mulao	4.56	0.43	0.16	0.00
Naxi	6.22	0.61	0.34	6.33
Nu	0.59	0.06	0.03	0.02
Oroqen	0.17	0.01	0.01	0.04

(*continued*)

Table 3.5 (continued)

Ethnic group	Total	Manufacturing	Construction	Transport, storage and post
Pumi	0.68	0.07	0.04	0.01
Qiang	4.29	0.31	0.15	0.72
Russian	0.38	0.04	0.02	0.09
Salar	2.44	0.19	0.12	2.76
She	36.26	6.87	1.23	0.15
Shui	8.62	0.72	0.34	0.00
Tajik	0.92	0.10	0.03	0.81
Tatar	0.11	0.01	0.00	0.21
Tibetan	155.29	10.24	21.53	11.42
Tu	5.78	0.49	0.28	0.07
Tujia	212.78	20.14	7.93	4.73
Uygur	186.48	19.46	6.72	0.01
Uzbek	0.28	0.03	0.01	5.11
Va	8.08	0.80	0.43	0.15
Xibe	4.40	0.68	0.21	0.11
Yao	58.10	5.88	1.84	0.01
Yi	143.83	12.93	6.89	0.01
Yugur	0.27	0.02	0.02	0.01
Zhuang	360.06	34.60	12.62	0.08

Table 3.6 Number of engaged persons in private enterprises and self-employed individuals at year-end (10,000 persons) (II)

Ethnic group	Wholesale and retail trades	Hotels and catering services	Leasing and business services	Services to households and other services
National total	14,495.2	2945.1	3038.4	2200.2
Achang	0.24	0.08	0.04	0.04
Bai	13.39	4.07	2.09	2.52
Baonan	0.13	0.04	0.02	0.02
Blang	0.66	0.20	0.10	0.12
Buyi	23.91	6.86	4.22	4.36
Dai	8.31	2.56	1.23	1.53
Daur	1.17	0.34	0.18	0.26
Deang	0.13	0.04	0.02	0.02
Derung	0.06	0.02	0.01	0.01
Dong	23.23	6.22	4.32	4.45
Dongxiang	4.10	1.16	0.52	0.73
Ewenki	0.32	0.08	0.05	0.07
Gaoshan	0.05	0.01	0.01	0.01

(continued)

Table 3.6 (continued)

Ethnic group	Wholesale and retail trades	Hotels and catering services	Leasing and business services	Services to households and other services
Gelao	4.66	1.34	0.82	0.85
Han	13,542.81	2692.47	2863.50	2027.74
Hani	10.33	3.18	1.53	1.91
Hezhe	0.03	0.01	0.00	0.01
Hui	94.58	25.58	17.10	17.38
Jing	0.21	0.04	0.04	0.03
Jingpo	0.95	0.29	0.14	0.18
Jino	0.15	0.05	0.02	0.03
Kazak	11.17	3.61	2.04	2.42
Kirgiz	1.43	0.46	0.26	0.31
Korean	19.83	4.76	2.46	3.90
Lahu	3.26	1.00	0.48	0.60
Lhoba	0.04	0.02	0.01	0.01
Li	12.88	4.23	3.82	2.57
Lisu	4.53	1.40	0.67	0.84
Manchu	93.78	21.52	15.42	18.25
Maonan	0.97	0.21	0.19	0.14
Miao	72.97	19.84	14.12	13.71
Monba	0.11	0.05	0.03	0.02
Mongol	59.43	14.76	9.48	12.26
Mulao	1.97	0.40	0.39	0.27
Naxi	2.22	0.69	0.33	0.41
Nu	0.21	0.07	0.03	0.04
Oroqen	0.07	0.02	0.01	0.02
Pumi	0.24	0.07	0.04	0.04
Qiang	1.88	0.60	0.31	0.34
Russian	0.15	0.04	0.03	0.03
Salar	0.91	0.37	0.14	0.21
She	16.46	1.93	3.09	1.46
Shui	3.26	0.93	0.58	0.59
Tajik	0.37	0.12	0.07	0.08
Tatar	0.04	0.01	0.01	0.01
Tibetan	52.58	22.16	11.57	10.89
Tu	2.18	0.85	0.33	0.48
Tujia	81.54	20.00	16.76	14.81
Uygur	75.15	24.26	13.74	16.27
Uzbek	0.11	0.04	0.02	0.02
Va	2.89	0.88	0.43	0.53
Xibe	1.62	0.40	0.28	0.34
Yao	24.35	5.13	4.86	3.85
Yi	54.08	16.70	8.38	9.95
Yugur	0.11	0.03	0.01	0.02
Zhuang	157.09	31.20	31.06	21.19

Table 3.7 Number of engaged persons in urban private enterprises and self-employed individuals at year-end (10,000 persons) (I)

Ethnic group	Total	Manufacturing	Construction	Transport, storage and post
National total	24,391.9	3007.9	1176.2	592.3
Achang	0.39	0.03	0.03	0.01
Bai	20.57	1.56	1.28	0.42
Baonan	0.18	0.01	0.01	0.00
Blang	1.06	0.08	0.07	0.02
Buyi	26.29	2.14	0.83	0.43
Dai	13.24	0.99	0.90	0.27
Daur	2.17	0.16	0.08	0.08
Deang	0.20	0.02	0.01	0.00
Derung	0.10	0.01	0.01	0.00
Dong	29.58	2.45	0.92	0.64
Dongxiang	5.73	0.38	0.40	0.09
Ewenki	0.56	0.04	0.02	0.02
Gaoshan	0.09	0.01	0.00	0.00
Gelao	5.05	0.39	0.15	0.08
Han	22,823.53	2874.67	1091.93	549.93
Hani	16.47	1.24	1.12	0.34
Hezhe	0.06	0.00	0.00	0.00
Hui	157.84	13.36	7.15	3.95
Jing	0.31	0.03	0.01	0.01
Jingpo	1.51	0.11	0.10	0.03
Jino	0.24	0.02	0.02	0.00
Kazak	24.48	2.45	0.88	0.65
Kirgiz	3.14	0.31	0.11	0.08
Korean	29.42	2.88	1.94	1.35
Lahu	5.19	0.39	0.35	0.11
Lhoba	0.11	0.01	0.02	0.00
Li	28.39	1.01	2.25	0.61
Lisu	7.18	0.54	0.49	0.15
Manchu	148.78	17.38	7.77	6.59
Maonan	1.32	0.10	0.05	0.04
Miao	101.99	7.98	4.08	2.13
Monba	0.33	0.02	0.06	0.00
Mongol	101.93	8.19	4.35	3.34
Mulao	2.81	0.23	0.10	0.09
Naxi	3.55	0.27	0.25	0.07
Nu	0.34	0.03	0.03	0.01
Oroqen	0.13	0.01	0.00	0.01
Pumi	0.39	0.03	0.03	0.01

(continued)

Table 3.7 (continued)

Ethnic group	Total	Manufacturing	Construction	Transport, storage and post
Qiang	2.54	0.17	0.14	0.05
Russian	0.31	0.03	0.01	0.01
Salar	2.00	0.12	0.09	0.09
She	24.30	3.33	0.90	0.34
Shui	3.62	0.29	0.12	0.06
Tajik	0.80	0.08	0.03	0.02
Tatar	0.10	0.01	0.00	0.00
Tibetan	131.67	8.04	19.86	2.46
Tu	4.63	0.30	0.20	0.19
Tujia	128.15	10.09	5.40	2.97
Uygur	164.62	16.48	5.90	4.39
Uzbek	0.24	0.02	0.01	0.01
Va	4.57	0.35	0.31	0.09
Xibe	2.80	0.37	0.14	0.13
Yao	37.67	3.29	1.34	1.04
Yi	79.38	5.84	4.89	1.57
Yugur	0.15	0.01	0.01	0.00
Zhuang	233.36	19.07	8.84	7.21

Table 3.8 Number of engaged persons in urban private enterprises and self-employed individuals at year-end (10,000 persons) (II)

Ethnic group	Wholesale and retail trades	Hotels and catering services	Leasing and business services	Services to households and other services
National total	9838.2	2151.5	2273.6	1563.6
Achang	0.15	0.05	0.03	0.03
Bai	7.87	2.76	1.49	1.65
Baonan	0.08	0.02	0.01	0.01
Blang	0.40	0.14	0.08	0.08
Buyi	11.08	4.02	1.73	2.35
Dai	5.00	1.76	0.96	1.04
Daur	0.93	0.27	0.14	0.22
Deang	0.08	0.03	0.01	0.02
Derung	0.04	0.01	0.01	0.01
Dong	12.56	3.95	2.21	2.50
Dongxiang	2.53	0.74	0.34	0.45
Ewenki	0.25	0.06	0.04	0.05
Gaoshan	0.04	0.01	0.01	0.00
Gelao	2.14	0.78	0.33	0.46

(continued)

Table 3.8 (continued)

Ethnic group	Wholesale and retail trades	Hotels and catering services	Leasing and business services	Services to households and other services
Han	9197.59	1967.24	2151.52	1442.46
Hani	6.21	2.18	1.19	1.29
Hezhe	0.02	0.01	0.00	0.01
Hui	63.90	19.41	12.17	12.39
Jing	0.14	0.03	0.03	0.02
Jingpo	0.57	0.20	0.11	0.12
Jino	0.09	0.03	0.02	0.02
Kazak	10.03	3.22	1.72	2.15
Kirgiz	1.29	0.41	0.22	0.28
Korean	11.66	3.05	1.46	2.65
Lahu	1.96	0.69	0.37	0.41
Lhoba	0.03	0.02	0.01	0.01
Li	10.07	3.54	3.06	2.11
Lisu	2.71	0.95	0.52	0.56
Manchu	58.04	14.67	9.23	12.07
Maonan	0.59	0.14	0.11	0.09
Miao	41.87	12.94	8.45	8.25
Monba	0.10	0.05	0.03	0.02
Mongol	44.54	10.64	6.89	9.57
Mulao	1.27	0.28	0.25	0.18
Naxi	1.34	0.47	0.26	0.28
Nu	0.13	0.05	0.03	0.03
Oroqen	0.05	0.02	0.01	0.01
Pumi	0.15	0.05	0.03	0.03
Qiang	1.03	0.33	0.23	0.19
Russian	0.13	0.04	0.02	0.03
Salar	0.77	0.33	0.11	0.18
She	12.00	1.44	2.52	1.06
Shui	1.52	0.55	0.24	0.32
Tajik	0.33	0.10	0.06	0.07
Tatar	0.04	0.01	0.01	0.01
Tibetan	44.32	19.44	9.89	9.37
Tu	1.81	0.74	0.28	0.41
Tujia	53.00	13.65	12.05	9.37
Uygur	67.46	21.64	11.58	14.45
Uzbek	0.10	0.03	0.02	0.02
Va	1.73	0.60	0.33	0.36
Xibe	1.10	0.29	0.17	0.23
Yao	16.56	3.70	3.41	2.54
Yi	30.81	10.69	6.01	6.29
Yugur	0.06	0.02	0.01	0.01
Zhuang	105.23	21.97	21.21	14.26

Table 3.9 Number of engaged persons in private enterprises at year-end (10,000 households, 10,000 persons)

Ethnic group	Number of households	Number of engaged persons	Urban area	Rural area
National total	3143.3	21,375.4	13,951.6	7423.7
Achang	0.05	0.34	0.21	0.13
Bai	2.65	18.68	10.81	7.87
Baonan	0.02	0.17	0.09	0.08
Blang	0.13	0.93	0.58	0.35
Buyi	4.96	33.16	10.89	22.27
Dai	1.62	11.60	7.19	4.41
Daur	0.20	1.24	0.90	0.34
Deang	0.02	0.18	0.11	0.07
Derung	0.01	0.08	0.05	0.03
Dong	4.73	31.37	13.05	18.32
Dongxiang	0.73	5.36	3.01	2.35
Ewenki	0.05	0.37	0.26	0.10
Gaoshan	0.01	0.07	0.05	0.03
Gelao	0.96	6.45	2.07	4.38
Han	2957.82	20,139.70	13,175.81	6963.90
Hani	2.01	14.45	8.94	5.51
Hezhe	0.01	0.02	0.02	0.01
Hui	22.30	122.50	75.06	47.45
Jing	0.04	0.26	0.16	0.11
Jingpo	0.18	1.33	0.82	0.51
Jino	0.03	0.21	0.13	0.08
Kazak	1.96	12.72	11.26	1.45
Kirgiz	0.25	1.63	1.44	0.19
Korean	3.18	20.12	12.51	7.61
Lahu	0.63	4.55	2.82	1.73
Lhoba	0.01	0.07	0.06	0.01
Li	3.48	21.32	16.50	4.82
Lisu	0.89	6.25	3.88	2.37
Manchu	21.68	118.68	69.59	49.09
Maonan	0.17	1.22	0.62	0.59
Miao	14.64	104.32	51.00	53.32
Monba	0.02	0.21	0.19	0.02
Mongol	9.97	70.60	48.62	21.97
Mulao	0.34	2.45	1.40	1.06
Naxi	0.44	3.09	1.93	1.16
Nu	0.04	0.30	0.19	0.11
Oroqen	0.01	0.07	0.05	0.02

(*continued*)

Table 3.9 (continued)

Ethnic group	Number of households	Number of engaged persons	Urban area	Rural area
Pumi	0.05	0.34	0.21	0.13
Qiang	0.47	1.50	1.25	0.24
Russian	0.03	0.19	0.15	0.04
Salar	0.18	1.00	0.71	0.28
She	2.41	20.34	12.51	7.83
Shui	0.67	4.50	1.50	3.00
Tajik	0.07	0.43	0.37	0.05
Tatar	0.01	0.05	0.04	0.01
Tibetan	9.89	78.16	67.55	10.62
Tu	0.42	2.46	1.75	0.72
Tujia	14.43	116.78	69.71	47.07
Uygur	13.22	85.70	75.81	9.89
Uzbek	0.02	0.13	0.11	0.02
Va	0.56	4.04	2.49	1.55
Xibe	0.35	2.14	1.30	0.84
Yao	4.58	31.63	20.06	11.57
Yi	11.35	67.41	41.11	26.29
Yugur	0.02	0.15	0.08	0.07
Zhuang	27.09	194.24	120.07	74.16

Table 3.10 Number of self-employed individuals at year-end (10,000 households, 10,000 persons)

Ethnic group	Number of households	Number of engaged persons	Urban area	Rural area
National total	7328.6	16,037.6	10,440.3	5597.4
Achang	0.18	0.34	0.18	0.17
Bai	9.87	18.65	9.75	8.89
Baonan	0.08	0.15	0.09	0.06
Blang	0.49	0.93	0.48	0.45
Buyi	16.62	30.29	15.40	14.89
Dai	6.16	11.73	6.05	5.68
Daur	0.76	1.61	1.27	0.34
Deang	0.10	0.18	0.09	0.09
Derung	0.04	0.08	0.04	0.03
Dong	15.62	29.27	16.53	12.73
Dongxiang	2.41	4.59	2.73	1.86
Ewenki	0.19	0.39	0.29	0.10
Gaoshan	0.02	0.06	0.04	0.02
Gelao	3.23	5.88	2.98	2.90

(continued)

Table 3.10 (continued)

Ethnic group	Number of households	Number of engaged persons	Urban area	Rural area
Han	6739.42	14,834.50	9647.72	5186.78
Hani	7.66	14.58	7.53	7.05
Hezhe	0.02	0.05	0.04	0.01
Hui	58.38	120.74	82.78	37.96
Jing	0.10	0.23	0.16	0.07
Jingpo	0.70	1.34	0.69	0.65
Jino	0.11	0.21	0.11	0.10
Kazak	8.54	14.99	13.22	1.77
Kirgiz	1.10	1.93	1.70	0.23
Korean	11.50	29.14	16.91	12.23
Lahu	2.41	4.60	2.37	2.22
Lhoba	0.02	0.05	0.05	0.00
Li	8.05	14.70	11.89	2.81
Lisu	3.37	6.42	3.30	3.12
Manchu	61.42	133.44	79.20	54.25
Maonan	0.51	1.08	0.69	0.39
Miao	47.85	89.85	50.99	38.86
Monba	0.07	0.16	0.15	0.01
Mongol	35.67	74.53	53.30	21.23
Mulao	0.96	2.11	1.41	0.70
Naxi	1.64	3.13	1.62	1.51
Nu	0.15	0.30	0.16	0.14
Oroqen	0.05	0.10	0.08	0.02
Pumi	0.18	0.34	0.18	0.16
Qiang	1.53	2.79	1.28	1.51
Russian	0.10	0.19	0.16	0.04
Salar	0.64	1.44	1.28	0.16
She	5.24	15.92	11.79	4.13
Shui	2.26	4.12	2.12	2.01
Tajik	0.28	0.49	0.43	0.06
Tatar	0.03	0.06	0.05	0.01
Tibetan	34.82	77.13	64.12	13.01
Tu	1.48	3.32	2.88	0.44
Tujia	44.17	96.00	58.43	37.56
Uygur	57.33	100.77	88.81	11.97
Uzbek	0.08	0.15	0.13	0.02
Va	2.11	4.04	2.09	1.95
Xibe	1.13	2.26	1.50	0.76
Yao	12.70	26.47	17.61	8.86
Yi	40.77	76.42	38.27	38.15
Yugur	0.06	0.12	0.07	0.05
Zhuang	74.06	165.83	113.29	52.54

Table 3.11 Total wage bill of employed persons in urban units

Ethnic group	(100 million yuan) Total	State-owned units	Urban collective-owned units	Units of other types of ownership
National total	141,480.0	51,126.6	2082.3	88,271.1
Achang	2.57	1.40	0.05	1.12
Bai	139.34	75.08	2.44	61.82
Baonan	1.21	0.74	0.02	0.45
Blang	6.96	3.78	0.13	3.05
Buyi	210.81	118.84	3.17	88.80
Dai	87.73	47.72	1.58	38.43
Daur	11.67	6.47	0.18	5.01
Deang	1.35	0.74	0.02	0.59
Derung	0.60	0.31	0.01	0.29
Dong	207.25	108.24	3.22	95.79
Dongxiang	39.06	23.54	0.60	14.93
Ewenki	2.79	1.53	0.04	1.22
Gaoshan	0.51	0.18	0.01	0.31
Gelao	40.92	23.15	0.61	17.15
Han	132,133.22	46,347.62	1955.56	83,830.05
Hani	108.93	59.29	1.96	47.68
Hezhe	0.40	0.21	0.01	0.19
Hui	1116.51	496.72	13.10	606.68
Jing	1.49	0.80	0.03	0.66
Jingpo	10.01	5.44	0.18	4.38
Jino	1.58	0.86	0.03	0.69
Kazak	161.55	87.59	0.99	72.97
Kirgiz	20.70	11.23	0.13	9.34
Korean	163.12	75.84	2.14	85.15
Lahu	34.28	18.66	0.62	15.00
Lhoba	0.46	0.37	0.00	0.08
Li	124.41	56.57	1.24	66.60
Lisu	47.86	26.03	0.87	20.97
Manchu	1016.29	419.97	14.84	581.48
Maonan	7.04	3.90	0.13	3.01
Miao	653.04	335.62	9.97	307.45
Monba	1.42	1.16	0.00	0.26
Mongol	533.40	280.33	8.10	244.98
Mulao	13.96	7.45	0.26	6.25
Naxi	23.63	12.83	0.42	10.38
Nu	2.22	1.22	0.04	0.96
Oroqen	0.71	0.38	0.01	0.31
Pumi	2.55	1.39	0.05	1.12

(*continued*)

Table 3.11 (continued)

Ethnic group	(100 million yuan) Total	State-owned units	Urban collective-owned units	Units of other types of ownership
Qiang	22.46	10.95	0.45	11.06
Russian	1.96	0.99	0.02	0.95
Salar	11.38	7.00	0.14	4.24
She	106.23	33.49	1.37	71.37
Shui	28.53	16.18	0.44	11.91
Tajik	5.27	2.83	0.03	2.41
Tatar	0.64	0.34	0.00	0.30
Tibetan	640.71	474.24	4.97	161.51
Tu	25.89	15.54	0.33	10.02
Tujia	638.59	280.99	8.37	349.22
Uygur	1086.00	587.77	6.67	491.56
Uzbek	1.61	0.86	0.01	0.74
Va	30.12	16.28	0.54	13.30
Xibe	18.29	8.08	0.25	9.95
Yao	195.53	92.38	3.45	99.70
Yi	576.46	306.73	10.51	259.21
Yugur	1.02	0.61	0.02	0.40
Zhuang	1106.15	578.39	21.23	506.53

Table 3.12 Indices of total wage bill of employed persons in urban units (preceding year = 100)

Ethnic group	Total	State-owned units	Urban collective-owned units	Units of other types of ownership
National average	108.9	104.6	94.0	112.0
Achang	110.86	106.40	90.71	118.20
Bai	110.21	106.59	91.77	116.32
Baonan	106.60	99.56	90.45	122.25
Blang	110.85	106.40	90.68	118.16
Buyi	107.19	106.06	103.85	108.92
Dai	110.88	106.40	90.76	118.21
Daur	105.24	101.97	96.77	110.68
Deang	110.87	106.39	90.71	118.24
Derung	110.47	105.89	91.10	117.54
Dong	107.27	107.32	97.75	107.84
Dongxiang	106.08	98.54	90.14	122.26
Ewenki	106.67	102.18	96.74	114.13
Gaoshan	107.02	105.95	93.99	109.09

(continued)

Table 3.12 (continued)

Ethnic group	Total	State-owned units	Urban collective-owned units	Units of other types of ownership
Gelao	107.12	106.07	104.06	108.75
Han	108.47	105.24	93.68	112.18
Hani	110.87	106.39	90.71	118.22
Hezhe	102.91	102.69	96.44	103.16
Hui	106.92	104.95	90.53	110.94
Jing	108.06	107.72	98.84	108.88
Jingpo	110.85	106.39	90.73	118.18
Jino	110.88	106.39	90.70	118.24
Kazak	101.63	91.95	94.59	116.51
Kirgiz	101.63	92.05	94.63	116.35
Korean	102.81	94.13	82.21	114.65
Lahu	110.84	106.40	90.67	118.15
Lhoba	114.08	110.59	72.11	140.77
Li	112.22	110.06	94.05	114.59
Lisu	110.85	106.41	90.89	118.12
Manchu	106.80	98.51	88.14	116.11
Maonan	107.72	107.36	100.38	108.59
Miao	107.79	107.18	96.34	109.29
Monba	114.44	110.87	71.00	142.22
Mongol	106.74	101.22	94.72	115.06
Mulao	107.94	107.68	99.49	108.65
Naxi	110.88	106.44	90.88	118.21
Nu	110.90	106.44	90.50	118.52
Oroqen	104.79	102.45	96.60	108.58
Pumi	110.86	106.38	90.75	118.20
Qiang	110.56	107.46	97.99	114.56
Russian	103.98	96.39	95.26	115.67
Salar	109.90	111.17	106.81	108.23
She	112.01	107.68	107.71	114.53
Shui	107.22	106.09	103.60	108.98
Tajik	101.88	92.43	94.52	116.37
Tatar	102.11	92.79	94.41	116.55
Tibetan	112.11	109.66	86.76	126.62
Tu	110.03	111.07	106.10	108.69
Tujia	107.08	106.76	91.27	107.79
Uygur	101.64	91.99	94.58	116.47
Uzbek	101.78	92.24	94.63	116.41
Va	110.73	106.36	90.49	117.93
Xibe	105.21	94.99	88.15	116.51
Yao	108.39	108.55	94.43	108.86
Yi	110.37	106.65	94.22	116.16
Yugur	106.57	99.34	89.94	122.59
Zhuang	108.35	107.88	98.18	109.41

Table 3.13 Average wage of employed persons in urban units (yuan)

Ethnic group	Total	Staff and workers	State-owned units	Urban collective-owned units	Units of other types of ownership
National average	82,413	84,744	89,474	60,664	79,453
Achang	75,730.41	80,521.82	97,016.10	80,152.91	59,269.03
Bai	75,737.25	80,333.56	94,665.46	78,448.15	60,923.72
Baonan	71,551.20	74,443.28	76,500.73	50,352.14	65,709.28
Blang	75,748.94	80,530.94	97,050.17	80,070.00	59,311.40
Buyi	78,362.54	82,569.41	85,051.92	85,719.13	70,754.32
Dai	75,754.86	80,544.39	97,009.65	80,104.77	59,305.78
Daur	70,137.31	72,856.12	70,744.58	68,358.93	69,992.11
Deang	75,712.81	80,517.78	96,989.29	80,234.08	59,207.19
Derung	75,515.08	79,819.18	94,402.34	76,284.73	61,507.68
Dong	75,426.42	79,082.71	83,383.41	70,658.51	68,297.24
Dongxiang	71,360.40	74,174.68	75,768.10	51,614.49	66,211.79
Ewenki	73,300.78	75,347.17	74,657.14	74,901.34	72,031.86
Gaoshan	74,083.79	76,320.36	85,159.83	60,383.14	68,810.54
Gelao	78,432.75	82,650.58	84,769.83	86,023.77	70,950.71
Han	76,209.32	78,548.48	89,534.98	60,095.62	70,706.63
Hani	75,742.67	80,540.66	97,049.13	80,207.12	59,258.68
Hezhe	64,163.10	68,417.79	64,474.81	53,106.29	65,794.79
Hui	76,593.85	79,220.48	84,702.25	62,522.44	71,135.49
Jing	71,386.61	74,364.75	78,547.65	53,944.82	65,079.48
Jingpo	75,731.92	80,521.62	96,953.18	80,145.36	59,302.13
Jino	75,757.15	80,556.87	97,035.80	80,176.31	59,275.88
Kazak	75,474.02	76,733.51	74,501.99	73,190.73	76,726.43
Kirgiz	75,345.48	76,632.61	74,380.38	73,045.48	76,618.93
Korean	68,379.78	70,776.35	70,346.21	54,159.58	67,728.89
Lahu	75,700.83	80,486.50	96,990.94	80,117.08	59,244.19
Lhoba	112,543.86	116,368.92	119,017.79	50,981.48	88,811.31
Li	76,076.65	77,982.24	84,199.83	56,124.77	70,709.41
Lisu	75,762.46	80,498.84	96,793.70	79,552.99	59,517.00
Manchu	69,657.29	72,007.63	71,194.82	48,866.07	69,683.49
Maonan	73,162.67	76,474.36	79,643.96	62,252.73	66,693.72
Miao	76,006.21	79,769.46	86,461.50	72,195.71	67,595.41
Monba	114,820.94	118,682.39	120,967.41	49,976.40	90,262.67
Mongol	73,246.09	75,164.08	75,087.12	70,595.56	71,700.76
Mulao	72,288.06	75,371.68	79,136.31	56,985.60	66,046.29
Naxi	76,004.81	80,741.35	97,002.89	79,473.47	59,721.48
Nu	76,333.05	81,089.31	97,389.49	79,563.94	59,832.59
Oroqen	68,336.78	71,499.36	68,992.26	63,796.86	68,624.79
Pumi	75,760.24	80,534.24	96,959.72	79,982.00	59,375.65

(*continued*)

Table 3.13 (continued)

Ethnic group	Total	Staff and workers	State-owned units	Urban collective-owned units	Units of other types of ownership
Qiang	77,726.64	80,508.76	90,423.41	59,335.27	68,930.49
Russian	76,017.19	77,616.86	76,674.58	73,349.18	75,914.65
Salar	83,559.69	85,274.12	90,395.67	64,724.66	74,501.04
She	78,145.24	80,259.71	104,224.39	69,337.76	70,197.59
Shui	78,066.29	82,261.02	84,812.21	84,914.75	70,395.40
Tajik	75,474.37	76,773.88	74,950.50	72,664.19	76,501.96
Tatar	75,801.57	77,184.48	75,627.18	71,844.35	76,522.20
Tibetan	95,815.70	98,921.75	103,990.97	55,841.47	79,356.88
Tu	83,087.96	84,908.83	90,762.48	64,497.25	73,960.19
Tujia	74,845.65	77,814.62	86,860.14	58,367.80	67,914.11
Uygur	75,488.29	76,748.51	74,558.45	73,172.87	76,729.13
Uzbek	75,633.72	76,912.80	74,934.43	72,937.79	76,765.16
Va	75,674.89	80,402.41	96,816.75	79,636.41	59,421.70
Xibe	69,556.74	71,404.36	69,853.19	49,401.12	70,583.18
Yao	72,482.46	75,481.31	82,284.30	54,245.92	65,459.69
Yi	76,557.30	80,732.54	93,784.12	75,045.12	63,211.96
Yugur	71,311.74	74,269.61	76,307.01	49,746.56	65,567.71
Zhuang	71,731.72	74,745.79	79,766.71	54,305.45	64,980.54

Table 3.14 Indices of average wage of employed persons in urban units (preceding year = 100)

Ethnic group	Total	Staff and workers	State-owned units	Urban collective-owned units	Units of other types of ownership
National average	110.9	111.3	110.3	109.8	111.4
Achang	109.51	109.51	108.52	114.60	112.97
Bai	109.54	109.70	108.45	113.79	112.71
Baonan	111.62	112.13	107.53	112.14	120.41
Blang	109.51	109.52	108.54	114.59	112.96
Buyi	109.17	110.03	106.53	110.01	112.84
Dai	109.52	109.53	108.54	114.60	112.98
Daur	109.93	110.76	106.88	113.70	114.76
Deang	109.51	109.51	108.51	114.65	112.99
Derung	109.71	109.81	108.80	113.54	112.84
Dong	109.73	110.49	108.03	110.15	111.72

(continued)

Table 3.14 (continued)

Ethnic group	Total	Staff and workers	State-owned units	Urban collective-owned units	Units of other types of ownership
Dongxiang	111.54	112.07	107.81	111.43	119.69
Ewenki	110.47	111.41	106.56	114.79	116.80
Gaoshan	111.06	111.58	110.24	110.35	112.05
Gelao	109.16	110.03	106.47	109.92	112.85
Han	110.68	111.10	110.39	109.23	111.77
Hani	109.51	109.51	108.52	114.63	112.97
Hezhe	108.76	109.33	107.15	112.56	111.16
Hui	111.09	111.72	109.56	107.80	113.45
Jing	110.56	110.70	109.21	111.44	112.06
Jingpo	109.51	109.52	108.51	114.59	112.98
Jino	109.51	109.52	108.52	114.64	112.99
Kazak	111.10	111.80	111.78	100.25	109.63
Kirgiz	111.07	111.77	111.74	100.36	109.62
Korean	110.57	110.96	105.30	110.07	117.97
Lahu	109.52	109.52	108.53	114.61	112.97
Lhoba	106.94	104.45	105.19	96.36	123.10
Li	111.85	112.37	113.42	98.25	111.38
Lisu	109.57	109.59	108.63	114.41	112.95
Manchu	109.90	110.42	108.34	109.60	111.57
Maonan	110.18	110.51	108.42	111.03	112.26
Miao	109.79	110.45	108.42	110.38	111.86
Monba	106.80	104.16	104.95	95.82	123.69
Mongol	110.61	111.46	107.10	113.24	116.03
Mulao	110.42	110.64	108.92	111.23	112.09
Naxi	109.56	109.57	108.61	114.36	113.00
Nu	109.47	109.44	108.48	114.30	113.11
Oroqen	109.58	110.33	106.86	113.72	113.86
Pumi	109.52	109.53	108.55	114.57	112.98
Qiang	111.87	112.27	112.44	107.34	112.40
Russian	110.85	111.62	109.73	106.11	112.46
Salar	112.56	113.31	109.01	106.45	117.19
She	110.34	110.59	111.37	112.99	111.01
Shui	109.19	110.02	106.60	110.14	112.81
Tajik	111.09	111.78	111.76	100.53	109.69
Tatar	111.09	111.77	111.57	101.07	110.10
Tibetan	109.61	108.66	107.78	102.18	119.38
Tu	112.42	113.15	108.99	106.97	117.07

(*continued*)

Table 3.14 (continued)

Ethnic group	Total	Staff and workers	State-owned units	Urban collective-owned units	Units of other types of ownership
Tujia	110.73	111.30	110.04	108.89	111.51
Uygur	111.10	111.80	111.79	100.26	109.62
Uzbek	111.10	111.79	111.77	100.40	109.66
Va	109.53	109.54	108.55	114.40	112.93
Xibe	110.24	110.72	109.10	107.29	110.83
Yao	110.52	110.84	109.76	111.06	111.32
Yi	110.13	110.34	109.38	112.10	112.81
Yugur	111.57	112.08	107.46	112.48	120.51
Zhuang	110.56	110.67	109.33	111.57	112.05

Table 3.15 Indices of average real wage of employed persons in urban units (preceding year = 100)

Ethnic group	Total	Staff and workers	State-owned units	Urban collective-owned units	Units of other types of ownership
National average	108.6	109.0	108.0	107.5	109.1
Achang	107.26	107.26	106.29	112.24	110.65
Bai	107.29	107.44	106.22	111.45	110.40
Baonan	109.32	109.82	105.32	109.83	117.93
Blang	107.26	107.27	106.31	112.23	110.64
Buyi	106.93	107.77	104.34	107.75	110.52
Dai	107.27	107.27	106.31	112.24	110.65
Daur	107.67	108.48	104.68	111.36	112.40
Deang	107.26	107.26	106.28	112.29	110.67
Derung	107.46	107.55	106.57	111.21	110.51
Dong	107.48	108.21	105.81	107.89	109.43
Dongxiang	109.25	109.76	105.59	109.14	117.22
Ewenki	108.20	109.12	104.36	112.43	114.40
Gaoshan	108.77	109.28	107.97	108.08	109.75
Gelao	106.91	107.77	104.28	107.66	110.53
Han	108.40	108.81	108.12	106.98	109.47
Hani	107.25	107.26	106.29	112.28	110.65
Hezhe	106.52	107.08	104.95	110.25	108.87
Hui	108.81	109.42	107.31	105.59	111.12
Jing	108.29	108.42	106.96	109.15	109.75
Jingpo	107.26	107.26	106.28	112.24	110.66

(*continued*)

Table 3.15 (continued)

Ethnic group	Total	Staff and workers	State-owned units	Urban collective-owned units	Units of other types of ownership
Jino	107.26	107.26	106.29	112.28	110.67
Kazak	108.82	109.50	109.49	98.19	107.38
Kirgiz	108.79	109.47	109.45	98.29	107.37
Korean	108.30	108.68	103.13	107.81	115.55
Lahu	107.26	107.27	106.30	112.25	110.65
Lhoba	104.74	102.30	103.02	94.38	120.57
Li	109.55	110.06	111.09	96.23	109.09
Lisu	107.32	107.33	106.39	112.06	110.63
Manchu	107.64	108.15	106.11	107.35	109.27
Maonan	107.91	108.24	106.19	108.75	109.95
Miao	107.54	108.18	106.19	108.11	109.56
Monba	104.60	102.02	102.79	93.85	121.14
Mongol	108.34	109.17	104.90	110.91	113.64
Mulao	108.15	108.36	106.68	108.94	109.79
Naxi	107.31	107.32	106.38	112.01	110.68
Nu	107.22	107.19	106.25	111.95	110.79
Oroqen	107.32	108.07	104.67	111.38	111.52
Pumi	107.27	107.28	106.31	112.21	110.66
Qiang	109.57	109.96	110.13	105.13	110.09
Russian	108.57	109.33	107.47	103.92	110.14
Salar	110.24	110.98	106.77	104.26	114.78
She	108.07	108.32	109.07	110.67	108.73
Shui	106.95	107.76	104.41	107.88	110.49
Tajik	108.80	109.48	109.46	98.47	107.44
Tatar	108.81	109.47	109.28	98.99	107.84
Tibetan	107.36	106.42	105.56	100.08	116.93
Tu	110.11	110.82	106.75	104.77	114.67
Tujia	108.45	109.01	107.78	106.65	109.22
Uygur	108.81	109.50	109.49	98.20	107.36
Uzbek	108.81	109.49	109.47	98.33	107.40
Va	107.28	107.29	106.32	112.05	110.60
Xibe	107.98	108.44	106.86	105.08	108.55
Yao	108.24	108.56	107.50	108.77	109.03
Yi	107.86	108.07	107.13	109.79	110.49
Yugur	109.28	109.78	105.25	110.17	118.03
Zhuang	108.29	108.40	107.08	109.28	109.75

Table 3.16 Average wage of employed persons in urban units by status of registration (yuan) (I)

Ethnic group	Total	State-owned units	Urban collective-owned units	Cooperative units	Joint ownership units
National average	82,413	89,474	60,664	77,751	72,107
Achang	75,730.41	97,016.10	80,152.91	63,338.90	50,418.02
Bai	75,737.25	94,665.46	78,448.15	72,809.93	50,774.51
Baonan	71,551.20	76,500.73	50,352.14	67,172.98	43,191.95
Blang	75,748.94	97,050.17	80,070.00	63,452.32	50,477.30
Buyi	78,362.54	85,051.92	85,719.13	145,648.49	54,530.83
Dai	75,754.86	97,009.65	80,104.77	63,374.60	50,536.51
Daur	70,137.31	70,744.58	68,358.93	83,366.65	47,452.43
Deang	75,712.81	96,989.29	80,234.08	63,244.57	50,280.37
Derung	75,515.08	94,402.34	76,284.73	67,177.74	51,230.42
Dong	75,426.42	83,383.41	70,658.51	120,362.67	51,974.78
Dongxiang	71,360.40	75,768.10	51,614.49	72,496.87	44,069.77
Ewenki	73,300.78	74,657.14	74,901.34	89,650.82	46,561.61
Gaoshan	74,083.79	85,159.83	60,383.14	82,152.77	64,540.09
Gelao	78,432.75	84,769.83	86,023.77	147,590.18	54,403.40
Han	76,209.32	89,534.98	60,095.62	77,801.68	64,727.24
Hani	75,742.67	97,049.13	80,207.12	63,280.90	50,384.10
Hezhe	64,163.10	64,474.81	53,106.29	61,937.12	50,766.19
Hui	76,593.85	84,702.25	62,522.44	82,451.90	58,025.37
Jing	71,386.61	78,547.65	53,944.82	116,122.41	47,290.62
Jingpo	75,731.92	96,953.18	80,145.36	63,552.27	50,392.83
Jino	75,757.15	97,035.80	80,176.31	63,279.51	50,380.20
Kazak	75,474.02	74,501.99	73,190.73	141,241.74	49,996.06
Kirgiz	75,345.48	74,380.38	73,045.48	140,581.50	50,024.17
Korean	68,379.78	70,346.21	54,159.58	56,525.52	52,745.71
Lahu	75,700.83	96,990.94	80,117.08	63,319.72	50,500.22
Lhoba	112,543.86	119,017.79	50,981.48	84,750.17	30,006.62
Li	76,076.65	84,199.83	56,124.77	71,457.71	71,168.15
Lisu	75,762.46	96,793.70	79,552.99	63,657.38	51,253.72
Manchu	69,657.29	71,194.82	48,866.07	58,979.91	41,751.93
Maonan	73,162.67	79,643.96	62,252.73	126,971.48	48,591.90
Miao	76,006.21	86,461.50	72,195.71	114,100.30	53,030.31
Monba	114,820.94	120,967.41	49,976.40	82,673.03	29,384.84
Mongol	73,246.09	75,087.12	70,595.56	85,988.69	46,233.59
Mulao	72,288.06	79,136.31	56,985.60	121,455.93	47,878.09
Naxi	76,004.81	97,002.89	79,473.47	63,809.07	51,221.27
Nu	76,333.05	97,389.49	79,563.94	63,819.43	50,225.65

(*continued*)

Table 3.16 (continued)

Ethnic group	Total	State-owned units	Urban collective-owned units	Cooperative units	Joint ownership units
Oroqen	68,336.78	68,992.26	63,796.86	75,473.05	48,284.19
Pumi	75,760.24	96,959.72	79,982.00	63,364.27	50,555.54
Qiang	77,726.64	90,423.41	59,335.27	77,378.29	82,196.66
Russian	76,017.19	76,674.58	73,349.18	118,373.82	49,614.12
Salar	83,559.69	90,395.67	64,724.66	80,319.20	35,444.93
She	78,145.24	104,224.39	69,337.76	83,683.99	68,953.51
Shui	78,066.29	84,812.21	84,914.75	144,286.18	53,983.07
Tajik	75,474.37	74,950.50	72,664.19	139,299.31	50,333.43
Tatar	75,801.57	75,627.18	71,844.35	135,702.59	50,280.76
Tibetan	95,815.70	103,990.97	55,841.47	78,931.86	43,623.47
Tu	83,087.96	90,762.48	64,497.25	79,345.07	37,259.28
Tujia	74,845.65	86,860.14	58,367.80	100,266.18	51,833.94
Uygur	75,488.29	74,558.45	73,172.87	141,128.40	50,073.58
Uzbek	75,633.72	74,934.43	72,937.79	140,207.90	50,314.97
Va	75,674.89	96,816.75	79,636.41	63,764.04	50,791.08
Xibe	69,556.74	69,853.19	49,401.12	66,424.77	40,809.64
Yao	72,482.46	82,284.30	54,245.92	99,741.51	49,433.38
Yi	76,557.30	93,784.12	75,045.12	76,510.46	59,638.25
Yugur	71,311.74	76,307.01	49,746.56	66,022.75	43,691.46
Zhuang	71,731.72	79,766.71	54,305.45	113,208.30	33,678.07

Table 3.17 Average wage of employed persons in urban units by status of registration (yuan) (II)

Ethnic group	Limited liability corporations	Share-holding corporations	Others	Units with funds from Hong Kong, Macau & Taiwan	Foreign funded units
National average	72,114	93,316	61,666	82,027	99,367
Achang	66,173.80	79,395.85	41,461.70	60,860.85	61,290.57
Bai	65,889.73	80,517.20	43,663.96	61,695.15	63,338.39
Baonan	62,934.39	74,696.65	44,650.29	65,165.27	89,937.72
Blang	66,171.42	79,416.91	41,552.99	60,883.85	61,332.76
Buyi	66,495.10	92,617.77	56,391.72	68,762.77	71,893.19
Dai	66,187.16	79,403.42	41,517.44	60,903.77	61,364.87
Daur	69,607.86	72,637.84	53,445.19	63,828.42	72,971.01
Deang	66,169.21	79,371.95	41,275.30	60,795.19	61,201.69

(continued)

Table 3.17 (continued)

Ethnic group	Limited liability corporations	Share-holding corporations	Others	Units with funds from Hong Kong, Macau & Taiwan	Foreign funded units
Derung	66,426.69	79,833.81	44,901.23	62,015.06	64,410.46
Dong	64,596.16	85,293.98	54,651.46	64,325.19	72,436.86
Dongxiang	63,416.71	76,427.73	44,447.08	65,727.40	90,194.67
Ewenki	71,832.24	72,594.03	58,314.87	68,040.13	76,251.24
Gaoshan	65,246.32	80,915.76	62,038.03	66,491.57	75,823.19
Gelao	66,539.47	93,023.03	56,488.91	68,849.30	71,988.73
Han	67,538.21	82,041.64	63,867.39	67,530.10	77,558.20
Hani	66,181.25	79,401.19	41,419.55	60,843.41	61,270.05
Hezhe	65,008.51	70,909.56	46,423.28	55,272.48	66,875.17
Hui	68,932.55	80,821.02	55,151.27	70,970.80	76,148.30
Jing	63,186.73	74,824.08	57,093.08	53,857.21	73,876.21
Jingpo	66,188.02	79,445.11	41,472.72	60,849.68	61,308.78
Jino	66,198.64	79,422.73	41,408.87	60,869.73	61,303.29
Kazak	72,419.29	104,287.62	40,998.77	74,148.76	80,937.14
Kirgiz	72,353.52	103,972.49	41,049.42	73,945.93	80,738.10
Korean	64,852.62	74,136.91	61,163.83	63,701.02	77,268.03
Lahu	66,138.70	79,354.58	41,472.14	60,825.35	61,254.83
Lhoba	87,652.57	88,609.30	49,520.22	72,559.11	121,750.54
Li	64,981.62	83,329.84	66,543.88	84,427.66	87,081.73
Lisu	66,149.73	79,292.46	42,098.11	61,191.83	61,775.34
Manchu	65,410.87	77,268.15	55,996.71	66,669.81	80,411.06
Maonan	63,972.63	79,697.34	56,944.87	57,513.15	73,527.34
Miao	65,004.55	85,409.77	53,810.27	65,268.24	71,277.15
Monba	89,063.66	89,126.13	49,577.32	73,455.46	124,861.22
Mongol	70,425.63	74,656.33	57,914.25	68,613.45	77,477.90
Mulao	63,687.97	77,226.83	57,412.85	55,409.35	74,074.90
Naxi	66,303.39	79,447.81	42,135.32	61,347.53	62,160.25
Nu	66,527.76	79,556.65	41,809.39	61,105.71	62,356.56
Oroqen	68,187.92	71,279.25	52,141.83	61,184.29	71,154.24
Pumi	66,198.79	79,395.72	41,627.67	60,933.85	61,476.98
Qiang	65,823.58	77,875.63	64,521.44	73,743.55	80,047.64
Russian	72,860.08	92,761.67	49,201.70	73,288.39	81,007.40
Salar	69,500.69	88,010.27	42,802.13	69,489.76	62,755.02
She	66,497.46	84,923.14	72,713.43	69,561.74	74,150.90
Shui	66,343.53	91,898.22	56,132.02	68,087.37	71,772.87
Tajik	72,235.60	103,550.23	41,676.95	73,860.76	80,761.88
Tatar	72,218.83	102,855.78	42,085.30	74,186.49	81,808.48
Tibetan	77,087.84	84,565.66	50,688.72	71,380.63	96,669.62

(*continued*)

Table 3.17 (continued)

Ethnic group	Limited liability corporations	Share-holding corporations	Others	Units with funds from Hong Kong, Macau & Taiwan	Foreign funded units
Tu	69,276.80	87,381.31	44,310.61	69,007.42	63,563.93
Tujia	64,868.18	80,152.24	56,121.54	64,106.24	74,889.70
Uygur	72,420.54	104,263.77	41,087.59	74,140.69	80,913.11
Uzbek	72,454.32	104,101.26	41,496.42	74,201.58	81,079.38
Va	66,101.17	79,370.70	41,900.18	60,945.60	61,456.44
Xibe	65,151.73	82,864.09	49,503.50	68,409.69	84,034.45
Yao	63,831.31	77,363.13	55,209.86	56,639.09	72,965.04
Yi	66,097.30	80,434.00	49,476.47	65,278.77	67,656.27
Yugur	62,849.92	74,172.12	45,066.53	65,247.78	91,131.22
Zhuang	63,619.21	75,387.04	56,665.46	53,884.79	73,518.24

Table 3.18 Total wage bill of employed persons in urban units (100 million yuan) (I)

Ethnic group	Total	Agriculture, forestry, animal husbandry and fishery	Mining	Manufacturing	Production and distribution of electricity, gas and water
National total	141,480.0	716.1	3413.4	30,385.0	3704.0
Achang	2.57	0.02	0.05	0.32	0.08
Bai	139.34	0.85	2.92	17.38	4.32
Baonan	1.21	0.01	0.05	0.14	0.06
Blang	6.96	0.05	0.15	0.86	0.21
Buyi	210.81	0.43	6.04	23.34	7.97
Dai	87.73	0.61	1.85	10.75	2.68
Daur	11.67	0.52	0.83	1.32	0.61
Deang	1.35	0.01	0.03	0.16	0.04
Derung	0.60	0.00	0.02	0.08	0.02
Dong	207.25	0.58	4.05	29.03	7.12
Dongxiang	39.06	0.44	1.88	4.39	1.99
Ewenki	2.79	0.10	0.19	0.34	0.16
Gaoshan	0.51	0.00	0.01	0.10	0.01

(*continued*)

Table 3.18 (continued)

Ethnic group	Total	Agriculture, forestry, animal husbandry and fishery	Mining	Manufacturing	Production and distribution of electricity, gas and water
Gelao	40.92	0.08	1.18	4.48	1.56
Han	132,133.22	628.33	3087.78	29,120.82	3373.74
Hani	108.93	0.76	2.31	13.36	3.32
Hezhe	0.40	0.02	0.03	0.05	0.01
Hui	1116.51	7.90	55.20	157.07	41.64
Jing	1.49	0.01	0.01	0.20	0.05
Jingpo	10.01	0.07	0.21	1.23	0.31
Jino	1.58	0.01	0.03	0.19	0.05
Kazak	161.55	2.06	12.54	15.87	6.27
Kirgiz	20.70	0.27	1.61	2.04	0.80
Korean	163.12	4.24	6.47	30.74	6.26
Lahu	34.28	0.24	0.73	4.21	1.05
Lhoba	0.46	0.00	0.01	0.01	0.01
Li	124.41	2.99	0.64	8.93	3.20
Lisu	47.86	0.33	1.02	5.89	1.47
Manchu	1016.29	14.24	39.67	177.16	34.35
Maonan	7.04	0.05	0.10	0.87	0.25
Miao	653.04	2.12	12.96	90.66	21.38
Monba	1.42	0.00	0.02	0.04	0.04
Mongol	533.40	14.93	32.91	70.94	28.59
Mulao	13.96	0.10	0.14	1.92	0.47
Naxi	23.63	0.16	0.50	2.88	0.72
Nu	2.22	0.01	0.05	0.27	0.07
Oroqen	0.71	0.03	0.05	0.08	0.03
Pumi	2.55	0.02	0.05	0.31	0.08
Qiang	22.46	0.05	0.47	3.33	0.82
Russian	1.96	0.03	0.13	0.21	0.08
Salar	11.38	0.14	0.75	1.23	0.48
She	106.23	0.23	0.26	27.30	2.43
Shui	28.53	0.07	0.81	3.11	1.08
Tajik	5.27	0.07	0.40	0.53	0.20
Tatar	0.64	0.01	0.05	0.06	0.02
Tibetan	640.71	2.93	17.34	40.43	22.30
Tu	25.89	0.30	1.60	3.16	1.07

(*continued*)

Table 3.18 (continued)

Ethnic group	Total	Agriculture, forestry, animal husbandry and fishery	Mining	Manufacturing	Production and distribution of electricity, gas and water
Tujia	638.59	2.20	7.49	113.23	17.91
Uygur	1086.00	13.80	84.05	107.18	42.05
Uzbek	1.61	0.02	0.12	0.16	0.06
Va	30.12	0.21	0.65	3.78	0.92
Xibe	18.29	0.24	0.97	3.30	0.65
Yao	195.53	1.12	1.43	36.24	5.90
Yi	576.46	2.98	12.68	73.59	19.05
Yugur	1.02	0.01	0.04	0.12	0.05
Zhuang	1106.15	8.99	8.38	164.18	35.95

Table 3.19 Total wage bill of employed persons in urban units (100 million yuan) (II)

Ethnic group	Construction	Transport, storage and post	Information transmission, computer service and software	Wholesale and retail trades	Hotels and catering services
National total	15,949.5	7273.3	6204.1	6628.5	1293.0
Achang	0.28	0.12	0.04	0.11	0.03
Bai	15.33	6.61	2.19	5.95	1.29
Baonan	0.12	0.08	0.02	0.03	0.01
Blang	0.76	0.33	0.10	0.30	0.07
Buyi	23.93	9.05	3.79	7.68	1.11
Dai	9.50	4.21	1.22	3.84	0.86
Daur	0.55	0.90	0.34	0.38	0.09
Deang	0.15	0.06	0.02	0.06	0.01
Derung	0.06	0.03	0.01	0.03	0.01
Dong	25.01	9.45	4.28	7.41	1.27
Dongxiang	3.89	2.67	0.52	0.86	0.22
Ewenki	0.12	0.22	0.08	0.09	0.02
Gaoshan	0.06	0.03	0.03	0.02	0.01
Gelao	4.59	1.76	0.74	1.50	0.21
Han	150,59.97	6736.33	5947.39	6294.93	1220.64
Hani	11.80	5.22	1.49	4.78	1.07

(continued)

Table 3.19 (continued)

Ethnic group	Construction	Transport, storage and post	Information transmission, computer service and software	Wholesale and retail trades	Hotels and catering services
Hezhe	0.02	0.03	0.02	0.02	0.00
Hui	91.27	65.52	49.14	47.61	8.97
Jing	0.19	0.08	0.03	0.05	0.01
Jingpo	1.08	0.48	0.14	0.44	0.10
Jino	0.17	0.08	0.02	0.07	0.02
Kazak	14.69	11.37	2.28	4.30	0.77
Kirgiz	1.88	1.46	0.29	0.55	0.10
Korean	9.14	10.39	6.64	6.43	1.18
Lahu	3.72	1.64	0.46	1.50	0.34
Lhoba	0.01	0.01	0.01	0.01	0.00
Li	4.75	10.02	4.39	5.88	5.33
Lisu	5.23	2.30	0.68	2.07	0.47
Manchu	60.43	68.28	56.29	43.38	8.91
Maonan	0.85	0.37	0.13	0.22	0.04
Miao	79.92	30.63	13.16	24.52	4.58
Monba	0.04	0.04	0.03	0.03	0.01
Mongol	27.59	40.44	16.24	16.83	3.89
Mulao	1.68	0.75	0.30	0.44	0.09
Naxi	2.55	1.13	0.36	1.03	0.23
Nu	0.24	0.10	0.03	0.10	0.02
Oroqen	0.03	0.05	0.02	0.03	0.01
Pumi	0.28	0.12	0.04	0.11	0.03
Qiang	3.15	1.19	0.82	0.70	0.15
Russian	0.15	0.14	0.06	0.07	0.01
Salar	0.83	0.89	0.21	0.31	0.06
She	20.00	4.04	3.57	4.16	0.93
Shui	3.27	1.23	0.49	1.03	0.15
Tajik	0.48	0.37	0.08	0.14	0.03
Tatar	0.06	0.04	0.01	0.02	0.00
Tibetan	36.19	27.33	11.17	14.27	4.44
Tu	1.96	1.96	0.47	0.73	0.14
Tujia	91.21	32.99	16.11	25.70	4.67
Uygur	98.76	76.38	15.48	29.04	5.22
Uzbek	0.15	0.11	0.03	0.04	0.01
Va	3.27	1.44	0.42	1.31	0.29
Xibe	1.26	1.34	0.70	0.65	0.14
Yao	22.19	10.12	4.98	6.83	1.54
Yi	67.79	28.10	11.65	22.77	4.87
Yugur	0.10	0.07	0.02	0.02	0.01
Zhuang	131.00	60.99	24.00	35.30	8.04

Table 3.20 Total wage bill of employed persons in urban units (100 million yuan) (III)

Ethnic group	Financial intermediation	Real estate	Leasing and business services	Scientific research, technical services, and geological prospecting	Management of water conservancy, environment and public facilities
National total	8907.3	3507.8	4453.3	5045.1	1456.5
Achang	0.12	0.06	0.05	0.08	0.03
Bai	6.68	3.32	2.60	4.09	1.69
Baonan	0.04	0.02	0.02	0.04	0.02
Blang	0.31	0.17	0.13	0.20	0.09
Buyi	11.33	5.04	3.77	5.33	2.07
Dai	3.97	2.09	1.61	2.59	1.10
Daur	0.76	0.17	0.26	0.36	0.20
Deang	0.06	0.03	0.02	0.04	0.02
Derung	0.03	0.01	0.01	0.02	0.01
Dong	12.01	4.86	3.90	5.33	2.16
Dongxiang	1.33	0.51	0.54	1.31	0.73
Ewenki	0.18	0.04	0.05	0.08	0.05
Gaoshan	0.03	0.01	0.02	0.02	0.01
Gelao	2.20	0.99	0.74	1.04	0.40
Han	8367.48	3312.33	4234.22	4749.35	1340.16
Hani	4.92	2.59	1.99	3.20	1.36
Hezhe	0.03	0.01	0.01	0.02	0.01
Hui	74.73	24.46	36.11	48.47	15.35
Jing	0.09	0.03	0.04	0.04	0.02
Jingpo	0.45	0.24	0.18	0.29	0.13
Jino	0.07	0.04	0.03	0.05	0.02
Kazak	6.40	1.85	3.59	4.01	2.08
Kirgiz	0.82	0.24	0.46	0.51	0.27
Korean	11.46	3.11	4.69	6.17	2.31
Lahu	1.55	0.82	0.62	1.00	0.43
Lhoba	0.03	0.00	0.01	0.01	0.00
Li	9.49	9.67	2.27	3.04	2.87
Lisu	2.17	1.14	0.87	1.42	0.60
Manchu	81.56	22.76	34.34	45.83	12.74
Maonan	0.41	0.16	0.16	0.17	0.08
Miao	36.82	16.30	12.31	17.59	7.09

(*continued*)

Table 3.20 (continued)

Ethnic group	Financial intermediation	Real estate	Leasing and business services	Scientific research, technical services, and geological prospecting	Management of water conservancy, environment and public facilities
Monba	0.08	0.01	0.03	0.04	0.01
Mongol	35.21	8.13	10.68	15.74	8.71
Mulao	0.83	0.32	0.35	0.35	0.17
Naxi	1.09	0.56	0.45	0.71	0.29
Nu	0.10	0.05	0.04	0.07	0.03
Oroqen	0.05	0.01	0.02	0.02	0.01
Pumi	0.12	0.06	0.05	0.08	0.03
Qiang	1.16	0.55	0.42	0.95	0.24
Russian	0.11	0.03	0.06	0.06	0.03
Salar	0.53	0.12	0.12	0.48	0.18
She	5.78	2.47	2.43	2.21	0.79
Shui	1.52	0.67	0.51	0.72	0.28
Tajik	0.21	0.06	0.12	0.13	0.07
Tatar	0.03	0.01	0.02	0.02	0.01
Tibetan	32.82	5.88	10.14	20.69	6.28
Tu	1.19	0.30	0.28	1.04	0.40
Tujia	35.99	16.53	12.36	19.00	7.45
Uygur	43.14	12.50	24.21	27.02	13.97
Uzbek	0.07	0.02	0.04	0.04	0.02
Va	1.37	0.72	0.55	0.88	0.38
Xibe	1.22	0.34	0.45	0.59	0.23
Yao	11.73	4.86	4.80	5.05	2.19
Yi	27.57	13.81	10.51	18.72	6.75
Yugur	0.04	0.01	0.02	0.04	0.02
Zhuang	65.06	25.53	28.14	27.46	13.39

Table 3.21 Total wage bill of employed persons in urban units (100 million yuan) (IV)

Ethnic group	Services to households and other services	Education	Health, social securities and social welfare	Culture, sports and entertainment	Public management and social organization
National total	423.8	15,928.1	8857.8	1450.7	15,882.8
Achang	0.01	0.49	0.20	0.03	0.48
Bai	0.46	25.75	10.79	1.41	25.68
Baonan	0.00	0.20	0.09	0.01	0.25
Blang	0.02	1.32	0.53	0.07	1.30
Buyi	0.55	39.35	16.28	1.84	41.93
Dai	0.30	16.62	6.70	0.87	16.34
Daur	0.05	1.58	0.77	0.14	1.86
Deang	0.00	0.26	0.10	0.01	0.25
Derung	0.00	0.10	0.04	0.01	0.10
Dong	0.52	34.33	17.50	2.05	36.41
Dongxiang	0.05	6.54	2.78	0.41	8.01
Ewenki	0.01	0.38	0.18	0.03	0.47
Gaoshan	0.00	0.06	0.03	0.01	0.06
Gelao	0.11	7.67	3.16	0.36	8.17
Han	400.23	14,531.21	8158.10	1346.90	14,223.31
Hani	0.38	20.67	8.32	1.08	20.31
Hezhe	0.00	0.05	0.03	0.01	0.05
Hui	2.92	142.13	74.00	15.14	158.88
Jing	0.00	0.24	0.15	0.01	0.23
Jingpo	0.03	1.90	0.76	0.10	1.86
Jino	0.01	0.30	0.12	0.02	0.29
Kazak	0.19	24.12	11.36	1.46	36.35
Kirgiz	0.03	3.09	1.46	0.19	4.65
Korean	0.88	20.31	11.13	2.05	19.55
Lahu	0.12	6.51	2.62	0.34	6.39
Lhoba	0.00	0.08	0.02	0.01	0.21
Li	0.30	19.00	9.51	1.61	20.53
Lisu	0.16	9.02	3.67	0.47	8.90
Manchu	4.88	117.37	64.14	13.12	116.86
Maonan	0.01	1.22	0.68	0.06	1.20
Miao	1.70	108.91	53.07	6.31	113.01

(*continued*)

Table 3.21 (continued)

Ethnic group	Services to households and other services	Education	Health, social securities and social welfare	Culture, sports and entertainment	Public management and social organization
Monba	0.00	0.24	0.07	0.03	0.64
Mongol	1.34	72.51	35.12	6.29	87.31
Mulao	0.03	2.30	1.38	0.13	2.22
Naxi	0.08	4.42	1.80	0.24	4.42
Nu	0.01	0.42	0.17	0.02	0.43
Oroqen	0.00	0.09	0.05	0.01	0.10
Pumi	0.01	0.48	0.19	0.03	0.47
Qiang	0.03	2.98	1.87	0.17	3.41
Russian	0.00	0.27	0.13	0.02	0.37
Salar	0.01	1.67	0.78	0.15	2.46
She	0.28	11.10	6.37	0.84	11.04
Shui	0.07	5.35	2.23	0.25	5.68
Tajik	0.01	0.78	0.37	0.05	1.17
Tatar	0.00	0.09	0.04	0.01	0.14
Tibetan	0.75	105.13	39.60	11.47	231.55
Tu	0.02	3.77	1.77	0.32	5.41
Tujia	1.51	88.22	51.55	6.59	87.88
Uygur	1.30	161.87	76.34	9.82	243.86
Uzbek	0.00	0.24	0.11	0.01	0.36
Va	0.10	5.67	2.30	0.30	5.57
Xibe	0.08	2.16	1.19	0.18	2.61
Yao	0.44	28.43	17.65	1.89	28.15
Yi	1.65	100.43	45.18	5.29	103.05
Yugur	0.00	0.17	0.07	0.01	0.20
Zhuang	2.02	178.75	109.16	9.99	169.80

Table 3.22 Average wage of employed persons in urban private units (yuan) (I)

Ethnic group	Total	Agriculture, forestry, animal husbandry and fishery	Mining	Manufac-turing	Production and distribution of electricity, gas and water
National average	49,575	36,375	44,096	49,275	44,239
Achang	43,663.76	41,775.43	36,705.23	45,550.91	39,251.72
Bai	43,442.70	39,976.17	38,614.16	44,968.90	40,667.17
Baonan	39,825.81	32,192.22	42,209.26	39,735.06	43,679.56
Blang	43,680.71	41,759.01	36,754.60	45,574.21	39,301.94
Buyi	43,785.13	30,652.65	49,915.19	43,914.92	53,122.61
Dai	43,643.34	41,735.23	36,692.98	45,535.73	39,255.11
Daur	38,776.67	33,856.18	43,984.59	40,747.84	42,487.10
Deang	43,604.86	41,758.19	36,636.69	45,513.32	39,198.85
Derung	43,695.99	40,354.81	38,395.60	45,357.62	40,290.31
Dong	42,573.50	31,980.52	47,368.00	42,571.37	47,254.73
Dongxiang	40,054.09	32,513.13	43,152.03	40,135.40	44,193.27
Ewenki	40,095.90	35,310.86	45,521.58	43,024.10	45,768.54
Gaoshan	44,488.42	34,292.29	42,571.97	44,343.64	42,716.08
Gelao	43,792.17	30,425.19	50,130.46	43,896.61	53,368.41
Han	45,896.99	35,742.28	44,342.00	45,962.01	44,684.86
Hani	43,649.42	41,772.97	36,673.92	45,550.62	39,244.67
Hezhe	36,466.52	30,659.34	39,220.97	36,061.22	34,288.82
Hui	42,978.89	34,119.80	43,811.77	44,145.06	46,411.74
Jing	40,653.91	33,927.23	43,332.99	41,760.91	40,989.13
Jingpo	43,652.02	41,730.47	36,721.69	45,539.79	39,273.10
Jino	43,632.54	41,745.34	36,653.35	45,534.45	39,213.62
Kazak	41,785.12	34,589.02	54,026.14	43,872.21	51,888.69
Kirgiz	41,730.86	34,561.45	53,903.07	43,799.85	51,722.50
Korean	36,742.45	27,391.99	35,852.85	36,418.88	32,852.93
Lahu	43,652.01	41,759.59	36,702.02	45,548.44	39,263.80
Lhoba	4258.66	3208.04	4403.94	4277.78	4401.30
Li	49,272.96	38,725.34	44,390.75	42,445.44	32,851.98
Lisu	43,630.08	41,589.96	36,860.97	45,488.36	39,434.68
Manchu	39,195.69	31,469.22	37,023.78	38,837.43	40,099.66
Maonan	41,299.54	32,778.35	45,283.24	42,160.03	44,454.43
Miao	43,441.99	33,557.59	46,760.77	43,719.49	47,042.08
Monba	2407.40	1773.84	1807.77	2371.38	2278.70
Mongol	40,131.47	34,512.61	44,168.05	42,470.95	45,302.86
Mulao	41,013.78	33,453.23	44,190.24	41,981.02	42,493.12
Naxi	43,474.01	41,405.29	36,723.44	45,316.64	39,268.04

(*continued*)

Table 3.22 (continued)

Ethnic group	Total	Agriculture, forestry, animal husbandry and fishery	Mining	Manufacturing	Production and distribution of electricity, gas and water
Nu	43,077.31	41,149.28	36,292.20	44,931.47	38,800.22
Oroqen	38,141.44	32,985.24	42,265.69	39,428.20	39,956.63
Pumi	43,628.97	41,681.95	36,723.16	45,513.65	39,265.68
Qiang	43,401.06	35,278.90	43,037.03	43,741.20	44,891.37
Russian	41,784.85	34,973.74	50,309.30	44,027.75	49,642.94
Salar	38,873.43	29,501.57	42,826.69	39,049.86	48,830.33
She	51,316.62	39,991.44	49,991.28	50,627.16	44,897.34
Shui	43,632.06	30,820.74	49,575.95	43,838.66	52,627.42
Tajik	41,910.95	34,615.40	53,739.99	43,940.90	51,614.08
Tatar	42,060.88	34,611.58	53,274.19	43,955.25	51,403.25
Tibetan	22,702.35	18,087.91	23,400.06	22,846.97	25,440.76
Tu	39,449.35	30,003.40	42,640.18	39,552.30	48,347.12
Tujia	43,515.87	33,474.14	46,464.43	43,711.41	43,922.73
Uygur	41,802.59	34,595.04	54,002.08	43,885.11	51,864.73
Uzbek	41,938.38	34,643.49	53,867.69	43,961.67	51,732.36
Va	43,775.89	41,758.28	36,958.31	45,640.30	39,521.89
Xibe	39,230.94	31,868.46	39,035.73	38,866.87	40,821.67
Yao	41,817.11	34,875.51	42,982.06	42,288.15	40,135.11
Yi	43,564.31	38,686.02	39,918.48	44,836.29	42,354.30
Yugur	40,033.85	32,358.97	42,146.77	39,907.56	43,520.00
Zhuang	40,957.69	34,547.74	42,731.49	42,069.35	40,557.92

Table 3.23 Average wage of employed persons in urban private units (yuan) (II)

Ethnic group	Construction	Transport, storage and post	Information transmission, computer service and software	Wholesale and retail trades	Hotels and catering services
National average	50,879	50,547	76,326	45,177	39,632
Achang	40,332.35	43,071.18	57,219.97	41,379.49	38,482.84
Bai	41,227.79	42,536.03	58,014.90	40,402.13	37,793.42
Baonan	38,493.99	40,673.82	40,931.76	39,798.13	37,844.17
Blang	40,381.52	43,098.25	57,205.36	41,390.21	38,482.20
Buyi	45,194.56	40,982.55	66,553.33	38,389.22	36,929.70

(continued)

Table 3.23 (continued)

Ethnic group	Construction	Transport, storage and post	Information transmission, computer service and software	Wholesale and retail trades	Hotels and catering services
Dai	40,327.30	43,031.01	57,165.39	41,354.58	38,460.62
Daur	39,262.44	42,886.64	39,332.37	36,121.84	35,367.28
Deang	40,258.98	42,991.08	57,123.38	41,330.37	38,448.09
Derung	41,415.90	43,602.97	56,437.75	41,106.55	38,162.32
Dong	44,980.28	40,571.90	61,276.01	36,832.34	34,976.46
Dongxiang	39,013.54	41,343.13	41,101.79	39,335.63	38,030.53
Ewenki	40,763.18	43,557.43	38,385.09	37,865.72	36,927.11
Gaoshan	45,994.12	44,739.05	55,930.03	41,464.05	36,864.16
Gelao	45,266.11	40,887.53	66,914.54	38,333.45	36,894.29
Han	47,650.25	47,260.64	58,344.76	42,302.24	38,151.88
Hani	40,320.01	43,041.40	57,199.04	41,365.47	38,475.56
Hezhe	36,094.26	40,741.57	43,589.47	33,260.35	32,088.95
Hui	44,459.04	45,064.30	49,335.62	40,403.68	36,877.99
Jing	40,514.86	40,812.44	48,818.87	39,257.83	33,727.82
Jingpo	40,339.33	43,038.69	57,260.02	41,363.47	38,463.93
Jino	40,294.45	43,009.82	57,186.93	41,344.13	38,454.89
Kazak	45,551.25	51,520.28	42,444.70	35,178.61	37,818.01
Kirgiz	45,466.20	51,437.18	42,444.66	35,147.44	37,758.92
Korean	38,555.30	37,050.96	42,663.26	32,825.28	32,851.32
Lahu	40,346.69	43,054.91	57,160.86	41,372.47	38,473.01
Lhoba	4413.81	4311.78	5739.83	3802.61	3512.07
Li	43,221.81	57,634.60	61,356.80	42,454.81	40,967.35
Lisu	40,438.10	43,056.24	56,860.87	41,301.15	38,427.85
Manchu	40,868.67	40,518.22	45,618.10	37,433.93	34,056.78
Maonan	41,632.91	40,570.14	53,482.44	38,900.02	34,399.52
Miao	45,095.07	41,903.32	61,369.19	38,015.97	35,930.05
Monba	2391.25	2422.52	3279.73	2200.86	1975.12
Mongol	41,300.76	43,101.69	39,734.33	38,054.51	36,553.73
Mulao	41,102.41	40,813.37	51,247.85	39,276.16	33,993.22
Naxi	40,276.40	42,875.23	56,738.21	41,142.65	38,270.56
Nu	39,846.62	42,518.60	56,414.51	40,815.52	37,946.31
Oroqen	38,363.98	42,074.91	40,633.45	35,475.88	34,426.50
Pumi	40,345.12	43,035.00	57,097.66	41,336.89	38,444.39
Qiang	44,665.07	43,353.68	47,934.09	39,203.91	36,802.68
Russian	44,065.05	48,391.23	42,705.59	36,894.12	37,703.77
Salar	40,508.09	46,294.88	40,379.69	43,517.51	33,788.52
She	53,298.45	51,878.31	73,286.20	47,067.08	40,499.92
Shui	44,934.96	40,906.93	65,757.27	38,389.50	36,834.64
Tajik	45,606.55	51,373.91	42,953.59	35,380.70	37,796.47

(continued)

Table 3.23 (continued)

Ethnic group	Construction	Transport, storage and post	Information transmission, computer service and software	Wholesale and retail trades	Hotels and catering services
Tatar	45,409.75	51,003.76	43,462.76	35,752.93	37,918.85
Tibetan	23,211.77	24,421.87	24,539.31	22,818.63	19,704.26
Tu	40,922.33	46,262.28	42,391.30	43,746.67	34,169.22
Tujia	46,881.71	43,018.91	57,201.69	37,757.37	35,551.72
Uygur	45,573.64	51,517.85	42,516.48	35,189.34	37,812.47
Uzbek	45,611.35	51,495.53	42,989.70	35,367.65	37,843.43
Va	40,591.20	43,252.55	57,213.92	41,468.88	38,535.63
Xibe	41,714.31	41,775.77	44,479.37	37,584.55	34,454.42
Yao	42,915.37	41,607.61	54,545.48	38,625.52	33,847.35
Yi	42,044.49	42,851.28	55,630.83	40,397.45	37,815.63
Yugur	38,510.34	40,482.19	41,409.22	39,848.88	38,042.95
Zhuang	40,581.32	41,168.19	49,917.36	39,763.09	33,967.03

Table 3.24 Average wage of employed persons in urban private units (yuan) (III)

Ethnic group	Financial intermed-iation	Real estate	Leasing and business services	Scientific research, technical services, and geological prospecting	Management of water conservancy, environment and public facilities
National average	62,943	51,393	53,382	61,876	42,409
Achang	36,689.98	45,891.22	46,352.13	55,944.51	37,514.22
Bai	40,601.62	46,642.24	45,148.40	54,050.14	36,861.77
Baonan	44,735.40	43,454.55	43,927.30	54,914.45	40,178.24
Blang	36,803.43	45,872.50	46,344.30	55,941.50	37,533.42
Buyi	60,197.84	52,598.19	39,830.65	44,944.18	32,634.73
Dai	36,699.10	45,854.78	46,323.02	55,910.02	37,518.44
Daur	43,492.28	37,421.08	40,041.54	44,395.16	34,331.05
Deang	36,564.64	45,800.18	46,290.73	55,925.85	37,474.47
Derung	39,517.92	45,788.72	45,791.34	54,640.44	37,481.99
Dong	57,447.42	50,270.50	39,999.00	45,753.81	33,849.19
Dongxiang	45,749.84	43,813.98	43,860.88	54,341.02	40,123.73
Ewenki	42,443.98	37,344.11	40,509.39	44,536.34	35,611.16
Gaoshan	51,473.47	48,006.53	44,760.69	50,405.83	38,097.64
Gelao	60,532.66	52,769.72	39,694.36	44,760.93	32,518.80

(continued)

Table 3.24 (continued)

Ethnic group	Financial intermed-iation	Real estate	Leasing and business services	Scientific research, technical services, and geological prospecting	Management of water conservancy, environment and public facilities
Han	52,647.99	48,133.66	46,176.37	52,349.22	39,608.42
Hani	36,665.54	45,841.04	46,332.50	55,942.95	37,498.82
Hezhe	46,426.75	38,360.69	40,105.69	44,880.86	31,765.28
Hui	48,228.44	43,676.82	41,824.72	50,802.19	38,341.95
Jing	48,043.05	46,563.80	40,999.41	47,587.79	34,259.05
Jingpo	36,727.64	45,879.79	46,320.74	55,918.12	37,500.47
Jino	36,672.21	45,833.70	46,316.99	55,940.61	37,497.31
Kazak	51,385.02	41,962.12	36,612.61	48,152.79	37,641.26
Kirgiz	51,324.48	41,915.11	36,637.30	48,093.20	37,572.60
Korean	44,419.96	36,583.12	35,811.51	45,163.15	31,449.78
Lahu	36,690.97	45,841.10	46,331.62	55,926.84	37,514.92
Lhoba	5387.55	4595.04	4082.09	4738.03	3493.19
Li	44,968.61	75,450.96	55,410.78	52,975.12	39,200.59
Lisu	36,952.45	45,845.24	46,251.95	55,702.56	37,627.49
Manchu	44,657.10	40,537.25	39,845.23	44,001.50	34,666.15
Maonan	51,553.99	48,105.83	40,383.65	46,560.66	33,581.23
Miao	56,397.85	50,449.43	41,396.28	47,664.26	34,976.48
Monba	2991.33	2478.46	2489.59	2862.80	2123.86
Mongol	42,536.72	38,055.25	40,026.74	44,674.23	35,639.22
Mulao	49,727.95	47,297.13	40,875.60	47,365.39	34,113.26
Naxi	36,954.09	45,716.76	46,093.15	55,514.54	37,474.15
Nu	36,406.28	45,240.23	45,692.29	55,129.38	37,014.26
Oroqen	44,010.35	37,632.48	40,198.18	44,437.29	33,582.94
Pumi	36,754.78	45,813.37	46,284.60	55,859.34	37,496.06
Qiang	47,116.47	46,894.39	44,130.99	48,494.31	41,713.39
Russian	49,563.55	41,001.08	38,920.83	47,493.56	37,265.23
Salar	32,814.45	32,156.75	31,556.41	56,929.05	37,341.60
She	65,840.80	55,344.23	50,763.38	56,685.99	41,654.18
Shui	59,466.61	52,255.15	39,821.76	45,014.15	32,607.70
Tajik	51,457.88	42,187.11	36,915.52	48,280.59	37,678.60
Tatar	51,858.61	42,519.81	37,480.04	48,827.60	37,913.08
Tibetan	22,114.09	22,187.16	21,507.93	29,371.19	21,852.18
Tu	33,670.48	33,511.89	32,918.45	57,078.83	37,664.04
Tujia	58,547.78	49,826.25	40,999.82	47,732.66	36,366.41
Uygur	51,408.10	41,983.43	36,634.88	48,148.46	37,639.58
Uzbek	51,574.95	42,245.95	36,895.33	48,333.42	37,722.92

(continued)

Table 3.24 (continued)

Ethnic group	Financial intermed-iation	Real estate	Leasing and business services	Scientific research, technical services, and geological prospecting	Management of water conservancy, environment and public facilities
Va	37,111.41	45,946.64	46,394.22	55,924.16	37,661.01
Xibe	42,497.41	40,565.69	39,798.85	43,696.73	34,572.59
Yao	49,041.63	47,498.53	42,300.52	49,466.23	35,985.11
Yi	42,174.51	46,869.37	44,952.99	52,594.41	38,085.95
Yugur	45,623.54	44,085.70	44,594.56	55,007.60	40,370.24
Zhuang	46,935.06	46,584.81	41,673.84	48,635.51	34,769.90

Table 3.25 Average wage of employed persons in urban private units (yuan) (IV)

Ethnic group	Services to households and other services	Education	Health, social securities and social welfare	Culture, sports and entertainment
National average	41,058	46,228	52,343	44,592
Achang	42,665.39	46,142.46	42,551.04	34,458.89
Bai	41,335.27	45,638.37	43,221.67	34,618.46
Baonan	37,263.91	44,236.51	42,343.21	35,416.87
Blang	42,675.46	46,155.70	42,601.68	34,501.69
Buyi	34,549.48	43,259.79	45,944.63	36,077.44
Dai	42,636.77	46,136.16	42,557.96	34,451.76
Daur	31,739.81	37,259.35	41,817.94	34,329.73
Deang	42,655.24	46,135.18	42,471.01	34,374.95
Derung	41,434.40	45,285.26	43,622.27	35,370.32
Dong	35,304.10	42,396.31	45,999.23	35,393.77
Dongxiang	37,011.23	43,902.95	43,378.80	35,630.51
Ewenki	31,935.94	38,846.05	43,227.61	35,861.93
Gaoshan	37,281.88	41,949.07	47,263.89	38,739.71
Gelao	34,407.35	43,237.53	45,979.99	36,082.39
Han	38,834.83	44,081.02	49,854.06	41,479.16
Hani	42,672.49	46,157.48	42,540.11	34,431.14
Hezhe	31,575.34	34,704.61	38,752.45	31,261.81
Hui	37,942.21	42,265.03	44,611.83	38,728.49
Jing	35,341.66	35,026.59	42,566.07	33,176.70
Jingpo	42,640.43	46,137.22	42,558.68	34,449.01
Jino	42,652.92	46,150.63	42,527.21	34,417.43

(continued)

Table 3.25 (continued)

Ethnic group	Services to households and other services	Education	Health, social securities and social welfare	Culture, sports and entertainment
Kazak	35,222.10	38,642.48	52,631.75	41,092.76
Kirgiz	35,175.02	38,577.85	52,504.57	40,997.67
Korean	33,201.76	38,690.43	42,226.81	32,324.46
Lahu	42,670.29	46,147.31	42,546.46	34,448.64
Lhoba	3497.74	4044.25	4642.20	3742.11
Li	32,439.98	34,453.85	44,534.22	46,487.39
Lisu	42,520.63	46,076.66	42,670.20	34,597.60
Manchu	34,224.06	39,836.67	44,022.47	35,148.52
Maonan	34,886.93	36,910.15	43,315.48	33,691.11
Miao	36,690.12	43,465.59	46,377.75	36,321.17
Monba	1980.02	2357.80	2706.67	2251.81
Mongol	32,770.02	39,402.35	43,775.59	36,098.56
Mulao	35,163.73	35,812.10	43,201.82	33,581.01
Naxi	42,327.45	45,906.89	42,540.62	34,468.00
Nu	42,045.79	45,485.03	42,052.60	34,047.42
Oroqen	31,700.50	36,579.61	40,793.43	33,359.23
Pumi	42,596.13	46,102.11	42,566.36	34,466.90
Qiang	37,264.78	43,589.51	47,932.60	40,286.14
Russian	34,350.03	39,584.85	49,400.27	39,607.50
Salar	40,666.15	42,201.75	36,705.10	42,035.71
She	41,127.53	42,507.92	55,513.50	42,159.63
Shui	34,625.01	42,987.08	45,679.29	35,856.42
Tajik	35,316.04	38,784.15	52,522.79	41,088.72
Tatar	35,487.54	39,299.37	52,308.68	41,081.19
Tibetan	21,548.78	23,880.57	23,297.67	22,236.67
Tu	40,699.56	42,534.55	37,617.19	42,018.59
Tujia	37,541.44	43,309.25	46,899.20	37,725.99
Uygur	35,227.36	38,650.00	52,642.45	41,101.09
Uzbek	35,285.12	38,763.27	52,674.22	41,183.35
Va	42,727.05	46,182.48	42,743.23	34,687.13
Xibe	34,123.73	38,522.11	46,218.19	35,614.19
Yao	36,721.40	38,972.49	45,642.80	35,143.95
Yi	40,225.38	45,092.06	44,373.39	36,196.11
Yugur	37,218.63	44,473.54	42,621.86	35,284.25
Zhuang	35,873.64	35,539.75	43,019.23	33,553.95

Table 3.26 Average wage of employed persons in urban units (yuan) (I)

Ethnic group	Total	Agriculture, forestry, animal husbandry and fishery	Mining	Manufacturing	Production and distribution of electricity, gas and water
National average	82,413	36,466	81,429	72,088	100,162
Achang	75,730.41	47,697.89	59,602.87	61,942.90	94,722.03
Bai	75,737.25	47,840.49	60,088.81	63,514.41	94,464.66
Baonan	71,551.20	46,765.38	86,852.40	68,316.69	79,368.88
Blang	75,748.94	47,722.91	59,732.31	61,973.40	94,735.66
Buyi	78,362.54	51,877.35	64,686.55	73,676.18	103,201.26
Dai	75,754.86	47,769.84	59,743.21	61,979.64	94,749.45
Daur	70,137.31	38,859.12	97,906.37	68,014.49	87,803.77
Deang	75,712.81	47,647.66	59,539.73	61,905.55	94,621.00
Derung	75,515.08	46,907.75	64,587.82	63,105.07	94,674.51
Dong	75,426.42	48,019.57	62,431.31	69,867.10	94,584.74
Dongxiang	71,360.40	45,218.12	88,685.86	68,672.36	80,220.89
Ewenki	73,300.78	42,543.57	104,234.40	69,611.48	93,345.92
Gaoshan	74,083.79	43,089.27	74,252.71	65,971.45	95,642.35
Gelao	78,432.75	51,919.07	64,714.46	73,908.63	103,295.94
Han	76,209.32	46,782.92	81,521.25	67,903.31	10,0882.11
Hani	75,742.67	47,693.78	59,575.25	61,948.07	94,732.42
Hezhe	64,163.10	32,819.63	80,255.69	65,099.07	76,965.78
Hui	76,593.85	47,109.01	92,854.17	66,664.37	97,945.67
Jing	71,386.61	42,515.25	62,385.35	61,276.73	91,919.40
Jingpo	75,731.92	47,689.59	59,645.12	61,965.73	94,726.87
Jino	75,757.15	47,704.70	59,616.55	61,967.18	94,699.67
Kazak	75,474.02	29,805.38	123,174.83	71,907.98	97,229.74
Kirgiz	75,345.48	29,796.14	122,805.61	71,828.92	97,051.74
Korean	68,379.78	35,387.93	71,872.41	72,059.82	84,214.25
Lahu	75,700.83	47,710.77	59,619.36	61,914.16	94,679.09
Lhoba	112,543.86	35,265.44	111,451.75	88,290.41	99,977.45
Li	76,076.65	44,037.84	68,854.43	67,343.82	89,613.77
Lisu	75,762.46	48,172.02	60,577.54	62,152.89	94,822.10
Manchu	69,657.29	25,559.72	76,012.40	69,630.64	83,387.67
Maonan	73,162.67	45,011.63	62,846.13	64,624.00	94,940.94
Miao	76,006.21	48,682.35	64,129.69	69,386.23	94,901.45
Monba	114,820.94	35,298.35	113,689.74	89,515.07	100,682.54
Mongol	73,246.09	40,009.05	99,183.89	69,695.75	92,204.38

(*continued*)

Table 3.26 (continued)

Ethnic group	Total	Agriculture, forestry, animal husbandry and fishery	Mining	Manufacturing	Production and distribution of electricity, gas and water
Mulao	72,288.06	43,540.40	63,207.50	62,775.66	93,665.04
Naxi	76,004.81	48,118.90	60,796.84	62,322.51	94,933.55
Nu	76,333.05	47,537.09	60,588.76	62,413.16	94,945.50
Oroqen	68,336.78	37,279.43	91,900.37	67,098.55	84,656.77
Pumi	75,760.24	47,721.60	59,893.81	62,021.01	94,767.12
Qiang	77,726.64	65,094.37	93,924.80	69,835.84	99,188.89
Russian	76,017.19	35,839.23	114,756.99	71,799.11	97,310.71
Salar	83,559.69	54,021.35	113,282.70	65,061.31	94,699.79
She	78,145.24	50,179.88	63,546.23	67,470.88	113,380.90
Shui	78,066.29	51,443.67	64,319.84	73,174.18	102,703.74
Tajik	75,474.37	30,346.33	121,757.33	71,734.67	97,181.25
Tatar	75,801.57	31,187.91	120,521.44	71,972.16	97,046.81
Tibetan	95,815.70	47,401.88	106,242.22	77,396.59	97,091.31
Tu	83,087.96	53,987.89	110,351.59	65,171.19	95,265.54
Tujia	74,845.65	44,361.85	68,601.45	68,062.00	90,599.59
Uygur	75,488.29	29,830.99	123,064.60	71,902.64	97,274.01
Uzbek	75,633.72	30,120.89	122,490.65	71,915.59	97,461.38
Va	75,674.89	47,890.92	60,107.68	61,981.63	94,674.05
Xibe	69,556.74	22,485.75	82,602.86	69,960.98	81,292.85
Yao	72,482.46	43,094.90	64,005.67	63,089.03	90,444.78
Yi	76,557.30	52,965.21	69,631.14	65,444.22	96,860.37
Yugur	71,311.74	46,744.78	85,552.69	68,494.94	79,108.84
Zhuang	71,731.72	42,517.68	63,379.27	61,125.53	92,653.03

Table 3.27 Average wage of employed persons in urban units (yuan) (II)

Ethnic group	Construction	Transport, storage and post	Information transmission, computer service and software	Wholesale and retail trades	Hotels and catering services
National average	60,501	88,508	147,678	80,551	48,260
Achang	49,242.41	88,950.68	85,542.33	59,717.62	39,297.37
Bai	51,008.64	88,083.82	89,113.56	61,072.13	39,944.60
Baonan	52,968.89	82,954.65	77,194.07	52,711.29	38,938.63
Blang	49,296.47	88,919.18	85,669.04	59,754.04	39,304.64
Buyi	62,299.37	86,225.01	108,869.13	71,302.42	43,856.67
Dai	49,274.25	88,952.79	85,603.96	59,759.58	39,290.63
Daur	51,830.80	80,614.25	80,019.05	59,563.73	46,436.62
Deang	49,208.55	88,979.61	85,284.40	59,667.26	39,248.54
Derung	50,961.95	87,753.52	88,759.93	60,395.31	40,168.89
Dong	59,026.15	84,130.13	104,866.71	66,956.95	42,683.19
Dongxiang	53,140.69	83,793.01	78,950.37	53,758.66	39,391.68
Ewenki	52,269.25	81,739.26	84,575.86	61,450.91	44,769.46
Gaoshan	58,186.08	81,450.58	102,192.47	63,589.64	43,930.33
Gelao	62,572.04	86,223.83	109,094.78	71,511.83	43,897.60
Han	58,832.77	83,147.05	109,961.64	64,736.68	44,175.50
Hani	49,247.72	88,961.14	85,496.43	59,726.52	39,272.70
Hezhe	50,623.57	76,457.09	71,485.87	55,005.63	49,627.12
Hui	58,176.18	83,732.22	97,227.30	61,361.85	43,426.92
Jing	55,378.36	82,188.12	93,797.25	60,875.68	39,495.73
Jingpo	49,289.23	88,950.36	85,546.95	59,731.21	39,288.76
Jino	49,249.32	88,971.40	85,482.02	59,729.90	39,259.50
Kazak	62,473.19	99,984.29	105,146.07	73,190.05	48,651.01
Kirgiz	62,349.08	99,767.02	104,839.92	73,034.89	48,685.16
Korean	51,113.60	76,648.12	84,310.06	54,606.84	43,753.89
Lahu	49,252.99	88,905.24	85,483.60	59,692.18	39,279.86
Lhoba	57,432.08	102,646.63	122,482.68	80,624.86	63,065.75
Li	46,989.08	84,726.67	117,476.63	64,976.90	55,413.63
Lisu	49,404.46	88,816.57	86,140.28	59,872.03	39,406.95
Manchu	55,357.88	77,605.06	94,027.09	56,646.27	45,873.35
Maonan	57,428.76	83,174.88	97,787.60	63,727.94	40,542.46
Miao	58,123.80	84,608.42	104,406.98	66,516.41	42,513.80
Monba	57,616.15	103,749.77	124,276.70	81,889.82	64,016.55
Mongol	53,508.32	81,774.22	88,169.47	61,167.98	44,582.02
Mulao	56,409.81	82,716.39	96,377.26	62,305.25	39,962.76
Naxi	49,490.53	88,931.98	86,507.64	60,069.80	39,521.26

(continued)

Table 3.27 (continued)

Ethnic group	Construction	Transport, storage and post	Information transmission, computer service and software	Wholesale and retail trades	Hotels and catering services
Nu	49,459.72	89,148.03	86,419.40	60,129.41	39,705.81
Oroqen	51,271.78	78,825.72	77,315.35	57,887.07	47,210.52
Pumi	49,328.32	88,911.16	85,672.83	59,770.18	39,331.07
Qiang	55,243.87	85,138.17	110,604.57	66,880.03	43,913.20
Russian	59,460.86	92,848.63	99,828.87	69,463.15	47,074.91
Salar	67,351.96	94,405.48	87,640.94	65,640.38	45,977.74
She	59,966.67	88,060.33	127,124.35	73,129.70	46,166.66
Shui	61,964.36	86,093.58	107,795.17	70,826.39	43,625.91
Tajik	62,337.73	99,403.98	105,155.37	72,879.95	48,473.95
Tatar	62,275.86	98,858.81	104,747.28	72,463.91	48,209.10
Tibetan	58,538.54	95,698.19	108,382.22	72,113.25	53,338.33
Tu	66,480.56	93,613.22	89,088.63	65,356.06	45,629.32
Tujia	58,551.62	81,818.39	108,018.68	63,457.77	42,329.62
Uygur	62,479.16	99,949.56	105,232.04	73,206.31	48,654.52
Uzbek	62,476.70	99,781.27	105,546.84	73,197.14	48,616.73
Va	49,439.32	88,735.12	85,851.67	59,718.47	39,382.62
Xibe	56,603.78	81,674.97	99,371.90	60,036.28	47,399.35
Yao	54,888.29	83,161.86	98,314.97	61,728.01	40,436.33
Yi	52,370.43	87,568.31	94,968.98	62,979.73	41,061.20
Yugur	52,593.95	82,383.21	77,195.77	52,315.50	38,657.31
Zhuang	55,024.36	82,784.38	94,176.65	60,858.17	39,421.80

Table 3.28 Average wage of employed persons in urban units (yuan) (III)

Ethnic group	Financial intermed-iation	Real estate	Leasing and business services	Scientific research, technical services, and geological prospecting	Management of water conservancy, environment and public facilities
National average	129,837	75,281	85,147	123,343	56,670
Achang	136,829.26	55,469.59	47,271.74	94,272.37	55,586.90
Bai	134,498.63	56,975.54	48,860.73	93,329.30	54,566.72
Baonan	75,242.27	50,603.26	59,083.29	94,223.75	55,302.48

(*continued*)

Table 3.28 (continued)

Ethnic group	Financial intermed-iation	Real estate	Leasing and business services	Scientific research, technical services, and geological prospecting	Management of water conservancy, environment and public facilities
Blang	136,771.34	55,540.80	47,301.64	94,384.45	55,629.59
Buyi	142,616.99	63,285.24	56,719.82	88,998.67	46,596.33
Dai	136,727.57	55,497.41	47,301.57	94,436.44	55,603.12
Daur	83,551.51	48,794.00	58,543.58	82,989.47	44,136.58
Deang	136,852.72	55,355.30	47,162.26	94,187.83	55,586.48
Derung	130,558.46	56,971.24	49,401.26	94,731.70	54,771.02
Dong	124,309.15	64,677.45	56,413.33	88,777.63	49,263.81
Dongxiang	76,025.17	50,763.50	58,738.19	93,649.94	54,387.22
Ewenki	88,749.64	48,290.54	55,318.09	82,556.25	45,775.06
Gaoshan	114,114.85	65,416.61	59,463.85	97,156.14	52,859.41
Gelao	143,170.69	63,382.82	56,835.49	88,745.33	46,368.46
Han	111,659.62	66,665.00	61,490.87	103,982.51	55,144.85
Hani	136,883.95	55,448.37	47,241.50	94,288.22	55,610.92
Hezhe	75,507.81	51,296.28	66,879.80	85,591.75	41,157.63
Hui	102,580.10	59,938.24	56,133.20	95,875.24	55,897.49
Jing	106,395.46	70,556.75	57,877.14	89,174.18	48,117.36
Jingpo	136,839.31	55,475.08	47,296.72	94,243.68	55,548.96
Jino	136,885.94	55,435.78	47,241.24	94,330.89	55,613.30
Kazak	99,905.03	52,751.97	54,669.86	89,658.36	51,468.45
Kirgiz	99,663.80	52,732.89	54,774.03	89,591.59	51,337.67
Korean	90,096.85	51,940.53	56,400.65	81,534.59	42,857.47
Lahu	136,759.28	55,462.38	47,245.18	94,267.58	55,587.19
Lhoba	209,358.88	80,822.18	99,097.92	123,697.11	53,531.62
Li	121,493.81	69,210.80	68,403.92	90,841.88	50,538.95
Lisu	135,552.82	55,713.71	47,553.61	95,115.04	55,551.81
Manchu	89,235.60	59,664.55	54,423.07	89,100.58	43,989.01
Maonan	115,978.51	68,915.54	57,655.41	88,609.56	47,314.27
Miao	127,380.01	63,908.46	55,129.94	91,581.45	50,745.23
Monba	214,398.54	81,928.80	101,996.83	126,193.11	53,954.00
Mongol	91,151.15	50,834.84	53,964.65	84,099.92	46,381.65
Mulao	110,745.68	70,354.34	58,230.85	89,439.90	47,896.63
Naxi	136,158.51	55,868.94	47,850.34	95,335.48	55,613.93
Nu	137,737.07	55,978.65	48,203.04	94,908.94	55,592.82
Oroqen	81,062.53	49,670.69	60,866.68	83,635.44	43,112.75
Pumi	136,546.71	55,537.77	47,383.80	94,435.63	55,597.60
Qiang	97,214.56	65,685.88	59,085.60	124,240.96	55,119.44

(*continued*)

Table 3.28 (continued)

Ethnic group	Financial intermed-iation	Real estate	Leasing and business services	Scientific research, technical services, and geological prospecting	Management of water conservancy, environment and public facilities
Russian	99,134.55	52,499.47	56,159.84	89,043.57	50,369.43
Salar	100,642.65	50,434.69	56,575.24	98,233.98	71,605.90
She	123,831.70	72,988.86	64,549.57	112,259.44	61,411.22
Shui	141,489.79	63,369.07	56,487.15	88,728.43	46,639.91
Tajik	100,273.20	53,245.55	54,865.85	90,055.03	51,565.02
Tatar	100,332.55	53,418.22	55,523.70	90,796.35	52,075.90
Tibetan	151,674.52	68,489.56	77,914.29	116,655.45	58,315.36
Tu	102,126.55	51,622.00	57,034.52	99,017.38	70,692.15
Tujia	113,096.61	66,538.45	55,583.40	97,492.43	55,298.30
Uygur	100,027.03	52,824.69	54,699.09	89,705.06	51,473.94
Uzbek	100,579.08	53,163.28	54,986.15	90,060.73	51,617.51
Va	136,122.20	55,686.42	47,529.27	94,404.87	55,520.94
Xibe	90,865.50	60,056.96	52,458.74	88,168.10	44,458.89
Yao	108,954.91	68,967.15	57,766.97	91,548.09	51,237.19
Yi	126,462.23	59,133.78	51,556.76	101,916.77	54,416.77
Yugur	74,846.25	50,885.62	59,406.01	94,347.00	54,835.21
Zhuang	108,330.75	70,505.27	57,906.84	90,302.00	48,795.04

Table 3.29 Average wage of employed persons in urban units (yuan) (IV)

Ethnic group	Services to households and other services	Education	Health, social securities and social welfare	Culture, sports and entertainment	Public management and social organization
National Average	55,343	92,383	98,118	98,621	87,932
Achang	46,215.07	101,159.71	87,550.45	83,483.66	98,062.03
Bai	47,060.94	97,978.64	88,282.98	84,416.36	94,541.82
Baonan	56,447.87	84,575.25	75,584.15	70,566.72	75,531.59
Blang	46,260.36	101,165.08	87,644.02	83,496.73	98,088.76
Buyi	44,223.55	85,333.40	87,649.23	87,408.87	80,700.81
Dai	46,222.53	101,094.97	87,604.53	83,475.08	98,056.23
Daur	51,431.79	83,336.27	76,419.62	69,991.94	73,066.46
Deang	46,183.97	101,161.82	87,454.45	83,421.46	98,038.11

(continued)

Table 3.29 (continued)

Ethnic group	Services to households and other services	Education	Health, social securities and social welfare	Culture, sports and entertainment	Public management and social organization
Derung	47,077.59	98,514.88	87,734.72	82,433.74	94,822.75
Dong	50,492.93	82,839.45	90,761.68	87,528.15	78,704.79
Dongxiang	56,265.22	83,487.49	76,203.10	70,883.32	74,384.82
Ewenki	48,153.35	85,685.64	77,486.20	72,279.42	74,818.47
Gaoshan	50,957.88	85,672.85	91,536.35	80,902.15	82,920.19
Gelao	44,064.29	85,018.36	87,502.72	87,506.33	80,291.46
Han	52,010.52	90,598.73	94,924.09	84,071.73	88,716.90
Hani	46,218.54	101,192.89	87,559.90	83,494.39	98,103.41
Hezhe	58,368.21	80,285.39	75,534.84	66,184.51	71,840.70
Hui	50,541.10	88,385.33	88,333.86	79,396.55	81,245.31
Jing	54,653.99	76,106.61	89,446.75	79,046.54	77,812.46
Jingpo	46,201.04	101,090.41	87,525.87	83,488.43	97,977.05
Jino	46,194.77	101,168.19	87,559.77	83,467.72	98,078.71
Kazak	50,452.40	78,316.74	85,683.33	79,851.49	69,046.76
Kirgiz	50,526.45	78,317.53	85,586.64	79,712.22	69,061.56
Korean	47,662.96	78,472.56	75,864.47	66,323.69	70,127.82
Lahu	46,218.52	101,117.69	87,539.86	83,442.52	98,024.86
Lhoba	102,701.31	134,341.12	121,887.24	106,746.48	115,838.47
Li	44,769.98	88,863.67	86,177.31	76,641.76	80,395.27
Lisu	46,273.68	100,628.22	87,790.00	83,325.10	97,800.49
Manchu	48,815.81	79,684.21	75,772.35	68,841.13	68,897.16
Maonan	51,892.87	77,773.90	88,704.46	81,224.78	77,777.02
Miao	49,327.85	86,467.09	91,265.83	86,562.40	82,448.96
Monba	105,420.59	136,729.42	123,812.57	108,452.37	117,849.01
Mongol	47,594.82	84,529.23	77,624.00	72,205.62	73,971.64
Mulao	53,721.89	76,784.79	89,569.52	80,442.30	77,912.92
Naxi	46,556.74	100,864.64	88,087.24	83,549.57	97,982.33
Nu	47,190.22	101,650.71	88,254.31	83,913.01	98,377.96

(*continued*)

Table 3.29 (continued)

Ethnic group	Services to households and other services	Education	Health, social securities and social welfare	Culture, sports and entertainment	Public management and social organization
Oroqen	53,337.63	82,564.86	75,973.02	68,682.58	72,862.53
Pumi	46,283.56	101,068.79	87,621.71	83,457.87	97,999.34
Qiang	49,183.21	83,210.64	98,273.01	80,298.71	90,043.29
Russian	49,643.35	82,813.14	84,477.65	78,751.70	73,093.24
Salar	47,713.36	98,546.09	79,197.56	80,163.85	90,699.19
She	59,146.00	99,389.88	114,471.14	90,911.96	106,230.24
Shui	44,527.88	85,093.36	87,480.06	87,029.52	80,647.34
Tajik	50,495.24	78,691.08	85,969.91	79,923.48	69,619.03
Tatar	50,771.44	79,546.93	86,219.25	80,274.28	70,393.60
Tibetan	75,511.18	112,276.93	103,941.13	92,475.87	102,567.89
Tu	48,091.72	98,440.41	80,237.24	80,712.61	91,252.16
Tujia	53,497.88	86,806.89	95,151.92	85,200.03	83,647.65
Uygur	50,457.45	78,348.59	85,756.91	79,904.69	69,106.18
Uzbek	50,517.70	78,662.52	86,093.57	80,188.33	69,530.70
Va	46,274.36	100,879.34	87,643.12	83,413.21	97,752.01
Xibe	51,368.93	77,838.80	75,795.99	69,477.28	67,051.92
Yao	55,916.57	80,461.29	92,926.53	84,723.84	80,120.68
Yi	46,789.61	94,354.94	90,462.55	82,979.17	93,822.57
Yugur	56,732.69	84,332.41	75,800.33	70,501.26	75,280.85
Zhuang	54,583.51	77,511.38	89,874.67	79,866.10	79,271.05

Table 3.30 Registered unemployed persons and unemployment rate in urban area

	Unemployed persons (10,000 persons)					Unemployment rate (%)				
Ethnic group	1990	2005	2011	2012	2018	1990	2005	2011	2012	2018
National total	383.20	839.00	922.00	917.00	790.57	2.50	4.20	4.10	4.10	3.39
Achang	0.01	0.01	0.01	0.01	0.02	2.50	4.16	4.04	4.02	3.38
Bai	0.38	0.63	0.74	0.80	0.93	2.67	4.17	4.01	3.95	2.78
Baonan	0.01	0.01	0.01	0.01	0.01	4.84	3.31	3.14	2.74	3.39
Blang	0.02	0.03	0.03	0.04	0.05	2.50	4.16	4.04	4.02	3.15
Buyi	0.89	1.04	1.08	1.09	1.29	4.01	4.18	3.62	3.30	3.40
Dai	0.22	0.36	0.44	0.48	0.57	2.51	4.17	4.04	4.02	3.64
Daur	0.08	0.10	0.12	0.13	0.14	3.16	4.28	3.85	3.83	3.40
Deang	0.00	0.01	0.01	0.01	0.01	2.50	4.17	4.05	4.03	3.37
Derung	0.00	0.00	0.00	0.00	0.00	2.51	4.13	3.95	3.91	3.16
Dong	0.85	1.37	1.41	1.41	1.46	3.55	4.18	3.76	3.57	2.74
Dongxiang	0.26	0.20	0.23	0.22	0.21	4.69	3.34	3.13	2.77	3.58
Ewenki	0.02	0.02	0.03	0.03	0.03	3.58	4.24	3.79	3.73	3.13
Gaoshan	0.00	0.00	0.00	0.00	0.00	2.81	3.87	3.46	3.34	3.15
Gelao	0.17	0.20	0.21	0.21	0.25	4.04	4.18	3.62	3.29	3.12
Han	345.49	660.90	691.13	687.37	726.47	2.56	3.79	3.50	3.39	3.40
Hani	0.27	0.44	0.55	0.60	0.71	2.50	4.16	4.04	4.02	3.85
Hezhe	0.00	0.00	0.00	0.00	0.00	2.22	4.33	3.98	4.01	3.19
Hui	4.61	5.94	6.65	6.41	7.03	3.65	3.91	3.61	3.47	2.42
Jing	0.01	0.01	0.01	0.01	0.01	3.79	4.11	3.45	3.40	3.39
Jingpo	0.02	0.04	0.05	0.05	0.07	2.51	4.16	4.04	4.02	3.40
Jino	0.00	0.01	0.01	0.01	0.01	2.50	4.17	4.04	4.02	2.36
Kazak	0.65	0.75	0.75	0.80	0.65	3.00	3.92	3.22	3.39	2.38

(*continued*)

Table 3.30 (continued)

	Unemployed persons (10,000 persons)					Unemployment rate (%)				
Ethnic group	1990	2005	2011	2012	2018	1990	2005	2011	2012	2018
Kirgiz	0.08	0.10	0.10	0.10	0.08	2.99	3.92	3.23	3.40	3.59
Korean	0.86	1.96	1.66	1.73	1.95	2.04	4.36	3.74	3.70	3.40
Lahu	0.08	0.14	0.17	0.19	0.22	2.50	4.16	4.04	4.02	2.85
Lhoba	0.00	0.00	0.00	0.00	0.00	0.26	0.37	3.23	2.66	2.35
Li	0.57	0.82	0.47	0.59	0.89	3.04	3.58	1.84	2.09	3.40
Lisu	0.12	0.20	0.24	0.26	0.32	2.53	4.18	4.05	4.02	3.67
Manchu	4.79	11.40	8.98	9.03	10.12	2.02	4.82	3.68	3.59	2.59
Maonan	0.03	0.04	0.04	0.04	0.04	3.93	4.14	3.50	3.36	3.20
Miao	2.35	3.99	4.09	4.13	4.40	3.24	4.18	3.77	3.59	2.85
Monba	0.00	0.00	0.00	0.01	0.01	0.13	0.16	3.22	2.62	3.53
Mongol	3.43	4.75	5.15	5.37	6.19	3.38	4.35	3.74	3.66	2.47
Mulao	0.06	0.09	0.09	0.09	0.08	3.86	4.11	3.46	3.37	3.39
Naxi	0.06	0.10	0.12	0.13	0.15	2.52	4.16	4.04	4.01	3.38
Nu	0.01	0.01	0.01	0.01	0.01	2.47	4.10	4.02	3.99	3.74
Oroqen	0.00	0.01	0.01	0.01	0.01	2.89	4.31	3.90	3.88	3.39
Pumi	0.01	0.01	0.01	0.01	0.02	2.51	4.16	4.04	4.02	3.46
Qiang	0.14	0.13	0.14	0.15	0.20	3.68	4.60	4.15	4.01	2.83
Russian	0.01	0.01	0.01	0.01	0.01	3.18	4.00	3.42	3.48	2.92
Salar	0.08	0.07	0.09	0.08	0.09	5.36	3.84	3.66	3.29	3.31
She	0.18	0.35	0.36	0.37	0.42	2.56	3.80	3.42	3.34	3.13
Shui	0.12	0.14	0.15	0.15	0.18	4.00	4.18	3.63	3.31	2.39
Tajik	0.02	0.02	0.02	0.03	0.02	2.98	3.91	3.23	3.39	2.40
Tatar	0.00	0.00	0.00	0.00	0.00	3.05	3.88	3.22	3.35	3.02
Tibetan	1.80	1.59	2.79	3.34	4.11	2.48	2.28	3.55	3.13	2.94
Tu	0.19	0.16	0.19	0.18	0.21	5.23	3.82	3.64	3.28	3.08
Tujia	1.67	5.14	5.13	4.68	4.44	2.19	4.21	3.90	3.74	2.36

Uygur	4.36	5.07	5.06	5.39	4.35	3.00	3.92	3.22	3.39	2.37
Uzbek	0.01	0.01	0.01	0.01	0.01	3.00	3.91	3.22	3.38	3.39
Va	0.07	0.12	0.15	0.16	0.20	2.51	4.15	4.03	4.01	3.60
Xibe	0.10	0.23	0.16	0.16	0.18	2.37	5.13	3.60	3.53	2.77
Yao	0.75	1.26	1.31	1.33	1.23	3.34	4.06	3.62	3.60	3.39
Yi	2.13	2.67	3.08	3.34	4.11	3.00	4.29	4.03	3.94	2.78
Yugur	0.01	0.01	0.01	0.01	0.01	4.82	3.29	3.12	2.72	2.43
Zhuang	4.93	6.72	6.93	7.02	6.39	3.72	4.09	3.46	3.42	3.39

4

Living Conditions and the Means of Livelihood

Data in this chapter show the people's living conditions and their changes in China, mainly include basic conditions and living conditions, income and expenditure, housing of households. Data of the year from 2013 onwards come from Household Survey on Income and Expenditure and Living Conditions. Data from 1978 to 2012 are estimated based on the historical data of Urban Household Survey and Rural Household Survey according to the definition of main income and consumption indicators of Household Survey on Income and Expenditure and Living Conditions.

The NBS has launched its reform on the household survey programme, to form an integrated survey, instead of the two separate urban and rural household surveys and has started household survey since the fourth quarter of 2012. The main contents of the survey include: income and expenditure of the household, and surveys of employment, social security participation, housing, family operation, production investment, and also influence factors of income distribution.

The household survey is conducted by selecting sampled houses randomly, deciding surveyed households, with all households in the province as the population, with stratified sampling, multi-stage sampling, probability sampling in proportion to population scale. 16,000

R. Guo, *China Ethnic Statistical Yearbook 2020*,
https://doi.org/10.1007/978-3-030-49024-9_4

communities of 1800 counties in the total country are selected, more than 1.6 million households in them are surveyed comprehensively, and then on this basis, randomly select about 160,000 households for keeping diaries. Communities and households surveyed rotate regularly. Survey on Income and Expenditures and Living Conditions is required that the sampling error should not exceed ±1%, with a confidence probability as 95%. Methods of collecting income and expenditure data are keeping diaries of the households, and questionnaires as assistance to collect other relevant data. All survey works are conducted by investigation team of NBS independently. Coding, check, entering of original data are conducted by investigation teams at city level with the same methods and data processing program, and then basic data are transferred to NBS to tabulate the data.

Urban Household Survey was conducted by the Office of Urban Household Surveys of the NBS prior to 2012. The main contents of the survey include persons in the household and the household composition; cash income and expenditure of the household; quantity of major commodities purchased and expenditure; the employment of household members; the housing condition; and the possession of durable consumer goods. The survey had covered only non-farm households prior to 2001. From 2002 to 2012, the survey covers the households in district areas of all city and county towns.

Sample cities and towns in urban areas are selected by using stratified random sampling method. Firstly, all the urban areas and towns of all provinces autonomous regions and municipalities directly under the Central Government) are stratified into three strata according to population size: large and medium-sized cities (at and above prefecture level), county cities and county towns; secondly, the sample size is decided by proportion of population in selected stratus to the provincial total; thirdly, cities and towns are arranged in ranking the annual average wages of the employed persons, then with the accumulative population in each city and town sample cities and towns are selected by systematic sampling scheme according to the size of the samples. The selection of sample households in urban areas is done by two steps: the first step is to have a one-off large sample survey; the second step is to select a small sample from the large sample to be used as regular sample households for diaries.

Rural Household Survey was organized by the Office of Rural Household Survey of the NBS prior to 2012. The main contents of the survey include the basic condition of rural households, housing conditions, income, consumption expenditure, consumption of major consumer goods and the quantity of durable consumer goods owned. Sample survey on rural households is conducted by first selecting sampled villages and then selecting households in the selected villages in each province, with all rural households in the province as the population. A combination of various sampling approaches is used to identify a total of 74,000 households selected from 7000 villages throughout the whole country. It is required that the sampling error should not exceed ±3%, with a confidence probability as 95%. In order to overcome the tedium of respondent households and to ensure that the sample is accurately representative over time and reflects the changing rural social and economic situation, a rotation sampling scheme is implemented, and the complete cycle of rotation is 5 years.

Table 4.1 Savings deposit of urban and rural households at year-end (100 million yuan)

Ethnic group	2007	2008	2009	2010	2011	2012	2018
National total	172534.2	217885.4	260771.7	303302.5	343635.9	399551.0	**28228.0**
Achang	2.5	3.1	3.8	4.6	5.4	6.27	16.24
Bai	135.0	167.8	205.7	250.1	291.7	341.09	895.93
Baonan	1.3	1.7	2.0	2.4	2.9	3.42	14.26
Blang	6.7	8.3	10.3	12.6	14.6	17.00	43.97
Buyi	166.3	208.0	248.9	300.4	361.1	437.55	1575.42
Dai	84.4	104.9	129.3	158.2	184.0	214.17	551.23
Daur	15.9	19.9	23.8	27.7	32.0	37.90	136.77
Deang	1.3	1.6	2.0	2.4	2.8	3.30	8.57
Derung	0.6	0.8	1.0	1.2	1.3	1.56	4.08
Dong	208.1	258.0	308.3	365.7	432.2	516.90	1453.42
Dongxiang	41.3	52.9	64.8	77.3	91.0	108.65	401.32
Ewenki	3.6	4.5	5.4	6.4	7.4	8.94	35.81
Gaoshan	0.6	0.7	0.9	1.0	1.2	1.37	3.45
Gelao	31.8	39.8	47.6	57.4	69.2	83.96	306.22
Han	161224.8	203873.8	243098.2	282215.2	320675.9	372678.70	771014.38
Hani	104.7	130.1	160.4	196.3	228.3	265.66	685.39
Hezhe	0.6	0.8	0.9	1.0	1.2	1.34	3.47
Hui	1215.9	1550.4	1872.9	2206.3	2536.3	3008.33	16944.91

(continued)

Table 4.1 (continued)

Ethnic group	2007	2008	2009	2010	2011	2012	2018
Jing	1.7	2.1	2.6	3.1	3.6	4.26	11.58
Jingpo	9.6	12.0	14.7	18.0	21.0	24.41	62.97
Jino	1.5	1.9	2.3	2.9	3.3	3.86	10.00
Kazak	139.3	173.2	206.9	251.8	299.8	358.09	1457.38
Kirgiz	18.0	22.3	26.7	32.4	38.6	46.05	186.62
Korean	265.4	330.2	389.3	439.0	495.5	576.59	1619.01
Lahu	33.0	41.0	50.5	61.8	71.9	83.69	215.33
Lhoba	0.2	0.2	0.3	0.3	0.4	0.50	18.03
Li	140.2	172.1	208.4	269.7	303.8	352.35	3853.51
Lisu	46.5	57.9	71.3	87.1	101.4	118.10	298.06
Manchu	1851.9	2339.9	2780.2	3177.5	3582.6	4146.77	8364.88
Maonan	7.4	9.1	11.0	13.3	15.6	18.60	54.17
Miao	646.3	802.9	965.5	1151.4	1360.1	1622.50	4728.11
Monba	0.6	0.7	0.9	1.0	1.2	1.54	56.68
Mongol	720.2	909.5	1097.9	1283.0	1487.1	1778.96	6608.24
Mulao	15.7	19.2	23.2	28.0	32.7	38.72	104.40
Naxi	22.8	28.3	34.9	42.6	49.6	57.81	154.11
Nu	2.1	2.6	3.2	3.9	4.6	5.35	16.26
Oroqen	1.0	1.3	1.5	1.8	2.0	2.36	7.68
Pumi	2.5	3.1	3.8	4.6	5.4	6.24	16.15
Qiang	27.9	36.1	43.3	51.1	60.4	72.65	86.94
Russian	1.9	2.4	2.9	3.5	4.1	4.84	19.18
Salar	9.8	12.7	15.6	18.9	22.6	27.53	391.66
She	111.5	140.9	170.9	197.3	223.3	256.06	624.36
Shui	22.6	28.2	33.8	40.9	49.1	59.52	213.50
Tajik	4.6	5.7	6.8	8.3	9.9	11.78	47.31
Tatar	0.6	0.7	0.8	1.0	1.2	1.43	5.73
Tibetan	416.2	519.5	632.4	753.5	896.0	1098.89	21490.70
Tu	23.0	29.9	36.4	44.1	52.5	63.60	848.79
Tujia	720.0	893.0	1075.6	1270.5	1488.6	1769.61	4270.08
Uygur	938.0	1165.6	1393.0	1694.7	2017.2	2408.74	9777.92
Uzbek	1.4	1.7	2.1	2.5	3.0	3.58	14.47
Va	29.2	36.3	44.8	54.7	63.6	74.00	188.43
Xibe	33.0	41.5	49.3	56.6	64.0	74.41	158.99
Yao	239.0	292.5	349.5	415.3	480.4	563.92	1243.15
Yi	587.5	740.5	902.5	1089.9	1278.1	1509.12	3323.39
Yugur	1.1	1.4	1.7	2.1	2.4	2.89	10.57
Zhuang	1297.8	1578.3	1907.8	2308.1	2677.8	3157.04	8084.37

Table 4.2 Per capita annual income of urban households by sources (yuan)

Ethnic group	Disposable income	Income from wages and salaries	Net business income	Income from properties	Income from transfers
National average	**28228.0**	**15829.0**	**4852.4**	**2378.5**	**5168.1**
Achang	20196.22	9695.92	4888.20	1969.96	3642.14
Bai	20485.87	9976.65	4809.06	1911.47	3788.69
Baonan	17817.92	9877.20	3282.42	1152.69	3505.61
Blang	20229.82	9717.29	4887.64	1970.13	3654.78
Buyi	18995.95	9860.11	4108.50	1380.08	3647.26
Dai	20191.41	9688.08	4883.93	1967.91	3651.48
Daur	26454.02	13734.51	6180.32	1382.73	5156.46
Deang	20130.84	9647.10	4882.30	1964.04	3637.40
Derung	21510.07	10690.50	4901.23	1946.88	3971.45
Dong	21538.36	11096.10	4542.78	1602.07	4297.41
Dongxiang	17991.35	9935.77	3429.75	1123.84	3501.98
Ewenki	28121.19	14906.73	6800.01	1507.66	4906.79
Gaoshan	26880.52	14703.18	4858.14	2189.34	5129.86
Gelao	18856.38	9795.17	4077.85	1359.23	3624.13
Han	28030.41	15678.61	4861.48	2316.38	5173.94
Hani	20190.42	9686.92	4887.10	1970.61	3645.79
Hezhe	23970.25	11931.47	4829.75	1351.89	5857.15
Hui	24100.83	13506.04	4280.84	1663.05	4650.89
Jing	21842.73	10598.99	5388.87	1521.12	4333.74
Jingpo	20186.31	9694.63	4884.04	1968.05	3639.58
Jino	20174.69	9676.00	4881.29	1968.65	3648.74
Kazak	21509.62	11661.82	5145.72	790.10	3912.00
Kirgiz	21546.14	11668.89	5150.74	794.21	3932.30
Korean	24572.24	12903.06	4981.80	1261.55	5425.84
Lahu	20196.99	9692.87	4888.76	1968.14	3647.21
Lhoba	18102.33	9411.23	4594.40	1188.93	2907.76
Li	24406.06	14156.92	4453.91	1881.55	3913.68
Lisu	20250.42	9726.98	4877.52	1952.43	3693.49
Manchu	27763.51	15020.32	4782.77	1593.24	6367.19
Maonan	20855.49	10241.20	5049.28	1444.23	4120.78
Miao	21550.07	11061.94	4523.77	1637.15	4327.21
Monba	18137.03	9423.73	4559.44	1229.53	2924.33
Mongol	27788.43	14807.73	6376.90	1488.92	5114.89
Mulao	21604.89	10593.43	5262.43	1515.82	4233.21
Naxi	20282.73	9749.07	4873.59	1959.82	3700.26
Nu	20261.83	9760.18	4889.72	1965.76	3646.18
Oroqen	25985.13	13359.29	5830.71	1401.91	5393.21
Pumi	20237.22	9722.51	4885.32	1968.60	3660.79
Qiang	22522.91	11128.71	4557.07	1457.35	5379.77

(*continued*)

Table 4.2 (continued)

Ethnic group	Disposable income	Income from wages and salaries	Net business income	Income from properties	Income from transfers
Russian	24867.82	13448.34	5677.43	1259.95	4482.09
Salar	20647.44	12028.28	3131.80	1110.56	4376.81
She	34062.66	19742.02	6019.31	3406.44	4894.88
Shui	18978.82	9790.60	4148.65	1374.53	3665.03
Tajik	21690.61	11768.73	5132.16	832.91	3956.80
Tatar	21826.20	11879.88	5040.52	909.71	3996.10
Tibetan	19418.20	10246.07	4160.40	1213.07	3798.66
Tu	21003.87	12245.70	3216.19	1210.49	4331.48
Tujia	24799.08	12766.13	4841.78	1785.91	5405.26
Uygur	21550.56	11685.00	5149.06	796.54	3919.96
Uzbek	21700.08	11788.45	5139.02	835.88	3936.73
Va	20338.75	9803.38	4897.67	1967.30	3670.40
Xibe	27935.74	14758.41	5135.49	1319.50	6722.34
Yao	23517.49	12023.76	5226.79	1823.65	4443.29
Yi	20668.64	10082.18	4704.94	1756.35	4125.18
Yugur	17928.97	9929.88	3275.22	1199.98	3523.90
Zhuang	21984.66	10755.36	5402.49	1586.47	4240.34

Table 4.3 Consumer price indices by category (preceding year=100) (I)

Ethnic group	General index	Food	Grain	Oil or fat	Meat, poultry and processed products	Eggs	Aquatic products
National average	102.1	**101.8**	100.8	**99.2**	**105.5**	**112.0**	**102.3**
Achang	101.58	100.24	100.5	96.37	103.79	107.98	102.62
Bai	101.63	100.31	101.4	96.47	104.17	108.09	102.47
Baonan	102.06	101.07	98.2	100.67	102.24	111.50	102.73
Blang	101.58	100.25	100.8	96.38	103.79	108.01	102.61
Buyi	101.77	100.40	100.2	95.30	106.12	108.99	102.73
Dai	101.58	100.24	102.1	96.37	103.79	107.99	102.61
Daur	101.90	101.81	100.9	97.97	103.21	111.59	102.91
Deang	101.58	100.24	101.6	96.36	103.77	107.98	102.62
Derung	101.67	100.55	100.9	96.87	104.03	108.88	102.56
Dong	101.89	100.57	99.9	96.81	106.09	108.62	102.17

(continued)

Table 4.3 (continued)

Ethnic group	General index	Food	Grain	Oil or fat	Meat, poultry and processed products	Eggs	Aquatic products
Dongxiang	102.05	101.13	101.3	100.59	102.27	111.86	103.14
Ewenki	101.86	102.18	100.4	97.49	103.39	111.60	103.35
Gaoshan	102.12	101.47	100.9	98.81	105.64	111.94	102.37
Gelao	101.76	100.38	101.1	95.24	106.15	108.99	102.74
Han	102.10	101.66	100.8	99.23	105.40	111.73	101.75
Hani	101.58	100.24	101.2	96.37	103.78	107.98	102.61
Hezhe	102.00	100.88	101.1	98.98	102.95	110.91	101.38
Hui	102.17	102.10	101.1	99.42	103.81	112.88	102.16
Jing	102.28	100.47	100.5	97.45	106.83	108.61	103.99
Jingpo	101.58	100.24	100.9	96.37	103.79	107.99	102.62
Jino	101.58	100.24	101.5	96.36	103.78	107.99	102.61
Kazak	102.03	102.82	100.9	99.31	103.37	116.48	107.10
Kirgiz	102.03	102.80	100.4	99.30	103.37	116.43	107.06
Korean	102.13	101.34	100.3	99.52	103.68	111.59	101.96
Lahu	101.58	100.24	100.2	96.38	103.79	108.01	102.61
Lhoba	101.74	101.72	100.3	99.34	101.59	103.69	104.18
Li	102.43	100.89	99.2	98.63	104.91	108.32	101.48
Lisu	101.59	100.28	102.4	96.42	103.84	108.04	102.57
Manchu	102.35	102.04	100.0	99.49	104.31	111.90	103.60
Maonan	102.15	100.43	102.1	96.81	106.70	108.66	103.77
Miao	101.84	100.59	100.5	96.79	105.77	109.01	102.10
Monba	101.72	101.74	100.5	99.44	101.40	103.29	104.21
Mongol	101.96	102.22	101.4	97.89	103.71	111.85	103.51
Mulao	102.24	100.47	98.2	97.21	106.79	108.60	103.98
Naxi	101.59	100.28	100.8	96.43	103.83	108.02	102.58
Nu	101.59	100.28	100.2	96.44	103.77	107.94	102.64
Oroqen	101.93	101.53	102.1	98.24	103.19	111.25	102.38
Pumi	101.59	100.25	100.9	96.39	103.79	108.02	102.60
Qiang	101.74	101.33	101.6	98.01	105.73	109.66	100.94
Russian	101.98	102.57	100.9	98.67	103.47	114.48	105.43
Salar	102.46	102.97	99.9	99.97	103.41	112.44	100.65
She	101.82	101.72	101.3	99.04	107.67	109.98	102.59
Shui	101.78	100.38	100.4	95.35	106.12	108.96	102.77
Tajik	102.03	102.78	100.9	99.30	103.44	116.34	106.93
Tatar	102.03	102.72	101.1	99.37	103.38	116.11	106.73
Tibetan	101.91	101.85	100.8	99.23	102.91	107.30	102.49
Tu	102.42	102.82	101.2	99.87	103.51	112.12	100.71
Tujia	101.94	101.08	101.1	98.58	105.68	110.11	100.62

(continued)

Table 4.3 (continued)

Ethnic group	General index	Food	Grain	Oil or fat	Meat, poultry and processed products	Eggs	Aquatic products
Uygur	102.03	102.82	101.1	99.31	103.38	116.47	107.09
Uzbek	102.03	102.80	100.5	99.31	103.41	116.37	107.02
Va	101.60	100.28	100.9	96.44	103.84	108.10	102.60
Xibe	102.35	102.32	101.5	99.58	104.52	112.46	104.90
Yao	102.15	100.62	100.9	98.00	106.22	108.27	103.11
Yi	101.65	100.56	100.4	96.70	104.58	108.56	102.16
Yugur	102.05	100.99	100.3	100.69	102.21	111.43	102.73
Zhuang	102.26	100.47	100.2	97.46	106.65	108.49	104.09

Table 4.4 Consumer price indices by category (preceding year=100) (II)

Ethnic group	Vegetables	Fresh vegetables	Dried and fresh melons and fruits	Fresh fruits	Dining out	Tobacco, liquor and articles
National average	**106.6**	107.1	**104.1**	**105.6**	**102.4**	**101.2**
Achang	104.38	104.61	104.50	106.10	101.49	100.21
Bai	104.46	104.72	104.27	105.81	101.51	100.34
Baonan	101.54	101.51	101.76	102.89	101.24	100.65
Blang	104.39	104.63	104.50	106.10	101.49	100.21
Buyi	103.82	104.16	102.85	104.14	102.04	100.73
Dai	104.39	104.63	104.50	106.10	101.48	100.21
Daur	106.28	106.80	104.40	105.92	101.64	101.28
Deang	104.36	104.59	104.51	106.11	101.48	100.20
Derung	104.78	105.06	104.47	106.10	101.59	100.38
Dong	104.47	104.84	102.89	104.05	101.83	100.89
Dongxiang	101.35	101.30	101.75	102.93	101.44	100.74
Ewenki	106.60	107.11	104.20	105.54	101.68	100.96
Gaoshan	105.92	106.39	103.66	105.15	102.21	101.24
Gelao	103.77	104.12	102.81	104.09	102.05	100.73
Han	106.69	107.23	104.17	105.81	102.24	101.21
Hani	104.38	104.61	104.51	106.12	101.48	100.20
Hezhe	106.43	107.05	105.02	106.82	101.28	101.89

(*continued*)

Table 4.4 (continued)

Ethnic group	Vegetables	Fresh vegetables	Dried and fresh melons and fruits	Fresh fruits	Dining out	Tobacco, liquor and articles
Hui	105.51	105.83	103.22	104.78	102.02	100.95
Jing	103.24	103.50	100.54	101.00	102.92	100.53
Jingpo	104.38	104.61	104.50	106.10	101.49	100.21
Jino	104.38	104.61	104.50	106.11	101.48	100.20
Kazak	99.67	99.45	101.35	103.02	104.43	101.62
Kirgiz	99.73	99.53	101.39	103.07	104.40	101.62
Korean	106.73	107.36	103.91	104.98	101.74	101.36
Lahu	104.39	104.62	104.51	106.12	101.49	100.21
Lhoba	103.09	103.20	101.52	101.20	104.83	100.77
Li	103.94	104.14	96.34	95.65	102.58	100.01
Lisu	104.50	104.75	104.47	106.08	101.47	100.25
Manchu	107.01	107.64	105.93	107.83	101.84	101.38
Maonan	103.28	103.56	101.07	101.71	102.71	100.59
Miao	104.64	105.01	103.03	104.31	101.77	100.75
Monba	103.07	103.17	101.43	101.01	104.92	100.77
Mongol	106.41	106.90	104.34	105.77	101.81	101.01
Mulao	103.24	103.51	100.73	101.25	102.85	100.57
Naxi	104.49	104.73	104.45	106.05	101.49	100.25
Nu	104.38	104.62	104.45	106.03	101.55	100.22
Oroqen	106.55	107.12	104.68	106.28	101.46	101.44
Pumi	104.41	104.64	104.50	106.11	101.49	100.22
Qiang	108.36	109.10	102.90	104.46	100.97	101.71
Russian	102.68	102.78	102.53	104.08	103.32	101.34
Salar	102.93	102.97	101.04	102.17	102.17	100.23
She	107.04	107.74	103.21	104.12	102.71	100.76
Shui	103.77	104.11	102.79	104.05	102.06	100.71
Tajik	99.89	99.70	101.43	103.10	104.35	101.60
Tatar	100.03	99.85	101.46	103.10	104.22	101.57
Tibetan	104.19	104.42	101.75	102.26	103.09	100.83
Tu	103.13	103.21	101.22	102.35	102.10	100.26
Tujia	105.86	106.38	103.69	105.28	101.89	100.74
Uygur	99.69	99.48	101.36	103.04	104.43	101.62
Uzbek	99.78	99.58	101.36	103.02	104.40	101.61
Va	104.46	104.70	104.50	106.11	101.50	100.23
Xibe	105.28	105.71	105.63	107.49	102.32	101.69
Yao	104.12	104.44	101.74	102.43	102.28	100.80
Yi	105.42	105.80	103.88	105.44	101.40	100.68
Yugur	101.60	101.58	101.81	102.95	101.18	100.66
Zhuang	103.23	103.49	100.68	101.16	102.88	100.53

Table 4.5 Consumer price indices by category (preceding year=100) (III)

Ethnic group	Clothing	Garments	Garments material	Footgear and hats	Clothing manufac-turing service	House-hold facilities, articles and services
National average	**101.2**	**101.4**	**101.9**	**100.4**	**104.1**	102.4
Achang	101.36	100.93	99.93	100.9	103.57	102.07
Bai	101.35	101.04	100.64	99.0	103.54	102.25
Baonan	101.06	100.82	102.35	100.2	105.76	103.25
Blang	101.36	100.93	99.94	100.8	103.57	102.07
Buyi	100.95	101.21	104.87	101.1	102.24	102.85
Dai	101.35	100.92	99.94	99.4	103.57	102.06
Daur	101.29	101.59	101.34	100.0	102.22	101.73
Deang	101.35	100.91	99.91	100.4	103.56	102.06
Derung	101.33	101.01	100.31	102.6	103.45	102.10
Dong	101.28	101.50	103.59	100.7	103.60	103.19
Dongxiang	100.88	100.61	102.28	99.7	105.67	102.87
Ewenki	101.60	101.89	101.99	100.2	102.32	102.19
Gaoshan	101.11	101.22	101.87	99.8	103.72	102.49
Gelao	100.94	101.21	104.95	100.1	102.20	102.86
Han	101.38	101.58	102.05	101.1	103.84	102.48
Hani	101.36	100.92	99.92	101.5	103.57	102.06
Hezhe	100.98	101.34	100.09	100.2	102.09	101.31
Hui	101.29	101.37	101.83	101.5	103.55	102.16
Jing	101.49	101.08	100.50	100.4	106.53	104.08
Jingpo	101.36	100.92	99.94	101.1	103.56	102.07
Jino	101.35	100.92	99.93	101.5	103.57	102.06
Kazak	98.89	98.63	101.43	99.8	103.68	97.89
Kirgiz	98.91	98.65	101.41	101.5	103.65	97.91
Korean	101.81	101.96	102.51	100.8	103.66	101.88
Lahu	101.36	100.92	99.93	101.0	103.57	102.06
Lhoba	102.12	101.75	101.28	99.5	107.89	101.17
Li	103.90	103.66	102.54	101.1	105.26	103.36
Lisu	101.35	100.95	100.06	101.0	103.59	102.08
Manchu	100.96	101.03	100.89	99.2	102.36	101.84
Maonan	101.34	101.11	101.69	100.5	105.45	103.82
Miao	101.29	101.44	103.19	100.0	103.39	102.97
Monba	102.17	101.78	101.21	100.9	108.20	101.13
Mongol	101.43	101.65	101.96	99.0	102.46	102.09
Mulao	101.44	101.11	100.96	100.2	106.12	104.00
Naxi	101.35	100.94	100.06	100.8	103.61	102.07
Nu	101.37	100.94	99.97	101.1	103.64	102.05

(*continued*)

Table 4.5 (continued)

Ethnic group	Clothing	Garments	Garments material	Footgear and hats	Clothing manufacturing service	Household facilities, articles and services
Oroqen	101.28	101.60	101.00	99.4	102.16	101.74
Pumi	101.36	100.93	99.95	100.0	103.58	102.06
Qiang	101.14	101.70	104.54	100.4	104.64	102.64
Russian	100.01	99.97	101.70	102.6	103.27	99.75
Salar	101.26	101.93	102.30	100.7	103.61	102.47
She	100.21	100.61	103.33	99.7	102.60	102.43
Shui	100.97	101.20	104.68	100.2	102.40	102.89
Tajik	98.97	98.72	101.44	99.8	103.67	98.05
Tatar	99.06	98.82	101.48	100.1	103.78	98.27
Tibetan	101.69	101.77	102.26	101.1	106.11	101.97
Tu	101.31	101.95	102.30	101.5	103.64	102.59
Tujia	101.34	101.49	102.18	100.2	104.10	102.97
Uygur	98.89	98.63	101.43	101.5	103.67	97.90
Uzbek	98.94	98.68	101.43	100.4	103.70	97.98
Va	101.37	100.96	99.99	101.1	103.57	102.08
Xibe	100.19	99.98	100.63	101.5	102.12	100.89
Yao	101.62	101.44	100.94	99.8	105.82	103.73
Yi	101.25	101.17	101.76	101.5	103.71	102.31
Yugur	101.08	100.81	102.34	100.8	105.84	103.34
Zhuang	101.52	101.08	100.29	101.0	106.50	104.01

Table 4.6 Consumer price indices by category (preceding year=100) (IV)

Ethnic group	Durable consumer goods	Interior decorations	Bed articles	Daily use household articles	Household services and maintenance and renovation	Health care and personal articles	Health care
National average	**102.3**	**100.5**	**100.7**	**101.4**	**101.0**	**104.3**	**104.4**
Achang	101.34	100.51	99.84	101.49	100.49	104.05	106.34
Bai	101.32	100.51	99.92	101.45	100.58	103.74	105.93
Baonan	100.76	100.37	99.61	101.01	100.83	107.92	104.56

(*continued*)

Table 4.6 (continued)

Ethnic group	Durable consumer goods	Interior decorations	Bed articles	Daily use household articles	Household services and maintenance and renovation	Health care and personal articles	Health care
Blang	101.35	100.50	99.84	101.49	100.49	104.06	106.33
Buyi	101.25	100.45	100.27	100.90	100.88	102.11	103.32
Dai	101.35	100.50	99.84	101.49	100.48	104.05	106.33
Daur	100.59	100.78	100.79	100.83	100.89	105.21	103.27
Deang	101.33	100.50	99.82	101.49	100.48	104.07	106.35
Derung	101.41	100.47	100.00	101.41	100.56	104.24	105.90
Dong	101.23	100.54	100.35	101.31	101.03	102.51	104.02
Dongxiang	100.76	100.33	99.55	101.05	100.82	108.40	104.21
Ewenki	100.86	101.22	100.96	100.77	100.66	103.40	102.85
Gaoshan	102.03	100.81	100.78	101.06	101.12	104.93	104.67
Gelao	101.24	100.44	100.26	100.89	100.88	102.07	103.26
Han	102.24	100.55	100.77	101.38	101.01	104.38	104.59
Hani	101.34	100.51	99.83	101.49	100.48	104.05	106.34
Hezhe	100.16	99.96	100.71	101.01	101.37	108.08	104.58
Hui	102.10	101.28	100.82	100.98	100.98	105.11	104.44
Jing	101.39	100.74	100.61	101.94	101.15	104.45	104.56
Jingpo	101.34	100.50	99.83	101.49	100.49	104.05	106.33
Jino	101.34	100.50	99.83	101.49	100.48	104.06	106.34
Kazak	101.25	100.00	99.04	100.90	101.11	112.44	101.32
Kirgiz	101.24	100.00	99.06	100.90	101.11	112.40	101.34
Korean	102.14	101.78	101.37	101.41	101.24	106.56	106.04
Lahu	101.34	100.51	99.83	101.49	100.49	104.06	106.34
Lhoba	101.58	102.18	101.18	100.93	102.24	102.29	103.93
Li	102.59	102.19	105.96	100.33	101.56	103.53	107.39
Lisu	101.41	100.48	99.87	101.48	100.49	104.03	106.29
Manchu	101.60	100.41	100.47	100.68	101.00	108.75	104.96
Maonan	101.32	100.67	100.51	101.67	101.09	103.77	104.19
Miao	101.42	100.44	100.35	101.32	100.94	102.81	104.26
Monba	101.62	102.25	101.21	100.93	102.29	102.14	103.93
Mongol	101.13	101.13	100.82	100.74	100.72	104.41	103.26
Mulao	101.35	100.69	100.56	101.84	101.13	104.15	104.40
Naxi	101.41	100.49	99.87	101.48	100.49	104.02	106.27
Nu	101.35	100.53	99.86	101.48	100.52	104.03	106.29
Oroqen	100.49	100.58	100.82	100.88	101.02	105.80	103.71
Pumi	101.35	100.51	99.84	101.49	100.49	104.06	106.32
Qiang	103.84	99.71	101.29	101.11	100.52	102.84	104.43

(continued)

Table 4.6 (continued)

Ethnic group	Durable consumer goods	Interior decorations	Bed articles	Daily use household articles	Household services and maintenance and renovation	Health care and personal articles	Health care
Russian	101.21	100.49	99.84	100.88	100.94	108.58	102.04
Salar	101.72	101.02	100.19	99.83	101.69	104.25	106.94
She	101.68	100.14	100.80	100.74	100.46	103.00	103.93
Shui	101.25	100.47	100.27	100.95	100.89	102.19	103.39
Tajik	101.28	100.01	99.10	100.91	101.11	112.18	101.42
Tatar	101.27	100.03	99.14	100.92	101.10	111.95	101.56
Tibetan	102.09	101.27	100.90	100.72	101.64	103.07	104.89
Tu	101.72	100.97	100.22	99.92	101.61	104.10	106.85
Tujia	101.95	100.08	100.24	101.60	101.09	103.33	103.96
Uygur	101.26	100.01	99.05	100.90	101.11	112.41	101.32
Uzbek	101.27	100.01	99.09	100.90	101.11	112.28	101.37
Va	101.37	100.51	99.86	101.48	100.50	104.06	106.32
Xibe	101.05	99.87	100.04	100.37	100.80	110.76	103.66
Yao	101.31	100.63	100.50	101.83	101.12	103.90	104.86
Yi	102.02	100.28	100.28	101.32	100.54	103.50	105.47
Yugur	100.74	100.35	99.61	101.06	100.80	107.93	104.50
Zhuang	101.38	100.71	100.56	101.94	101.12	104.47	104.70

Table 4.7 Consumer price indices by category (preceding year=100) (V)

Ethnic group	Medical appliances and articles	Traditional Chinese medicine	Western medicine	Health care appliances and articles	Health care services	Personal articles and services	Cosmetics
National average	**104.3**	105.02	100.30	102.54	100.70	102.63	101.27
Achang	102.18	104.76	98.90	100.51	100.34	103.07	101.62
Bai	102.00	105.21	99.31	100.62	100.40	103.04	101.47
Baonan	110.40	108.32	102.33	100.63	102.64	102.47	103.70
Blang	102.19	104.76	98.91	100.52	100.34	103.07	101.62
Buyi	101.21	108.01	100.82	99.84	100.62	102.79	100.29
Dai	102.18	104.76	98.90	100.51	100.34	103.07	101.62

(*continued*)

Table 4.7 (continued)

Ethnic group	Medical appliances and articles	Traditional Chinese medicine	Western medicine	Health care appliances and articles	Health care services	Personal articles and services	Cosmetics
Daur	106.39	105.53	100.90	101.15	100.33	103.47	101.06
Deang	102.20	104.76	98.90	100.50	100.34	103.08	101.63
Derung	102.85	104.86	99.27	100.77	100.43	102.99	101.58
Dong	101.52	106.94	101.13	100.92	100.70	102.88	100.74
Dongxiang	111.22	108.39	102.41	100.77	102.51	102.59	103.68
Ewenki	103.76	105.01	100.51	101.08	100.58	103.40	101.47
Gaoshan	105.15	104.98	100.81	101.86	100.70	102.86	101.52
Gelao	101.19	108.10	100.86	99.80	100.63	102.79	100.26
Han	104.25	105.07	100.42	102.03	100.76	102.76	101.35
Hani	102.18	104.76	98.90	100.51	100.34	103.07	101.63
Hezhe	110.38	106.39	101.50	101.25	99.80	103.55	100.12
Hui	105.33	105.20	100.37	102.55	100.84	102.92	101.70
Jing	104.36	103.64	100.90	100.56	100.82	102.76	101.05
Jingpo	102.19	104.77	98.91	100.51	100.34	103.07	101.62
Jino	102.19	104.77	98.90	100.51	100.34	103.07	101.63
Kazak	117.13	107.31	101.94	102.14	100.40	103.33	101.96
Kirgiz	117.07	107.30	101.93	102.13	100.39	103.33	101.94
Korean	106.95	106.15	100.50	101.39	100.02	103.39	100.97
Lahu	102.19	104.76	98.90	100.52	100.34	103.07	101.63
Lhoba	101.19	103.54	97.97	100.06	102.15	101.65	100.90
Li	100.53	106.50	101.35	103.57	100.39	102.55	100.67
Lisu	102.17	104.78	98.89	100.53	100.37	103.05	101.60
Manchu	111.45	104.97	101.09	101.10	100.21	103.28	101.45
Maonan	103.48	104.82	100.93	100.30	100.78	102.76	100.82
Miao	101.81	106.78	100.78	100.92	100.65	102.82	100.85
Monba	100.97	103.37	97.75	100.05	102.23	101.58	100.88
Mongol	105.14	104.97	100.54	101.12	100.57	103.29	101.54
Mulao	103.99	104.09	100.92	100.45	100.81	102.75	100.95
Naxi	102.18	104.78	98.89	100.54	100.38	103.04	101.59
Nu	102.18	104.74	98.89	100.52	100.38	103.05	101.61
Oroqen	107.19	105.68	101.03	101.15	100.19	103.49	100.79
Pumi	102.20	104.76	98.91	100.52	100.35	103.07	101.62
Qiang	101.66	105.57	98.63	101.25	101.47	102.22	100.59
Russian	111.40	106.31	101.28	101.76	100.49	103.30	101.76
Salar	102.21	104.26	99.55	100.66	101.39	101.01	100.73
She	102.46	104.19	100.42	102.97	101.91	101.93	101.53
Shui	101.30	107.86	100.81	99.84	100.62	102.80	100.32

(continued)

Table 4.7 (continued)

Ethnic group	Medical appliances and articles	Traditional Chinese medicine	Western medicine	Health care appliances and articles	Health care services	Personal articles and services	Cosmetics
Tajik	116.72	107.23	101.90	102.13	100.41	103.30	101.94
Teatar	116.38	107.26	101.90	102.08	100.49	103.27	102.00
Tibetan	101.81	104.36	98.62	100.45	101.87	101.66	100.95
Tu	102.11	104.35	99.59	100.67	101.40	101.10	100.81
Tujia	102.96	106.40	101.29	102.37	100.76	102.76	101.18
Uygur	117.09	107.30	101.93	102.14	100.40	103.33	101.95
Uzbek	116.88	107.26	101.91	102.14	100.40	103.31	101.94
Va	102.21	104.76	98.94	100.56	100.36	103.06	101.62
Xibe	115.21	104.90	101.20	101.30	100.28	103.01	101.36
Yao	103.29	104.40	100.95	101.21	100.79	102.85	101.23
Yi	101.93	105.36	99.04	100.64	100.68	102.81	101.19
Yugur	110.52	108.43	102.41	100.64	102.68	102.52	103.78
Zhuang	104.30	103.55	100.79	100.55	100.81	102.77	101.11

Table 4.8 Consumer price indices by category (preceding year=100) (VI)

Ethnic group	Transport and Communications	Transport	Transport Facility	Fuels for Transport Facility	Use and Maintenance of Transport Facility	Traffic Fee
National average	**101.7**	**103.2**	**98.5**	**112.6**	**102.8**	**101.3**
Achang	101.74	103.59	100.09	112.02	101.69	98.89
Bai	101.84	103.68	99.94	112.14	101.68	99.23
Baonan	101.18	102.67	100.03	112.03	101.33	100.01
Blang	101.74	103.58	100.08	112.03	101.69	98.89
Buyi	102.04	103.96	99.00	112.57	101.11	99.33
Dai	101.74	103.58	100.08	112.02	101.68	98.89
Daur	101.30	102.39	97.34	112.85	101.40	102.16
Deang	101.74	103.59	100.10	112.02	101.68	98.87
Derung	101.68	103.44	99.69	112.15	101.79	99.31
Dong	102.21	104.00	99.10	112.64	101.71	100.66

(continued)

Table 4.8 (continued)

Ethnic group	Transport and Communications	Transport	Transport Facility	Fuels for Transport Facility	Use and Maintenance of Transport Facility	Traffic Fee
Dongxiang	101.17	102.61	99.80	112.00	101.35	100.11
Ewenki	101.37	102.18	96.41	112.97	101.26	102.32
Gaoshan	101.67	103.15	98.68	112.64	102.72	100.92
Gelao	102.05	103.97	99.00	112.58	101.09	99.31
Han	101.60	103.12	98.40	112.63	102.66	101.11
Hani	101.74	103.59	100.09	112.02	101.69	98.88
Hezhe	101.18	102.95	99.36	112.67	101.85	101.88
Hui	101.69	103.18	99.91	112.41	101.98	100.38
Jing	101.66	103.09	97.92	112.31	102.68	100.91
Jingpo	101.74	103.59	100.09	112.03	101.69	98.89
Jino	101.74	103.59	100.09	112.02	101.68	98.88
Kazak	101.19	102.20	97.66	111.88	101.79	100.86
Kirgiz	101.20	102.20	97.67	111.89	101.79	100.88
Korean	100.99	102.42	98.24	112.73	103.61	100.54
Lahu	101.74	103.59	100.09	112.03	101.69	98.89
Lhoba	101.47	103.61	100.14	111.54	101.45	101.86
Li	103.26	105.12	99.92	111.21	102.56	107.82
Lisu	101.72	103.56	99.99	112.03	101.66	98.94
Manchu	101.15	102.51	98.21	112.88	102.54	101.20
Maonan	101.76	103.32	98.16	112.39	102.26	100.48
Miao	102.03	103.86	99.09	112.55	101.59	100.36
Monba	101.47	103.63	100.19	111.49	101.43	101.98
Mongol	101.36	102.26	96.82	112.93	101.59	101.92
Mulao	101.70	103.19	97.98	112.35	102.53	100.75
Naxi	101.72	103.56	100.00	112.03	101.66	98.95
Nu	101.73	103.58	100.07	112.02	101.69	98.95
Oroqen	101.27	102.55	97.89	112.83	101.54	102.10
Pumi	101.74	103.58	100.07	112.03	101.69	98.90
Qiang	101.24	102.80	96.93	112.13	100.81	100.84
Russian	101.28	102.24	97.21	112.33	101.65	101.43
Salar	101.51	103.45	101.74	112.53	101.47	98.84
She	101.27	102.84	98.96	112.38	101.62	99.09
Shui	102.03	103.93	98.99	112.56	101.17	99.35
Tajik	101.21	102.23	97.68	111.90	101.81	100.87
Tatar	101.21	102.26	97.78	111.91	101.81	100.87
Tibetan	101.41	103.35	99.84	111.91	101.28	100.79
Tu	101.53	103.47	101.60	112.53	101.53	98.91
Tujia	101.96	103.77	98.89	112.71	101.81	101.70

(continued)

Table 4.8 (continued)

Ethnic group	Transport and Communications	Transport	Transport Facility	Fuels for Transport Facility	Use and Maintenance of Transport Facility	Traffic Fee
Uygur	101.20	102.20	97.66	111.88	101.80	100.87
Uzbek	101.21	102.22	97.67	111.89	101.81	100.89
Va	101.74	103.58	100.05	112.04	101.71	98.94
Xibe	101.40	102.67	98.95	112.77	102.80	101.06
Yao	101.99	103.54	98.59	112.47	102.64	101.35
Yi	101.64	103.41	99.09	112.11	101.38	99.47
Yugur	101.17	102.66	99.97	112.02	101.33	100.06
Zhuang	101.66	103.11	97.99	112.30	102.71	100.84

Table 4.9 Consumer price indices by category (preceding year=100) (VII)

Ethnic group	Communications	Education, Culture and Recreation	Education	Education Articles	Education Services
National average	**98.8**	**102.2**	**102.9**	**102.5**	**102.9**
Achang	98.74	102.34	102.32	101.54	102.37
Bai	98.87	102.38	102.23	101.57	102.28
Baonan	98.48	100.67	100.88	100.73	100.90
Blang	98.73	102.34	102.32	101.55	102.38
Buyi	99.31	103.31	101.76	102.48	101.73
Dai	98.74	102.33	102.32	101.54	102.37
Daur	99.21	101.62	101.88	100.81	101.94
Deang	98.73	102.34	102.31	101.53	102.37
Derung	98.77	102.28	102.37	101.78	102.41
Dong	99.46	102.67	101.95	101.82	101.98
Dongxiang	98.55	100.59	100.81	100.65	100.82
Ewenki	99.78	101.11	101.09	100.62	101.14
Gaoshan	99.03	102.42	103.18	102.64	103.22
Gelao	99.32	103.34	101.74	102.49	101.71
Han	98.88	102.21	102.83	102.87	102.84
Hani	98.74	102.34	102.32	101.54	102.37
Hezhe	97.96	102.83	103.72	101.45	103.83
Hui	98.91	102.15	102.70	103.09	102.64

(*continued*)

Table 4.9 (continued)

Ethnic group	Communications	Education, Culture and Recreation	Education	Education Articles	Education Services
Jing	99.18	102.55	103.18	102.14	103.28
Jingpo	98.74	102.34	102.32	101.54	102.37
Jino	98.73	102.34	102.32	101.54	102.37
Kazak	98.76	101.29	101.39	101.07	101.40
Kirgiz	98.76	101.31	101.41	101.07	101.43
Korean	98.40	102.41	102.87	103.48	102.84
Lahu	98.74	102.34	102.32	101.55	102.38
Lhoba	98.67	100.60	100.44	100.40	100.46
Li	100.35	102.68	104.10	100.86	104.46
Lisu	98.73	102.31	102.32	101.56	102.38
Manchu	98.58	102.24	103.13	102.99	103.14
Maonan	99.24	102.78	102.79	102.24	102.86
Miao	99.19	102.67	102.04	101.87	102.08
Monba	98.68	100.49	100.39	100.29	100.41
Mongol	99.60	101.32	101.44	101.21	101.47
Mulao	99.20	102.64	103.03	102.18	103.12
Naxi	98.72	102.31	102.32	101.55	102.37
Nu	98.73	102.31	102.29	101.54	102.34
Oroqen	98.89	101.97	102.41	101.04	102.49
Pumi	98.74	102.33	102.32	101.56	102.38
Qiang	98.61	101.51	102.54	102.13	102.58
Russian	99.11	101.28	101.39	101.03	101.41
Salar	97.44	104.11	103.99	103.76	104.00
She	98.46	102.26	102.82	102.91	102.81
Shui	99.31	103.29	101.80	102.47	101.77
Tajik	98.76	101.33	101.44	101.13	101.46
Tatar	98.73	101.32	101.45	101.12	101.46
Tibetan	98.35	101.61	101.76	101.55	101.78
Tu	97.54	103.98	103.87	103.66	103.88
Tujia	98.99	102.12	102.16	101.36	102.24
Uygur	98.76	101.30	101.39	101.08	101.41
Uzbek	98.76	101.31	101.42	101.09	101.44
Va	98.74	102.34	102.33	101.57	102.39
Xibe	98.88	101.99	102.98	102.71	102.99
Yao	99.31	102.23	102.75	101.65	102.86
Yi	98.77	102.22	102.32	101.81	102.36
Yugur	98.51	100.57	100.82	100.65	100.83
Zhuang	99.15	102.51	103.17	102.09	103.27

Table 4.10 Consumer price indices by category (preceding year=100) (VIII)

Ethnic group	Cultural and Recreational Articles	Durable Consumer Goods for Culture and Recreation	Other Articles	Cultural and Recreational Services	Touring and Outing
National average	**101.4**	**98.3**	**101.9**	**100.8**	**103.3**
Achang	102.36	98.74	101.94	102.10	106.02
Bai	102.55	98.89	101.80	101.82	106.64
Baonan	100.29	99.15	100.59	100.62	101.10
Blang	102.36	98.74	101.94	102.09	106.02
Buyi	105.15	98.93	101.40	100.09	115.20
Dai	102.35	98.72	101.95	102.09	106.01
Daur	101.13	98.60	101.45	100.03	103.46
Deang	102.36	98.74	101.94	102.10	106.04
Derung	102.15	98.69	101.86	101.81	105.51
Dong	103.44	99.47	101.27	100.56	109.51
Dongxiang	100.20	99.06	100.64	100.54	100.74
Ewenki	101.13	99.51	101.77	100.03	102.69
Gaoshan	101.30	98.82	101.86	100.65	103.28
Gelao	105.23	98.94	101.38	100.05	115.47
Han	101.31	98.52	101.90	100.80	103.09
Hani	102.36	98.74	101.94	102.10	106.03
Hezhe	101.18	96.81	100.84	100.09	104.89
Hui	101.30	98.86	101.85	100.63	104.18
Jing	101.51	98.93	102.26	101.27	103.44
Jingpo	102.36	98.74	101.94	102.09	106.04
Jino	102.36	98.73	101.94	102.10	106.03
Kazak	101.11	97.88	100.99	99.97	105.99
Kirgiz	101.11	97.87	100.99	99.97	105.98
Korean	101.60	99.39	101.59	100.18	103.82
Lahu	102.35	98.74	101.94	102.09	106.01
Lhoba	100.73	100.32	100.40	101.29	100.80
Li	100.59	100.02	103.03	100.96	99.15
Lisu	102.30	98.67	101.96	102.06	105.90
Manchu	100.68	98.22	101.32	100.21	102.35
Maonan	102.54	98.95	102.00	100.93	106.79
Miao	103.36	99.20	101.37	100.72	109.27
Monba	100.59	100.36	100.37	101.34	100.30
Mongol	101.11	99.39	101.72	100.11	102.88
Mulao	101.93	98.93	102.13	101.12	104.81
Naxi	102.30	98.67	101.96	102.05	105.89
Nu	102.32	98.76	101.92	102.07	105.92

(*continued*)

Table 4.10 (continued)

Ethnic group	Cultural and Recreational Articles	Durable Consumer Goods for Culture and Recreation	Other Articles	Cultural and Recreational Services	Touring and Outing
Oroqen	101.13	98.14	101.30	100.06	103.71
Pumi	102.35	98.73	101.94	102.09	105.99
Qiang	100.49	96.30	102.58	100.80	101.74
Russian	101.14	98.53	101.34	100.05	104.67
Salar	104.32	98.94	100.31	101.30	120.24
She	101.38	98.28	101.96	100.98	103.03
Shui	105.04	98.95	101.44	100.15	114.83
Tajik	101.11	97.90	101.01	100.01	105.89
Tatar	101.09	97.94	101.00	100.04	105.73
Tibetan	101.46	99.03	100.90	101.20	105.44
Tu	104.16	98.94	100.40	101.29	119.14
Tujia	101.99	99.21	101.06	100.86	104.99
Uygur	101.11	97.88	100.99	99.98	105.98
Uzbek	101.11	97.89	101.00	99.99	105.92
Va	102.33	98.74	101.94	102.07	105.94
Xibe	100.22	97.75	101.12	100.15	101.75
Yao	101.40	99.36	101.71	101.31	102.95
Yi	102.16	98.08	102.06	101.51	105.88
Yugur	100.15	99.16	100.62	100.60	100.40
Zhuang	101.46	98.90	102.21	101.35	103.29

Table 4.11 Consumer price indices by category (preceding year=100) (IX)

Ethnic group	Health Care	Medicine and Medical Instrument	Medical Services	Other Articles and Services	Other Articles	Other Services
National average	**104.3**	**104.4**	**104.3**	**101.2**	**99.1**	**102.8**
Achang	104.05	105.4	102.18	100.79	100.31	101.63
Bai	103.74	101.5	102.00	100.76	100.15	101.64
Baonan	107.92	104.4	110.40	100.78	98.87	102.44
Blang	104.06	104.0	102.19	100.79	100.31	101.64
Buyi	102.11	104.6	101.21	100.66	99.71	101.41
Dai	104.05	103.4	102.18	100.79	100.31	101.64

(continued)

Table 4.11 (continued)

Ethnic group	Health Care	Medicine and Medical Instrument	Medical Services	Other Articles and Services	Other Articles	Other Services
Daur	105.21	104.6	106.39	100.37	99.13	101.36
Deang	104.07	103.2	102.20	100.78	100.32	101.63
Derung	104.24	107.6	102.85	100.81	100.09	101.77
Dong	102.51	107.3	101.52	100.70	99.36	101.82
Dongxiang	108.40	104.5	111.22	100.74	98.75	102.47
Ewenki	103.40	105.6	103.76	100.59	99.50	101.47
Gaoshan	104.93	102.3	105.15	101.14	99.12	102.78
Gelao	102.07	105.5	101.19	100.65	99.70	101.40
Han	104.38	102.6	104.25	101.14	99.16	102.75
Hani	104.05	104.2	102.18	100.78	100.32	101.63
Hezhe	108.08	101.4	110.38	100.01	98.55	101.12
Hui	105.11	107.2	105.33	101.00	99.02	102.73
Jing	104.45	104.1	104.36	101.29	98.64	103.40
Jingpo	104.05	102.6	102.19	100.78	100.31	101.63
Jino	104.06	107.6	102.19	100.79	100.32	101.63
Kazak	112.44	104.4	117.13	100.13	97.68	102.41
Kirgiz	112.40	106.1	117.07	100.13	97.68	102.39
Korean	106.56	101.1	106.95	100.59	99.32	101.57
Lahu	104.06	104.0	102.19	100.79	100.31	101.63
Lhoba	102.29	104.4	101.19	101.06	99.14	103.04
Li	103.53	104.3	100.53	101.76	97.97	104.80
Lisu	104.03	103.9	102.17	100.83	100.29	101.71
Manchu	108.75	101.3	111.45	101.11	99.13	102.62
Maonan	103.77	106.4	103.48	101.13	98.90	102.89
Miao	102.81	105.3	101.81	100.73	99.48	101.80
Monba	102.14	105.4	100.97	101.12	99.16	103.13
Mongol	104.41	101.5	105.14	100.73	99.45	101.76
Mulao	104.15	104.4	103.99	101.23	98.73	103.21
Naxi	104.02	104.0	102.18	100.83	100.29	101.71
Nu	104.03	104.6	102.18	100.79	100.29	101.66
Oroqen	105.80	103.4	107.19	100.29	99.02	101.29
Pumi	104.06	104.6	102.20	100.79	100.31	101.65
Qiang	102.84	103.2	101.66	102.37	99.44	104.18
Russian	108.58	107.6	111.40	100.40	98.45	102.13
Salar	104.25	107.3	102.21	100.50	99.44	101.53
She	103.00	104.5	102.46	100.48	98.89	101.74
Shui	102.19	105.6	101.30	100.68	99.69	101.48
Tajik	112.18	102.3	116.72	100.16	97.72	102.42
Tatar	111.95	105.5	116.38	100.20	97.78	102.43

(continued)

Table 4.11 (continued)

Ethnic group	Health Care	Medicine and Medical Instrument	Medical Services	Other Articles and Services	Other Articles	Other Services
Tibetan	103.07	102.6	101.81	101.24	99.31	102.93
Tu	104.10	104.2	102.11	100.54	99.46	101.58
Tujia	103.33	101.4	102.96	100.65	99.05	102.00
Uygur	112.41	107.2	117.09	100.14	97.68	102.41
Uzbek	112.28	104.1	116.88	100.15	97.70	102.42
Va	104.06	102.6	102.21	100.79	100.29	101.66
Xibe	110.76	107.6	115.21	100.72	98.61	102.44
Yao	103.90	104.4	103.29	101.06	98.85	102.90
Yi	103.50	106.1	101.93	101.21	100.01	102.31
Yugur	107.93	101.1	110.52	100.81	98.87	102.48
Zhuang	104.47	104.0	104.30	101.29	98.69	103.38

Table 4.12 Ownership of major durable consumer goods per 100 urban households at year-end (I)

Ethnic group	Automobile (unit)	Motorcycle (unit)	Electric Bicycle (unit)	Washing Machine (set)	Refrigerator (set)
National average	**41.0**	**19.5**	**55.0**	**97.7**	**100.9**
Achang	52.65	32.74	38.69	100.27	97.55
Bai	49.87	32.21	35.38	100.60	98.40
Baonan	30.73	12.55	24.50	99.74	97.88
Blang	52.57	32.66	38.68	100.28	97.58
Buyi	40.22	25.60	17.15	101.37	101.12
Dai	52.56	32.70	38.52	100.28	97.55
Daur	37.68	12.01	30.68	97.96	101.90
Deang	52.66	32.77	38.43	100.29	97.52
Derung	49.83	29.65	39.65	99.83	98.25
Dong	38.06	29.91	27.72	101.51	102.17
Dongxiang	31.01	12.34	25.52	99.80	98.21
Ewenki	45.17	14.60	38.37	98.79	103.37
Gaoshan	39.22	20.43	63.01	97.59	100.36
Gelao	40.00	25.68	16.13	101.42	101.15
Han	40.39	20.21	57.71	98.07	100.91

(continued)

Table 4.12 (continued)

Ethnic group	Automobile (unit)	Motorcycle (unit)	Electric Bicycle (unit)	Washing Machine (set)	Refrigerator (set)
Hani	52.65	32.74	38.59	100.29	97.55
Hezhe	22.02	7.47	14.96	95.89	98.42
Hui	41.06	14.81	48.97	99.42	100.19
Jing	40.58	32.28	84.38	98.51	102.46
Jingpo	52.61	32.74	38.52	100.28	97.55
Jino	52.60	32.74	38.35	100.28	97.53
Kazak	38.34	10.00	30.01	99.61	103.01
Kirgiz	38.19	9.97	29.91	99.57	102.98
Korean	31.57	8.98	13.23	96.44	99.04
Lahu	52.62	32.68	38.79	100.29	97.56
Lhoba	45.01	15.26	22.20	99.44	103.37
Li	39.63	30.97	82.26	90.91	96.95
Lisu	52.15	32.29	38.44	100.27	97.65
Manchu	36.12	8.19	30.90	96.75	100.13
Maonan	40.27	30.63	66.63	99.38	102.24
Miao	39.39	28.95	26.23	101.13	101.55
Monba	45.32	14.79	21.86	99.46	103.45
Mongol	44.26	13.84	37.68	98.61	102.90
Mulao	40.39	31.79	77.21	98.84	102.40
Naxi	52.09	32.24	38.20	100.26	97.66
Nu	52.46	32.34	38.68	100.24	97.68
Oroqen	33.43	10.93	26.96	97.31	100.90
Pumi	52.50	32.57	38.68	100.27	97.58
Qiang	33.88	19.46	28.34	99.71	100.93
Russian	41.53	11.92	34.41	99.31	103.10
Salar	39.17	12.93	11.42	98.25	99.38
She	38.12	27.60	57.97	90.10	98.52
Shui	40.38	25.91	19.61	101.35	101.16
Tajik	38.32	10.38	30.78	99.55	102.95
Tatar	38.20	10.36	30.46	99.57	102.75
Tibetan	40.65	15.77	21.06	99.30	101.47
Tu	39.25	14.22	13.48	98.16	99.24
Tujia	35.23	30.64	25.61	100.34	103.36
Uygur	38.36	10.05	30.14	99.60	103.02
Uzbek	38.41	10.33	30.59	99.55	102.96
Va	52.46	32.38	39.27	100.26	97.66
Xibe	32.95	7.44	18.40	96.17	100.85
Yao	39.50	34.66	63.13	99.59	102.12
Yi	46.02	28.24	33.29	100.25	98.88
Yugur	30.53	12.63	25.38	99.78	97.81
Zhuang	41.32	33.03	83.24	98.45	102.14

Table 4.13 Ownership of major durable consumer goods per 100 urban households at year-end (II)

Ethnic group	Microwave Oven (set)	Color TV Set (set)	Air Conditioner (set)	Water Heater (set)	Exhaust Fan (set)	Mobile Phone (set)	Computer (set)	Camera (set)
National average	**55.2**	**121.3**	**142.2**	**97.2**	**79.1**	**243.1**	**73.1**	**20.2**
Achang	58.85	107.54	9.00	99.50	76.12	253.05	64.07	15.52
Bai	55.79	108.49	24.88	99.21	74.21	257.22	63.95	15.09
Baonan	49.65	102.03	14.44	82.57	84.02	244.69	59.17	19.99
Blang	58.89	107.68	9.80	99.51	76.15	253.01	64.09	15.53
Buyi	40.96	107.44	39.62	94.64	57.29	280.50	55.65	9.85
Dai	58.83	107.60	9.29	99.49	76.09	253.02	64.02	15.50
Daur	41.49	102.09	23.11	77.18	83.12	222.27	60.28	16.29
Deang	58.88	107.44	8.02	99.46	76.13	253.00	63.99	15.49
Derung	57.33	108.71	28.33	98.09	76.62	250.41	64.56	16.10
Dong	43.95	111.84	97.66	98.26	64.44	276.41	64.41	13.49
Dongxiang	48.91	102.01	15.75	83.65	84.42	243.29	59.11	19.81
Ewenki	43.91	103.10	25.95	78.43	81.61	226.78	62.78	18.00
Gaoshan	52.79	116.23	137.29	96.69	75.05	246.53	70.77	18.14
Gelao	40.51	107.07	38.91	94.52	56.77	281.32	55.35	9.67
Han	53.68	120.19	142.15	97.35	78.07	245.29	71.60	19.04
Hani	58.90	107.59	8.75	99.51	76.14	253.02	64.06	15.51
Hezhe	37.62	101.31	25.43	74.17	85.60	214.97	56.96	13.19
Hui	52.91	107.80	70.94	92.43	82.00	240.69	65.91	17.96
Jing	63.36	110.84	152.04	102.88	65.74	268.30	78.33	19.92
Jingpo	58.78	107.47	8.93	99.47	76.07	253.09	64.06	15.51
Jino	58.88	107.52	8.60	99.46	76.12	253.01	64.02	15.50
Kazak	41.21	100.19	29.80	92.04	86.40	220.95	55.07	15.17
Kirgiz	41.14	100.21	29.81	91.88	86.40	220.83	55.08	15.13
Korean	46.77	101.65	30.28	78.06	85.57	221.98	63.19	15.35
Lahu	58.86	107.60	9.33	99.50	76.15	252.99	64.07	15.52

Lhoba	46.72	120.84	22.92	52.39	48.39	213.92	45.67	13.96
Li	33.72	103.96	146.85	96.86	64.00	274.35	65.05	13.59
Lisu	58.57	107.93	12.51	99.43	76.04	252.81	63.92	15.48
Manchu	56.29	105.14	62.72	86.05	83.05	215.68	65.53	21.41
Maonan	57.37	109.33	122.64	100.68	62.79	272.60	72.38	17.24
Miao	45.81	112.19	89.36	98.12	66.18	272.58	63.32	13.54
Monba	47.02	121.81	20.90	50.27	47.46	211.68	45.19	14.12
Mongol	46.92	103.96	35.24	81.07	81.56	226.31	63.04	18.62
Mulao	60.92	110.07	142.52	102.06	64.41	270.30	76.32	18.99
Naxi	58.50	108.06	12.59	99.22	75.90	252.70	63.83	15.47
Nu	58.70	108.00	10.46	98.79	75.73	252.33	63.90	15.55
Oroqen	40.80	102.13	25.34	76.27	83.62	220.38	59.79	15.61
Pumi	58.83	107.68	9.84	99.43	76.14	252.87	64.05	15.53
Qiang	46.36	120.93	139.43	97.44	72.11	249.17	58.11	13.50
Russian	43.73	102.63	35.19	87.39	84.29	224.18	59.28	16.94
Salar	52.28	97.64	6.60	75.63	79.81	235.82	53.29	14.67
She	52.28	133.01	175.77	105.57	71.15	249.17	76.88	17.27
Shui	41.99	107.49	41.84	94.98	57.62	280.08	56.33	10.16
Tajik	41.61	100.77	33.73	92.21	86.09	221.87	55.59	15.28
Tatar	42.19	100.96	33.40	91.85	86.12	222.67	55.96	15.65
Tibetan	48.36	114.36	42.49	69.28	62.89	228.55	50.77	14.32
Tu	52.31	98.86	13.99	77.05	79.23	237.86	54.59	14.90
Tujia	46.68	119.93	155.32	100.69	72.90	267.31	69.35	15.85
Uygur	41.24	100.28	30.40	92.09	86.37	221.01	55.14	15.18
Uzbek	41.44	100.49	32.38	92.20	86.18	221.57	55.48	15.28
Va	58.70	107.70	12.32	99.49	76.27	252.80	64.24	15.67
Xibe	53.05	103.94	45.87	86.94	86.45	210.30	57.91	20.36
Yao	56.45	112.34	154.52	102.78	69.81	268.19	77.13	19.25
Yi	53.38	111.21	48.21	98.36	72.86	255.06	61.42	14.29
Yugur	49.82	102.36	16.24	82.93	84.12	245.26	59.74	20.32
Zhuang	63.58	110.07	148.89	102.99	66.34	267.45	78.59	20.10

Table 4.14 Per capita net income of rural households (yuan)

Ethnic group	1990	1995	2000	2005	2010	2011	2012	2018
National average	686.31	1577.74	2253.42	3254.93	5919.01	6977.29	7916.58	**19853.1**
Achang	543.08	1020.14	1492.68	2063.04	3985.32	4761.08	5460.00	14322.22
Bai	543.34	1064.01	1543.03	2137.30	4079.75	4862.03	5568.00	14669.05
Baonan	446.68	899.57	1443.12	2013.02	3502.27	4012.33	4630.80	14781.38
Blang	542.15	1018.97	1495.98	2068.78	3995.13	4773.00	5473.28	14346.61
Buyi	452.75	1123.81	1438.81	1973.10	3634.74	4334.23	4963.41	14135.98
Dai	542.78	1019.07	1492.20	2062.84	3985.04	4760.82	5459.75	14329.83
Daur	671.72	1423.80	2092.15	3101.75	5814.46	7011.71	8004.18	18797.35
Deang	541.69	1014.43	1484.52	2051.15	3966.72	4739.01	5435.63	14283.47
Derung	560.89	1098.75	1641.15	2301.74	4367.80	5214.96	5967.31	15260.31
Dong	547.06	1282.23	1760.53	2435.63	4433.43	5226.00	5958.06	15916.20
Dongxiang	460.46	911.59	1453.33	2041.48	3572.22	4095.29	4733.68	14826.09
Ewenki	634.05	1300.62	2092.32	3074.01	5693.86	6841.02	7824.48	19611.61
Gaoshan	682.40	1603.12	2372.79	3414.65	6171.88	7306.48	8299.37	18900.42
Gelao	447.60	1115.97	1423.84	1947.22	3588.35	4280.37	4903.18	14066.62
Han	709.39	1673.09	2491.84	3590.78	6439.14	7636.87	8657.82	19724.82
Hani	542.78	1018.77	1491.26	2061.27	3983.14	4758.37	5456.90	14319.04
Hezhe	767.38	1771.46	2211.18	3325.73	6348.72	7707.04	8736.72	17701.44
Hui	620.96	1299.25	1980.70	2887.72	5285.15	6222.49	7110.66	17559.61
Jing	640.02	1453.05	1892.74	2545.06	4628.90	5351.26	6137.48	15223.63
Jingpo	543.00	1020.46	1491.98	2061.56	3982.42	4757.41	5455.83	14319.68
Jino	542.13	1016.32	1489.06	2058.35	3978.60	4753.31	5451.40	14316.53
Kazak	683.04	1136.98	1619.29	2483.31	4643.78	5443.11	6393.96	16196.38
Kirgiz	684.42	1144.25	1626.22	2493.52	4664.73	5471.01	6423.52	16215.59
Korean	801.36	1688.86	2161.66	3393.99	6435.69	7750.06	8831.03	18188.44
Lahu	542.43	1018.82	1492.91	2064.02	3988.05	4764.43	5463.72	14321.85
Lhoba	648.41	1224.60	1410.87	2178.88	4284.66	5077.31	5904.29	12190.42

Li	686.71	1508.48	2156.90	2968.81	5220.90	6370.28	7317.97	17430.17
Lisu	543.11	1023.23	1503.77	2083.93	4016.42	4799.80	5503.63	14408.84
Manchu	778.64	1729.24	2368.50	3609.25	6651.98	7966.53	9029.71	19943.94
Maonan	585.85	1359.79	1751.15	2355.57	4295.67	4994.32	5729.14	14798.74
Miao	509.28	1166.55	1720.67	2395.71	4399.04	5217.26	5952.41	15883.05
Monba	662.05	1241.20	1411.82	2189.68	4309.75	5101.39	5932.04	12158.07
Mongol	650.38	1334.44	2096.86	3108.52	5749.22	6891.96	7877.74	19518.99
Mulao	623.79	1434.90	1857.68	2494.13	4529.87	5245.38	6014.09	15176.00
Naxi	544.38	1025.90	1505.54	2088.13	4024.66	4808.12	5513.01	14426.52
Nu	546.99	1031.59	1503.47	2084.04	4020.09	4800.46	5505.05	14350.64
Oroqen	699.66	1535.56	2149.65	3195.36	6015.18	7270.46	8276.03	18610.41
Pumi	544.05	1023.29	1497.79	2072.17	4000.85	4779.27	5480.47	14357.77
Qiang	558.89	1163.28	1908.06	2807.84	5095.44	6136.66	7010.06	17677.95
Russian	675.96	1246.10	1872.39	2817.37	5224.94	6178.10	7155.14	17990.14
Salar	554.33	1032.27	1510.58	2179.16	3905.82	4631.66	5383.33	16441.62
She	824.94	2172.95	3244.15	4670.63	7935.46	9318.52	10509.90	23274.64
Shui	456.85	1125.26	1439.90	1970.89	3635.28	4330.27	4961.21	14089.62
Tajik	681.22	1147.60	1643.32	2512.33	4690.93	5502.08	6453.91	16292.92
Tatar	679.10	1157.47	1658.25	2529.81	4710.34	5517.46	6463.28	16411.81
Tibetan	590.87	1131.76	1522.63	2272.21	4271.37	5079.77	5878.63	14394.74
Tu	560.46	1074.86	1571.75	2249.37	4016.55	4763.20	5520.00	16616.55
Tujia	518.66	1173.95	2063.06	2902.13	5335.20	6330.84	7197.42	18434.78
Uygur	683.86	1140.14	1623.91	2489.83	4655.39	5457.25	6409.30	16217.91
Uzbek	685.98	1152.77	1641.33	2511.06	4688.36	5495.42	6448.96	16304.23
Va	543.21	1026.46	1510.96	2092.58	4033.96	4819.33	5524.90	14412.88
Xibe	800.79	1640.99	2220.49	3452.70	6459.58	7728.56	8788.38	20240.07
Yao	667.82	1502.80	2062.16	2799.48	5049.32	5877.84	6704.44	16811.33
Yi	536.40	1068.62	1597.36	2253.08	4244.00	5083.16	5821.40	15209.71
Yugur	445.72	907.47	1458.91	2033.33	3533.85	4042.21	4659.18	14836.88
Zhuang	647.55	1462.66	1908.62	2555.24	4644.72	5373.48	6161.13	15348.18

Table 4.15 Per capita annual net income of rural households by sources (yuan)

Ethnic group	Disposable Income	Income from Wages and Salaries	Net Business Income	Net Income from Properties	Net Income from Transfers
National average	**28228.0**	**15829.0**	**4852.4**	**2378.5**	**5168.1**
Achang	20196.22	9695.92	4888.20	1969.96	3642.14
Bai	20485.87	9976.65	4809.06	1911.47	3788.69
Baonan	17817.92	9877.20	3282.42	1152.69	3505.61
Blang	20229.82	9717.29	4887.64	1970.13	3654.78
Buyi	18995.95	9860.11	4108.50	1380.08	3647.26
Dai	20191.41	9688.08	4883.93	1967.91	3651.48
Daur	26454.02	13734.51	6180.32	1382.73	5156.46
Deang	20130.84	9647.10	4882.30	1964.04	3637.40
Derung	21510.07	10690.50	4901.23	1946.88	3971.45
Dong	21538.36	11096.10	4542.78	1602.07	4297.41
Dongxiang	17991.35	9935.77	3429.75	1123.84	3501.98
Ewenki	28121.19	14906.73	6800.01	1507.66	4906.79
Gaoshan	26880.52	14703.18	4858.14	2189.34	5129.86
Gelao	18856.38	9795.17	4077.85	1359.23	3624.13
Han	28030.41	15678.61	4861.48	2316.38	5173.94
Hani	20190.42	9686.92	4887.10	1970.61	3645.79
Hezhe	23970.25	11931.47	4829.75	1351.89	5857.15
Hui	24100.83	13506.04	4280.84	1663.05	4650.89
Jing	21842.73	10598.99	5388.87	1521.12	4333.74
Jingpo	20186.31	9694.63	4884.04	1968.05	3639.58
Jino	20174.69	9676.00	4881.29	1968.65	3648.74
Kazak	21509.62	11661.82	5145.72	790.10	3912.00
Kirgiz	21546.14	11668.89	5150.74	794.21	3932.30
Korean	24572.24	12903.06	4981.80	1261.55	5425.84
Lahu	20196.99	9692.87	4888.76	1968.14	3647.21
Lhoba	18102.33	9411.23	4594.40	1188.93	2907.76
Li	24406.06	14156.92	4453.91	1881.55	3913.68
Lisu	20250.42	9726.98	4877.52	1952.43	3693.49
Manchu	27763.51	15020.32	4782.77	1593.24	6367.19
Maonan	20855.49	10241.20	5049.28	1444.23	4120.78
Miao	21550.07	11061.94	4523.77	1637.15	4327.21
Monba	18137.03	9423.73	4559.44	1229.53	2924.33
Mongol	27788.43	14807.73	6376.90	1488.92	5114.89
Mulao	21604.89	10593.43	5262.43	1515.82	4233.21
Naxi	20282.73	9749.07	4873.59	1959.82	3700.26
Nu	20261.83	9760.18	4889.72	1965.76	3646.18
Oroqen	25985.13	13359.29	5830.71	1401.91	5393.21
Pumi	20237.22	9722.51	4885.32	1968.60	3660.79
Qiang	22522.91	11128.71	4557.07	1457.35	5379.77

(continued)

Table 4.15 (continued)

Ethnic group	Disposable Income	Income from Wages and Salaries	Net Business Income	Net Income from Properties	Net Income from Transfers
Russian	24867.82	13448.34	5677.43	1259.95	4482.09
Salar	20647.44	12028.28	3131.80	1110.56	4376.81
She	34062.66	19742.02	6019.31	3406.44	4894.88
Shui	18978.82	9790.60	4148.65	1374.53	3665.03
Tajik	21690.61	11768.73	5132.16	832.91	3956.80
Tatar	21826.20	11879.88	5040.52	909.71	3996.10
Tibetan	19418.20	10246.07	4160.40	1213.07	3798.66
Tu	21003.87	12245.70	3216.19	1210.49	4331.48
Tujia	24799.08	12766.13	4841.78	1785.91	5405.26
Uygur	21550.56	11685.00	5149.06	796.54	3919.96
Uzbek	21700.08	11788.45	5139.02	835.88	3936.73
Va	20338.75	9803.38	4897.67	1967.30	3670.40
Xibe	27935.74	14758.41	5135.49	1319.50	6722.34
Yao	23517.49	12023.76	5226.79	1823.65	4443.29
Yi	20668.64	10082.18	4704.94	1756.35	4125.18
Yugur	17928.97	9929.88	3275.22	1199.98	3523.90
Zhuang	21984.66	10755.36	5402.49	1586.47	4240.34

Table 4.16 Per capita consumption expenditure of rural households (yuan) (I)

Ethnic group	Consumption expenditure	Food	Clothing	Residence	Household facilities and articles
National average	**12124.3**	**3645.6**	**647.7**	**2660.6**	**720.5**
Achang	9168.75	2704.80	373.11	1895.37	561.43
Bai	9473.38	2784.25	408.03	2003.60	579.38
Baonan	9146.53	2719.53	573.90	1733.07	517.82
Blang	9185.28	2710.48	374.92	1898.65	562.73
Buyi	9374.26	2672.67	505.98	2169.47	578.55
Dai	9179.72	2711.35	374.45	1896.83	562.68
Daur	12144.47	3340.29	714.22	2203.38	562.86
Deang	9143.59	2695.28	372.28	1888.62	560.21
Derung	9719.10	2881.52	430.31	2014.71	584.03
Dong	10686.82	3105.41	531.92	2462.28	643.79
Dongxiang	9126.09	2714.03	585.96	1728.69	525.64
Ewenki	12596.52	3474.11	714.26	2336.32	584.01
Gaoshan	12131.85	3614.71	651.71	2712.59	716.50
Gelao	9325.49	2657.28	504.64	2160.27	576.26

(continued)

Table 4.16 (continued)

Ethnic group	Consumption expenditure	Food	Clothing	Residence	Household facilities and articles
Han	12712.46	3836.87	672.40	2810.20	752.44
Hani	9166.16	2702.79	373.24	1894.67	561.45
Hezhe	11626.66	3187.31	698.60	2048.50	527.49
Hui	11029.78	3144.42	688.59	2229.08	674.95
Jing	10697.74	3233.24	348.22	2482.81	610.04
Jingpo	9165.44	2703.07	373.42	1894.99	561.30
Jino	9163.57	2704.34	373.23	1892.69	561.33
Kazak	9427.23	2825.34	797.94	1718.76	610.17
Kirgiz	9453.18	2830.10	797.39	1722.45	609.46
Korean	11270.37	3116.20	655.30	2054.40	481.50
Lahu	9170.80	2703.76	374.29	1895.64	562.02
Lhoba	7854.59	2771.46	943.85	1306.97	383.96
Li	10920.29	4489.25	327.43	2173.91	519.83
Lisu	9265.83	2753.11	383.57	1911.34	570.09
Manchu	11671.50	3133.78	685.46	2346.84	619.20
Maonan	10282.24	3057.70	384.09	2386.42	598.48
Miao	10550.53	3123.82	526.46	2368.68	642.64
Monba	7787.32	2789.81	963.47	1266.07	376.11
Mongol	12265.85	3382.87	706.60	2323.45	592.30
Mulao	10598.82	3189.23	363.16	2459.02	608.84
Naxi	9272.34	2757.09	386.42	1913.76	569.86
Nu	9192.42	2718.85	385.37	1899.05	561.12
Oroqen	12090.56	3318.41	706.00	2184.43	553.49
Pumi	9197.15	2714.50	376.61	1901.25	563.30
Qiang	12705.11	4533.45	714.65	2502.19	857.04
Russian	10879.04	3136.08	767.40	2046.96	621.03
Salar	10233.72	3020.66	706.47	1807.10	508.41
She	15273.53	5092.92	726.03	3786.78	807.70
Shui	9366.43	2667.35	496.90	2166.95	577.07
Tajik	9521.37	2858.64	792.19	1749.59	613.91
Tatar	9587.26	2868.39	786.52	1774.97	616.93
Tibetan	9501.25	3211.92	810.83	1689.64	522.13
Tu	10379.17	3087.39	691.02	1870.00	519.17
Tujia	12394.85	3713.73	649.87	2696.20	758.52
Uygur	9443.22	2830.38	797.99	1723.70	611.08
Uzbek	9503.78	2853.05	794.20	1745.04	613.69
Va	9225.01	2723.05	379.89	1905.86	566.08
Xibe	11182.76	3058.01	688.78	2170.12	583.34
Yao	11438.43	3484.93	430.15	2614.15	658.76
Yi	10160.29	3203.09	482.54	2091.47	644.73
Yugur	9176.31	2722.01	568.03	1755.06	522.60
Zhuang	10708.43	3256.31	341.40	2464.02	610.34

Table 4.17 Per capita consumption expenditure of rural households (yuan) (II)

Ethnic group	Transport and communications	Education, culture and recreation	Health care and medical services	Miscellaneous Goods and Services Miscellaneous
National average	**1690.0**	**1301.6**	**1240.1**	**218.3**
Achang	1511.36	1155.72	850.21	116.75
Bai	1499.26	1193.16	879.23	126.46
Baonan	1117.27	1184.96	1136.61	163.37
Blang	1513.00	1156.03	852.27	117.20
Buyi	1400.99	1170.91	730.80	144.89
Dai	1511.31	1153.81	852.09	117.19
Daur	1909.75	1582.14	1596.32	235.51
Deang	1508.60	1153.89	848.58	116.14
Derung	1546.19	1192.31	932.60	137.41
Dong	1453.26	1338.32	983.89	167.94
Dongxiang	1110.87	1180.40	1121.61	158.90
Ewenki	2053.47	1687.07	1504.21	243.07
Gaoshan	1674.49	1310.22	1233.27	218.36
Gelao	1391.41	1168.95	722.44	144.24
Han	1780.62	1329.94	1296.44	233.56
Hani	1511.89	1155.29	850.16	116.69
Hezhe	1683.34	1409.65	1839.56	232.21
Hui	1640.24	1225.13	1231.63	195.74
Jing	1534.83	1248.92	1077.06	162.62
Jingpo	1510.18	1155.48	850.21	116.79
Jino	1510.42	1154.38	850.45	116.73
Kazak	1301.85	1011.68	1018.50	143.01
Kirgiz	1306.73	1016.04	1027.07	143.94
Korean	1775.06	1399.07	1553.93	234.91
Lahu	1511.40	1155.51	851.38	116.81
Lhoba	1420.64	488.15	389.82	149.74
Li	1129.96	1367.01	721.35	191.55
Lisu	1514.22	1148.57	864.74	120.19
Manchu	1820.81	1330.88	1494.18	240.36
Maonan	1491.88	1225.86	981.29	156.53
Miao	1460.56	1303.29	961.06	164.03
Monba	1424.70	448.44	367.99	150.73
Mongol	1984.58	1589.59	1448.21	238.25
Mulao	1525.35	1244.38	1047.04	161.80
Naxi	1514.91	1146.70	863.13	120.47
Nu	1515.46	1146.78	847.38	118.40
Oroqen	1866.49	1548.73	1675.14	237.87
Pumi	1513.78	1154.89	854.98	117.85

(continued)

Table 4.17 (continued)

Ethnic group	Transport and communications	Education, culture and recreation	Health care and medical services	Miscellaneous Goods and Services Miscellaneous
Qiang	1580.07	940.15	1340.32	237.26
Russian	1629.99	1276.05	1215.24	186.30
Salar	1674.61	982.13	1298.14	236.19
She	2001.75	1432.18	1138.32	287.86
Shui	1404.41	1171.35	738.35	144.05
Tajik	1313.34	1022.07	1026.11	145.53
Tatar	1321.71	1031.86	1039.40	147.49
Tibetan	1494.16	732.53	851.12	188.93
Tu	1675.00	1010.82	1289.83	235.94
Tujia	1603.40	1480.27	1263.11	229.75
Uygur	1304.21	1012.92	1019.58	143.36
Uzbek	1311.48	1018.66	1023.03	144.63
Va	1514.67	1157.80	859.25	118.41
Xibe	1728.33	1279.21	1448.60	226.37
Yao	1536.05	1372.35	1165.75	176.28
Yi	1516.54	1096.77	972.00	153.14
Yugur	1109.66	1198.36	1138.57	162.00
Zhuang	1543.16	1249.82	1081.11	162.28

Table 4.18 Per Capita Consumption Expenditure of Rural Households (2018) (I)

Ethnic group	Consumption Expenditure	Food, Tobacco and Liquor	Clothing	Residence	Household Facilities, Articles and Services
National Average	**12124.3**	**3645.6**	**647.7**	**2660.6**	**720.5**
Achang	9168.75	2704.80	373.11	1895.37	561.43
Bai	9473.38	2784.25	408.03	2003.60	579.38
Baonan	9146.53	2719.53	573.90	1733.07	517.82
Blang	9185.28	2710.48	374.92	1898.65	562.73
Buyi	9374.26	2672.67	505.98	2169.47	578.55
Dai	9179.72	2711.35	374.45	1896.83	562.68
Daur	12144.47	3340.29	714.22	2203.38	562.86
Deang	9143.59	2695.28	372.28	1888.62	560.21
Derung	9719.10	2881.52	430.31	2014.71	584.03

(continued)

Table 4.18 (continued)

Ethnic group	Consumption Expenditure	Food, Tobacco and Liquor	Clothing	Residence	Household Facilities, Articles and Services
Dong	10686.82	3105.41	531.92	2462.28	643.79
Dongxiang	9126.09	2714.03	585.96	1728.69	525.64
Ewenki	12596.52	3474.11	714.26	2336.32	584.01
Gaoshan	12131.85	3614.71	651.71	2712.59	716.50
Gelao	9325.49	2657.28	504.64	2160.27	576.26
Han	12712.46	3836.87	672.40	2810.20	752.44
Hani	9166.16	2702.79	373.24	1894.67	561.45
Hezhe	11626.66	3187.31	698.60	2048.50	527.49
Hui	11029.78	3144.42	688.59	2229.08	674.95
Jing	10697.74	3233.24	348.22	2482.81	610.04
Jingpo	9165.44	2703.07	373.42	1894.99	561.30
Jino	9163.57	2704.34	373.23	1892.69	561.33
Kazak	9427.23	2825.34	797.94	1718.76	610.17
Kirgiz	9453.18	2830.10	797.39	1722.45	609.46
Korean	11270.37	3116.20	655.30	2054.40	481.50
Lahu	9170.80	2703.76	374.29	1895.64	562.02
Lhoba	7854.59	2771.46	943.85	1306.97	383.96
Li	10920.29	4489.25	327.43	2173.91	519.83
Lisu	9265.83	2753.11	383.57	1911.34	570.09
Manchu	11671.50	3133.78	685.46	2346.84	619.20
Maonan	10282.24	3057.70	384.09	2386.42	598.48
Miao	10550.53	3123.82	526.46	2368.68	642.64
Monba	7787.32	2789.81	963.47	1266.07	376.11
Mongol	12265.85	3382.87	706.60	2323.45	592.30
Mulao	10598.82	3189.23	363.16	2459.02	608.84
Naxi	9272.34	2757.09	386.42	1913.76	569.86
Nu	9192.42	2718.85	385.37	1899.05	561.12
Oroqen	12090.56	3318.41	706.00	2184.43	553.49
Pumi	9197.15	2714.50	376.61	1901.25	563.30
Qiang	12705.11	4533.45	714.65	2502.19	857.04
Russian	10879.04	3136.08	767.40	2046.96	621.03
Salar	10233.72	3020.66	706.47	1807.10	508.41
She	15273.53	5092.92	726.03	3786.78	807.70
Shui	9366.43	2667.35	496.90	2166.95	577.07
Tajik	9521.37	2858.64	792.19	1749.59	613.91
Tatar	9587.26	2868.39	786.52	1774.97	616.93
Tibetan	9501.25	3211.92	810.83	1689.64	522.13
Tu	10379.17	3087.39	691.02	1870.00	519.17
Tujia	12394.85	3713.73	649.87	2696.20	758.52

(*continued*)

Table 4.18 (continued)

Ethnic group	Consumption Expenditure	Food, Tobacco and Liquor	Clothing	Residence	Household Facilities, Articles and Services
Uygur	9443.22	2830.38	797.99	1723.70	611.08
Uzbek	9503.78	2853.05	794.20	1745.04	613.69
Va	9225.01	2723.05	379.89	1905.86	566.08
Xibe	11182.76	3058.01	688.78	2170.12	583.34
Yao	11438.43	3484.93	430.15	2614.15	658.76
Yi	10160.29	3203.09	482.54	2091.47	644.73
Yugur	9176.31	2722.01	568.03	1755.06	522.60
Zhuang	10708.43	3256.31	341.40	2464.02	610.34

Table 4.19 Per Capita Consumption Expenditure of Rural Households (2018) (II)

Ethnic group	Transport and Communications	Education, Culture and Recreation	Health Care and Medical Services	Miscellaneous Goods and Services
National average	**1690.0**	**1301.6**	**1240.1**	**218.3**
Achang	1511.36	1155.72	850.21	116.75
Bai	1499.26	1193.16	879.23	126.46
Baonan	1117.27	1184.96	1136.61	163.37
Blang	1513.00	1156.03	852.27	117.20
Buyi	1400.99	1170.91	730.80	144.89
Dai	1511.31	1153.81	852.09	117.19
Daur	1909.75	1582.14	1596.32	235.51
Deang	1508.60	1153.89	848.58	116.14
Derung	1546.19	1192.31	932.60	137.41
Dong	1453.26	1338.32	983.89	167.94
Dongxiang	1110.87	1180.40	1121.61	158.90
Ewenki	2053.47	1687.07	1504.21	243.07
Gaoshan	1674.49	1310.22	1233.27	218.36
Gelao	1391.41	1168.95	722.44	144.24
Han	1780.62	1329.94	1296.44	233.56
Hani	1511.89	1155.29	850.16	116.69
Hezhe	1683.34	1409.65	1839.56	232.21
Hui	1640.24	1225.13	1231.63	195.74
Jing	1534.83	1248.92	1077.06	162.62

(*continued*)

Table 4.19 (continued)

Ethnic group	Transport and Communications	Education, Culture and Recreation	Health Care and Medical Services	Miscellaneous Goods and Services
Jingpo	1510.18	1155.48	850.21	116.79
Jino	1510.42	1154.38	850.45	116.73
Kazak	1301.85	1011.68	1018.50	143.01
Kirgiz	1306.73	1016.04	1027.07	143.94
Korean	1775.06	1399.07	1553.93	234.91
Lahu	1511.40	1155.51	851.38	116.81
Lhoba	1420.64	488.15	389.82	149.74
Li	1129.96	1367.01	721.35	191.55
Lisu	1514.22	1148.57	864.74	120.19
Manchu	1820.81	1330.88	1494.18	240.36
Maonan	1491.88	1225.86	981.29	156.53
Miao	1460.56	1303.29	961.06	164.03
Monba	1424.70	448.44	367.99	150.73
Mongol	1984.58	1589.59	1448.21	238.25
Mulao	1525.35	1244.38	1047.04	161.80
Naxi	1514.91	1146.70	863.13	120.47
Nu	1515.46	1146.78	847.38	118.40
Oroqen	1866.49	1548.73	1675.14	237.87
Pumi	1513.78	1154.89	854.98	117.85
Qiang	1580.07	940.15	1340.32	237.26
Russian	1629.99	1276.05	1215.24	186.30
Salar	1674.61	982.13	1298.14	236.19
She	2001.75	1432.18	1138.32	287.86
Shui	1404.41	1171.35	738.35	144.05
Tajik	1313.34	1022.07	1026.11	145.53
Tatar	1321.71	1031.86	1039.40	147.49
Tibetan	1494.16	732.53	851.12	188.93
Tu	1675.00	1010.82	1289.83	235.94
Tujia	1603.40	1480.27	1263.11	229.75
Uygur	1304.21	1012.92	1019.58	143.36
Uzbek	1311.48	1018.66	1023.03	144.63
Va	1514.67	1157.80	859.25	118.41
Xibe	1728.33	1279.21	1448.60	226.37
Yao	1536.05	1372.35	1165.75	176.28
Yi	1516.54	1096.77	972.00	153.14
Yugur	1109.66	1198.36	1138.57	162.00
Zhuang	1543.16	1249.82	1081.11	162.28

Table 4.20 Per capita consumption of major foods by rural households (kg) (I)

Ethnic group	Grain (Unprocessed)	Cereal	Edible Oil and Fats	Edible Vegetable Oil	Vegetable and Edible Mushroom
National average	**148.5**	**137.9**	**9.9**	**9.0**	**87.5**
Achang	132.35	124.38	6.24	4.31	75.22
Bai	133.46	125.09	6.63	4.66	76.09
Baonan	160.90	149.07	8.43	8.25	63.25
Blang	132.59	124.58	6.28	4.34	75.42
Buyi	119.73	108.89	5.77	4.18	73.23
Dai	132.61	124.61	6.27	4.33	75.41
Daur	172.28	159.25	9.48	9.22	81.69
Deang	132.38	124.42	6.23	4.30	75.13
Derung	137.30	128.46	6.96	5.21	78.24
Dong	136.82	127.08	8.03	6.02	79.07
Dongxiang	162.23	150.98	8.75	8.59	65.05
Ewenki	177.51	164.23	7.44	7.12	82.53
Gaoshan	144.15	134.15	9.29	8.36	85.18
Gelao	119.19	108.33	5.72	4.13	73.14
Han	148.44	137.29	10.14	9.29	89.93
Hani	132.40	124.42	6.24	4.31	75.24
Hezhe	158.52	144.77	13.37	13.22	81.31
Hui	144.72	135.70	9.06	8.57	77.40
Jing	152.01	146.03	8.45	6.67	79.40
Jingpo	132.35	124.37	6.24	4.31	75.21
Jino	132.52	124.53	6.25	4.32	75.34
Kazak	169.83	168.43	13.42	13.17	78.52
Kirgiz	169.76	168.25	13.43	13.18	78.59
Korean	152.65	138.40	11.32	11.13	86.26
Lahu	132.43	124.44	6.25	4.32	75.26
Lhoba	203.62	198.69	14.09	8.03	32.71
Li	109.83	105.66	8.51	6.38	80.58
Lisu	133.71	125.60	6.40	4.49	76.30
Manchu	147.17	134.15	10.04	9.75	88.17
Maonan	143.34	136.12	7.64	5.90	77.35
Miao	138.02	127.85	8.09	6.05	82.63
Monba	206.87	202.13	14.33	8.07	30.58
Mongol	170.68	157.92	7.79	7.43	83.12
Mulao	148.71	142.25	8.14	6.38	78.78
Naxi	133.99	125.90	6.44	4.50	76.13
Nu	133.72	125.76	6.41	4.42	74.70
Oroqen	168.15	154.59	10.41	10.18	81.88
Pumi	132.70	124.69	6.29	4.37	75.40

(*continued*)

Table 4.20 (continued)

Ethnic group	Grain (Unprocessed)	Cereal	Edible Oil and Fats	Edible Vegetable Oil	Vegetable and Edible Mushroom
Qiang	177.98	165.92	11.91	10.40	113.02
Russian	170.89	164.58	10.93	10.62	80.65
Salar	139.94	134.06	9.79	9.17	47.55
She	156.93	146.19	10.61	9.06	94.19
Shui	120.60	109.96	5.80	4.21	73.16
Tajik	169.34	167.61	13.33	13.04	79.06
Tatar	168.47	166.31	13.10	12.83	78.46
Tibetan	180.97	173.82	12.22	8.73	55.40
Tu	139.83	133.45	9.63	8.96	50.00
Tujia	152.35	141.05	11.24	9.15	102.27
Uygur	169.78	168.36	13.42	13.16	78.61
Uzbek	169.34	167.82	13.36	13.09	78.74
Va	132.78	124.73	6.32	4.42	75.66
Xibe	151.16	139.67	11.06	10.76	88.44
Yao	153.76	146.87	9.39	7.28	82.64
Yi	143.60	134.16	7.75	5.98	85.45
Yugur	161.14	148.99	8.33	8.17	64.01
Zhuang	151.73	145.86	8.38	6.59	79.59

Table 4.21 Per capita consumption of major foods by rural households (kg) (II)

Ethnic group	Products of Meat	Pork	Beef	Mutton
National average	**27.5**	**23.0**	**1.1**	**1.0**
Achang	33.07	30.80	1.18	0.43
Bai	32.79	30.55	1.12	0.41
Baonan	18.02	12.91	1.10	2.87
Blang	33.08	30.80	1.18	0.43
Buyi	30.71	29.30	0.59	0.21
Dai	33.15	30.87	1.18	0.43
Daur	29.31	21.35	1.50	4.39
Deang	33.07	30.79	1.18	0.45
Derung	32.12	29.26	1.17	0.72
Dong	31.48	29.44	0.81	0.32
Dongxiang	17.96	12.10	1.02	3.74
Ewenki	32.23	23.38	1.67	5.26
Gaoshan	26.82	22.52	1.05	0.98
Gelao	30.74	29.38	0.58	0.19
Han	27.71	23.26	1.04	0.84

(continued)

Table 4.21 (continued)

Ethnic group	Products of Meat	Pork	Beef	Mutton
Hani	33.08	30.81	1.18	0.43
Hezhe	24.05	19.87	0.87	0.74
Hui	22.03	14.33	2.53	3.47
Jing	33.40	30.73	0.97	0.51
Jingpo	33.06	30.78	1.18	0.43
Jino	33.13	30.86	1.18	0.43
Kazak	22.34	1.45	3.82	16.45
Kirgiz	22.38	1.63	3.79	16.31
Korean	24.92	21.33	0.92	0.52
Lahu	33.04	30.76	1.18	0.43
Lhoba	21.56	6.41	10.79	4.00
Li	31.67	28.75	1.25	0.57
Lisu	33.38	31.05	1.17	0.43
Manchu	23.92	19.64	0.88	0.94
Maonan	32.76	30.48	0.85	0.42
Miao	32.41	30.31	0.82	0.33
Monba	21.45	5.84	11.24	4.01
Mongol	30.67	22.23	1.71	4.82
Mulao	33.30	30.76	0.92	0.47
Naxi	33.35	30.97	1.22	0.45
Nu	32.86	30.36	1.33	0.50
Oroqen	28.02	21.56	1.24	2.96
Pumi	33.07	30.76	1.18	0.44
Qiang	44.95	40.90	1.00	0.37
Russian	26.27	10.61	2.93	11.51
Salar	26.97	9.89	8.77	7.66
She	32.67	28.77	1.20	0.51
Shui	30.77	29.33	0.61	0.22
Tajik	22.60	2.27	3.73	15.92
Tatar	22.43	2.74	3.62	15.35
Tibetan	28.12	15.71	7.64	3.79
Tu	27.32	11.51	8.19	6.86
Tujia	32.73	29.95	0.90	0.41
Uygur	22.38	1.52	3.81	16.41
Uzbek	22.53	1.93	3.77	16.17
Va	32.94	30.61	1.17	0.44
Xibe	24.33	17.40	1.44	3.62
Yao	33.75	30.90	1.06	0.49
Yi	36.09	33.43	1.06	0.39
Yugur	17.75	13.27	0.79	2.51
Zhuang	33.78	31.07	1.00	0.51

Table 4.22 Per capita consumption of major foods by rural households (kg) (III)

Ethnic group	Poultry	Aquatic Products	Eggs	Milk and Dairy Products	Dried and Fresh Melons and Fruits	Sugar
National average	**8.0**	**7.8**	**8.4**	**6.9**	**39.9**	**1.3**
Achang	6.40	2.37	3.92	2.30	18.52	1.02
Bai	6.41	2.83	4.08	2.40	21.23	1.02
Baonan	3.96	1.02	5.72	6.75	69.61	1.83
Blang	6.40	2.38	3.95	2.34	18.62	1.03
Buyi	3.66	1.75	2.77	2.16	24.50	0.79
Dai	6.41	2.35	3.93	2.32	18.53	1.03
Daur	4.94	4.66	7.65	9.78	44.32	1.52
Deang	6.36	2.29	3.89	2.29	18.45	1.02
Derung	6.49	3.31	4.84	3.43	22.94	1.12
Dong	7.35	5.06	4.54	2.64	31.88	0.97
Dongxiang	3.97	0.99	5.65	6.89	69.34	1.76
Ewenki	5.10	4.34	7.43	11.60	41.35	1.45
Gaoshan	8.29	8.10	8.55	6.55	40.20	1.33
Gelao	3.60	1.66	2.69	2.08	24.39	0.79
Han	8.31	8.89	8.90	7.27	40.83	1.37
Hani	6.38	2.34	3.91	2.30	18.51	1.03
Hezhe	5.25	6.36	8.70	5.43	50.31	1.70
Hui	5.62	3.70	7.18	8.23	50.13	1.39
Jing	16.58	7.38	4.71	2.73	28.95	1.05
Jingpo	6.40	2.35	3.92	2.30	18.56	1.02
Jino	6.39	2.33	3.91	2.30	18.48	1.03
Kazak	3.43	0.73	3.47	11.11	41.17	1.07
Kirgiz	3.45	0.80	3.52	11.06	41.20	1.07
Korean	4.89	6.07	9.17	5.43	41.15	1.36
Lahu	6.38	2.34	3.94	2.32	18.61	1.03
Lhoba	0.98	0.66	2.40	11.46	6.62	4.34
Li	17.26	22.89	3.85	1.81	17.32	0.90
Lisu	6.45	2.41	4.06	2.49	18.94	1.05
Manchu	3.88	5.99	9.45	6.33	42.21	1.18
Maonan	13.32	5.72	4.09	2.45	27.78	0.97
Miao	6.81	4.79	4.73	2.97	29.93	1.12
Monba	0.86	0.54	2.30	11.83	5.48	4.50
Mongol	4.75	4.34	7.55	10.71	40.01	1.37
Mulao	15.53	6.83	4.48	2.60	28.63	1.03
Naxi	6.43	2.42	4.03	2.52	18.83	1.07
Nu	6.33	2.40	3.94	2.50	18.54	1.08
Oroqen	5.12	5.33	8.10	8.50	46.00	1.57
Pumi	6.40	2.38	3.96	2.37	18.69	1.03
Qiang	9.44	5.38	8.32	8.23	30.74	2.07

(*continued*)

Table 4.22 (continued)

Ethnic group	Poultry	Aquatic Products	Eggs	Milk and Dairy Products	Dried and Fresh Melons and Fruits	Sugar
Russian	4.20	2.45	5.30	11.27	41.41	1.22
Salar	2.76	0.75	2.75	11.68	23.07	1.85
She	11.10	17.51	7.61	7.31	37.19	1.80
Shui	4.04	1.83	2.79	2.14	24.43	0.79
Tajik	3.63	1.01	3.65	10.97	41.12	1.09
Tatar	3.64	1.07	3.79	10.83	42.44	1.11
Tibetan	3.47	1.61	3.94	10.47	18.73	3.14
Tu	3.36	1.42	3.03	11.10	24.15	1.83
Tujia	7.42	8.91	6.94	4.26	36.63	1.44
Uygur	3.46	0.77	3.49	11.10	41.12	1.07
Uzbek	3.63	0.96	3.55	11.01	41.07	1.07
Va	6.41	2.45	4.10	2.45	19.22	1.04
Xibe	3.43	5.61	7.80	6.57	37.47	1.09
Yao	15.08	8.40	5.58	2.87	33.04	1.16
Yi	6.91	3.09	5.00	3.92	22.57	1.29
Yugur	4.08	1.12	5.90	6.55	71.34	1.82
Zhuang	16.81	7.44	4.70	2.63	28.38	1.07

Table 4.23 Main Durable Goods Owned Per 100 Rural Households at Year-end (I)

Ethnic group	Automobile (unit)	Motorcycle (unit)	Electric Bicycle (unit)	Washing Machine (set)	Refrigerator (set)	Microwave Oven (set)	Color TV Set (set)
National average	**22.3**	**57.4**	**64.9**	**88.5**	**95.9**	**17.7**	**116.6**
Achang	25.28	76.17	19.18	83.22	79.92	11.61	102.74
Bai	23.84	73.87	18.75	84.56	82.14	11.03	103.45
Baonan	21.50	60.60	48.34	96.58	85.50	7.46	110.53
Blang	25.26	75.98	19.32	83.27	80.03	11.67	102.84
Buyi	19.78	53.99	15.34	93.01	86.77	7.32	101.16
Dai	25.26	76.06	19.06	83.27	79.97	11.60	102.77
Daur	22.24	55.24	43.82	92.13	99.89	7.25	105.08
Deang	25.31	76.24	18.84	83.25	79.84	11.52	102.63
Derung	24.45	71.96	26.79	84.34	83.14	12.34	104.71
Dong	17.35	65.81	21.04	88.93	91.83	9.69	105.87
Dongxiang	20.87	60.12	51.72	96.66	86.43	7.39	110.31

(*continued*)

Table 4.23 (continued)

Ethnic group	Automobile (unit)	Motorcycle (unit)	Electric Bicycle (unit)	Washing Machine (set)	Refrigerator (set)	Microwave Oven (set)	Color TV Set (set)
Ewenki	25.49	59.36	49.16	92.79	101.99	7.56	106.07
Gaoshan	21.91	58.90	68.45	88.47	96.46	18.59	116.13
Gelao	19.65	53.91	14.42	93.19	86.72	7.08	100.74
Han	22.70	56.36	68.05	88.80	96.78	20.08	118.92
Hani	25.30	76.12	19.09	83.26	79.92	11.62	102.76
Hezhe	16.01	46.75	28.80	89.97	94.91	8.08	104.56
Hui	26.92	56.66	66.79	95.02	95.17	14.14	110.19
Jing	16.08	88.81	52.54	74.16	94.05	20.33	104.90
Jingpo	25.28	76.18	19.08	83.28	79.93	11.56	102.70
Jino	25.28	76.14	18.82	83.25	79.90	11.57	102.71
Kazak	19.42	60.24	76.87	94.90	101.75	7.61	101.02
Kirgiz	19.37	60.10	76.45	94.84	101.72	7.61	101.05
Korean	21.36	55.67	29.13	91.03	96.02	9.38	105.67
Lahu	25.29	76.02	19.37	83.30	79.97	11.61	102.78
Lhoba	31.03	87.62	22.13	78.26	73.92	4.06	105.65
Li	10.44	91.07	63.67	45.97	77.49	12.42	102.61
Lisu	25.13	75.27	19.64	83.50	80.39	11.57	103.04
Manchu	23.59	54.06	56.54	92.04	98.49	13.71	109.78
Maonan	16.84	80.03	42.11	79.34	92.20	16.75	103.24
Miao	18.26	63.90	20.01	88.30	90.57	9.96	105.95
Monba	31.64	88.64	21.68	77.61	72.95	4.06	105.91
Mongol	25.38	59.27	51.79	92.74	101.28	8.77	106.73
Mulao	16.35	85.86	48.29	76.42	93.49	19.08	104.24
Naxi	25.14	75.32	19.47	83.44	80.35	11.58	103.13
Nu	25.38	76.10	19.73	83.21	80.02	11.63	103.06
Oroqen	20.63	52.95	39.30	91.45	98.52	7.74	105.26
Pumi	25.27	75.90	19.46	83.32	80.08	11.66	102.87
Qiang	17.83	49.18	30.98	90.09	95.71	10.49	112.78
Russian	22.47	58.98	66.96	94.06	101.75	9.06	104.23
Salar	34.31	72.00	20.89	92.50	94.63	9.69	96.88
She	19.65	62.04	55.60	82.33	100.32	27.48	139.90
Shui	19.69	55.27	16.47	92.38	86.88	7.83	101.07
Tajik	19.43	60.19	76.29	94.56	101.55	7.97	101.48
Tatar	19.78	59.84	75.38	94.76	101.00	8.34	102.08
Tibetan	28.51	74.54	23.92	84.99	83.66	6.73	105.22
Tu	33.48	72.26	21.64	92.12	94.06	10.28	98.33
Tujia	16.85	67.57	24.40	86.47	98.06	11.87	113.88
Uygur	19.42	60.24	76.90	94.87	101.77	7.67	101.08
Uzbek	19.46	60.49	76.60	94.62	101.63	7.93	101.31

(continued)

Table 4.23 (continued)

Ethnic group	Automobile (unit)	Motorcycle (unit)	Electric Bicycle (unit)	Washing Machine (set)	Refrigerator (set)	Microwave Oven (set)	Color TV Set (set)
Va	25.26	75.52	20.57	83.46	80.34	11.69	102.95
Xibe	19.00	57.66	53.53	90.50	99.31	11.67	107.40
Yao	16.06	87.79	39.83	78.65	94.60	17.24	107.45
Yi	22.60	66.15	21.89	86.26	85.05	10.78	105.30
Yugur	21.17	60.04	49.29	96.67	85.20	7.71	111.22
Zhuang	16.50	90.59	51.04	74.35	93.43	20.36	104.55

Table 4.24 Main Durable Goods Owned Per 100 Rural Households at Year-end (II)

Ethnic group	Air Conditioner (set)	Water Heater (set)	Exhaust Fan (set)	Mobile Phone (set)	Computer (set)	Camera (set)
National average	**65.2**	**68.7**	**26.0**	**257.0**	**26.9**	**2.5**
Achang	2.61	71.36	8.86	278.53	10.25	1.48
Bai	8.12	69.74	10.35	279.69	11.74	1.48
Baonan	2.15	35.68	13.53	296.29	20.69	1.76
Blang	2.96	71.38	8.93	278.41	10.32	1.48
Buyi	8.31	54.24	8.84	286.47	11.86	0.89
Dai	2.67	71.34	8.84	278.47	10.24	1.48
Daur	5.12	20.84	14.92	230.64	21.27	1.32
Deang	2.09	71.24	8.72	278.60	10.14	1.47
Derung	11.49	68.23	11.76	272.25	13.14	1.63
Dong	31.55	63.05	15.94	286.45	18.05	1.37
Dongxiang	2.13	36.59	13.45	289.89	20.36	1.68
Ewenki	6.40	24.26	16.16	236.13	21.73	1.50
Gaoshan	65.90	68.50	25.16	259.49	27.45	2.40
Gelao	7.58	53.80	8.57	287.05	11.68	0.85
Han	73.02	71.14	28.65	256.05	28.48	2.83
Hani	2.52	71.36	8.83	278.52	10.23	1.48
Hezhe	8.43	14.58	13.87	225.49	22.29	1.21
Hui	36.42	65.35	22.10	262.91	24.20	2.24
Jing	38.26	73.54	12.49	292.39	19.95	1.02
Jingpo	2.55	71.28	8.86	278.55	10.27	1.47

(*continued*)

Table 4.24 (continued)

Ethnic group	Air Conditioner (set)	Water Heater (set)	Exhaust Fan (set)	Mobile Phone (set)	Computer (set)	Camera (set)
Jino	2.34	71.26	8.78	278.54	10.20	1.47
Kazak	3.14	44.16	14.13	203.00	13.63	0.93
Kirgiz	3.19	43.86	14.12	203.00	13.70	0.93
Korean	8.42	17.78	15.43	237.38	27.19	1.45
Lahu	2.81	71.38	8.88	278.45	10.30	1.48
Lhoba	4.87	13.58	2.80	250.99	5.20	1.49
Li	54.20	64.89	9.95	276.78	10.39	1.02
Lisu	3.92	71.26	9.02	277.74	10.47	1.51
Manchu	27.13	34.74	23.60	228.49	28.52	2.50
Maonan	29.24	67.99	11.02	292.01	17.66	0.92
Miao	29.10	63.72	14.91	283.25	16.70	1.44
Monba	4.23	11.52	2.15	250.24	4.63	1.54
Mongol	10.78	28.62	17.53	236.32	22.59	1.68
Mulao	35.63	71.55	12.27	292.69	19.34	1.02
Naxi	3.97	71.03	9.03	277.71	10.45	1.51
Nu	3.35	70.54	9.02	277.84	10.37	1.49
Oroqen	7.00	19.16	14.93	230.18	21.99	1.33
Pumi	3.04	71.25	8.95	278.25	10.36	1.49
Qiang	49.42	69.26	14.62	255.49	17.10	2.42
Russian	9.62	39.05	16.40	218.16	17.90	1.39
Salar	2.30	34.76	17.48	278.93	15.56	2.05
She	88.21	91.19	44.93	255.03	33.07	3.48
Shui	8.55	54.90	8.63	286.80	11.91	0.87
Tajik	5.23	44.96	14.50	204.83	14.03	0.98
Tatar	6.14	44.98	14.92	208.58	14.60	1.09
Tibetan	12.90	32.07	8.91	262.25	10.74	1.83
Tu	6.13	37.34	18.12	280.69	16.26	2.10
Tujia	61.87	72.77	23.98	276.32	24.28	2.15
Uygur	3.46	44.30	14.19	203.01	13.68	0.94
Uzbek	4.61	44.83	14.47	204.19	13.91	0.98
Va	4.24	71.46	9.31	277.82	10.69	1.50
Xibe	9.71	30.69	22.00	216.44	23.51	1.94
Yao	48.07	74.85	18.72	290.17	22.33	1.60
Yi	16.00	68.76	10.37	273.06	12.28	1.66
Yugur	3.21	36.26	13.71	297.50	21.18	1.80
Zhuang	37.95	74.35	12.78	292.70	19.87	1.10

Table 4.25 Housing conditions of rural households

Ethnic group	Per capita floor space of houses (sq.m/person)	Value of houses (yuan/sq.m)	House structures (sq.m/person)	
			Reinforced concrete structure	Brick and wood structure
National average	37.09	681.90	17.12	16.35
Achang	31.81	591.27	10.12	8.54
Bai	32.70	577.66	11.01	10.42
Baonan	24.48	545.02	4.35	10.06
Blang	31.88	590.80	10.18	8.59
Buyi	30.15	543.96	11.02	15.95
Dai	31.83	590.87	10.15	8.54
Daur	25.44	652.09	1.74	18.45
Deang	31.76	590.11	10.05	8.49
Derung	32.28	605.47	10.76	10.34
Dong	35.86	513.66	16.13	17.21
Dongxiang	24.49	541.31	4.21	10.24
Ewenki	25.44	579.18	1.97	17.77
Gaoshan	37.65	713.42	19.21	16.24
Gelao	29.94	540.59	10.89	16.01
Han	38.58	716.68	18.86	17.00
Hani	31.83	591.18	10.12	8.54
Hezhe	25.98	855.39	2.25	20.36
Hui	31.21	659.51	9.09	16.47
Jing	35.91	491.68	27.14	6.84
Jingpo	31.79	590.97	10.11	8.55
Jino	31.80	591.32	10.09	8.52
Kazak	27.19	487.76	2.83	14.19
Kirgiz	27.19	491.09	2.82	14.26
Korean	26.20	717.25	2.09	22.27
Lahu	31.85	590.41	10.15	8.57
Lhoba	29.44	353.11	2.13	16.74
Li	25.64	849.75	12.73	12.68
Lisu	31.99	588.51	10.27	8.76
Manchu	29.80	816.41	5.91	22.50
Maonan	34.13	497.26	22.91	9.18
Miao	35.33	526.13	15.09	16.27
Monba	29.40	354.51	1.65	16.84
Mongol	26.75	596.24	3.31	18.33
Mulao	35.17	496.58	25.58	7.75
Naxi	32.00	590.36	10.28	8.77
Nu	31.90	589.09	10.14	8.73
Oroqen	25.73	712.50	2.10	19.14
Pumi	31.86	591.71	10.16	8.61

(*continued*)

Table 4.25 (continued)

Ethnic group	Per capita floor space of houses (sq.m/person)	Value of houses (yuan/sq.m)	House structures (sq.m/person)	
			Reinforced concrete structure	Brick and wood structure
Qiang	37.86	510.30	16.28	15.32
Russian	27.26	567.81	3.26	15.90
Salar	29.11	522.71	4.54	13.77
She	50.85	878.13	36.79	11.78
Shui	30.26	539.58	11.41	15.59
Tajik	27.53	493.91	3.35	14.26
Tatar	27.44	515.39	3.33	14.23
Tibetan	30.87	430.59	5.83	15.12
Tu	29.52	532.96	5.61	13.55
Tujia	41.85	508.17	20.66	18.06
Uygur	27.25	488.68	2.90	14.22
Uzbek	27.38	496.40	3.17	14.19
Va	31.98	590.11	10.26	8.81
Xibe	28.82	768.06	5.26	21.02
Yao	38.07	504.99	24.21	11.30
Yi	33.28	562.80	11.90	11.25
Yugur	24.44	557.48	4.52	9.99
Zhuang	35.54	498.37	26.62	6.46

Note: All data are as of 2012

Table 4.26 Electricity consumption (100 million kwh)

Ethnic group	2000	2005	2010	2011	2012	2018
Achang	0.22	0.45	0.81	0.97	1.06	1.35
Bai	12.52	24.57	43.83	51.90	56.60	73.23
Baonan	0.20	0.33	0.57	0.66	0.72	0.95
Blang	0.60	1.22	2.19	2.63	2.87	3.67
Buyi	24.62	42.15	72.29	81.68	90.21	127.38
Dai	7.54	15.33	27.58	33.02	36.07	46.09
Daur	1.53	3.13	6.44	7.66	8.29	13.28
Deang	0.12	0.24	0.43	0.51	0.56	0.71
Derung	0.06	0.11	0.20	0.23	0.25	0.33
Dong	23.16	39.30	68.05	76.19	82.26	114.52
Dongxiang	5.99	10.00	16.97	19.78	21.85	30.54
Ewenki	0.34	0.83	1.85	2.23	2.41	3.94
Gaoshan	0.05	0.09	0.15	0.17	0.18	0.24
Gelao	4.80	8.18	14.00	15.81	17.48	24.72

(continued)

Table 4.26 (continued)

Ethnic group	2000	2005	2010	2011	2012	2018
Han	12595.97	22976.44	38702.90	43178.69	45394.31	62259.31
Hani	9.37	19.06	34.31	41.09	44.88	57.35
Hezhe	0.06	0.08	0.11	0.12	0.12	0.15
Hui	143.54	275.68	503.14	612.70	650.33	914.03
Jing	0.17	0.27	0.52	0.59	0.61	0.90
Jingpo	0.86	1.75	3.15	3.77	4.12	5.27
Jino	0.14	0.28	0.50	0.60	0.65	0.83
Kazak	12.42	21.04	44.86	56.84	73.83	144.56
Kirgiz	1.60	2.70	5.75	7.28	9.45	18.48
Korean	23.76	32.64	49.62	54.09	55.33	67.54
Lahu	2.95	6.01	10.81	12.95	14.14	18.08
Lhoba	0.00	0.01	0.03	0.03	0.04	0.09
Li	6.65	13.89	26.75	31.08	34.82	54.26
Lisu	4.13	8.39	15.07	18.02	19.67	25.16
Manchu	163.42	255.12	413.65	454.96	469.20	589.02
Maonan	0.82	1.35	2.51	2.82	2.98	4.34
Miao	69.86	118.36	205.59	232.62	251.30	348.08
Monba	0.01	0.01	0.09	0.10	0.11	0.25
Mongol	69.56	155.46	332.10	396.51	427.32	682.17
Mulao	1.58	2.61	4.91	5.49	5.75	8.40
Naxi	2.01	4.07	7.32	8.75	9.55	12.23
Nu	0.19	0.38	0.68	0.82	0.89	1.15
Oroqen	0.10	0.18	0.34	0.40	0.43	0.66
Pumi	0.22	0.45	0.80	0.96	1.05	1.34
Qiang	1.96	3.55	5.84	6.60	6.91	9.29
Russian	0.17	0.34	0.72	0.88	1.04	1.86
Salar	2.17	4.06	8.98	10.80	11.64	14.47
She	8.51	16.94	29.12	32.98	34.32	49.68
Shui	3.33	5.71	9.84	11.12	12.28	17.34
Tajik	0.41	0.69	1.46	1.85	2.39	4.65
Tatar	0.05	0.08	0.18	0.22	0.28	0.54
Tibetan	39.43	72.76	167.16	197.90	213.98	300.16
Tu	4.86	9.11	19.89	23.86	25.65	31.79
Tujia	66.35	102.74	176.57	196.36	206.03	286.70
Uygur	83.38	141.34	301.15	381.44	495.33	969.67
Uzbek	0.12	0.21	0.44	0.56	0.73	1.42
Va	2.61	5.29	9.51	11.37	12.40	15.91
Xibe	3.00	4.56	7.43	8.32	8.95	12.52
Yao	20.10	34.59	62.43	69.71	72.89	102.42
Yi	51.79	99.82	174.81	205.22	222.33	290.86
Yugur	0.16	0.27	0.45	0.52	0.57	0.75
Zhuang	120.79	202.97	384.30	431.51	450.01	653.19

[a]Data are provided by the Association of Power Generation Enterprises

5

Agricultural Production and Other Rural Activity

The data in this chapter show the basic conditions of agricultural production and rural economy, including mainly cultivated land, quantity of agricultural machinery, output of agriculture, forestry, animal husbandry and fishery, output of major products, facilities of water conservancy and efforts to eliminate water-logging and combat alkalinity, productive fixed assets owned by rural households, basic conditions of State-owned farms. Statistics on agriculture cover all agricultural production activities except horse raising for military purpose and agricultural production activities undertaken by agriculture research institutions. In other words, included in agriculture statistics are production activities in agriculture, forestry, animal husbandry and fishery undertaken by rural economic units of various types and by rural households; production activities of farms specializing in agriculture, forestry, animal husbandry and fishery; production activities in agriculture undertaken by government agencies, institutions, schools and military units; production activities in agriculture undertaken by collective farms run by townships and villages; and production activities in agriculture, forestry, animal husbandry and fishery undertaken by manufacturing and mining enterprises.

R. Guo, *China Ethnic Statistical Yearbook 2020*,
https://doi.org/10.1007/978-3-030-49024-9_5

Data on agricultural production are provided by the Department of Rural Social and Economic Survey of the NBS using data from *The Statistical Survey System on Agriculture, Forestry, Animal Husbandry and Fishery; The Statistical Reporting System on Agricultural Output and Price* and *The Statistical Reporting System on the Basic Condition of Social and Economic Activities of Counties.*

The Statistical Survey System on Agriculture, Forestry, Animal Husbandry and Fishery is composed of three parts: (i) the sample survey conducted by the nation taking the province as the population on major farm crops such as grain and cotton, on animal husbandry such as hog, cattle, sheep and poultry, and a sample survey on 362 pig output counties taking the county as the population; (ii) the comprehensive reporting system, statistical reporting forms are used on agricultural production conditions, tropical farm crops, garden crops, agricultural facilities and other poultry; and (iii) the statistical reporting forms of forestry and fishery industries from forestry department and fishery department. *The Statistical Reporting System on the Basic Condition of Social and Economic Activities of Counties* is a special survey designed by the NBS to understand the basic conditions of social and economic activities at county, township and rural level and the energy consumption of the units engaged in agriculture, forestry, animal husbandry and fishery. Under this survey system, a complete enumeration is conducted every 3 years to collect information on the basic conditions of all towns, townships and villages, and a complete enumeration is conducted every year in counties administratively designated towns.

Data on fixed assets, sales of farm products of rural households are collected and compiled by the Office of Household Surveys of the NBS through the *System of Rural Household Survey.*

Table 5.1 Gross output value of agriculture, forestry, animal husbandry and fishery (100 million yuan)

Ethnic groups	Total	Farming	Forestry	Animal husbandry	Fishery
National total	113579.5	61452.6	5432.6	28697.4	12131.5
Achang	3.29	1.79	0.32	0.99	0.08
Bai	179.37	98.68	16.38	52.21	5.09
Baonan	1.18	0.81	0.02	0.25	0.00

(continued)

Table 5.1 (continued)

Ethnic groups	Total	Farming	Forestry	Animal husbandry	Fishery
Blang	8.90	4.84	0.85	2.67	0.23
Buyi	303.17	190.04	21.23	71.00	6.22
Dai	112.29	61.08	10.78	33.75	2.80
Daur	18.20	10.37	0.60	6.52	0.28
Deang	1.74	0.95	0.17	0.52	0.04
Derung	0.72	0.39	0.06	0.21	0.03
Dong	289.26	168.28	20.30	69.45	14.81
Dongxiang	41.43	28.96	0.80	8.37	0.14
Ewenki	3.91	2.04	0.13	1.60	0.06
Gaoshan	0.43	0.23	0.02	0.11	0.05
Gelao	59.18	37.23	4.14	13.81	1.13
Han	102035.21	54844.31	4819.15	25567.84	11479.75
Hani	139.53	75.87	13.41	41.93	3.48
Hezhe	0.67	0.42	0.02	0.19	0.02
Hui	962.49	564.28	31.17	275.18	42.18
Jing	2.49	1.38	0.19	0.55	0.26
Jingpo	12.81	6.97	1.23	3.85	0.32
Jino	2.02	1.10	0.19	0.61	0.05
Kazak	245.75	171.63	4.24	53.82	1.91
Kirgiz	31.57	22.03	0.55	6.93	0.25
Korean	189.35	97.83	6.57	70.64	7.64
Lahu	43.96	23.91	4.21	13.21	1.10
Lhoba	0.23	0.11	0.00	0.11	0.00
Li	245.62	117.65	17.64	39.77	60.43
Lisu	61.37	33.42	5.81	18.47	1.55
Manchu	1050.16	518.54	38.45	349.77	95.64
Maonan	11.64	6.68	0.87	2.59	0.93
Miao	862.59	501.28	61.80	213.61	41.23
Monba	0.67	0.30	0.01	0.33	0.00
Mongol	698.65	358.99	23.89	279.39	19.21
Mulao	22.67	12.74	1.72	4.99	2.13
Naxi	29.80	16.22	2.82	8.98	0.75
Nu	2.78	1.51	0.26	0.84	0.07
Oroqen	1.12	0.65	0.04	0.38	0.02
Pumi	3.26	1.77	0.31	0.98	0.08
Qiang	26.79	15.46	1.34	8.33	0.94
Russian	2.55	1.64	0.06	0.70	0.03
Salar	8.99	4.19	0.23	4.25	0.09
She	72.15	31.33	6.07	12.18	19.96
Shui	41.74	26.05	2.94	9.78	0.94
Tajik	7.92	5.51	0.14	1.74	0.07
Tatar	0.92	0.64	0.02	0.20	0.01

(*continued*)

Table 5.1 (continued)

Ethnic groups	Total	Farming	Forestry	Animal husbandry	Fishery
Tibetan	431.33	214.57	12.89	185.35	5.82
Tu	20.19	9.36	0.57	9.35	0.36
Tujia	724.37	391.32	41.49	176.76	70.35
Uygur	1649.14	1151.25	28.58	361.26	13.13
Uzbek	2.41	1.68	0.04	0.53	0.02
Va	38.39	20.88	3.63	11.51	1.02
Xibe	22.17	11.76	0.69	6.54	2.12
Yao	265.38	142.58	20.27	62.30	25.93
Yi	736.67	414.40	59.80	217.50	19.68
Yugur	0.96	0.66	0.02	0.19	0.00
Zhuang	1772.84	976.76	138.19	394.91	179.69

Table 5.2 Indices of gross output value of agriculture, forestry, animal husbandry and fishery (preceding year=100)

Ethnic group	Total	Farming	Forestry	Animal husbandry	Fishery
National average	103.5	103.9	106.5	101.7	102.7
Achang	106.25	106.74	109.89	104.19	109.74
Bai	106.10	106.62	109.69	103.95	108.02
Baonan	103.77	105.36	105.31	102.51	96.94
Blang	106.23	106.72	109.86	104.18	109.71
Buyi	106.85	108.21	108.30	104.26	95.73
Dai	106.25	106.73	109.86	104.18	109.73
Daur	103.17	103.97	103.36	101.51	101.32
Deang	106.27	106.75	109.91	104.21	109.79
Derung	105.64	106.08	108.95	103.71	108.08
Dong	105.65	106.47	108.41	103.06	100.07
Dongxiang	103.85	105.40	105.20	102.52	97.59
Ewenki	102.98	103.81	101.83	101.85	98.55
Gaoshan	103.51	103.56	106.84	100.91	102.48
Gelao	106.90	108.28	108.32	104.32	95.45
Han	103.13	103.32	106.44	100.64	102.35
Hani	106.25	106.74	109.89	104.19	109.75
Hezhe	103.25	103.92	106.23	100.32	105.68
Hui	103.66	103.57	106.43	102.13	101.82
Jing	105.54	106.68	106.44	102.64	104.52
Jingpo	106.25	106.74	109.90	104.19	109.71
Jino	106.25	106.74	109.88	104.19	109.74
Kazak	105.14	105.25	108.55	103.33	109.40
Kirgiz	105.12	105.24	108.52	103.30	109.39

(continued)

Table 5.2 (continued)

Ethnic group	Total	Farming	Forestry	Animal husbandry	Fishery
Korean	102.46	102.86	98.31	101.90	99.18
Lahu	106.24	106.73	109.88	104.18	109.75
Lhoba	105.40	107.68	104.70	102.53	101.97
Li	104.25	105.23	105.56	103.84	101.00
Lisu	106.18	106.67	109.64	104.14	109.61
Manchu	102.57	102.17	103.71	102.36	101.71
Maonan	105.97	107.22	106.91	103.15	101.96
Miao	105.57	106.31	108.05	103.35	100.70
Monba	105.36	107.75	104.39	102.36	101.92
Mongol	103.01	103.57	102.25	102.21	99.19
Mulao	105.71	106.91	106.62	102.81	103.41
Naxi	106.17	106.67	109.67	104.11	109.55
Nu	106.21	106.72	109.77	104.11	109.57
Oroqen	103.13	103.90	103.90	101.14	102.27
Pumi	106.22	106.71	109.84	104.16	109.69
Qiang	103.93	104.63	101.80	102.42	104.84
Russian	104.09	104.32	106.59	102.30	104.45
Salar	104.43	103.90	113.84	104.28	104.68
She	103.30	104.42	105.22	97.34	103.31
Shui	106.83	108.18	108.29	104.25	96.14
Tajik	105.08	105.19	108.47	103.26	109.16
Tatar	104.96	105.06	108.71	103.04	108.48
Tibetan	104.80	106.07	106.12	103.01	103.17
Tu	104.43	104.04	113.20	104.13	104.36
Tujia	103.94	104.12	107.41	102.61	101.22
Uygur	105.13	105.24	108.55	103.31	109.40
Uzbek	105.10	105.20	108.61	103.24	109.24
Va	106.18	106.67	109.81	104.12	109.58
Xibe	103.04	102.90	105.43	102.90	104.43
Yao	105.00	105.69	107.45	102.25	105.62
Yi	105.68	106.33	107.46	103.72	106.81
Yugur	103.69	105.31	105.15	102.32	96.47
Zhuang	105.58	106.70	106.57	102.71	105.06

Table 5.3 Major agricultural machinery at year-end

Ethnic group	Total power of agricultural machinery (10,000 kw)
National total	100371.7
Achang	2.16
Bai	123.57
Baonan	1.43
Blang	5.86

(continued)

Table 5.3 (continued)

Ethnic group	Total power of agricultural machinery (10,000 kw)
Buyi	199.72
Dai	73.77
Daur	20.68
Deang	1.14
Derung	0.51
Dong	230.63
Dongxiang	46.69
Ewenki	4.67
Gaoshan	0.37
Gelao	38.83
Han	90674.10
Hani	91.76
Hezhe	0.72
Hui	972.32
Jing	1.87
Jingpo	8.43
Jino	1.33
Kazak	184.67
Kirgiz	23.79
Korean	238.37
Lahu	28.99
Lhoba	0.58
Li	92.68
Lisu	40.43
Manchu	948.33
Maonan	8.51
Miao	655.10
Monba	1.79
Mongol	790.42
Mulao	16.89
Naxi	19.77
Nu	1.90
Oroqen	1.27
Pumi	2.15
Qiang	17.19
Russian	2.25
Salar	10.21
She	30.43
Shui	27.62
Tajik	5.96
Tatar	0.70
Tibetan	733.94

(*continued*)

Table 5.3 (continued)

Ethnic group	Total power of agricultural machinery (10,000 kw)
Tu	22.62
Tujia	607.14
Uygur	1239.34
Uzbek	1.81
Va	25.56
Xibe	15.01
Yao	219.02
Yi	481.91
Yugur	1.17
Zhuang	1323.66

Table 5.4 Original value of productive fixed assets of rural households at year-end (yuan/household)

Ethnic group	Total original value	Agriculture	Industry	Construction	Transport, postal and tele-communication services
National average	16974.09	11406.20	1109.48	361.18	2283.42
Achang	18968.58	14341.50	239.36	79.83	3732.60
Bai	17532.01	13021.22	245.05	106.75	3471.18
Baonan	20156.81	13816.39	137.90	83.68	2571.77
Blang	18955.75	14326.74	243.53	81.55	3724.88
Buyi	12198.27	8080.81	189.92	196.35	2512.25
Dai	18948.38	14332.02	234.49	79.48	3726.35
Daur	29797.02	26089.63	193.09	244.60	1884.01
Deang	19009.96	14391.55	227.92	79.20	3743.63
Derung	18794.01	14100.77	339.63	133.84	3426.43
Dong	11099.50	7207.24	283.48	227.77	2223.66
Dongxiang	21207.58	14882.41	226.59	179.87	2529.07
Ewenki	28897.84	25257.07	148.35	245.05	1995.36
Gaoshan	15213.18	10188.29	887.42	291.49	2170.96
Gelao	12015.33	7964.03	153.41	195.44	2492.87
Han	15284.69	9757.43	1235.37	329.64	2103.70
Hani	18978.98	14351.97	237.64	79.72	3737.21
Hezhe	29766.14	26065.97	234.40	116.01	1593.40

(continued)

Table 5.4 (continued)

Ethnic group	Total original value	Agriculture	Industry	Construction	Transport, postal and tele-communication services
Hui	20570.22	14263.88	755.76	379.53	3066.78
Jing	12054.17	9016.06	297.71	242.25	1686.18
Jingpo	18949.75	14329.73	234.18	80.20	3730.46
Jino	18974.43	14361.59	229.60	79.11	3734.68
Kazak	34996.79	29010.99	1284.99	1428.67	2311.99
Kirgiz	34983.75	29022.81	1277.61	1417.68	2303.50
Korean	25661.57	21680.38	309.03	376.08	1738.25
Lahu	18965.95	14337.88	240.06	80.17	3730.91
Lhoba	49576.46	40738.28	113.49	1497.99	5966.87
Li	11446.22	8778.72	396.07	49.14	827.23
Lisu	18851.42	14242.07	245.27	80.98	3671.75
Manchu	23797.48	17197.08	1065.16	479.76	3005.35
Maonan	11894.02	8641.35	237.62	230.16	1874.70
Miao	12211.38	8265.02	278.44	216.85	2352.91
Monba	50972.68	41985.74	76.70	1540.55	6117.72
Mongol	27342.91	23027.85	337.66	330.18	2266.86
Mulao	11863.13	8732.49	288.54	242.83	1738.98
Naxi	18973.55	14342.99	246.30	87.65	3684.51
Nu	19438.67	14715.06	259.23	105.39	3757.74
Oroqen	29427.69	25751.61	184.23	178.17	1806.42
Pumi	18976.33	14345.51	242.42	82.15	3720.45
Qiang	13785.68	10218.05	316.79	109.56	1428.95
Russian	31530.89	26329.19	891.31	938.31	2233.27
Salar	22049.75	15788.92	148.51	262.50	3358.22
She	14154.91	6816.54	2291.67	330.82	2475.17
Shui	12245.79	8183.86	177.33	195.19	2502.69
Tajik	34308.67	28374.43	1268.24	1391.02	2295.86
Tatar	33695.13	27695.98	1246.23	1334.58	2320.56
Tibetan	33579.04	26670.59	130.78	801.91	4202.10
Tu	21124.12	14945.22	179.31	233.33	3290.05
Tujia	10810.17	7198.59	373.03	294.98	1888.85
Uygur	34942.32	28961.69	1286.68	1427.09	2309.87
Uzbek	34588.71	28624.59	1282.68	1408.94	2303.32
Va	18901.42	14263.82	259.19	84.26	3689.14
Xibe	26849.13	20043.89	1015.46	714.58	3309.34
Yao	11354.99	7993.84	344.46	251.91	1855.90
Yi	16774.15	12506.83	247.91	100.39	2959.19
Yugur	19818.11	13478.50	137.35	63.39	2546.32
Zhuang	12281.22	9209.56	292.51	239.24	1756.36

Note: All data are as of 2012

Table 5.5 Original value of productive fixed assets of rural households at year-end (yuan/household)

Ethnic group	Wholesale and retail trades and catering services	Social services	Education, culture, and health care	Others
National average	1279.80	261.14	121.18	151.69
Achang	413.96	16.29	60.63	84.41
Bai	479.61	40.88	79.72	87.59
Baonan	2834.27	259.41	166.34	287.04
Blang	416.64	16.89	60.83	84.69
Buyi	831.67	62.80	214.99	109.48
Dai	414.84	17.01	60.58	83.61
Daur	962.27	121.35	107.33	194.74
Deang	408.65	14.84	60.19	83.99
Derung	563.71	60.48	71.81	97.33
Dong	748.09	133.39	161.74	114.12
Dongxiang	2711.10	253.60	170.27	254.67
Ewenki	868.85	92.48	83.91	206.77
Gaoshan	1191.07	235.18	129.05	119.72
Gelao	824.66	58.98	216.81	109.12
Han	1310.62	279.65	121.48	146.80
Hani	412.05	15.83	60.49	84.08
Hezhe	1239.43	194.02	148.77	174.15
Hui	1599.01	208.55	106.32	190.39
Jing	476.39	85.73	64.24	185.62
Jingpo	413.38	16.43	60.90	84.47
Jino	410.28	15.50	60.26	83.42
Kazak	606.53	122.85	163.60	67.17
Kirgiz	607.60	123.27	163.49	67.79
Korean	1179.39	180.83	119.62	77.99
Lahu	414.86	16.59	60.89	84.60
Lhoba	1037.36	79.21	13.18	130.08
Li	1221.68	86.49	63.66	23.24
Lisu	440.44	25.44	62.16	83.30
Manchu	1490.18	342.18	128.80	88.98
Maonan	559.26	76.22	106.10	168.61
Miao	730.63	112.83	151.13	103.57
Monba	1041.20	76.36	4.41	129.99
Mongol	968.85	135.74	91.13	184.64
Mulao	513.11	85.76	81.67	179.75
Naxi	441.90	25.58	62.06	82.55
Nu	433.78	20.63	60.90	85.94
Oroqen	1054.95	144.59	116.40	191.31

(continued)

Table 5.5 (continued)

Ethnic group	Wholesale and retail trades and catering services	Social services	Education, culture, and health care	Others
Pumi	421.91	18.54	60.85	84.50
Qiang	1261.51	310.48	106.62	33.71
Russian	763.39	123.86	129.32	122.25
Salar	1625.06	129.84	55.79	680.92
She	1560.59	387.66	187.77	104.69
Shui	808.03	59.09	207.92	111.68
Tajik	621.78	126.17	161.62	69.54
Tatar	725.12	134.11	161.15	77.40
Tibetan	1326.21	150.68	48.65	248.13
Tu	1631.13	138.21	59.77	647.10
Tujia	704.63	165.18	105.98	78.93
Uygur	603.65	123.17	163.38	66.80
Uzbek	614.40	125.06	162.05	67.66
Va	432.85	21.22	62.47	88.47
Xibe	1286.32	299.66	122.11	57.77
Yao	542.99	144.84	70.66	150.40
Yi	693.99	102.40	90.68	72.76
Yugur	2883.62	266.20	168.82	273.91
Zhuang	458.66	84.62	58.45	181.82

Note: All data are as of 2012

Table 5.6 Number of major productive fixed assets per 100 rural households at year-end

Ethnic group	Motor vehicles (set)	Large and medium tractors (set)	Mini and walking tractors (set)	Motorized threshing machines (set)	Carts with rubber tyres (set)	Pumps (unit)	Draught animals (unit)	Commodity animals (unit)
National average	4.04	4.40	20.49	11.49	4.31	25.46	26.36	86.13
Achang	4.36	3.20	14.49	18.08	1.89	20.42	56.29	78.88
Bai	4.20	2.81	12.46	17.92	1.75	20.08	52.49	71.84
Baonan	3.79	5.32	32.48	14.75	11.27	15.51	47.11	91.85
Blang	4.36	3.20	14.50	18.09	1.89	20.45	56.19	78.76
Buyi	3.83	1.32	2.13	16.84	0.63	11.35	50.88	49.41
Dai	4.36	3.19	14.44	18.17	1.88	20.47	56.25	78.68
Daur	4.32	15.77	48.20	6.71	9.08	33.17	28.82	211.60
Deang	4.37	3.22	14.55	18.12	1.91	20.37	56.56	79.29
Derung	4.31	3.65	15.81	16.58	2.72	21.68	49.83	83.71
Dong	3.29	1.17	4.79	17.93	1.37	18.91	36.64	39.66

(*continued*)

Table 5.6 (continued)

Ethnic group	Motor vehicles (set)	Large and medium tractors (set)	Mini and walking tractors (set)	Motorized threshing machines (set)	Carts with rubber tyres (set)	Pumps (unit)	Draught animals (unit)	Commodity animals (unit)
Dongxiang	3.75	5.95	32.14	13.95	13.10	15.45	48.33	118.17
Ewenki	4.82	12.59	48.23	8.42	10.73	36.54	36.38	252.11
Gaoshan	3.73	3.99	20.05	11.94	3.90	27.92	18.84	64.53
Gelao	3.81	1.27	1.77	16.90	0.58	11.05	51.19	48.59
Han	3.74	3.89	18.44	11.44	3.73	26.83	15.37	56.03
Hani	4.37	3.20	14.50	18.10	1.89	20.41	56.36	78.79
Hezhe	3.17	21.77	47.16	3.92	2.32	27.78	7.84	79.97
Hui	4.80	6.47	30.20	8.77	6.21	22.89	27.71	113.24
Jing	2.07	2.15	19.04	26.95	3.90	30.43	38.25	42.07
Jingpo	4.36	3.20	14.49	18.08	1.90	20.39	56.29	78.77
Jino	4.37	3.21	14.49	18.14	1.88	20.39	56.40	78.85
Kazak	4.61	13.12	36.60	2.50	31.76	10.22	62.60	483.12
Kirgiz	4.60	13.24	36.73	2.48	31.50	10.41	62.05	479.83
Korean	4.07	14.66	43.88	6.26	5.81	31.42	18.31	120.99
Lahu	4.37	3.21	14.55	18.08	1.89	20.49	56.21	78.69
Lhoba	11.71	6.94	53.79	13.00	7.40	1.69	351.70	738.44
Li	0.69	0.40	3.47	4.20	1.10	23.52	22.24	155.82
Lisu	4.34	3.15	14.23	18.40	1.87	20.90	55.38	78.21
Manchu	5.16	9.01	25.28	4.90	8.73	31.57	19.09	99.62
Maonan	2.50	1.87	14.50	24.64	3.05	25.34	42.16	42.77
Miao	3.47	1.36	5.19	17.79	1.27	18.72	38.91	46.71
Monba	12.04	6.99	55.52	13.18	7.35	1.00	366.37	766.19
Mongol	4.97	10.76	42.33	8.32	11.11	35.11	35.52	230.83
Mulao	2.22	1.99	17.13	26.09	3.59	28.31	39.56	41.30
Naxi	4.37	3.16	14.34	18.38	1.89	20.72	56.72	81.03
Nu	4.48	3.26	15.13	17.96	2.00	20.15	60.57	89.07
Oroqen	4.00	17.30	47.77	6.09	6.54	32.44	21.78	164.96
Pumi	4.36	3.22	14.58	18.09	1.91	20.52	56.15	79.10
Qiang	3.02	0.91	2.97	29.90	0.95	36.59	24.66	54.25
Russian	4.73	12.09	39.44	5.02	22.49	20.42	50.88	375.21
Salar	6.45	4.68	49.27	9.95	4.17	6.56	36.71	170.85
She	3.81	1.42	4.63	10.69	1.49	13.05	11.43	62.91
Shui	3.78	1.37	2.83	17.22	0.74	12.00	50.86	49.40
Tajik	4.57	12.81	35.94	2.87	30.81	10.78	61.12	468.90
Tatar	4.56	12.47	35.68	3.22	29.86	10.92	60.14	451.70
Tibetan	8.14	4.85	40.33	16.69	5.04	11.68	190.22	415.69
Tu	6.22	4.33	46.55	10.53	3.61	7.53	35.57	153.56
Tujia	3.04	1.17	6.96	14.97	1.75	24.45	22.20	35.62
Uygur	4.61	13.10	36.52	2.51	31.69	10.29	62.44	482.20
Uzbek	4.58	12.92	36.14	2.69	31.24	10.45	61.80	475.52
Va	4.36	3.22	14.62	17.96	1.94	20.81	55.29	78.24
Xibe	5.01	9.19	20.55	4.71	15.71	30.99	30.91	168.14
Yao	2.39	1.65	14.03	23.42	3.25	28.55	30.81	37.15
Yi	3.93	2.36	9.93	21.24	1.48	23.88	47.00	68.66
Yugur	3.68	5.25	31.64	14.97	11.14	15.98	46.38	82.86
Zhuang	2.12	2.17	19.14	26.83	3.94	30.19	38.91	42.91

Note: All data are as of 2012

Table 5.7 Output of major farm products per hectare (kg/hectare) (I)

Ethnic group	Cereals	Cotton	Peanuts	Rapeseeds	Sesame
National average	6120	1819	3752	2027	1645
Achang	4997.70	384.23	1716.27	2049.64	842.42
Bai	5106.39	514.78	1841.60	1996.12	936.89
Baonan	4779.16	1582.19	3796.40	2053.44	60.04
Blang	5005.49	385.35	1721.42	2053.01	844.03
Buyi	4936.25	974.90	2236.43	1747.40	1356.32
Dai	5002.09	386.12	1715.88	2052.79	844.45
Daur	6357.73	942.10	2881.99	1583.97	1268.82
Deang	4991.93	382.70	1707.47	2051.43	835.75
Derung	5206.45	535.26	1990.82	2013.70	985.10
Dong	5498.28	1078.64	2466.09	1666.80	1642.53
Dongxiang	4973.19	1666.91	3967.37	2114.74	167.67
Ewenki	6253.69	1234.36	2754.61	1603.86	916.00
Gaoshan	6064.78	1048.45	3380.66	1903.84	1814.02
Gelao	4920.06	977.27	2230.27	1740.16	1359.35
Han	6096.44	1000.49	3367.71	2044.94	1616.77
Hani	4997.84	384.07	1713.50	2052.21	839.99
Hezhe	6502.05	141.53	2980.61	1364.86	2015.89
Hui	5695.42	904.25	3290.77	2180.83	939.65
Jing	5454.60	1026.93	2921.96	1051.59	3706.42
Jingpo	4996.80	386.08	1717.72	2049.33	843.90
Jino	4997.56	381.39	1708.48	2049.05	838.64
Kazak	6843.42	2047.96	4444.08	2789.57	1495.97
Kirgiz	6845.22	2029.43	4430.14	2776.65	1505.09
Korean	6644.81	367.38	3147.14	642.50	1817.44
Lahu	5002.18	386.12	1722.78	2054.61	842.53
Lhoba	5691.83	95.18	2945.50	2537.31	136.96
Li	5301.34	55.89	2699.62	108.88	1367.02
Lisu	5035.71	403.55	1742.29	2062.20	860.97
Manchu	6300.32	1501.83	3023.99	1531.12	2436.63
Maonan	5292.08	1025.53	2746.47	1210.39	3163.48
Miao	5481.97	924.70	2344.78	1754.72	1433.59
Monba	5701.99	48.54	2938.33	2573.45	67.47
Mongol	6217.57	1365.88	2807.96	1648.10	1180.37
Mulao	5391.69	1024.50	2864.72	1114.84	3528.20
Naxi	5037.98	401.20	1742.78	2062.61	857.63
Nu	5020.07	388.00	1748.66	2059.47	839.12
Oroqen	6385.56	701.56	2873.87	1492.89	1488.65
Pumi	5008.85	389.95	1728.15	2052.81	847.68
Qiang	6308.57	989.92	2571.49	2389.78	1559.98
Russian	6575.58	1708.96	3744.23	2311.46	1269.91
Salar	3848.47	273.73	658.35	1972.69	77.80

(*continued*)

Table 5.7 (continued)

Ethnic group	Cereals	Cotton	Peanuts	Rapeseeds	Sesame
She	6284.33	1016.03	2901.35	1789.78	1441.89
Shui	4943.93	972.52	2248.58	1727.12	1430.40
Tajik	6817.80	2008.87	4401.04	2757.19	1503.99
Tatar	6736.72	1984.60	4367.65	2725.58	1442.16
Tibetan	5307.82	387.14	2320.44	2349.60	404.68
Tu	3922.91	289.78	784.39	1961.10	142.41
Tujia	6176.21	903.64	2714.68	1898.24	1414.60
Uygur	6846.33	2044.89	4441.42	2787.81	1500.24
Uzbek	6827.90	2024.45	4419.17	2767.39	1506.43
Va	5028.91	398.39	1762.15	2058.62	858.27
Xibe	6501.70	2040.16	3049.27	1865.73	2849.85
Yao	5724.41	999.73	2779.40	1353.75	2831.15
Yi	5352.33	619.11	2009.94	2109.88	1098.24
Yugur	4803.19	1612.30	3888.20	2041.17	69.83
Zhuang	5429.39	970.21	2880.13	1094.63	3649.37

Table 5.8 Output of major farm products per hectare (kg/hectare) (II)

Ethnic group	Jute and ambary hemp	Sugarcane	Beetroots	Flue-cured tobacco
National average	5008	76,891	52,174	2103
Achang	19.19	62827.62	52.02	2044.47
Bai	177.41	61076.17	298.08	2016.05
Baonan	6.27	179.00	64780.90	2969.70
Blang	26.60	62714.55	66.91	2043.76
Buyi	94.61	59104.48	256.21	1693.17
Dai	25.36	62780.64	132.93	2046.49
Daur	24.39	666.46	43352.20	3338.45
Deang	9.42	62813.96	135.97	2046.92
Derung	242.57	55492.18	4873.72	2105.58
Dong	1043.56	57481.01	953.68	1830.07
Dongxiang	2.79	133.07	66928.36	2849.65
Ewenki	49.87	1480.60	41242.74	3758.18
Gaoshan	2624.83	46398.85	12626.37	2106.20
Gelao	76.36	59274.95	94.55	1693.86
Han	1833.91	39220.29	13718.74	2018.93
Hani	13.82	62835.78	51.99	2045.98
Hezhe	83.67	2161.25	41596.36	2697.45
Hui	935.79	18481.76	22990.64	2383.76

(*continued*)

Table 5.8 (continued)

Ethnic group	Jute and ambary hemp	Sugarcane	Beetroots	Flue-cured tobacco
Jing	2895.85	79564.13	341.23	1632.54
Jingpo	19.47	62778.30	99.35	2048.48
Jino	13.91	62785.83	109.94	2047.27
Kazak	1.13	50.56	74032.32	10.29
Kirgiz	2.87	91.85	73706.50	33.69
Korean	61.29	1537.55	40865.02	2571.52
Lahu	30.71	62804.49	48.09	2048.44
Lhoba	101.29	3577.87	1412.47	147.02
Li	2852.56	63561.03	99.57	105.90
Lisu	63.23	61948.56	675.91	2048.49
Manchu	64.78	1278.67	50450.32	2642.77
Maonan	2161.80	75046.07	141.27	1646.53
Miao	887.88	56228.39	1296.32	1841.43
Monba	58.94	1692.39	729.31	76.53
Mongol	161.07	3361.37	42255.47	3410.63
Mulao	2622.70	78295.92	192.74	1640.52
Naxi	70.08	61861.54	615.45	2034.80
Nu	33.30	61697.23	204.01	2011.14
Oroqen	56.02	1434.15	41773.39	3259.54
Pumi	30.58	62505.98	273.45	2045.06
Qiang	1867.00	38842.07	17246.11	2055.68
Russian	66.71	1959.18	58297.23	1467.82
Salar	23.33	564.70	25379.81	386.44
She	3075.01	56698.82	229.64	1622.82
Shui	153.85	59979.13	166.41	1688.42
Tajik	67.43	1416.16	71950.63	77.95
Tatar	47.80	1254.07	71239.83	184.27
Tibetan	458.11	10965.83	13368.33	815.34
Tu	126.33	4661.69	23758.02	564.79
Tujia	1845.67	47153.88	9700.01	1877.32
Uygur	10.72	230.54	73782.15	12.56
Uzbek	45.23	1096.16	72693.53	36.97
Va	62.04	62031.90	190.58	2055.76
Xibe	30.58	797.10	58993.47	2224.87
Yao	2485.81	70357.03	109.42	1862.72
Yi	537.18	55755.14	4878.82	2011.33
Yugur	20.08	594.11	65238.34	3086.95
Zhuang	2825.07	80296.36	158.27	1669.64

Table 5.9 Per capita output of major farm products (kg)

Ethnic group	Grain	Cereal	Cotton	Oil-bearing Crops	Pork, Beef and Mutton	Total Aquatic Products	Milk
National average	472	438	4.4	24.7	46.8	46.4	22.1
Achang	386.40	328.85	0.02	12.80	78.21	13.89	12.12
Bai	380.51	322.61	0.15	16.32	74.70	14.94	10.28
Baonan	434.28	349.68	8.41	27.55	38.04	1.00	19.53
Blang	386.71	329.10	0.03	12.87	78.08	13.80	12.10
Buyi	297.11	211.06	0.10	30.42	52.81	9.18	1.84
Dai	386.50	328.74	0.02	12.92	78.21	13.62	12.08
Daur	1517.69	1368.32	8.71	49.35	77.31	10.97	174.35
Deang	387.01	329.26	0.17	12.79	78.40	13.35	12.21
Derung	428.23	371.27	1.52	15.94	73.03	19.23	19.09
Dong	336.18	278.77	0.50	30.00	57.36	25.52	1.52
Dongxiang	455.59	375.94	23.71	26.86	38.70	1.42	23.53
Ewenki	1400.63	1261.22	0.52	69.49	88.16	8.97	203.64
Gaoshan	488.27	456.40	2.43	30.19	50.41	53.16	23.70
Gelao	293.91	206.83	0.06	30.75	52.54	8.53	1.47
Han	489.68	454.66	2.13	25.70	46.83	46.75	20.81
Hani	386.78	329.14	0.02	12.78	78.26	13.60	12.11
Hezhe	1780.50	1605.67	1.05	6.72	53.68	18.85	107.38
Hui	519.34	473.41	18.33	26.82	49.71	22.99	75.54
Jing	287.59	268.31	0.17	14.35	56.57	65.16	2.53
Jingpo	386.49	328.89	0.05	12.86	78.15	13.72	12.13
Jino	387.05	329.25	0.00	12.80	78.29	13.43	12.09
Kazak	609.11	598.55	206.37	27.49	56.43	7.12	78.75
Kirgiz	622.67	610.45	204.63	27.30	56.48	7.30	79.36
Korean	1299.23	1232.54	0.23	24.15	59.30	24.31	40.50
Lahu	387.51	329.99	0.02	12.93	78.20	13.66	12.13
Lhoba	317.11	305.06	2.34	17.82	78.47	3.95	98.97
Li	166.53	145.58	0.02	10.20	52.26	178.85	0.43
Lisu	388.26	330.05	0.03	13.68	77.86	13.76	12.13
Manchu	749.07	706.88	1.03	20.22	55.41	58.88	50.37
Maonan	283.02	245.80	0.05	18.78	55.29	49.91	1.84
Miao	343.01	279.99	0.51	28.14	59.00	22.84	2.96
Monba	308.48	298.37	0.27	17.51	79.57	1.62	102.64
Mongol	1172.46	1063.80	5.47	61.89	81.89	19.12	165.75
Mulao	279.40	253.58	0.07	16.04	55.47	59.30	1.96
Naxi	386.78	328.76	0.06	13.64	77.78	13.68	12.42

(continued)

Table 5.9 (continued)

Ethnic group	Grain	Cereal	Cotton	Oil-bearing Crops	Pork, Beef and Mutton	Total Aquatic Products	Milk
Nu	385.30	328.72	0.15	12.92	77.90	14.04	13.54
Oroqen	1599.28	1441.28	0.42	37.92	71.06	14.74	156.62
Pumi	388.57	331.00	0.07	12.99	78.04	13.78	12.29
Qiang	419.01	339.87	0.25	43.22	64.82	18.64	7.89
Russian	866.71	810.07	118.70	43.05	67.15	9.26	121.28
Salar	220.07	155.03	7.62	43.87	56.12	3.21	50.26
She	175.02	152.45	0.28	9.81	30.46	140.74	3.12
Shui	298.41	214.49	0.18	29.72	53.37	10.48	1.90
Tajik	605.20	593.55	199.53	27.33	56.15	8.40	76.80
Tatar	596.46	582.04	190.85	27.18	55.22	8.12	74.54
Tibetan	320.66	276.19	0.36	30.17	68.99	5.72	62.54
Tu	223.20	158.04	2.63	42.24	55.14	6.40	46.37
Tujia	400.02	351.92	1.51	34.99	58.66	40.26	1.92
Uygur	609.10	598.65	205.94	27.49	56.45	7.30	78.64
Uzbek	603.33	592.69	202.68	27.28	56.20	8.31	77.61
Va	389.77	332.63	0.07	13.35	77.68	14.49	12.30
Xibe	613.23	588.40	37.97	20.15	55.98	75.75	46.09
Yao	317.55	297.07	0.41	19.01	59.34	55.03	2.38
Yi	386.40	319.49	0.06	23.25	71.70	14.38	9.81
Yugur	441.35	355.69	5.84	26.78	37.16	1.32	18.54
Zhuang	282.26	263.47	0.10	13.50	57.26	64.13	2.70

Table 5.10 Per capita major farm products sold by rural households (kg)

Ethnic group	Grain	Cotton	Oil-bearing crops	Tobacco	Vegetables	Fruits
National average	529.75	22.98	18.52	4.80	164.13	71.04
Achang	107.93	0.19	6.02	35.93	275.59	42.05
Bai	110.89	2.27	6.76	31.50	237.49	40.63
Baonan	305.49	29.97	26.25	0.08	190.50	67.51
Blang	108.85	0.25	6.05	35.82	274.99	41.93
Buyi	59.59	0.37	8.24	14.22	71.18	8.46
Dai	107.15	0.14	6.07	35.88	274.70	41.94
Daur	1873.60	16.29	73.97	0.90	202.45	12.37
Deang	107.65	0.38	6.04	36.09	275.65	41.91
Derung	221.18	4.53	10.50	29.59	259.90	47.65
Dong	118.55	9.66	9.36	10.72	75.74	34.06

(*continued*)

Table 5.10 (continued)

Ethnic group	Grain	Cotton	Oil-bearing crops	Tobacco	Vegetables	Fruits
Dongxiang	364.57	56.83	28.56	0.07	203.38	76.27
Ewenki	1305.95	1.55	103.05	0.45	227.98	6.32
Gaoshan	546.02	11.70	18.31	5.70	171.44	69.14
Gelao	53.83	0.21	8.21	14.05	67.39	7.17
Han	556.04	17.57	17.03	4.43	171.97	72.61
Hani	108.12	0.17	6.00	36.01	275.43	41.88
Hezhe	3096.50	2.99	8.48	2.05	131.11	10.76
Hui	558.83	42.19	24.37	4.02	217.95	62.39
Jing	147.54	0.71	3.85	4.36	149.27	56.68
Jingpo	108.62	0.25	6.05	35.89	275.03	42.01
Jino	108.83	0.09	6.03	36.01	275.07	41.82
Kazak	1007.05	371.20	66.02	0.01	297.09	154.29
Kirgiz	1030.94	368.04	65.55	0.03	295.69	152.95
Korean	2607.62	1.86	36.10	1.03	154.19	24.27
Lahu	109.33	0.23	6.07	35.91	275.39	41.92
Lhoba	110.69	4.81	5.72	0.69	15.49	8.58
Li	55.91	0.14	9.14	0.73	266.37	102.45
Lisu	109.11	0.27	6.49	35.13	271.87	42.34
Manchu	1444.07	9.21	24.53	2.17	265.79	101.25
Maonan	112.45	0.20	4.80	6.52	124.66	42.29
Miao	115.20	8.13	9.49	13.84	104.84	33.58
Monba	84.42	0.67	5.10	0.21	7.90	5.39
Mongol	1162.13	11.53	89.56	1.10	238.47	29.74
Mulao	126.93	0.37	4.08	4.83	137.72	50.53
Naxi	107.74	0.24	6.43	35.00	269.86	42.18
Nu	110.23	0.52	6.07	35.12	270.62	41.89
Oroqen	2216.32	1.65	55.48	1.26	181.73	9.52
Pumi	113.23	0.34	6.19	35.67	274.20	42.03
Qiang	101.24	0.50	21.61	7.13	131.73	50.39
Russian	1046.06	214.47	77.38	0.34	265.28	96.24
Salar	143.79	15.69	44.71	0.08	85.64	14.35
She	145.21	2.35	3.62	8.78	158.44	136.89
Shui	62.10	0.44	8.03	14.26	75.23	9.49
Tajik	991.14	359.28	64.28	0.16	292.73	151.26
Tatar	962.91	344.33	62.49	0.19	288.14	147.21
Tibetan	105.77	2.07	18.91	2.56	67.93	20.32
Tu	132.70	7.30	41.55	0.86	88.78	15.39
Tujia	237.15	34.66	22.45	8.09	106.15	61.90
Uygur	1006.77	370.47	65.89	0.03	296.73	154.12
Uzbek	993.13	364.67	64.99	0.08	294.66	152.88
Va	116.87	0.71	6.39	35.25	275.79	42.49

(*continued*)

Table 5.10 (continued)

Ethnic group	Grain	Cotton	Oil-bearing crops	Tobacco	Vegetables	Fruits
Xibe	1330.73	68.80	32.77	2.70	315.99	135.33
Yao	147.02	6.98	5.50	7.08	132.86	59.05
Yi	101.85	0.22	10.60	25.55	212.31	40.38
Yugur	307.69	25.81	24.92	0.11	192.82	68.58
Zhuang	134.71	0.33	3.59	5.64	158.59	56.36

Note: All data are as of 2012

Table 5.11 Sales of livestock, poultry, small animals and fishery per capita rural household (kg)

Ethnic group	Pork	Mutton	Beef	Poultry	Poultry eggs	Milk	Aquatic products
National average	30.74	3.32	3.34	8.09	10.13	9.32	9.71
Achang	37.40	0.57	1.78	2.37	2.68	17.62	2.06
Bai	35.70	0.56	1.70	2.38	2.47	14.49	2.46
Baonan	9.94	5.22	5.69	1.23	5.93	2.20	0.05
Blang	37.40	0.57	1.78	2.39	2.76	17.52	2.06
Buyi	22.85	0.62	1.83	2.74	0.94	0.44	0.99
Dai	37.47	0.56	1.78	2.32	2.66	17.56	2.04
Daur	18.02	28.21	13.95	3.15	4.60	99.33	1.23
Deang	37.35	0.58	1.80	2.26	2.64	17.70	1.94
Derung	36.20	2.05	2.48	3.97	4.78	18.89	3.09
Dong	26.98	0.51	1.33	3.22	1.55	0.11	5.01
Dongxiang	9.75	6.38	6.41	1.48	6.36	2.93	0.04
Ewenki	15.04	39.40	16.03	2.68	5.45	131.73	0.93
Gaoshan	37.34	2.95	3.14	8.54	10.38	8.08	10.42
Gelao	22.41	0.60	1.82	2.67	0.78	0.13	0.90
Han	34.07	2.23	2.41	9.96	11.60	6.88	11.41
Hani	37.40	0.56	1.78	2.34	2.69	17.63	2.00
Hezhe	28.16	2.58	8.23	4.88	3.13	31.78	3.09
Hui	22.93	7.19	7.31	6.54	8.56	26.32	3.60
Jing	26.59	0.52	1.37	7.55	2.12	0.60	8.81
Jingpo	37.35	0.57	1.78	2.36	2.66	17.60	2.02
Jino	37.44	0.56	1.79	2.29	2.67	17.64	1.98
Kazak	4.81	22.46	16.75	4.27	9.32	10.94	0.01
Kirgiz	5.05	22.32	16.69	4.28	9.26	11.30	0.05
Korean	52.37	3.04	8.54	11.72	18.12	10.75	1.98
Lahu	37.44	0.57	1.77	2.37	2.72	17.58	2.01
Lhoba	3.59	5.11	11.34	0.73	1.05	5.63	0.80

(continued)

Table 5.11 (continued)

Ethnic group	Pork	Mutton	Beef	Poultry	Poultry eggs	Milk	Aquatic products
Li	32.91	0.49	1.29	15.92	0.38	0.09	42.42
Lisu	37.79	0.58	1.81	2.41	2.73	17.17	2.17
Manchu	54.42	4.88	8.46	17.44	28.30	13.97	3.72
Maonan	25.04	0.52	1.49	6.26	1.50	0.08	6.45
Miao	28.95	0.59	1.48	3.37	2.98	2.19	4.96
Monba	2.39	5.13	11.62	0.56	0.60	5.83	0.47
Mongol	23.50	32.65	14.51	5.89	10.61	104.83	1.42
Mulao	25.91	0.50	1.40	7.13	1.75	0.11	8.01
Naxi	37.66	0.59	1.85	2.35	2.69	17.11	2.18
Nu	36.87	0.66	1.93	2.39	2.74	17.34	2.09
Oroqen	21.74	20.99	12.16	3.91	4.49	82.06	1.97
Pumi	37.40	0.59	1.80	2.39	2.75	17.54	2.07
Qiang	51.54	0.62	2.59	4.01	2.38	0.27	8.63
Russian	10.04	27.77	15.73	4.24	8.42	55.60	0.72
Salar	3.65	10.27	9.75	0.52	1.18	7.94	0.16
She	44.71	0.52	0.57	6.40	4.52	0.82	25.04
Shui	22.82	0.61	1.81	2.81	1.03	0.61	1.15
Tajik	5.72	21.79	16.27	4.46	9.37	10.83	0.36
Tatar	6.04	21.04	15.81	4.43	9.26	10.66	0.38
Tibetan	15.14	5.06	8.58	1.24	1.35	5.02	2.18
Tu	5.84	9.30	8.95	0.85	1.33	7.75	1.19
Tujia	30.98	0.63	1.04	3.84	8.70	0.15	16.37
Uygur	4.94	22.41	16.72	4.30	9.34	10.95	0.06
Uzbek	5.31	22.10	16.48	4.38	9.25	10.90	0.33
Va	37.45	0.61	1.78	2.74	2.91	17.30	2.11
Xibe	61.28	6.72	11.09	21.73	31.99	6.51	4.64
Yao	30.14	0.42	1.07	6.03	1.71	1.34	9.51
Yi	39.66	0.59	2.01	2.82	2.39	10.90	3.69
Yugur	10.37	4.86	5.39	1.35	6.12	2.46	0.13
Zhuang	27.26	0.48	1.35	7.50	1.87	1.33	9.01

Note: All data are as of 2012

Table 5.12 Price indices for means of agricultural production by category (preceding year=100) (I)

Ethnic group	General index	Farm handtools	Forage	Commodity animals	Semi-mechanized farm Tools	Mechanized farm machinery
National average	103.1	103.8	102.9	89.5	101.4	101.8
Achang	101.64	103.11	102.90	86.05	100.39	100.60

(continued)

Table 5.12 (continued)

Ethnic group	General index	Farm handtools	Forage	Commodity animals	Semi-mechanized farm Tools	Mechanized farm machinery
Bai	101.29	102.82	102.35	86.27	100.39	100.69
Baonan	104.08	105.15	101.75	99.09	102.18	102.89
Blang	101.38	102.85	102.64	85.84	100.14	100.34
Buyi	98.86	102.59	100.16	85.93	100.44	99.98
Dai	101.58	103.08	102.85	86.01	100.35	100.55
Daur	102.06	106.76	99.70	93.52	100.37	100.32
Deang	101.63	103.11	102.89	86.05	100.38	100.59
Derung	99.51	100.91	100.46	84.58	98.27	98.45
Dong	100.21	102.23	100.35	86.56	100.85	101.63
Dongxiang	104.25	105.15	101.87	99.23	102.13	102.78
Ewenki	101.83	107.38	99.42	95.41	100.69	100.03
Gaoshan	97.17	97.93	97.47	82.65	95.45	95.80
Gelao	98.65	102.42	99.95	85.80	100.29	99.81
Han	96.90	97.56	96.90	83.84	95.51	95.77
Hani	101.58	103.06	102.85	86.00	100.34	100.54
Hezhe	100.94	104.22	99.01	87.75	98.42	99.68
Hui	98.83	99.88	98.77	89.79	98.01	96.33
Jing	101.48	103.65	100.64	78.69	100.79	103.19
Jingpo	101.64	103.11	102.90	86.06	100.40	100.60
Jino	101.45	102.93	102.72	85.90	100.21	100.41
Kazak	104.89	102.61	102.19	98.42	100.44	100.60
Kirgiz	104.87	102.66	102.18	98.32	100.44	100.62
Korean	101.41	101.04	102.00	92.31	98.39	99.18
Lahu	101.58	103.05	102.85	85.99	100.33	100.53
Lhoba	100.04	101.52	99.75	99.07	99.07	99.04
Li	101.97	102.75	100.52	90.57	99.98	103.72
Lisu	101.65	103.23	102.93	86.12	100.43	100.63
Manchu	99.46	98.48	99.98	82.01	97.72	97.93
Maonan	100.84	103.49	100.53	80.38	100.83	102.50
Miao	94.72	96.70	95.09	81.99	95.14	95.71
Monba	99.72	101.28	99.43	99.32	98.74	98.71
Mongol	101.66	105.62	100.00	93.10	100.40	99.86
Mulao	101.19	103.55	100.51	79.27	100.77	102.90
Naxi	101.49	103.09	102.77	86.05	100.27	100.49
Nu	101.61	103.08	102.84	86.27	100.38	100.58
Oroqen	101.82	106.22	99.64	91.78	99.99	100.27
Pumi	101.60	103.09	102.86	86.04	100.36	100.56
Qiang	101.58	107.01	103.36	88.06	100.97	101.58
Russian	101.65	102.36	99.25	95.09	98.65	98.48
Salar	102.00	101.01	100.25	95.44	101.00	101.33
She	102.19	102.69	102.10	92.35	100.62	100.74
Shui	99.04	102.71	100.27	85.72	100.52	100.15
Tajik	104.22	102.05	101.61	97.54	99.89	100.06
Tatar	103.73	101.69	101.14	97.16	99.51	99.70
Tibetan	101.57	103.45	101.35	96.15	100.65	100.90

(continued)

Table 5.12 (continued)

Ethnic group	General index	Farm handtools	Forage	Commodity animals	Semi-mechanized farm Tools	Mechanized farm machinery
Tu	102.00	101.25	100.38	95.07	101.05	101.39
Tujia	83.09	83.25	82.22	74.84	82.73	84.10
Uygur	104.84	102.56	102.15	98.34	100.40	100.56
Uzbek	104.59	102.37	101.94	98.00	100.20	100.39
Va	101.34	102.75	102.59	85.79	100.10	100.29
Xibe	101.38	99.76	101.64	81.88	99.28	99.73
Yao	101.93	103.01	100.99	82.96	101.12	103.36
Yi	101.30	104.13	102.71	86.57	100.55	100.79
Yugur	103.74	104.93	101.41	98.72	101.86	102.57
Zhuang	101.69	103.75	100.85	78.96	100.87	103.25

Table 5.13 Price indices for means of agricultural production by category (preceding year=100) (II)

Ethnic group	Chemical fertilizer	Pesticide and its appliances	Oil for farm machinery	Other means of agricultural production	Service for agricultural production
National average	107.4	104.8	112.6	101.3	102.8
Achang	108.42	103.38	109.46	102.61	102.79
Bai	107.64	103.02	109.44	102.07	102.33
Baonan	108.22	101.36	111.51	101.03	103.81
Blang	108.14	103.12	109.18	102.35	102.52
Buyi	103.94	100.19	107.68	99.41	100.23
Dai	108.36	103.32	109.41	102.57	102.75
Daur	105.75	102.47	111.44	100.00	101.36
Deang	108.42	103.36	109.44	102.62	102.78
Derung	105.71	101.06	107.49	99.96	100.37
Dong	104.75	101.84	109.98	100.08	101.27
Dongxiang	108.62	101.22	111.58	101.14	104.03
Ewenki	106.11	101.44	111.47	98.63	100.31
Gaoshan	101.42	98.30	106.43	95.25	96.68
Gelao	103.69	99.96	107.45	99.21	100.03
Han	100.97	98.43	105.85	95.24	96.42
Hani	108.36	103.32	109.39	102.56	102.73
Hezhe	103.00	103.49	109.91	101.43	101.83
Hui	103.12	98.62	107.23	95.79	97.75
Jing	106.32	102.86	112.44	100.78	105.77

(continued)

Table 5.13 (continued)

Ethnic group	Chemical fertilizer	Pesticide and its appliances	Oil for farm machinery	Other means of agricultural production	Service for agricultural production
Jingpo	108.41	103.38	109.46	102.61	102.79
Jino	108.22	103.18	109.25	102.44	102.60
Kazak	111.85	101.70	112.38	101.02	105.32
Kirgiz	111.80	101.75	112.39	101.05	105.31
Korean	105.05	101.57	110.49	97.53	99.86
Lahu	108.36	103.32	109.40	102.55	102.72
Lhoba	99.51	99.22	105.25	100.82	99.13
Li	106.42	102.20	112.07	101.09	100.00
Lisu	108.39	103.40	109.51	102.62	102.84
Manchu	103.40	100.16	109.58	98.02	99.14
Maonan	105.75	102.20	111.32	100.47	104.53
Miao	99.29	96.25	103.62	94.79	95.64
Monba	98.91	98.81	104.73	100.60	98.78
Mongol	106.13	101.31	111.46	98.53	100.34
Mulao	106.03	102.56	111.99	100.59	105.32
Naxi	108.19	103.22	109.34	102.47	102.68
Nu	108.26	103.32	109.40	102.57	102.72
Oroqen	104.99	102.94	111.16	100.49	101.51
Pumi	108.36	103.34	109.44	102.56	102.75
Qiang	106.74	103.55	111.03	102.23	104.18
Russian	107.44	99.69	109.87	98.11	101.27
Salar	105.83	105.88	112.33	98.32	101.59
She	105.73	103.95	110.74	100.82	100.76
Shui	104.15	100.37	107.93	99.56	100.51
Tajik	111.07	101.18	111.74	100.44	104.64
Tatar	110.44	100.72	111.21	99.99	104.11
Tibetan	103.60	102.43	109.07	101.16	101.65
Tu	105.80	105.73	112.25	98.54	101.64
Tujia	86.16	84.44	91.82	82.50	82.99
Uygur	111.80	101.67	112.34	100.97	105.27
Uzbek	111.50	101.49	112.11	100.77	105.03
Va	108.06	103.12	109.13	102.22	102.45
Xibe	105.75	101.10	112.17	99.92	102.18
Yao	106.43	103.61	112.63	101.18	104.63
Yi	107.44	103.05	109.68	102.14	102.88
Yugur	107.84	100.84	111.07	100.74	103.47
Zhuang	106.62	103.09	112.56	101.03	106.01

Table 5.14 Producer price indices for farm products

Ethnic group	General index	Planting products	Forestry products	Animal husbandry	Fishery products
National average	**99.1**	**101.2**	**98.9**	**95.6**	**102.6**
Achang	96.93	100.65	105.82	89.05	100.25
Bai	96.40	100.54	104.42	88.93	99.82
Baonan	101.69	101.39	4.71	102.28	94.24
Blang	96.93	100.65	105.75	89.06	100.19
Buyi	93.00	101.41	97.05	86.15	99.37
Dai	96.94	100.66	105.82	89.08	100.25
Daur	101.75	104.54	102.38	95.99	99.49
Deang	96.92	100.65	105.78	89.02	100.22
Derung	97.63	101.08	103.56	90.60	100.03
Dong	94.31	100.22	98.88	88.60	98.91
Dongxiang	102.21	102.00	13.46	102.62	95.23
Ewenki	101.84	105.04	100.76	97.90	99.26
Gaoshan	99.78	101.78	98.18	95.53	80.62
Gelao	92.87	101.44	96.91	86.01	99.37
Han	100.18	101.75	96.36	96.38	94.34
Hani	96.93	100.66	105.85	89.03	100.26
Hezhe	101.06	103.30	102.01	90.73	98.79
Hui	101.74	102.46	60.18	100.06	92.22
Jing	97.25	99.33	102.53	91.74	103.12
Jingpo	96.93	100.66	105.79	89.05	100.23
Jino	96.94	100.68	105.79	89.04	100.27
Kazak	106.31	105.94	120.91	106.20	107.70
Kirgiz	106.26	105.92	121.04	106.04	107.64
Korean	104.38	107.80	104.94	93.75	96.80
Lahu	96.93	100.65	105.84	89.05	100.03
Lhoba	9.17	9.49	9.02	8.74	9.13
Li	97.09	97.57	90.83	95.30	102.36
Lisu	97.04	100.69	105.69	89.34	100.30
Manchu	103.64	105.44	101.05	99.81	103.10
Maonan	95.98	99.87	100.90	90.12	102.18
Miao	94.88	100.72	99.11	88.96	99.09
Monba	5.00	5.08	4.42	4.81	4.91
Mongol	102.19	105.05	99.88	98.82	98.88
Mulao	96.76	99.54	101.81	91.19	102.81
Naxi	96.65	100.30	105.20	88.96	99.86
Nu	95.60	99.24	104.25	87.87	98.90

(continued)

Table 5.14 (continued)

Ethnic group	General index	Planting products	Forestry products	Animal husbandry	Fishery products
Oroqen	101.47	104.16	102.01	94.33	99.17
Pumi	96.93	100.63	105.67	89.09	100.17
Qiang	100.13	101.74	101.13	98.59	101.00
Russian	104.28	105.40	110.13	102.66	103.78
Salar	100.48	97.79	5.53	104.84	99.25
She	100.84	101.37	105.31	94.78	103.99
Shui	93.13	101.35	97.38	86.28	99.54
Tajik	106.08	105.80	120.05	105.84	107.33
Tatar	105.91	105.66	114.73	105.68	106.74
Tibetan	55.37	55.18	27.32	55.89	54.86
Tu	100.31	97.95	9.53	104.11	99.12
Tujia	96.23	100.56	98.60	91.21	99.06
Uygur	106.28	105.93	121.09	106.16	107.64
Uzbek	106.18	105.85	120.42	106.00	107.51
Va	97.00	100.68	105.68	89.22	99.89
Xibe	104.01	105.42	106.98	101.56	104.54
Yao	96.98	99.14	102.24	92.18	101.09
Yi	97.37	101.05	103.54	91.34	100.32
Yugur	101.79	101.63	4.26	102.18	94.11
Zhuang	97.39	99.33	102.85	91.92	103.15

6

Education, Science and Technological Progress

Data in this chapter show the development of China's education and the basic conditions on China's scientific and technological development.

Data on education cover the situations on education funded by government and non-government agencies, and the education with and without academic credentials including higher education (education of postgraduates, general higher education and adult education), secondary education (senior and junior high schools), elementary education (primary schools), preschool education, special education (schools for the blind, deaf-mutes and mentally retarded) and their expenditure. The main indicators include the number of schools, the number of students enrolled, the number of new students enrolled, the number of graduates, the number of staff and workers, the number of full-time teachers, sources and outlay of education funding, and education expenditure from the State budget.

The Ministry of Education provides statistical data on education undertakings and education funding. Data on technical training schools are provided by Ministry of Human Resources and Social Security. Detailed information can be found in "Statistical Yearbook on China's Education" compiled by Department of Planning and Development,

R. Guo, *China Ethnic Statistical Yearbook 2020*,
https://doi.org/10.1007/978-3-030-49024-9_6

Ministry of Education; and the "Statistical Yearbook on National Education Funding" compiled by the Department of Finance, Ministry of Education.

Data on technology mainly include: data on scientific and technological activities (R&D) all over the country, including industrial enterprises, scientific and technological institutions under the government and institutions of higher education, data on domestic and foreign patents application accepted and granted, data on production, research and development activities of high-tech enterprises, data on scientific and technological papers; data on import and export trade of high-technological products; data on technological markets; main economic indicators of high and new-tech industrial enterprises in development zones; data on the scientific and technological activities in the system of associations for science and technology; data on operation institutions and activities of the polytechnic departments of meteorology, earthquake, surveying and mapping, product quality supervision, inspection and quarantine.

Data on research and development (R&D) activities of enterprises and institutions all over the country mainly include industrial enterprises above designated size, scientific research and technological development institutions and scientific and technological information and literature institutions of prefecture level and above cities under the government with independent accounting, full-time universities and colleges, affiliated hospitals and relatively R&D-intensive industries (such as agriculture, forestry, animal husbandry, fishery, construction, transport, storage and post, information transmission, software and information technology service, financial intermediation, leasing and business services, scientific research and technical services, management of water conservancy, environment and public facilities, health and social service, culture, sports and entertainment).

Data on the general national information and R&D activities of enterprises and institutions are from National Bureau of Statistics; data on scientific and technological institutions under the government are from Ministry of Science and Technology, and State Administration of Science, Technology and Industry for National Defense; data on R&D of scientific research and technical service enterprises and institutions, scientific and technological papers, technological markets information and high and new-tech industrial enterprises in development zones are from Ministry of Science and Technology; data on scientific and technological activities in institutions of higher education are from Ministry of Education; data on import and export trade of high-technological products are from General Administration of Customs; The China Association for Science and Technology provides data on the scientific and technological activities of associations for science and technology. Data on the development of surveying and mapping, meteorology, earthquake, product quality supervision and inspection and quarantine are provided separately by the State Bureau of Surveying, Mapping and Geoinformation, China Meteorological Administration, China Earthquake Administration, General Administration of Quality Supervision, Inspection and Quarantine, and State Intellectual Property Office.

Data on the Internet development come from China Telecom, China Mobile, and China Unicom.

Table 6.1 Number of students in undergraduate or specialized courses in institutions of higher education

Ethnic group	Entrants	Enrollment	Anticipated graduates for next year	Graduates with degrees or diplomas
National total	**7909931**	**28310348**	**3807417**	**7876732**
Achang	169	615	75	163
Bai	9637	34385	4132	9139
Baonan	90	316	44	83
Blang	458	1666	204	441
Buyi	18267	58246	5758	15209
Dai	5769	20982	2574	5558
Daur	722	2666	373	747
Deang	89	324	40	86
Derung	39	141	18	38
Dong	18311	60345	6486	16172
Dongxiang	2842	9952	1360	2597
Ewenki	164	608	79	174
Gaoshan	29	103	14	28
Gelao	3574	11360	1115	2963

(*continued*)

Table 6.1 (continued)

Ethnic group	Entrants	Enrollment	Anticipated graduates for next year	Graduates with degrees or diplomas
Han	7282743	26136389	3542523	7293892
Hani	7162	26058	3198	6903
Hezhe	26	97	16	27
Hui	60799	216409	28900	58713
Jing	145	484	50	128
Jingpo	658	2394	294	634
Jino	104	378	46	100
Kazak	7741	25407	2164	6208
Kirgiz	995	3269	281	800
Korean	12207	45617	7708	12397
Lahu	2259	8218	1008	2178
Lhoba	12	43	6	12
Li	8918	30874	3906	8612
Lisu	3168	11507	1410	3051
Manchu	65825	243437	40598	67161
Maonan	683	2245	227	592
Miao	54364	181744	20188	48723
Monba	34	126	19	36
Mongol	32168	118791	16012	33593
Mulao	1331	4414	452	1167
Naxi	1541	5600	688	1485
Nu	143	520	64	138
Oroqen	45	167	25	47
Pumi	167	609	75	161
Qiang	1690	5833	680	1583
Russian	93	323	35	84
Salar	471	1622	194	447
She	4557	16147	2329	4519
Shui	2499	7984	789	2084
Tajik	254	838	73	206
Tatar	30	100	9	25
Tibetan	23878	85442	11282	23595
Tu	1107	3827	465	1057
Tujia	51918	179731	22617	49399
Uygur	52028	170809	14570	41761
Uzbek	77	253	22	62
Va	1986	7221	886	1917
Xibe	1163	4264	699	1163
Yao	16491	55958	6193	15107
Yi	40818	143843	16989	38300
Yugur	75	266	38	70
Zhuang	102881	345018	36010	91453

Table 6.2 Situations on teachers and staff in regular schools (institutions) of higher education

Ethnic group	Full-time teachers	Senior	Sub-senior	Middle	Junior	No rank
National total	**1672753**	**217874**	**504719**	**655883**	**178390**	**115887**
Achang	32	3	9	12	5	3
Bai	1820	194	516	666	259	185
Baonan	19	2	6	7	2	1
Blang	88	9	24	33	13	9
Buyi	3084	300	949	914	505	416
Dai	1103	117	307	411	160	107
Daur	163	22	54	63	14	10
Deang	17	2	5	6	2	2
Derung	8	1	2	3	1	1
Dong	3215	337	966	1096	417	400
Dongxiang	591	69	192	231	66	33
Ewenki	37	4	12	14	3	3
Gaoshan	6	1	2	2	1	0
Gelao	601	58	185	177	99	82
Han	1550288	203237	468279	609973	164695	104104
Hani	1369	146	381	510	199	133
Hezhe	6	1	2	2	0	0
Hui	13519	1958	4094	4772	1686	1009
Jing	24	3	6	9	2	4
Jingpo	126	13	35	47	18	12
Jino	20	2	6	7	3	2
Kazak	1411	102	389	577	151	193
Kirgiz	182	13	50	74	19	25
Korean	2872	479	956	1077	278	82
Lahu	432	46	120	161	63	42
Lhoba	3	0	1	1	0	0
Li	1647	213	476	602	172	182
Lisu	606	64	168	226	88	58
Manchu	15773	2520	5167	6252	1238	596
Maonan	111	12	31	41	11	17
Miao	9748	1035	2906	3371	1303	1133
Monba	9	1	3	4	1	1
Mongol	7189	901	2326	2801	687	473
Mulao	217	24	60	83	18	33
Naxi	296	32	82	110	43	28
Nu	27	3	8	10	4	3
Oroqen	10	2	4	4	1	1

(*continued*)

Table 6.2 (continued)

Ethnic group	Full-time teachers	Senior	Sub-senior	Middle	Junior	No rank
Pumi	32	3	9	12	5	3
Qiang	325	36	88	124	56	21
Russian	19	2	6	8	2	2
Salar	108	16	34	31	17	10
She	960	123	289	388	103	57
Shui	421	41	129	126	68	57
Tajik	47	3	13	19	5	6
Tatar	6	0	2	2	1	1
Tibetan	5577	635	1659	2044	852	386
Tu	249	37	79	73	38	23
Tujia	10062	1212	3094	3777	1086	893
Uygur	9487	687	2614	3878	1012	1295
Uzbek	14	1	4	6	1	2
Va	380	40	106	142	55	37
Xibe	272	39	88	112	22	12
Yao	2847	319	791	1121	239	377
Yi	7692	821	2149	2816	1194	712
Yugur	16	2	5	6	2	1
Zhuang	16813	1854	4549	6623	1279	2508

Table 6.3 Statistics on Secondary Vocational Schools

Ethnic group	Schools (unit)	Educational Personnel	Full-time Teachers	Graduates	With Professional Qualification Certificates	Entrants	Enrolment	Estimated Graduates for Next Year
National total	**7850**	**799593**	**635461**	**3969770**	**2997739**	**4285024**	**12136280**	**4056047**
Achang	0	20	17	114	74	148	404	127
Bai	15	1096	912	6392	4247	8064	22140	6980
Baonan	0	11	9	41	34	51	133	42
Blang	1	54	45	308	199	401	1093	343
Buyi	16	1781	1472	12728	9011	13927	39450	12741
Dai	10	683	572	3892	2522	5066	13799	4328
Daur	1	91	68	321	194	299	943	322
Deang	0	11	9	60	39	78	214	67
Derung	0	5	4	25	16	31	85	27
Dong	17	1759	1418	11604	8300	13017	36875	11882
Dongxiang	4	349	291	1291	1075	1643	4252	1332
Ewenki	0	23	17	78	46	73	232	79
Gaoshan	0	3	2	15	11	17	47	16
Gelao	3	346	286	2494	1765	2723	7718	2492
Han	7116	732159	582211	3604842	2755907	3844339	10921688	3668125
Hani	13	849	711	4828	3123	6292	17145	5373
Hezhe	0	3	2	9	6	7	25	9
Hui	69	6543	5224	33694	23171	39650	108337	34654
Jing	0	14	10	94	57	123	338	108
Jingpo	1	78	65	444	287	578	1574	493
Jino	0	12	10	70	45	91	249	78

(*continued*)

Table 6.3 (continued)

Ethnic group	Schools (unit)	Educational Personnel	Full-time Teachers	Graduates	With Professional Qualification Certificates	Entrants	Enrolment	Estimated Graduates for Next Year
Kazak	11	925	724	4634	3189	6815	17155	4954
Kirgiz	1	119	93	594	408	871	2194	634
Korean	16	1208	913	3529	1984	2947	10037	3625
Lahu	4	268	224	1522	985	1982	5402	1693
Lhoba	0	2	2	6	1	11	26	8
Li	12	1022	738	5448	1743	7188	19450	5788
Lisu	6	375	313	2140	1402	2767	7523	2371
Manchu	81	7306	5530	26678	16376	24874	78705	27906
Maonan	1	66	51	455	289	572	1579	505
Miao	55	5307	4314	34195	24339	38659	108782	34972
Monba	0	6	6	18	3	33	78	23
Mongol	55	4314	3255	15443	9244	15148	46821	15824
Mulao	1	129	98	874	543	1127	3099	988
Naxi	3	182	153	1039	680	1345	3657	1152
Nu	0	17	14	96	62	125	341	107
Oroqen	0	5	4	19	11	16	53	18
Pumi	0	20	17	113	73	147	399	125
Qiang	2	180	141	1216	1083	1211	3054	1172
Russian	0	12	9	51	33	66	175	53
Salar	1	65	52	420	269	579	1547	427
She	4	447	377	2367	2118	2602	7343	2476
Shui	2	244	201	1739	1223	1921	5432	1752
Tajik	0	30	24	152	104	221	558	162
Tatar	0	4	3	18	12	26	65	19
Tibetan	30	3555	3088	16219	9238	22530	56618	17526

Tu	2	150	121	956	621	1296	3479	969
Tujia	45	4415	3532	24898	18667	27385	77800	24897
Uygur	72	6210	4860	31126	21424	45744	115184	33274
Uzbek	0	9	7	46	31	67	169	49
Va	3	234	196	1329	863	1724	4702	1476
Xibe	1	123	93	490	293	488	1521	513
Yao	17	1619	1238	10176	6669	12717	35258	11222
Yi	58	4579	3762	28182	20542	33317	89499	29677
Yugur	0	9	8	33	28	41	107	34
Zhuang	96	10111	7580	67049	40827	88390	241937	76881

Table 6.4 Statistics on Regular Senior Secondary Schools

Ethnic group	Schools (unit)	Educational Personnel	Full-time Teachers	Graduates	Entrants	Enrolment
National total	**13737**	**2742521**	**1812584**	**7792443**	**7927063**	**23753709**
Achang	0	74	47	206	242	692
Bai	23	4098	2671	11849	13584	39124
Baonan	0	41	30	133	116	368
Blang	1	201	128	558	655	1874
Buyi	39	7444	5540	27320	27943	83424
Dai	14	2541	1618	7034	8261	23629
Daur	2	293	194	789	732	2322
Deang	0	39	25	109	128	366
Derung	0	16	11	46	52	150
Dong	35	6691	4817	23260	24616	72593
Dongxiang	8	1324	970	4205	3657	11696
Ewenki	0	72	46	188	172	544
Gaoshan	0	10	7	29	30	90
Gelao	8	1457	1087	5374	5488	16393
Han	12431	2494622	1645101	7054298	7149727	21428237
Hani	18	3155	2011	8736	10268	29363
Hezhe	0	8	6	24	23	72
Hui	131	24540	17033	73204	72668	219493
Jing	0	45	31	153	187	529
Jingpo	2	290	185	804	944	2700
Jino	0	46	29	127	149	426
Kazak	23	4802	3027	12037	11177	37190
Kirgiz	3	614	387	1541	1431	4761
Korean	19	3280	2299	9687	9333	29467
Lahu	6	994	634	2754	3236	9255
Lhoba	0	7	6	22	25	70
Li	19	4474	2219	9495	9506	28366
Lisu	8	1390	884	3848	4500	12884
Manchu	111	19928	14014	56240	55068	171742
Maonan	1	229	163	805	932	2678
Miao	106	20374	14273	68396	72265	213245
Monba	0	22	19	65	76	208
Mongol	72	13423	8853	35919	33528	105433
Mulao	2	427	299	1474	1758	5006
Naxi	4	677	431	1874	2191	6273
Nu	0	63	41	175	206	588
Oroqen	0	17	11	46	43	136
Pumi	0	74	47	204	239	684
Qiang	3	648	373	1791	1725	5193

(continued)

Table 6.4 (continued)

Ethnic group	Schools (unit)	Educational Personnel	Full-time Teachers	Graduates	Entrants	Enrolment
Russian	0	50	32	127	118	385
Salar	2	300	209	848	894	2691
She	10	1870	1088	4500	4633	13883
Shui	5	1010	751	3701	3811	11354
Tajik	1	155	98	390	363	1206
Tatar	0	18	12	46	43	142
Tibetan	76	13433	10135	38692	42108	120742
Tu	5	678	473	1931	2031	6099
Tujia	81	16007	10858	50574	52484	155347
Uygur	156	32216	20303	80747	75012	249532
Uzbek	0	47	30	118	110	366
Va	5	868	554	2410	2823	8080
Xibe	2	387	277	1106	1029	3314
Yao	28	5406	3631	17244	20252	57830
Yi	90	17123	10866	49395	54155	157729
Yugur	0	34	25	110	95	302
Zhuang	176	32616	22295	108867	133248	376629

Table 6.5 Statistics on Regular Junior Secondary Schools

Ethnic group	Schools (unit)	Full-time Teachers	City	Township	Rural	Enrolment	City	Township	Rural
National total	**51982**	**3638999**	**1296529**	**1779144**	**563326**	**46525854**	**16918809**	**23122983**	**6484062**
Achang	1	106	21	55	31	1489	288	787	414
Bai	78	5843	1179	3099	1564	81920	16549	44397	20973
Baonan	1	53	12	29	13	588	148	324	117
Blang	4	287	56	148	83	4028	782	2128	1119
Buyi	166	10704	2324	6705	1675	150632	32304	95716	22611
Dai	46	3615	699	1868	1048	50802	9821	26851	14131
Daur	5	343	137	166	40	3699	1567	1771	361
Deang	1	56	11	29	16	788	151	416	220
Derung	0	23	5	12	6	313	70	163	79
Dong	156	9722	2315	5820	1587	136720	32725	83169	20826
Dongxiang	30	1719	376	908	435	18733	4784	10006	3943
Ewenki	1	77	31	40	6	841	358	427	56
Gaoshan	0	14	4	7	2	180	60	93	27
Gelao	33	2096	454	1318	325	29515	6312	18816	4387
Han	47361	3301764	1201955	1603849	495960	42128152	15669737	20774038	5684377
Hani	57	4494	869	2321	1305	63164	12193	33373	17598
Hezhe	0	12	5	5	2	123	56	53	15
Hui	446	32545	10291	15688	6565	413310	137645	203453	72211
Jing	1	71	17	44	10	1082	259	675	148
Jingpo	5	413	80	213	120	5802	1123	3067	1613
Jino	1	65	13	34	19	916	177	484	255
Kazak	63	5816	1480	2280	2056	62545	18547	24407	19591
Kirgiz	8	745	190	292	262	8009	2383	3125	2501

Korean	80	4766	2046	1890	830	48964	22870	19195	6899
Lahu	18	1416	274	732	411	19908	3849	10520	5539
Lhoba	0	12	3	7	2	144	30	85	30
Li	66	4334	1630	2135	569	58369	24777	27067	6525
Lisu	25	1970	385	1020	566	27635	5395	14626	7614
Manchu	394	27241	12284	11160	3796	302677	137198	127203	38276
Maonan	5	352	82	220	50	5265	1210	3328	727
Miao	448	28899	6979	16893	5027	403637	98168	239570	65899
Monba	0	36	8	21	6	434	90	255	89
Mongol	193	15148	5937	7607	1604	168386	69434	83085	15868
Mulao	9	664	162	411	91	10063	2398	6304	1361
Naxi	12	960	188	497	275	13449	2629	7118	3702
Nu	1	90	18	47	26	1263	246	668	348
Oroqen	0	21	9	10	2	221	97	104	20
Pumi	1	105	20	54	30	1471	286	777	408
Qiang	14	766	211	430	124	9785	2877	5563	1345
Russian	1	59	18	25	16	637	214	269	155
Salar	6	356	97	182	77	4687	1309	2461	917
She	29	2135	807	1001	327	28116	11459	12996	3660
Shui	22	1460	315	915	230	20604	4392	13095	3116
Tajik	2	188	48	74	66	2035	607	800	628
Tatar	0	22	6	9	8	239	71	95	73
Tibetan	242	18840	4589	10722	3529	233928	55481	133370	45077
Tu	13	810	224	416	170	10698	3033	5636	2028
Tujia	351	22004	6895	11709	3399	294424	94980	158126	41318
Uygur	425	39032	9949	15302	13781	419916	124657	163884	131375

(continued)

Table 6.5 (continued)

Ethnic group	Schools (unit)	Full-time Teachers	City	Township	Rural	Enrolment	City	Township	Rural
Uzbek	1	57	15	22	20	617	184	241	191
Va	16	1237	244	639	355	17354	3413	9165	4776
Xibe	7	531	232	198	101	5471	2517	2014	940
Yao	115	8073	2146	4633	1295	118547	31434	69221	17892
Yi	334	23317	5018	12640	5660	320965	69711	177212	74041
Yugur	1	44	10	24	10	482	122	266	94
Zhuang	646	50808	12586	30893	7329	774613	187694	476987	109932

Table 6.6 Statistics on Regular Primary Schools

Ethnic group	Schools (unit)	Full-time Teachers	City	Township	Rural	Enrolment	City	Township	Rural
National total	**161811**	**6091908**	**2002078**	**2225601**	**1864229**	**103392541**	**37221569**	**39506834**	**26664138**
Achang	9	183	31	50	102	3040	597	868	1576
Bai	443	9953	1784	3002	5166	168200	34738	53509	79953
Baonan	4	96	17	35	44	1295	316	528	452
Blang	23	494	84	136	275	8222	1618	2350	4254
Buyi	580	17410	3522	7315	6574	310885	69877	140640	100368
Dai	296	6236	1049	1715	3471	103680	20332	29628	53720
Daur	9	542	183	234	124	7191	2959	3049	1183
Deang	5	97	16	27	54	1607	313	458	836
Derung	2	39	8	11	20	645	146	195	303
Dong	494	15913	3650	6636	5627	289842	72526	129197	88120
Dongxiang	115	3092	554	1105	1434	42060	10145	16507	15409
Ewenki	2	129	44	60	25	1739	735	779	225
Gaoshan	1	23	7	8	8	401	132	154	115
Gelao	113	3406	688	1438	1280	60904	13674	27681	19548
Han	144144	5508817	1860052	2022217	1626548	93691247	34561211	35984235	23145801
Hani	368	7752	1302	2128	4322	128872	25228	36758	66886
Hezhe	0	15	6	6	4	192	89	75	29
Hui	1741	55747	15087	19157	21503	904835	280734	327674	296426
Jing	4	132	30	46	56	2419	599	883	937
Jingpo	34	712	120	196	396	11844	2326	3384	6134
Jino	5	112	19	31	63	1869	366	533	970
Kazak	228	10727	2050	3126	5551	164106	36751	46673	80682
Kirgiz	29	1372	263	400	708	20970	4713	5969	10289

(*continued*)

Table 6.6 (continued)

Ethnic group	Schools (unit)	Full-time Teachers	City	Township	Rural	Enrolment	City	Township	Rural
Korean	216	7262	2720	2463	2078	88513	42035	30832	15647
Lahu	116	2443	411	672	1361	40628	7963	11607	21058
Lhoba	1	25	4	7	13	361	60	107	193
Li	227	8302	2574	2946	2781	136773	53381	50870	32522
Lisu	159	3394	576	945	1873	56436	11157	16329	28950
Manchu	1087	42345	16704	14068	11573	624423	283961	203510	136952
Maonan	20	630	138	232	260	11530	2763	4490	4277
Miao	1545	47415	10839	19030	17546	847860	214280	363555	270025
Monba	3	75	12	22	41	1090	178	320	592
Mongol	500	25523	8525	10992	6007	357072	144537	148982	63553
Mulao	38	1216	279	431	507	22376	5554	8362	8460
Naxi	77	1655	282	461	913	27499	5445	7948	14107
Nu	7	156	26	43	87	2589	510	742	1338
Oroqen	1	31	11	13	6	400	176	170	54
Pumi	9	181	31	50	100	3003	591	859	1553
Qiang	22	1234	314	556	364	20777	6022	9668	5087
Russian	2	106	25	35	46	1579	436	505	638
Salar	17	606	137	229	239	10321	2619	4128	3574
She	98	3623	1375	1363	885	65838	27076	25727	13035
Shui	80	2385	479	994	912	42604	9507	19112	13985
Tajik	7	347	67	102	178	5317	1207	1523	2587
Tatar	1	41	8	12	21	622	143	179	300
Tibetan	1147	35645	6503	12074	17068	548223	112066	191809	244349
Tu	39	1376	321	521	533	23480	6167	9400	7912
Tujia	961	35171	10605	14447	10119	634484	209228	274647	150608
Uygur	1530	71972	13785	20977	37210	1101543	247098	313397	541047

Uzbek	2	105	20	31	54	1616	366	461	789
Va	100	2131	365	590	1176	35448	7058	10203	18186
Xibe	19	817	309	243	265	11920	5318	3257	3345
Yao	437	14383	3701	5120	5562	265467	73605	99722	92139
Yi	1536	39299	7509	13065	18725	661453	145548	230420	285485
Yugur	3	79	14	29	36	1058	262	433	364
Zhuang	3010	94605	21979	31934	40692	1736847	438008	616684	682155

Table 6.7 Student-Teacher Ratio by Level of Regular Schools (number of teachers=1)

Ethnic group	Primary School	Junior Secondary School	Regular Senior Secondary School	Secondary Vocational School	Regular Institution of Higher Education
National average	16.97	12.79	13.10	19.10	17.56
Achang	16.63	14.06	14.60	24.13	20.40
Bai	16.92	14.01	14.63	24.26	20.00
Baonan	13.50	10.99	12.06	14.44	17.39
Blang	16.63	14.05	14.60	24.10	20.39
Buyi	17.85	14.06	15.04	26.86	18.22
Dai	16.63	14.05	14.60	24.13	20.41
Daur	13.04	10.79	12.05	13.86	16.79
Deang	16.62	14.06	14.61	24.15	20.42
Derung	16.48	13.65	14.24	22.99	19.85
Dong	18.27	14.03	15.06	25.98	18.18
Dongxiang	13.51	10.90	12.05	14.60	17.57
Ewenki	13.35	10.93	11.73	13.53	17.23
Gaoshan	17.11	13.11	13.90	21.05	17.72
Gelao	17.88	14.08	15.08	26.99	18.20
Han	16.87	12.67	13.08	19.16	17.65
Hani	16.63	14.06	14.60	24.13	20.41
Hezhe	12.33	10.57	12.74	13.58	15.67
Hui	16.19	12.64	12.95	20.95	17.74
Jing	18.38	15.29	17.05	32.31	18.36
Jingpo	16.63	14.05	14.60	24.13	20.40
Jino	16.62	14.05	14.61	24.12	20.41
Kazak	15.30	10.75	12.29	23.70	19.00
Kirgiz	15.27	10.75	12.29	23.61	18.97
Korean	12.14	10.24	12.86	11.12	17.31
Lahu	16.63	14.06	14.60	24.11	20.40
Lhoba	14.76	12.07	10.99	13.81	15.18
Li	16.49	13.46	12.78	26.34	17.72
Lisu	16.63	14.02	14.58	24.03	20.38
Manchu	14.40	10.94	12.25	14.11	17.15
Maonan	18.31	15.02	16.63	31.24	18.30
Miao	17.91	13.93	14.91	25.19	18.42
Monba	14.61	12.01	10.81	13.26	15.06
Mongol	13.84	11.05	11.92	14.47	17.42
Mulao	18.39	15.18	16.88	31.91	18.31
Naxi	16.62	14.01	14.56	24.00	20.35

(continued)

Table 6.7 (continued)

Ethnic group	Primary School	Junior Secondary School	Regular Senior Secondary School	Secondary Vocational School	Regular Institution of Higher Education
Nu	16.60	14.01	14.53	23.92	20.30
Oroqen	12.84	10.75	12.24	13.52	16.43
Pumi	16.62	14.04	14.58	24.08	20.39
Qiang	16.84	12.78	13.93	21.65	19.31
Russian	14.65	10.86	12.02	19.57	18.29
Salar	17.07	13.17	12.87	29.88	16.08
She	18.15	13.12	12.75	20.30	16.35
Shui	17.87	14.11	15.12	27.09	18.26
Tajik	15.35	10.82	12.34	23.60	18.96
Tatar	15.26	10.80	12.27	23.13	18.89
Tibetan	15.67	12.47	12.17	19.33	16.48
Tu	17.07	13.20	12.91	29.13	16.18
Tujia	18.04	13.28	14.20	21.76	18.05
Uygur	15.31	10.76	12.29	23.70	19.00
Uzbek	15.34	10.80	12.31	23.68	18.98
Va	16.64	14.03	14.58	24.00	20.36
Xibe	14.35	10.20	11.92	16.07	17.46
Yao	18.48	14.67	16.00	28.57	18.38
Yi	16.82	13.70	14.47	23.76	19.86
Yugur	13.39	10.93	12.04	13.86	17.42
Zhuang	18.35	15.25	16.95	32.04	18.47

Table 6.8 Number of Students per 100 000 Population by Level

Ethnic group	Pre-school education	Primary education	Junior secondary	Senior secondary	Higher education
National average	3350	7438	3347	2828	2658
Achang	2987.58	7904.32	3872.30	3144.74	2171.44
Bai	3143.99	8118.01	3953.30	3242.71	2217.47
Baonan	3687.87	7351.06	3345.03	3003.75	2217.52
Blang	2987.54	7898.44	3869.36	3143.26	2174.59
Buyi	4276.69	10236.69	4962.61	4297.81	2265.85
Dai	2986.67	7897.17	3869.23	3143.07	2172.25
Daur	2264.23	4935.66	2562.75	2372.75	2174.80
Deang	2986.07	7904.72	3874.17	3145.88	2168.62
Derung	3018.32	7695.26	3735.92	3083.21	2242.29
Dong	3989.32	9332.18	4410.91	3775.70	2424.54
Dongxiang	3896.61	7527.82	3370.79	3033.07	2222.55
Ewenki	2381.36	5226.44	2535.09	2422.38	2073.42
Gaoshan	3649.19	8129.29	3659.22	3030.88	2643.77
Gelao	4305.32	10303.18	4996.04	4330.66	2265.65
Han	3309.81	7385.22	3336.80	2812.27	2671.13
Hani	2984.40	7899.57	3871.47	3143.61	2171.39
Hezhe	1575.43	3874.42	2508.45	2129.68	2497.28
Hui	3623.64	7926.94	3634.46	3083.32	2434.09
Jing	4407.80	9640.31	4315.11	3711.79	2585.67
Jingpo	2990.72	7910.14	3874.92	3147.42	2171.89
Jino	2981.92	7893.77	3869.49	3142.84	2172.34
Kazak	6357.91	9913.68	3778.61	3627.69	1956.56
Kirgiz	6312.96	9854.65	3765.86	3613.08	1960.73
Korean	1686.86	4407.73	2449.56	2119.68	2941.64
Lahu	2988.20	7904.43	3872.78	3144.37	2172.69
Lhoba	3680.31	9547.45	3827.25	2574.95	1701.20
Li	4046.67	9030.09	3859.04	3400.60	2307.58
Lisu	2988.28	7865.47	3850.66	3132.96	2177.83
Manchu	2258.60	5376.22	2625.45	2324.64	2776.54
Maonan	4431.22	9904.82	4532.85	3917.24	2500.08
Miao	3812.76	9010.97	4296.00	3681.42	2418.76
Monba	3636.03	9522.00	3794.01	2505.98	1674.40
Mongol	2566.69	5595.10	2648.87	2501.46	2196.68
Mulao	4440.06	9773.01	4402.56	3801.36	2554.89
Naxi	2992.50	7871.26	3849.55	3130.60	2177.93
Nu	3001.62	7923.97	3866.03	3131.91	2167.21
Oroqen	1964.75	4527.48	2518.53	2270.14	2279.33
Pumi	2986.30	7889.72	3864.00	3139.16	2174.79

(continued)

Table 6.8 (continued)

Ethnic group	Pre-school education	Primary education	Junior secondary	Senior secondary	Higher education
Qiang	3151.51	6718.36	3164.97	2807.21	2411.59
Russian	4713.42	8020.20	3267.18	3116.75	2077.78
Salar	3682.69	8073.08	3669.17	3589.16	1569.07
She	3971.77	8008.08	3424.59	2821.37	2414.04
Shui	4274.62	10217.34	4943.99	4278.28	2274.81
Tajik	6255.44	9828.51	3765.90	3604.41	1980.37
Tatar	6122.59	9685.14	3728.62	3560.53	2008.50
Tibetan	3502.15	8402.21	3607.70	2870.04	1842.38
Tu	3620.71	8033.37	3662.76	3547.01	1630.62
Tujia	3371.61	7589.31	3526.23	3017.32	2758.26
Uygur	6350.78	9908.46	3777.55	3625.20	1959.42
Uzbek	6309.34	9879.59	3771.82	3614.62	1972.62
Va	2994.92	7895.18	3864.89	3139.76	2182.06
Xibe	2870.72	5518.47	2573.62	2463.68	2683.28
Yao	4015.79	8971.72	4015.93	3418.30	2563.02
Yi	3176.59	7837.59	3800.44	3182.09	2248.23
Yugur	3645.50	7282.87	3322.85	2969.50	2260.00
Zhuang	4361.11	9571.00	4272.44	3673.45	2568.41

Table 6.9 Basic statistics on educational funds (10000 yuan)

Ethnic group	Government appropriation for education	Budgetary (Public Expenditure on Education)	Funds from private schools	Donations and fund-raising for running schools	Income from teaching research and other auxiliary activity	Tuition and miscellaneous fees	Other educational funds
Achang	9204.91	7924.89	50.23	16.99	1125.08	912.05	261.28
Bai	495223.25	431935.95	2941.11	837.27	63894.02	51613.24	19880.76
Baonan	4424.40	3941.45	6.25	2.29	367.25	294.40	108.06
Blang	24910.58	21448.65	135.16	46.11	3049.59	2471.93	705.48
Buyi	825861.85	762784.47	6613.51	764.89	105491.83	82794.70	112627.99
Dai	313951.99	270297.82	1698.88	580.75	38390.96	31118.25	8892.28
Daur	34583.19	29155.18	76.24	21.45	3640.65	3045.58	840.67
Deang	4866.94	4189.61	26.14	8.97	591.13	479.09	137.77
Derung	1990.23	1718.96	11.04	3.43	260.55	211.65	56.57
Dong	729446.93	676614.60	6230.73	677.97	118630.06	94609.27	71269.54
Dongxiang	140848.10	125960.65	170.56	68.79	11226.50	9009.67	3486.41
Ewenki	8604.30	7053.55	22.76	6.76	878.31	727.61	246.64
Gaoshan	1122.21	999.41	8.64	1.69	212.92	175.42	32.01
Gelao	161252.81	149086.23	1295.18	146.15	20527.32	16101.16	22382.73
Han	284942890.72	256207090.36	2089884.23	460497.73	56702475.82	46734459.01	7238972.80
Hani	390399.44	336108.79	2106.89	721.80	47644.56	38620.82	11080.56
Hezhe	939.85	845.44	2.04	0.32	135.30	116.38	8.99
Hui	3023134.14	2658285.66	12954.20	3712.51	370712.53	300411.71	83766.20
Jing	5225.32	4789.49	36.43	5.47	917.54	737.03	108.64
Jingpo	35837.83	30862.28	194.19	66.04	4381.44	3552.40	1025.74
Jino	5668.50	4879.13	30.55	10.48	691.48	560.49	160.52

Kazak	532936.48	488264.33	357.41	162.46	21797.06	15927.40	17426.43
Kirgiz	68198.49	62476.34	46.38	20.81	2820.75	2067.05	2223.03
Korean	404028.72	363511.84	1429.96	246.08	69477.30	59271.77	6201.59
Lahu	122877.22	105794.61	664.96	227.21	15028.01	12184.03	3477.86
Lhoba	2508.00	2298.31	0.66	1.76	35.38	26.94	7.67
Li	444850.61	361760.55	16464.69	170.05	79343.43	63257.11	11969.04
Lisu	170596.62	146973.68	929.73	316.66	21058.61	17064.27	4779.73
Manchu	2279678.39	1986355.72	6718.21	1072.51	433865.88	358246.16	25643.64
Maonan	26061.41	23995.68	187.67	25.23	4188.64	3342.68	1521.22
Miao	2250740.12	2050577.30	19391.69	2604.65	354278.81	282333.32	198202.44
Monba	7800.58	7144.88	1.19	5.45	99.65	75.63	14.71
Mongol	1603403.11	1331148.59	4442.51	1216.92	180376.17	148104.42	45062.77
Mulao	49153.33	45154.90	349.05	50.37	8468.42	6795.49	1804.75
Naxi	83988.48	72410.25	452.19	154.49	10255.67	8307.87	2336.44
Nu	8056.86	6961.80	41.71	14.47	948.07	768.35	218.89
Oroqen	1957.36	1669.60	4.49	1.15	234.31	198.01	39.55
Pumi	9108.86	7845.34	49.12	16.80	1113.88	902.96	256.81
Qiang	59279.11	52458.20	493.10	136.68	11497.53	9190.48	934.41
Russian	5825.02	5166.35	8.06	2.90	380.14	298.52	180.73
Salar	43909.18	38577.34	159.09	29.59	2519.88	1703.15	1711.55
She	204079.16	187216.81	1995.29	591.02	44406.28	36244.36	9026.61
Shui	112375.03	103761.73	884.86	104.90	14342.80	11256.15	14933.76
Tajik	17244.51	15787.85	14.18	5.66	758.12	559.98	559.94
Tatar	2040.13	1865.40	1.73	0.69	93.97	69.96	65.53
Tibetan	3078837.01	2789769.37	4506.24	2540.72	111864.47	84470.63	30218.87
Tu	97939.16	86024.24	386.54	73.14	6389.98	4473.60	3858.00
Tujia	1765137.98	1603282.19	17088.61	2246.19	357657.33	287718.58	92083.78
Uygur	3576524.77	3276694.79	2452.41	1099.97	147580.47	107996.17	116862.02

(continued)

Table 6.9 (continued)

Ethnic group	Government appropriation for education	Budgetary (Public Expenditure on Education)	Funds from private schools	Donations and fund-raising for running schools	Income from teaching research and other auxiliary activity	Tuition and miscellaneous fees	Other educational funds
Uzbek	5251.45	4808.59	4.29	1.69	226.68	167.04	170.84
Va	107053.17	92245.68	584.57	197.24	13235.56	10739.33	3015.24
Xibe	45072.98	39128.38	72.80	13.56	7240.86	5823.40	763.88
Yao	604951.92	553298.60	4948.96	735.43	120451.36	97911.86	13602.66
Yi	1942470.00	1697561.66	12311.95	3551.26	268000.34	215516.74	76274.31
Yugur	3591.86	3199.20	4.87	1.89	313.39	253.08	84.02
Zhuang	3791793.38	3457812.95	26489.24	4315.58	674724.46	544255.68	67113.59

Table 6.10 Statistics on R&D Activities and Patents of Industrial Enterprises

Ethnic group	Full-time Equivalent of R&D Personnel (man-year)	Expenditure on R&D (10 000 yuan)	R&D Projects (unit)	Number of Patent Applications (piece)	Inventions	Number of Inventions In Force (piece)
National total	**2981234**	**129548264**	**472299**	**957298**	**371569**	**1094200**
Achang	20	900	4	5	2	6
Bai	1292	57492	215	346	126	382
Baonan	5	319	1	2	1	2
Blang	56	2482	10	15	5	15
Buyi	2109	79397	311	640	268	697
Dai	688	30586	120	180	60	190
Daur	83	4984	13	21	9	26
Deang	10	462	2	3	1	3
Derung	6	281	1	2	1	2
Dong	3224	140589	473	942	401	1124
Dongxiang	168	10227	28	73	26	70
Ewenki	23	1419	4	6	2	7
Gaoshan	9	383	1	3	1	3
Gelao	397	14933	57	122	52	136
Han	2886996	124981433	457078	928157	359901	1059331
Hani	857	38132	150	224	75	235
Hezhe	3	128	0	1	0	1
Hui	12359	634281	2224	3970	1609	4673
Jing	13	602	2	5	2	5
Jingpo	79	3497	14	21	7	22
Jino	12	546	2	3	1	3

(continued)

Table 6.10 (continued)

Ethnic group	Full-time Equivalent of R&D Personnel (man-year)	Expenditure on R&D (10 000 yuan)	R&D Projects (unit)	Number of Patent Applications (piece)	Inventions	Number of Inventions In Force (piece)
Kazak	397	30548	74	243	85	222
Kirgiz	52	3942	10	31	11	29
Korean	1345	69503	224	384	160	570
Lahu	272	12097	47	71	24	74
Lhoba	1	32	0	0	0	0
Li	417	21743	101	127	54	240
Lisu	383	17064	67	101	34	107
Manchu	12004	665126	1992	3100	1311	4867
Maonan	59	2614	9	20	8	23
Miao	9573	420403	1482	2768	1135	3200
Monba	2	88	0	1	0	1
Mongol	4830	287820	745	1266	502	1544
Mulao	131	5769	20	46	19	54
Naxi	188	8309	33	50	17	53
Nu	18	785	3	5	2	5
Oroqen	5	300	1	1	1	2
Pumi	20	903	4	5	2	6
Qiang	295	12945	45	99	40	135
Russian	10	618	2	4	1	4
Salar	30	1746	5	19	7	15
She	3182	114934	555	867	264	708
Shui	272	10497	40	83	35	91
Tajik	15	1099	3	9	3	8

Tatar	2	137	0	1	0	1
Tibetan	2134	94652	323	766	300	901
Tu	119	5701	20	60	23	53
Tujia	13672	643641	2110	3834	1589	4424
Uygur	2747	208594	508	1653	579	1522
Uzbek	5	324	1	3	1	2
Va	250	11274	44	66	23	69
Xibe	203	11581	35	54	23	85
Yao	3388	145631	482	1129	478	1441
Yi	5431	236773	884	1597	599	1902
Yugur	5	284	1	2	1	2
Zhuang	10889	479738	1650	3951	1629	4749

Table 6.11 Three Kinds of Domestic Patent Applications and Granted (piece)

Ethnic group	Applications	Inventions	Utility Models	Designs	Granted	Inventions	Utility Models	Designs
National total	**4146772**	**1393815**	**2063860**	**689097**	**2335411**	**345959**	**1471759**	**517693**
Achang	31	8	20	3	17	2	13	2
Bai	1905	555	1148	201	1029	126	749	154
Baonan	18	4	11	3	9	1	7	1
Blang	84	22	53	8	47	5	35	6
Buyi	4217	1403	2365	448	1946	216	1355	374
Dai	1043	279	666	98	581	67	440	74
Daur	129	40	76	13	74	13	52	9
Deang	16	4	10	1	9	1	7	1
Derung	9	3	5	1	5	1	4	1
Dong	4658	1630	2380	648	2300	315	1481	503
Dongxiang	557	124	348	86	287	27	219	41
Ewenki	29	8	18	3	17	2	12	2
Gaoshan	13	4	6	2	7	1	5	2
Gelao	811	270	456	85	371	41	258	71
Han	3968075	1327596	1974870	665609	2235790	326704	1409671	499415
Hani	1291	344	827	120	719	82	546	91
Hezhe	6	2	3	1	4	1	2	0
Hui	21303	7542	11550	2210	11845	2071	8129	1645
Jing	27	11	12	4	13	2	8	3
Jingpo	119	32	76	11	66	8	50	8
Jino	19	5	12	2	10	1	8	1
Kazak	1002	253	646	104	659	64	502	93
Kirgiz	130	33	83	13	85	8	65	12
Korean	2700	1049	1399	253	1463	317	959	187
Lahu	408	109	261	38	227	26	172	29
Lhoba	2	1	1	0	1	0	1	0
Li	1177	386	611	180	604	87	377	140

Lisu	584	158	369	56	326	38	245	43
Manchu	18845	7319	9567	1960	10558	2305	6824	1429
Maonan	130	52	61	17	62	10	38	13
Miao	13812	4684	7309	1819	7048	946	4656	1446
Monba	7	2	3	1	4	0	2	1
Mongol	6273	1945	3655	673	3583	532	2545	505
Mulao	270	110	120	41	133	23	80	30
Naxi	289	79	181	28	162	19	121	22
Nu	27	7	17	3	15	2	11	2
Oroqen	9	3	5	1	5	1	4	1
Pumi	31	8	20	3	17	2	13	2
Qiang	575	202	275	98	328	44	200	84
Russian	18	6	10	2	11	2	8	2
Salar	107	32	66	9	63	8	48	6
She	4057	1080	2144	833	2496	260	1576	660
Shui	557	187	312	57	254	29	178	47
Tajik	36	9	23	4	23	2	17	3
Tatar	5	1	3	1	3	0	2	0
Tibetan	5569	1764	2894	911	3097	370	1979	748
Tu	297	86	177	34	173	20	128	25
Tujia	16130	5746	8223	2160	8783	1344	5730	1709
Uygur	6821	1734	4376	712	4479	440	3402	637
Uzbek	11	3	7	1	7	1	5	1
Va	370	100	235	35	207	24	156	27
Xibe	290	111	152	27	161	33	109	20
Yao	4730	1684	2145	901	2537	386	1486	665
Yi	9443	2942	5309	1192	5192	639	3566	986
Yugur	16	4	10	2	8	1	6	1
Zhuang	21395	8559	9349	3488	10841	1894	6400	2547

Table 6.12 Transaction value in technical markets (10000 yuan)

Ethnic group	2005	2006	2007	2008	2009	2010	2011	2012	2018
National total	15513694	18181813	22265261	26652288	30390024	39065753	47635589	64370683	**176974213**
Achang	131	71	84	48	90	98	108	379	764.31
Bai	7464	5032	5847	4568	6594	7598	8638	21490	57328.46
Baonan	112	139	173	198	234	286	353	483	1231.93
Blang	357	194	227	133	244	269	292	1020	2078.70
Buyi	2426	2045	2463	3971	3962	9409	14751	13043	152633.17
Dai	4516	2496	2949	1753	3205	3494	3828	13119	26916.94
Daur	955	1098	1471	1602	2001	2702	2901	6543	6579.43
Deang	69	38	44	25	48	52	57	201	400.03
Derung	39	31	36	33	43	52	59	124	275.68
Dong	9333	9214	9935	11814	11439	15107	18643	19932	156672.25
Dongxiang	3406	4165	5038	5709	6599	8085	9867	13633	33602.55
Ewenki	216	240	284	294	388	578	582	1631	1158.27
Gaoshan	69	85	103	120	140	176	211	276	658.59
Gelao	452	410	492	810	795	1890	2947	2542	30077.76
Han	14785404	16659829	20278701	24171461	27430833	34792745	42830708	55837372	163971618.11
Hani	5586	3031	3573	2054	3834	4165	4540	16029	32298.83
Hezhe	53	68	101	118	140	167	199	281	557.99
Hui	145861	181060	228915	267075	314660	396087	497046	648207	1563092.28
Jing	63	26	31	44	43	67	84	89	510.97
Jingpo	515	283	336	200	365	400	439	1499	3043.08
Jino	82	46	55	33	60	65	71	240	486.19
Kazak	5583	5386	5159	5362	1262	3612	3636	4523	4595.12
Kirgiz	715	689	666	693	172	472	477	607	617.15
Korean	21167	25525	32415	37000	42594	49007	60490	78718	285427.49
Lahu	1744	931	1097	618	1170	1271	1384	4982	10077.14
Lhoba	4	5	6	8	9	11	13	17	44.30

Li	1872	1676	1569	6081	1459	5924	6462	2200	16750.25
Lisu	2407	1314	1552	923	1706	1840	2023	7029	15871.84
Manchu	221929	256385	314376	353603	422959	506260	612042	845671	1863071.09
Maonan	205	63	75	132	116	229	325	272	2980.52
Miao	32390	34081	33938	41635	38563	55437	63790	74181	472411.54
Monba	21	28	33	37	43	49	57	69	167.67
Mongol	51954	56986	66508	70551	89135	123587	132868	307285	335132.36
Mulao	544	242	291	435	413	647	831	827	5617.94
Naxi	1254	768	913	635	1049	1169	1311	3831	8549.94
Nu	112	62	73	44	80	88	97	324	666.82
Oroqen	69	83	116	130	160	205	229	435	572.68
Pumi	134	76	90	57	100	111	123	394	812.90
Qiang	795	1074	1265	1773	2204	2274	2807	4488	37443.93
Russian	163	197	231	257	277	379	430	721	1069.53
Salar	471	786	1377	1874	2097	2771	3897	4619	16814.58
She	4354	3827	4603	5783	6340	8580	9517	12280	44203.90
Shui	332	233	280	459	462	1196	1902	1681	19920.23
Tajik	193	190	186	197	69	151	158	197	300.70
Tatar	34	38	41	46	36	53	61	79	153.08
Tibetan	10862	15823	24298	32698	37897	46785	63767	82324	384750.09
Tu	990	1597	2841	3914	4348	5746	8136	9644	36431.44
Tujia	59835	69642	67333	85518	79040	107782	119161	145865	791836.69
Uygur	37917	36679	35244	36711	9307	25217	25543	31779	34799.02
Uzbek	63	64	65	70	33	61	67	85	134.32
Va	1578	867	1020	636	1110	1231	1347	4461	9416.16
Xibe	3567	3618	4269	4682	5472	6304	7638	10791	22255.15
Yao	11842	9146	10098	12478	11443	13808	15180	19064	96859.82
Yi	24422	17866	21076	20012	28912	31958	38463	87518	412737.24
Yugur	111	141	174	199	237	291	355	486	1168.28
Zhuang	46525	17902	21443	31578	29050	43784	53920	62727	360237.22

Table 6.13 Main indicators on Internet development (year-end)

Ethnic group	Broad band subscribers port of Internet (10000 ports)	Mobile Internet Subscribers (10 000 subscribers) Mobile Internet	Broadband subscribers of Internet (10000 subscribers)
National total	86752.3	127481.5	40738.2
Achang	1.59	3.15	0.82
Bai	86.61	171.78	44.77
Baonan	0.79	1.48	0.49
Blang	4.30	8.52	2.23
Buyi	134.67	283.20	64.08
Dai	54.15	107.40	28.06
Daur	8.04	13.12	3.45
Deang	0.83	1.66	0.43
Derung	0.38	0.70	0.19
Dong	142.19	273.60	70.83
Dongxiang	25.85	46.51	15.53
Ewenki	1.82	3.24	0.82
Gaoshan	0.31	0.45	0.14
Gelao	26.01	55.21	12.36
Han	80126.58	117193.68	37763.68
Hani	67.14	133.39	34.81
Hezhe	0.28	0.40	0.11
Hui	695.98	1045.03	319.78
Jing	1.42	2.15	0.64
Jingpo	6.17	12.25	3.19
Jino	0.97	1.94	0.51
Kazak	113.55	134.96	43.82
Kirgiz	14.57	17.32	5.62
Korean	118.97	173.79	45.71
Lahu	21.17	42.02	10.98
Lhoba	0.22	0.30	0.09
Li	116.63	149.47	45.17
Lisu	29.96	58.74	15.50
Manchu	762.80	1037.26	298.60
Maonan	6.20	10.21	2.81
Miao	441.56	828.75	219.49
Monba	0.67	0.90	0.27
Mongol	363.30	608.93	160.00
Mulao	12.73	19.95	5.72
Naxi	14.64	28.64	7.55

(*continued*)

Table 6.13 (continued)

Ethnic group	Broad band subscribers port of Internet (10000 ports)	Mobile Internet Subscribers (10 000 subscribers) Mobile Internet	Broadband subscribers of Internet (10000 subscribers)
Nu	1.36	2.67	0.70
Oroqen	0.49	0.78	0.21
Pumi	1.57	3.11	0.82
Qiang	20.08	27.35	9.75
Russian	1.24	1.70	0.50
Salar	7.45	11.78	3.31
She	67.33	83.78	32.86
Shui	18.52	38.62	8.81
Tajik	3.69	4.42	1.43
Tatar	0.43	0.53	0.17
Tibetan	374.16	538.27	165.74
Tu	16.92	27.11	7.63
Tujia	426.94	701.98	217.13
Uygur	762.72	906.66	294.37
Uzbek	1.12	1.34	0.43
Va	18.68	36.76	9.66
Xibe	14.87	18.34	5.41
Yao	156.24	254.95	74.45
Yi	400.93	713.75	201.60
Yugur	0.65	1.23	0.41
Zhuang	1021.02	1566.50	458.87

7

Health Care and Social Security

Data on public health are mainly from the Information Center under the Ministry of Health. Data on civil affairs are from the Ministry of Civil Affairs based on statistical reporting form scheme. Data on disabled persons are from the China Disabled Persons Federation. For detailed information please refer to *Annual Statistical Yearbook on National Health Care* (Ministry of Health of the People's Republic of China), *Statistical Yearbook on Civil Affairs of China* (Department of Financial and Planning, Ministry of Civil Affairs) and *China Statistical Yearbook on the Work for Persons with Disabilities* (China Disabled Persons Federation).

Data on labor and social security mainly include revenue and expenses of social insurance fund, urban employee basic pension insurance, urban basic medical care insurance, unemployment insurance, etc. Data are from the Ministry of Human Resources and Social Security.

R. Guo, *China Ethnic Statistical Yearbook 2020*,
https://doi.org/10.1007/978-3-030-49024-9_7

Table 7.1 Medical technical personnel in health care institutions per 1000 persons (person)

Ethnic group	Medical technical personnel			Licensed (assistant) doctors			Registered nurses		
	Total	City	County	Total	City	County	Total	City	County
National total	6.83	10.91	4.63	2.59	4.01	1.82	2.94	5.08	1.80
Achang	6.26	13.02	4.97	2.07	4.53	1.59	2.84	6.30	2.18
Bai	6.33	12.61	4.86	2.13	4.41	1.60	2.85	6.11	2.10
Baonan	6.07	9.70	4.20	2.29	3.50	1.65	2.48	4.54	1.46
Blang	6.26	13.00	4.97	2.07	4.53	1.60	2.84	6.29	2.18
Buyi	6.81	9.84	4.31	2.27	3.46	1.40	3.03	4.80	1.80
Dai	6.26	13.00	4.97	2.07	4.53	1.59	2.84	6.29	2.18
Daur	6.98	12.66	4.96	2.72	4.68	2.04	2.84	5.78	1.72
Deang	6.25	13.03	4.97	2.07	4.54	1.59	2.83	6.30	2.18
Derung	6.36	12.64	4.89	2.17	4.45	1.65	2.85	6.08	2.09
Dong	6.66	10.48	4.34	2.38	3.72	1.57	2.91	5.12	1.75
Dongxiang	6.11	9.91	4.34	2.30	3.60	1.69	2.50	4.61	1.55
Ewenki	7.31	13.45	5.18	2.85	4.95	2.15	2.97	6.14	1.82
Gaoshan	6.72	11.15	4.32	2.54	4.07	1.71	2.89	5.26	1.66
Gelao	6.82	9.78	4.29	2.27	3.44	1.38	3.03	4.77	1.79
Han	6.79	10.82	4.68	2.58	3.96	1.88	2.93	5.09	1.80
Hani	6.26	13.02	4.97	2.07	4.53	1.59	2.84	6.30	2.18
Hezhe	6.33	10.69	4.27	2.46	3.99	1.76	2.57	4.89	1.41
Hui	6.97	11.58	4.71	2.62	4.23	1.85	2.95	5.39	1.74
Jing	6.52	9.26	4.17	2.17	3.18	1.35	2.86	4.40	1.68
Jingpo	6.26	13.01	4.96	2.07	4.53	1.59	2.84	6.29	2.17
Jino	6.26	13.01	4.97	2.07	4.53	1.59	2.84	6.30	2.18
Kazak	7.09	14.44	6.42	2.55	5.46	2.26	2.91	6.42	2.55
Kirgiz	7.08	14.42	6.40	2.55	5.45	2.25	2.91	6.41	2.54
Korean	6.74	11.04	4.77	2.75	4.41	2.02	2.81	4.98	1.76
Lahu	6.26	13.01	4.97	2.07	4.53	1.59	2.84	6.29	2.18
Lhoba	5.67	8.68	3.81	2.43	3.81	1.59	1.75	3.17	0.93
Li	6.82	13.85	4.24	2.38	4.85	1.48	3.20	6.85	1.86
Lisu	6.27	12.90	4.96	2.08	4.50	1.60	2.84	6.24	2.17
Manchu	6.82	10.84	4.23	2.78	4.23	1.86	2.88	4.97	1.52
Maonan	6.61	9.30	4.19	2.19	3.21	1.35	2.91	4.45	1.70
Miao	6.64	10.63	4.43	2.35	3.76	1.58	2.93	5.19	1.81
Monba	5.63	8.58	3.79	2.43	3.80	1.60	1.70	3.08	0.89
Mongol	7.25	13.06	5.05	2.84	4.84	2.09	2.98	5.98	1.81
Mulao	6.57	9.25	4.18	2.19	3.18	1.35	2.88	4.40	1.68
Naxi	6.27	12.89	4.96	2.08	4.50	1.60	2.84	6.23	2.16
Nu	6.25	12.93	4.95	2.08	4.52	1.60	2.82	6.24	2.16
Oroqen	6.80	12.02	4.72	2.65	4.45	1.95	2.77	5.50	1.61

(continued)

Table 7.1 (continued)

Ethnic group	Medical technical personnel Total	City	County	Licensed (assistant) doctors Total	City	County	Registered nurses Total	City	County
Pumi	6.26	12.99	4.96	2.07	4.53	1.60	2.84	6.28	2.17
Qiang	6.75	9.10	4.73	2.46	3.21	1.77	2.97	4.39	1.89
Russian	7.24	13.98	5.84	2.69	5.23	2.19	2.97	6.28	2.22
Salar	7.23	13.77	4.88	2.63	4.69	1.90	2.87	6.49	1.55
She	6.76	11.03	4.96	2.52	4.07	1.87	2.94	5.07	2.02
Shui	6.80	9.84	4.31	2.26	3.46	1.39	3.02	4.80	1.80
Tajik	7.07	14.31	6.35	2.54	5.41	2.24	2.91	6.38	2.52
Tatar	7.06	14.17	6.25	2.55	5.35	2.22	2.90	6.32	2.46
Tibetan	6.27	9.99	4.27	2.46	3.85	1.70	2.31	4.28	1.31
Tu	7.16	13.49	4.83	2.61	4.60	1.88	2.86	6.37	1.55
Tujia	6.69	10.48	4.54	2.52	3.74	1.80	2.97	5.16	1.82
Uygur	7.09	14.44	6.42	2.55	5.46	2.26	2.91	6.42	2.54
Uzbek	7.09	14.40	6.38	2.55	5.44	2.25	2.91	6.41	2.53
Va	6.27	12.96	4.96	2.08	4.52	1.60	2.84	6.27	2.17
Xibe	6.98	11.61	4.47	2.72	4.45	1.82	3.03	5.36	1.70
Yao	6.47	10.44	4.28	2.30	3.66	1.54	2.81	5.01	1.70
Yi	6.45	11.57	4.82	2.20	4.05	1.62	2.89	5.60	2.05
Yugur	6.05	9.54	4.14	2.28	3.45	1.63	2.47	4.47	1.45
Zhuang	6.51	9.46	4.21	2.16	3.25	1.36	2.86	4.49	1.70

Table 7.2 Village clinics

Ethnic group	Village clinics (unit) Total	Run by village	Township hospitals	Jointly run	Run by private	Others	Villages with clinics as % of total
National total	622001	342062	65495	28353	141623	44468	94.0
Achang	11	8	1	0	0	1	99.89
Bai	683	465	72	27	65	54	99.85
Baonan	11	4	3	1	3	1	99.95
Blang	29	22	3	1	1	2	99.88
Buyi	1683	728	229	45	521	159	99.57
Dai	370	275	40	16	11	28	99.92
Daur	64	28	12	2	17	5	99.53
Deang	6	4	1	0	0	0	99.97
Derung	3	2	0	0	0	0	99.41
Dong	1682	890	162	44	443	143	99.62
Dongxiang	331	125	86	17	73	30	99.98
Ewenki	17	7	3	1	5	1	99.57
Gaoshan	2	1	0	0	1	0	97.25

(*continued*)

Table 7.2 (continued)

Ethnic group	Village clinics (unit) Total	Run by village	Township hospitals	Jointly run	Run by private	Others	Villages with clinics as % of total
Gelao	330	142	45	9	103	31	99.76
Han	565184	314003	55754	25959	129535	39934	94.98
Hani	458	341	50	20	13	34	99.91
Hezhe	1	1	0	0	0	0	98.84
Hui	5350	2417	935	364	1143	491	97.16
Jing	10	7	0	0	3	0	99.83
Jingpo	42	31	5	2	1	3	99.91
Jino	7	5	1	0	0	1	99.94
Kazak	687	139	369	72	35	73	99.98
Kirgiz	88	18	47	9	4	9	99.97
Korean	718	333	96	56	199	34	98.99
Lahu	145	108	16	6	4	11	99.89
Lhoba	6	2	2	0	0	1	99.72
Li	461	154	39	5	235	28	99.91
Lisu	209	152	22	9	10	15	99.89
Manchu	5546	2602	313	119	2250	262	98.87
Maonan	53	31	4	1	14	3	99.88
Miao	4734	2535	482	136	1171	410	99.62
Monba	17	7	7	0	0	2	99.61
Mongol	3256	1315	510	113	1076	243	99.55
Mulao	99	63	6	1	25	4	99.73
Naxi	103	75	12	5	5	8	99.85
Nu	10	7	1	0	0	1	99.77
Oroqen	4	2	1	0	1	0	99.38
Pumi	11	8	1	0	0	1	99.89
Qiang	207	103	13	9	69	12	99.94
Russian	9	3	3	1	1	1	99.08
Salar	92	36	15	11	19	11	99.82
She	338	194	20	7	87	30	87.03
Shui	228	100	31	6	70	21	99.79
Tajik	22	5	12	2	1	2	99.89
Tatar	3	1	1	0	0	0	99.61
Tibetan	7147	2986	2380	312	575	894	99.94
Tu	205	83	31	25	43	23	99.66
Tujia	4033	2407	374	193	736	324	99.55
Uygur	4614	938	2471	479	233	493	99.97
Uzbek	7	1	4	1	0	1	99.86
Va	129	95	14	6	4	10	99.67
Xibe	88	35	13	3	34	4	99.57
Yao	1288	858	59	21	278	72	99.93
Yi	3461	2061	325	146	684	244	99.92
Yugur	9	4	2	0	2	1	99.83
Zhuang	7275	4913	336	78	1688	260	99.90

Table 7.3 Number of beds in health institutions by urban and rural areas (bed)

Ethnic group	Beds of Medical Institutions			Beds of Medical Institutions per 1000 Population			Beds of Township Health Centers per 1000 Rural Population
	Total	Urban	Rural	Total	Urban	Rural	
National total/ average	8404088	4141427	4262661	6.03	8.70	4.56	1.43
Achang	233.23	65.85	167.37	6.03	10.34	5.22	1.32
Bai	12883.37	3791.97	9091.40	6.18	10.26	5.15	1.33
Baonan	109.84	48.08	61.76	6.22	8.92	4.69	1.36
Blang	631.64	179.05	452.59	6.03	10.33	5.22	1.33
Buyi	20654.89	6612.91	14041.98	6.76	8.61	4.55	1.15
Dai	7968.45	2253.14	5715.32	6.03	10.33	5.22	1.33
Daur	924.52	489.06	435.46	6.42	11.47	4.56	1.23
Deang	123.34	34.67	88.68	6.03	10.35	5.23	1.32
Derung	51.06	16.72	34.34	6.07	10.15	5.10	1.35
Dong	20760.25	7285.83	13474.42	6.64	9.36	4.64	1.38
Dongxiang	3514.48	1455.51	2058.97	6.28	9.03	4.86	1.38
Ewenki	208.64	106.57	102.07	6.28	11.24	4.58	1.28
Gaoshan	29.78	14.32	15.45	6.00	9.11	4.24	1.35
Gelao	4028.36	1286.92	2741.44	6.78	8.58	4.54	1.15
Han	7659091.82	3839512.72	3819579.11	6.05	8.92	4.49	1.43
Hani	9896.78	2791.74	7105.05	6.03	10.34	5.22	1.32
Hezhe	32.16	20.12	12.04	6.56	11.72	4.13	1.09
Hui	71058.87	34234.06	36824.81	6.18	9.30	4.63	1.31
Jing	133.42	57.38	76.04	5.28	6.65	3.74	1.61
Jingpo	908.21	256.54	651.67	6.03	10.34	5.22	1.32
Jino	143.69	40.58	103.11	6.03	10.34	5.23	1.32
Kazak	12102.54	2688.13	9414.41	7.19	11.29	7.11	1.51

(continued)

Table 7.3 (continued)

Ethnic group	Beds of Medical Institutions			Beds of Medical Institutions per 1000 Population			Beds of Township Health Centers per 1000 Rural Population
	Total	Urban	Rural	Total	Urban	Rural	
Kirgiz	1552.82	349.02	1203.80	7.18	11.30	7.08	1.51
Korean	12685.08	7239.88	5445.20	6.37	10.50	4.52	1.13
Lahu	3118.70	880.74	2237.96	6.03	10.34	5.22	1.32
Lhoba	19.24	9.54	9.70	5.02	7.21	3.60	1.51
Li	7465.28	3868.96	3596.31	4.90	9.41	3.22	0.92
Lisu	4371.12	1251.84	3119.28	6.06	10.28	5.24	1.35
Manchu	75693.84	45400.65	30293.19	6.61	9.95	4.57	1.33
Maonan	662.22	262.68	399.54	5.67	7.06	3.93	1.49
Miao	62851.27	22346.31	40504.96	6.64	9.38	4.78	1.42
Monba	57.65	29.31	28.34	4.95	7.11	3.54	1.51
Mongol	40541.85	20501.37	20040.48	6.39	10.91	4.70	1.31
Mulao	1248.36	525.46	722.89	5.42	6.77	3.79	1.56
Naxi	2126.61	612.41	1514.20	6.06	10.27	5.22	1.34
Nu	197.47	56.69	140.78	6.01	10.27	5.19	1.32
Oroqen	56.37	32.09	24.29	6.43	11.49	4.36	1.18
Pumi	230.99	65.63	165.36	6.03	10.33	5.22	1.32
Qiang	2224.58	948.37	1276.21	7.16	8.44	5.62	2.15
Russian	132.75	43.67	89.08	6.79	11.10	6.00	1.41
Salar	833.34	373.13	460.21	6.47	10.79	4.94	1.11
She	4406.64	2127.97	2278.67	5.29	7.91	4.14	1.07
Shui	2814.99	902.31	1912.68	6.71	8.57	4.53	1.17
Tajik	392.97	90.00	302.97	7.15	11.21	7.02	1.51
Tatar	46.29	11.09	35.19	7.10	11.12	6.89	1.50

Tibetan	37812.19	17545.82	20266.37	5.89	8.41	4.42	1.56
Tu	1883.64	855.39	1028.26	6.40	10.60	4.85	1.12
Tujia	57162.85	24414.36	32748.49	6.82	9.68	5.05	1.77
Uygur	81248.12	18089.64	63158.48	7.19	11.29	7.10	1.51
Uzbek	119.04	26.97	92.07	7.16	11.24	7.05	1.51
Va	2726.15	781.46	1944.69	6.04	10.31	5.21	1.33
Xibe	1481.69	824.27	657.42	7.10	10.63	5.19	1.43
Yao	16967.32	7031.28	9936.05	5.72	8.33	4.19	1.60
Yi	54266.96	17779.67	36487.29	6.43	9.62	5.26	1.53
Yugur	90.27	40.20	50.07	6.19	8.82	4.63	1.36
Zhuang	95993.30	41243.78	54749.53	5.24	6.74	3.77	1.61

Table 7.4 Hospitaliztion services in health institutions

Ethnic group	Number of inpatients (10000 persons)	Patients discharged (10000 persons)	Surgical operation of hospitalized (10000 person-times)	Inpatients per 100 outpatient and emergency visits (person)
National Total	**25454.3**	**25384.7**	**6171.6**	**4.5**
Achang	0.77	0.77	0.18	5.39
Bai	42.39	42.20	9.74	5.80
Baonan	0.33	0.32	0.05	6.17
Blang	2.08	2.07	0.50	5.40
Buyi	68.42	67.96	13.74	6.95
Dai	26.28	26.17	6.27	5.40
Daur	2.26	2.26	0.49	5.93
Deang	0.41	0.41	0.10	5.40
Derung	0.16	0.16	0.04	5.43
Dong	68.50	68.22	13.30	7.28
Dongxiang	10.53	10.49	1.56	6.20
Ewenki	0.51	0.51	0.11	5.42
Gaoshan	0.09	0.09	0.02	5.24
Gelao	13.36	13.27	2.67	7.00
Han	23172.25	23110.19	5690.55	5.20
Hani	32.65	32.50	7.79	5.40
Hezhe	0.08	0.08	0.02	6.83
Hui	208.42	207.75	44.21	5.18
Jing	0.48	0.48	0.10	5.33
Jingpo	3.00	2.98	0.71	5.40
Jino	0.47	0.47	0.11	5.40
Kazak	36.75	36.73	7.38	6.30
Kirgiz	4.71	4.70	0.95	6.30
Korean	30.88	30.73	6.85	5.91
Lahu	10.29	10.24	2.45	5.40
Lhoba	0.04	0.04	0.01	3.25
Li	20.22	20.23	4.41	3.39
Lisu	14.38	14.32	3.42	5.40
Manchu	188.88	187.88	43.47	5.55
Maonan	2.33	2.32	0.46	5.79
Miao	206.12	205.25	41.47	7.00
Monba	0.11	0.11	0.02	3.07
Mongol	101.23	100.93	20.97	5.40
Mulao	4.46	4.44	0.90	5.48
Naxi	6.99	6.96	1.66	5.39
Nu	0.65	0.64	0.15	5.35
Oroqen	0.14	0.14	0.03	6.15

(continued)

Table 7.4 (continued)

Ethnic group	Number of inpatients (10000 persons)	Patients discharged (10000 persons)	Surgical operation of hospitalized (10000 person-times)	Inpatients per 100 outpatient and emergency visits (person)
Pumi	0.76	0.76	0.18	5.39
Qiang	6.82	6.79	1.50	5.60
Russian	0.38	0.38	0.08	5.82
Salar	2.16	2.16	0.36	5.76
She	13.66	13.64	3.70	3.88
Shui	9.35	9.29	1.87	6.90
Tajik	1.19	1.19	0.24	6.27
Tatar	0.14	0.14	0.03	6.23
Tibetan	92.11	91.77	17.65	4.49
Tu	4.94	4.93	0.86	5.69
Tujia	185.85	185.47	38.66	7.16
Uygur	246.72	246.57	49.63	6.29
Uzbek	0.36	0.36	0.07	6.26
Va	8.98	8.94	2.14	5.40
Xibe	3.75	3.74	0.87	5.61
Yao	58.27	58.16	12.04	6.12
Yi	175.45	174.61	40.19	5.63
Yugur	0.27	0.27	0.04	6.16
Zhuang	344.62	343.66	71.26	5.22

Table 7.5 Statistics on Medical Aid

Ethnic group	Aid for Basic Medical Insurance (10 000 persons)	Outpatient and Hospitalization Medical Aid (10 000 persons)	Expenses of Aid for Basic Medical Insurance (10 000 yuan)	Expenses for Outpatient and Hospitalization Medical Aid (10 000 yuan)
National total	**6692.3**	**5361.0**	**1026748.8**	**2970236.8**
Achang	0.53	0.15	51.66	79.12
Bai	25.85	7.36	2483.53	4311.31
Baonan	0.54	0.03	45.46	66.18
Blang	1.43	0.41	139.62	214.88
Buyi	25.54	5.29	1677.38	6954.08

(*continued*)

Table 7.5 (continued)

Ethnic group	Aid for Basic Medical Insurance (10 000 persons)	Outpatient and Hospitalization Medical Aid (10 000 persons)	Expenses of Aid for Basic Medical Insurance (10 000 yuan)	Expenses for Outpatient and Hospitalization Medical Aid (10 000 yuan)
Dai	18.04	5.07	1758.92	2702.13
Daur	0.84	0.33	116.35	431.61
Deang	0.28	0.08	27.43	41.92
Derung	0.10	0.03	10.23	17.83
Dong	18.61	5.67	1507.24	6382.44
Dongxiang	16.75	0.99	1449.12	2036.62
Ewenki	0.17	0.09	19.58	104.67
Gaoshan	0.02	0.02	2.76	9.10
Gelao	4.95	0.98	316.28	1353.90
Han	5758.45	5052.01	914318.89	2687256.53
Hani	22.48	6.33	2193.69	3359.42
Hezhe	0.03	0.01	4.80	12.10
Hui	123.08	39.45	14592.23	31969.76
Jing	0.10	0.03	12.80	29.43
Jingpo	2.06	0.58	200.77	307.91
Jino	0.33	0.09	31.83	48.80
Kazak	25.11	2.84	4473.47	6109.59
Kirgiz	3.20	0.37	571.20	782.21
Korean	10.46	4.60	1268.67	4012.64
Lahu	7.07	1.99	689.92	1057.80
Lhoba	0.02	0.01	0.59	22.66
Li	7.30	10.26	1281.60	2432.37
Lisu	9.70	2.75	943.31	1475.94
Manchu	36.27	30.53	3303.58	18746.20
Maonan	0.59	0.11	58.43	165.01
Miao	67.11	27.63	5891.06	20847.55
Monba	0.04	0.02	1.26	70.16
Mongol	33.36	16.49	3766.97	18601.68
Mulao	0.99	0.21	113.54	287.39
Naxi	4.71	1.34	458.06	726.92
Nu	0.44	0.13	43.05	69.55
Oroqen	0.05	0.02	6.74	24.53
Pumi	0.52	0.15	50.92	78.50
Qiang	1.36	0.75	77.01	656.70
Russian	0.22	0.04	36.41	65.84
Salar	1.50	0.34	286.08	720.48
She	2.66	6.52	602.53	1896.43

(continued)

Table 7.5 (continued)

Ethnic group	Aid for Basic Medical Insurance (10 000 persons)	Outpatient and Hospitalization Medical Aid (10 000 persons)	Expenses of Aid for Basic Medical Insurance (10 000 yuan)	Expenses for Outpatient and Hospitalization Medical Aid (10 000 yuan)
Shui	3.50	0.71	233.66	935.82
Tajik	0.80	0.10	142.85	197.15
Tatar	0.10	0.01	16.81	23.27
Tibetan	47.65	14.46	5030.37	32745.63
Tu	3.40	0.79	625.56	1585.37
Tujia	37.52	39.83	4883.91	20757.63
Uygur	167.82	19.12	29952.79	40954.56
Uzbek	0.24	0.03	43.59	59.80
Va	6.09	1.74	595.26	922.33
Xibe	1.17	0.47	144.18	437.65
Yao	12.45	4.33	1528.90	4292.71
Yi	91.09	27.56	8244.03	17699.15
Yugur	0.46	0.03	37.28	53.01
Zhuang	80.82	18.50	9980.86	21290.38

Table 7.6 Beds of Civil Affairs Institutions with Accommodations (10000 bed)

Ethnic group	Number of Beds	The Aged	Child Welfare and Assistance	Mental Illness	Other	Beds in Elderly Care Institutions per 1 000 Senior Citizens (bed)
National total	**408.1**	**379.4**	**9.7**	**6.3**	**12.7**	**29.15**
Achang	0.01	0.00	0.00	0.00	0.00	0.01
Bai	0.32	0.28	0.01	0.01	0.01	0.77
Baonan	0.00	0.00	0.00	0.00	0.00	0.02
Blang	0.01	0.01	0.00	0.00	0.00	0.03
Buyi	0.71	0.62	0.03	0.03	0.03	2.52
Dai	0.18	0.16	0.01	0.01	0.01	0.41
Daur	0.05	0.05	0.00	0.00	0.00	0.23
Deang	0.00	0.00	0.00	0.00	0.00	0.01
Derung	0.00	0.00	0.00	0.00	0.00	0.00
Dong	0.69	0.61	0.02	0.03	0.03	2.00
Dongxiang	0.07	0.05	0.01	0.00	0.01	0.62
Ewenki	0.01	0.01	0.00	0.00	0.00	0.07
Gaoshan	0.00	0.00	0.00	0.00	0.00	0.00

(*continued*)

Table 7.6 (continued)

Ethnic group	Number of Beds	The Aged	Child Welfare and Assistance	Mental Illness	Other	Beds in Elderly Care Institutions per 1 000 Senior Citizens (bed)
Gelao	0.14	0.12	0.01	0.01	0.01	0.49
Han	381.23	356.45	8.08	5.39	11.14	741.90
Hani	0.22	0.19	0.01	0.01	0.01	0.52
Hezhe	0.00	0.00	0.00	0.00	0.00	0.00
Hui	2.67	2.35	0.14	0.04	0.12	18.83
Jing	0.00	0.00	0.00	0.00	0.00	0.01
Jingpo	0.02	0.02	0.00	0.00	0.00	0.05
Jino	0.00	0.00	0.00	0.00	0.00	0.01
Kazak	0.34	0.25	0.05	0.02	0.01	1.12
Kirgiz	0.04	0.03	0.01	0.00	0.00	0.14
Korean	0.87	0.81	0.02	0.03	0.02	1.60
Lahu	0.07	0.06	0.00	0.00	0.00	0.16
Lhoba	0.00	0.00	0.00	0.00	0.00	0.01
Li	0.09	0.08	0.00	0.00	0.01	1.90
Lisu	0.10	0.09	0.00	0.00	0.00	0.23
Manchu	3.99	3.76	0.05	0.04	0.14	7.32
Maonan	0.02	0.02	0.00	0.00	0.00	0.07
Miao	2.09	1.86	0.07	0.08	0.08	5.94
Monba	0.00	0.00	0.00	0.00	0.00	0.03
Mongol	2.19	2.04	0.05	0.04	0.06	11.04
Mulao	0.03	0.03	0.00	0.00	0.00	0.12
Naxi	0.05	0.04	0.00	0.00	0.00	0.11
Nu	0.00	0.00	0.00	0.00	0.00	0.01
Oroqen	0.00	0.00	0.00	0.00	0.00	0.01
Pumi	0.01	0.00	0.00	0.00	0.00	0.01
Qiang	0.12	0.10	0.00	0.00	0.01	0.11
Russian	0.01	0.00	0.00	0.00	0.00	0.02
Salar	0.02	0.01	0.00	0.00	0.00	0.57
She	0.22	0.21	0.00	0.00	0.01	0.60
Shui	0.09	0.08	0.00	0.00	0.00	0.34
Tajik	0.01	0.01	0.00	0.00	0.00	0.04
Tatar	0.00	0.00	0.00	0.00	0.00	0.00
Tibetan	1.77	0.71	0.44	0.02	0.59	15.57
Tu	0.04	0.03	0.01	0.00	0.00	1.24
Tujia	2.40	2.21	0.06	0.05	0.07	4.85
Uygur	2.30	1.70	0.34	0.16	0.10	7.49
Uzbek	0.00	0.00	0.00	0.00	0.00	0.01
Va	0.06	0.05	0.00	0.00	0.00	0.14
Xibe	0.07	0.06	0.00	0.00	0.00	0.12

(continued)

Table 7.6 (continued)

Ethnic group	Number of Beds	The Aged	Child Welfare and Assistance	Mental Illness	Other	Beds in Elderly Care Institutions per 1 000 Senior Citizens (bed)
Yao	0.47	0.41	0.02	0.01	0.02	1.28
Yi	1.76	1.55	0.07	0.07	0.08	3.20
Yugur	0.00	0.00	0.00	0.00	0.00	0.02
Zhuang	2.36	2.05	0.13	0.08	0.10	8.63

Table 7.7 Statistics on social relief (10000 persons)

Ethnic group	Number of Urban Residents Receiving Minimum Living Allowance	Number of Rural Residents Receiving Minimum Living Allowance	Rural Households with Centralized Livelihood Guaranteed in Five Aspects	Rural Households with Decentralized Livelihood Guaranteed in Five Aspects
National total	1007.0	3519.1	86.2	368.8
Achang	0.04	0.20	0.00	0.01
Bai	2.04	10.62	0.07	0.48
Baonan	0.03	0.15	0.00	0.01
Blang	0.10	0.55	0.00	0.02
Buyi	2.83	18.61	0.25	0.45
Dai	1.32	6.92	0.03	0.29
Daur	0.24	0.59	0.01	0.04
Deang	0.02	0.11	0.00	0.00
Derung	0.01	0.04	0.00	0.00
Dong	2.55	13.79	0.23	0.86
Dongxiang	1.06	4.83	0.02	0.17
Ewenki	0.05	0.15	0.00	0.01
Gaoshan	0.00	0.01	0.00	0.00
Gelao	0.55	3.65	0.05	0.09
Han	885.16	2994.39	79.35	337.74
Hani	1.63	8.61	0.04	0.36
Hezhe	0.01	0.01	0.00	0.00
Hui	13.18	51.80	0.55	2.54
Jing	0.01	0.09	0.00	0.01
Jingpo	0.15	0.79	0.00	0.03
Jino	0.02	0.13	0.00	0.01

(continued)

Table 7.7 (continued)

Ethnic group	Number of Urban Residents Receiving Minimum Living Allowance	Number of Rural Residents Receiving Minimum Living Allowance	Rural Households with Centralized Livelihood Guaranteed in Five Aspects	Rural Households with Decentralized Livelihood Guaranteed in Five Aspects
Kazak	3.58	13.36	0.08	0.11
Kirgiz	0.46	1.71	0.01	0.01
Korean	3.34	4.18	0.12	0.55
Lahu	0.51	2.71	0.01	0.11
Lhoba	0.00	0.02	0.00	0.00
Li	0.81	2.69	0.03	0.36
Lisu	0.72	3.76	0.02	0.16
Manchu	11.94	20.48	0.55	2.87
Maonan	0.05	0.51	0.01	0.04
Miao	8.28	42.39	0.64	2.42
Monba	0.01	0.06	0.00	0.00
Mongol	8.95	27.01	0.28	1.71
Mulao	0.08	0.91	0.01	0.09
Naxi	0.35	1.83	0.01	0.08
Nu	0.03	0.17	0.00	0.01
Oroqen	0.01	0.03	0.00	0.00
Pumi	0.04	0.20	0.00	0.01
Qiang	0.35	1.26	0.04	0.13
Russian	0.04	0.13	0.00	0.00
Salar	0.17	0.71	0.01	0.03
She	0.34	1.29	0.04	0.10
Shui	0.38	2.54	0.03	0.07
Tajik	0.11	0.43	0.00	0.00
Tatar	0.01	0.05	0.00	0.00
Tibetan	6.95	33.33	1.29	1.81
Tu	0.38	1.58	0.01	0.07
Tujia	6.92	22.90	0.58	2.73
Uygur	24.01	89.48	0.54	0.77
Uzbek	0.03	0.13	0.00	0.00
Va	0.44	2.34	0.01	0.10
Xibe	0.28	0.62	0.01	0.04
Yao	1.39	9.31	0.13	1.21
Yi	8.66	42.73	0.48	2.20
Yugur	0.03	0.13	0.00	0.00
Zhuang	5.51	67.52	0.58	7.70

Table 7.8 Medical aid of civil affairs offices (10000 persons or person-times)

	Medical aid in urban areas		Medical aid in rural areas			
Ethnic group	Medical aid	Aid for medical insurance	Medical aid	Aid for cooperative medical care	Expenses of urban medical aid	Expense of rural medical aid
National total	689.90	1387.10	1483.80	4490.40	708801.60	1329104.80
Achang	0.01	0.08	0.06	0.39	17.59	61.77
Bai	0.75	4.04	2.89	20.70	946.47	3288.99
Baonan	0.02	0.02	0.04	0.07	16.57	42.04
Blang	0.04	0.22	0.15	1.06	47.69	167.04
Buyi	0.52	4.10	3.29	41.01	1069.89	5534.32
Dai	0.48	2.74	1.89	13.36	601.37	2109.69
Daur	0.13	0.46	0.13	0.64	170.80	179.59
Deang	0.01	0.04	0.03	0.21	9.34	32.76
Derung	0.00	0.02	0.01	0.07	4.09	12.46
Dong	0.91	3.62	3.44	27.99	1261.28	4541.64
Dongxiang	0.46	0.69	1.16	2.13	540.40	1252.64
Ewenki	0.02	0.10	0.03	0.16	32.45	40.26
Gaoshan	0.00	0.00	0.00	0.02	2.12	4.41
Gelao	0.10	0.80	0.64	8.08	206.30	1083.00
Han	614.75	1190.43	1314.05	3791.88	631051.17	1166855.88
Hani	0.59	3.41	2.34	16.63	746.11	2621.97
Hezhe	0.01	0.02	0.00	0.02	7.45	6.25
Hui	12.47	19.53	24.84	47.78	9385.31	16735.77
Jing	0.00	0.01	0.02	0.12	6.31	28.77
Jingpo	0.05	0.31	0.21	1.53	68.38	240.37
Jino	0.01	0.05	0.03	0.24	10.87	38.09
Kazak	2.27	6.55	3.14	10.23	2716.85	2277.78
Kirgiz	0.29	0.84	0.40	1.31	348.83	291.77
Korean	1.96	4.40	1.55	4.53	2233.48	1966.30
Lahu	0.19	1.07	0.74	5.23	234.71	824.68
Lhoba	0.00	0.00	0.00	0.00	0.86	11.85
Li	0.87	2.44	1.63	5.66	1275.72	2305.36
Lisu	0.27	1.48	1.06	7.20	331.77	1149.57
Manchu	5.04	12.02	6.17	21.57	6353.02	6999.63
Maonan	0.02	0.08	0.11	0.83	30.12	153.50
Miao	3.79	13.05	12.06	86.35	4190.71	14140.97
Monba	0.00	0.00	0.01	0.00	2.42	36.73
Mongol	4.27	16.47	6.29	28.13	5551.07	7213.10

(continued)

Table 7.8 (continued)

	Medical aid in urban areas		Medical aid in rural areas			
Ethnic group	Medical aid	Aid for medical insurance	Medical aid	Aid for cooperative medical care	Expenses of urban medical aid	Expense of rural medical aid
Mulao	0.04	0.13	0.22	1.31	55.34	273.66
Naxi	0.13	0.72	0.51	3.49	161.29	562.51
Nu	0.01	0.07	0.05	0.32	14.80	53.14
Oroqen	0.01	0.03	0.01	0.03	10.89	10.81
Pumi	0.01	0.08	0.05	0.39	17.49	61.06
Qiang	0.29	0.35	0.92	1.51	211.32	462.05
Russian	0.02	0.07	0.03	0.11	25.90	24.80
Salar	0.46	0.41	0.88	0.82	223.91	410.07
She	0.24	0.31	0.68	2.11	239.38	639.59
Shui	0.07	0.56	0.45	5.54	145.92	752.99
Tajik	0.07	0.21	0.10	0.33	87.03	73.70
Tatar	0.01	0.02	0.01	0.04	10.12	8.89
Tibetan	7.41	6.93	18.72	19.40	4531.17	18319.01
Tu	0.99	0.88	1.90	1.84	482.61	905.23
Tujia	5.64	13.16	12.11	44.27	4603.87	9592.44
Uygur	15.22	43.91	21.04	68.62	18210.53	15249.70
Uzbek	0.02	0.06	0.03	0.10	26.50	22.33
Va	0.16	0.93	0.64	4.50	204.64	713.31
Xibe	0.12	0.31	0.16	0.50	147.41	138.25
Yao	0.89	2.22	3.00	13.11	990.98	3160.58
Yi	4.13	14.92	15.14	77.47	4255.38	13510.54
Yugur	0.01	0.01	0.03	0.05	12.96	34.04
Zhuang	3.49	10.69	17.57	89.23	4398.42	20484.47

Note: All data are as of 2012.

Table 7.9 Statistics on urban employee basic pension insurance

Ethnic group	Urban employee basic pension insurance contributors at year-end (10000 persons)	Number of staff and workers	Number of retirees	Revenue and expenses(100 million yuan)		
				Revenue	Expenses	Balance at year-end
National total	**41901.6**	**30104.0**	**11797.7**	**51167.6**	**44644.9**	**50901.3**
Achang	0.50	0.36	0.14	0.71	0.56	0.92
Bai	29.70	21.33	8.37	41.60	32.68	50.45
Baonan	0.32	0.21	0.11	0.40	0.37	0.33
Blang	1.37	0.98	0.39	1.93	1.53	2.50
Buyi	56.50	43.17	13.32	70.15	55.99	70.96
Dai	17.21	12.30	4.91	24.37	19.20	31.57
Daur	4.52	2.73	1.78	6.32	6.33	2.35
Deang	0.26	0.19	0.08	0.37	0.29	0.48
Derung	0.14	0.10	0.04	0.19	0.16	0.21
Dong	61.83	45.22	16.61	82.52	65.55	74.94
Dongxiang	10.49	7.00	3.50	13.38	12.19	12.09
Ewenki	1.00	0.62	0.38	1.46	1.42	0.83
Gaoshan	0.14	0.10	0.04	0.17	0.15	0.16
Gelao	10.96	8.40	2.56	13.59	10.79	13.79
Han	38987.77	28108.68	10879.08	47085.01	40997.89	47602.60
Hani	21.27	15.21	6.07	30.19	23.78	39.03
Hezhe	0.17	0.10	0.07	0.22	0.23	-0.01
Hui	318.54	225.85	92.69	420.21	373.94	383.07
Jing	0.45	0.31	0.14	0.65	0.58	0.42
Jingpo	1.96	1.40	0.56	2.77	2.18	3.59
Jino	0.31	0.22	0.09	0.44	0.35	0.57
Kazak	47.06	32.79	14.28	70.49	62.25	81.43
Kirgiz	6.06	4.21	1.84	9.06	8.02	10.36
Korean	69.77	41.98	27.80	86.31	83.09	30.85
Lahu	6.71	4.80	1.91	9.51	7.49	12.28
Lhoba	0.06	0.04	0.01	0.13	0.11	0.16
Li	41.84	30.49	11.35	52.74	43.23	39.03
Lisu	9.67	6.87	2.79	13.55	10.75	17.47
Manchu	437.91	276.43	161.48	544.89	568.29	197.90
Maonan	2.07	1.48	0.59	2.92	2.54	2.07
Miao	189.10	136.37	52.73	247.40	199.15	235.59
Monba	0.17	0.13	0.04	0.39	0.33	0.49

(continued)

Table 7.9 (continued)

Ethnic group	Urban employee basic pension insurance contributors at year-end (10000 persons)	Number of staff and workers	Number of retirees	Revenue and expenses(100 million yuan)		
				Revenue	Expenses	Balance at year-end
Mongol	196.51	123.00	73.50	276.69	273.10	159.76
Mulao	4.16	2.95	1.21	5.95	5.20	4.18
Naxi	4.74	3.38	1.36	6.67	5.29	8.63
Nu	0.43	0.31	0.12	0.62	0.49	0.80
Oroqen	0.29	0.17	0.12	0.39	0.39	0.09
Pumi	0.50	0.36	0.14	0.71	0.56	0.92
Qiang	9.46	6.20	3.27	10.75	9.43	13.73
Russian	0.58	0.39	0.19	0.85	0.77	0.85
Salar	3.07	2.12	0.94	4.54	4.53	1.66
She	27.47	21.19	6.28	26.41	22.77	31.36
Shui	7.61	5.80	1.82	9.57	7.67	9.47
Tajik	1.54	1.07	0.47	2.29	2.02	2.63
Tatar	0.18	0.13	0.06	0.27	0.24	0.31
Tibetan	127.15	90.67	36.48	211.68	190.52	213.75
Tu	7.03	4.91	2.12	10.15	10.03	4.09
Tujia	209.97	142.73	67.24	267.75	231.51	208.04
Uygur	316.38	220.45	95.93	473.68	418.26	547.07
Uzbek	0.47	0.33	0.14	0.70	0.61	0.81
Va	6.01	4.30	1.71	8.42	6.67	10.79
Xibe	8.51	5.31	3.20	10.56	11.39	4.02
Yao	59.58	43.02	16.56	82.71	66.55	75.56
Yi	152.71	105.94	46.77	195.16	160.73	244.78
Yugur	0.26	0.18	0.09	0.33	0.30	0.29
Zhuang	325.92	230.16	95.77	470.18	409.62	340.83

Table 7.10 Statistics of unemployment insurance

Ethnic group	Unemployment insurance contributors at year-end (10000 persons)	Beneficiaries of unemployment insurance fund (10000 persons)	Revenue and expenses (100 million yuan)		
			Revenue	Expenses	Balance at year-end
National total	**19643.5**	**223.1**	**1171.1**	**915.3**	**5817.0**
Achang	0.22	0.00	0.01	0.01	0.05
Bai	13.07	0.21	0.82	0.52	2.89
Baonan	0.12	0.00	0.01	0.00	0.03
Blang	0.61	0.01	0.04	0.02	0.15
Buyi	23.39	0.21	1.40	0.97	4.41
Dai	7.64	0.14	0.50	0.32	1.85
Daur	1.49	0.02	0.11	0.06	0.33
Deang	0.12	0.00	0.01	0.00	0.03
Derung	0.06	0.00	0.00	0.00	0.01
Dong	26.23	0.26	1.41	0.95	4.13
Dongxiang	4.11	0.03	0.26	0.16	0.82
Ewenki	0.36	0.00	0.03	0.01	0.07
Gaoshan	0.07	0.00	0.00	0.00	0.01
Gelao	4.54	0.04	0.27	0.19	0.85
Han	18461.66	208.40	1095.04	861.37	2707.94
Hani	9.46	0.17	0.61	0.39	2.30
Hezhe	0.05	0.00	0.00	0.00	0.01
Hui	141.24	1.52	9.43	6.95	24.77
Jing	0.18	0.00	0.01	0.01	0.04
Jingpo	0.87	0.02	0.06	0.04	0.21
Jino	0.14	0.00	0.01	0.01	0.03
Kazak	22.26	0.23	1.30	1.10	3.97
Kirgiz	2.85	0.03	0.17	0.14	0.51
Korean	23.05	0.24	1.54	1.08	4.86
Lahu	2.98	0.05	0.19	0.12	0.72
Lhoba	0.02	0.00	0.00	0.00	0.01
Li	27.77	0.36	1.16	0.91	4.18
Lisu	4.23	0.08	0.29	0.18	1.02
Manchu	159.13	2.07	9.97	8.01	30.84
Maonan	0.84	0.01	0.06	0.04	0.17
Miao	81.25	0.86	4.43	3.02	13.09
Monba	0.07	0.00	0.01	0.00	0.02
Mongol	71.11	0.77	5.36	3.11	14.25
Mulao	1.74	0.02	0.12	0.08	0.34
Naxi	2.09	0.04	0.14	0.09	0.50

(*continued*)

Table 7.10 (continued)

Ethnic group	Unemployment insurance contributors at year-end (10000 persons)	Beneficiaries of unemployment insurance fund (10000 persons)	Revenue and expenses (100 million yuan)		
			Revenue	Expenses	Balance at year-end
Nu	0.19	0.00	0.01	0.01	0.05
Oroqen	0.09	0.00	0.01	0.00	0.02
Pumi	0.22	0.00	0.01	0.01	0.05
Qiang	3.28	0.12	0.39	0.30	0.60
Russian	0.26	0.00	0.02	0.01	0.05
Salar	0.97	0.01	0.09	0.07	0.32
She	14.00	0.12	0.66	0.46	2.05
Shui	3.13	0.03	0.19	0.13	0.60
Tajik	0.73	0.01	0.04	0.04	0.13
Tatar	0.09	0.00	0.01	0.00	0.02
Tibetan	44.56	0.62	5.32	2.51	13.65
Tu	2.30	0.02	0.21	0.16	0.71
Tujia	89.69	0.81	4.26	2.92	11.62
Uygur	149.69	1.54	8.71	7.40	26.69
Uzbek	0.22	0.00	0.01	0.01	0.04
Va	2.67	0.05	0.17	0.11	0.64
Xibe	3.13	0.04	0.18	0.16	0.63
Yao	27.44	0.32	1.48	0.97	4.21
Yi	60.77	1.48	5.13	3.65	13.07
Yugur	0.10	0.00	0.01	0.00	0.02
Zhuang	139.25	2.07	9.13	6.27	27.37

Table 7.11 Persons covered of urban basic medical care insurance (10000 persons)

Ethnic group	Persons covered at year-end	Urban workers	Staff and workers	Retirees	Urban non-employment
National total	**134458.6**	**31680.8**	**23307.5**	**8373.3**	**102777.8**
Achang	3.62	0.41	0.29	0.12	3.21
Bai	201.10	23.36	16.54	6.83	177.73
Baonan	1.69	0.23	0.16	0.08	1.46
Blang	9.81	1.12	0.79	0.33	8.69
Buyi	355.47	38.83	28.63	10.20	316.64
Dai	123.74	14.11	9.95	4.16	109.63

(continued)

Table 7.11 (continued)

Ethnic group	Persons covered at year-end	Urban workers	Staff and workers	Retirees	Urban non-employment
Daur	12.01	3.13	2.08	1.06	8.87
Deang	1.91	0.22	0.15	0.06	1.70
Derung	0.79	0.11	0.08	0.03	0.68
Dong	342.40	42.21	30.56	11.65	300.20
Dongxiang	53.31	7.86	5.34	2.53	45.45
Ewenki	2.83	0.70	0.48	0.22	2.13
Gaoshan	0.49	0.11	0.08	0.03	0.39
Gelao	69.49	7.50	5.54	1.96	61.99
Han	122802.13	29571.04	21824.29	7746.75	93231.09
Hani	153.69	17.48	12.31	5.16	136.21
Hezhe	0.39	0.12	0.07	0.05	0.27
Hui	1081.96	233.95	166.88	67.07	848.02
Jing	2.63	0.32	0.23	0.09	2.31
Jingpo	14.12	1.61	1.13	0.47	12.51
Jino	2.23	0.25	0.18	0.08	1.98
Kazak	152.40	39.22	28.20	11.01	113.18
Kirgiz	19.54	5.04	3.62	1.42	14.50
Korean	182.22	49.07	31.18	17.89	133.15
Lahu	48.44	5.51	3.88	1.63	42.93
Lhoba	0.38	0.05	0.04	0.01	0.33
Li	150.94	36.35	26.29	10.06	114.59
Lisu	67.73	7.84	5.53	2.32	59.88
Manchu	1038.53	332.50	211.92	120.58	706.03
Maonan	12.65	1.46	1.07	0.40	11.18
Miao	1020.12	130.73	94.35	36.39	889.39
Monba	1.16	0.16	0.12	0.04	1.00
Mongol	557.30	140.68	95.80	44.87	416.62
Mulao	24.38	2.99	2.19	0.80	21.39
Naxi	33.00	3.86	2.72	1.13	29.14
Nu	3.08	0.36	0.25	0.10	2.73
Oroqen	0.72	0.20	0.13	0.07	0.53
Pumi	3.59	0.41	0.29	0.12	3.17
Qiang	32.15	6.23	4.43	1.79	25.93
Russian	1.73	0.46	0.33	0.13	1.28
Salar	11.91	2.15	1.43	0.72	9.76
She	81.33	21.26	17.03	4.23	60.07
Shui	48.59	5.24	3.85	1.39	43.35
Tajik	4.98	1.28	0.92	0.36	3.70
Tatar	0.59	0.15	0.11	0.04	0.44
Tibetan	641.67	98.20	71.10	27.10	543.48

(continued)

Table 7.11 (continued)

Ethnic group	Persons covered at year-end	Urban workers	Staff and workers	Retirees	Urban non-employment
Tu	27.35	4.95	3.33	1.61	22.41
Tujia	855.59	139.89	99.50	40.39	715.71
Uygur	1023.57	263.59	189.58	74.01	759.98
Uzbek	1.51	0.39	0.28	0.11	1.12
Va	42.35	4.90	3.46	1.44	37.45
Xibe	18.88	6.71	4.23	2.48	12.16
Yao	302.11	43.30	32.18	11.11	258.81
Yi	836.13	112.28	79.75	32.53	723.85
Yugur	1.40	0.20	0.13	0.06	1.21
Zhuang	1886.53	239.19	175.66	63.53	1647.34

Table 7.12 Revenue and expenses of urban basic medical care insurance (100 million yuan)

Ethnic group	Revenue			Expenses		
	Total	Workers	Non-employment	Total	Workers	Non-employment
National total	**21384.2**	**13537.8**	**7846.4**	**17822.5**	**10706.6**	**7115.9**
Achang	0.46	0.23	0.23	0.38	0.18	0.21
Bai	24.93	12.57	12.36	20.80	9.50	11.31
Baonan	0.20	0.10	0.10	0.18	0.08	0.10
Blang	1.25	0.63	0.62	1.04	0.48	0.56
Buyi	35.00	16.71	18.28	30.24	12.13	18.11
Dai	15.80	7.99	7.81	13.12	6.06	7.06
Daur	1.99	1.31	0.68	1.73	1.09	0.63
Deang	0.24	0.12	0.12	0.20	0.09	0.11
Derung	0.11	0.06	0.05	0.09	0.04	0.04
Dong	36.40	17.51	18.89	30.72	12.95	17.77
Dongxiang	6.36	3.21	3.15	5.78	2.71	3.07
Ewenki	0.46	0.30	0.16	0.40	0.25	0.16
Gaoshan	0.08	0.05	0.03	0.06	0.04	0.03
Gelao	6.77	3.22	3.55	5.86	2.33	3.53
Han	19741.11	12593.48	7147.63	16483.85	9965.03	6518.81
Hani	19.62	9.92	9.70	16.29	7.52	8.78
Hezhe	0.07	0.05	0.02	0.06	0.04	0.02

(*continued*)

Table 7.12 (continued)

Ethnic group	Revenue Total	Workers	Non-employment	Expenses Total	Workers	Non-employment
Hui	183.86	116.88	66.98	152.59	92.94	59.64
Jing	0.30	0.13	0.17	0.22	0.10	0.13
Jingpo	1.80	0.91	0.89	1.50	0.69	0.81
Jino	0.29	0.14	0.14	0.24	0.11	0.13
Kazak	29.02	19.21	9.81	23.14	15.96	7.18
Kirgiz	3.72	2.46	1.26	2.97	2.05	0.92
Korean	26.32	17.22	9.10	22.76	14.76	8.00
Lahu	6.18	3.12	3.06	5.13	2.36	2.77
Lhoba	0.07	0.04	0.03	0.04	0.02	0.02
Li	20.25	12.79	7.46	14.45	8.48	5.97
Lisu	8.66	4.39	4.28	7.18	3.32	3.86
Manchu	175.55	124.19	51.36	156.57	109.10	47.47
Maonan	1.38	0.59	0.79	1.06	0.43	0.62
Miao	113.85	56.40	57.44	96.28	42.74	53.53
Monba	0.21	0.13	0.08	0.13	0.07	0.06
Mongol	90.05	58.73	31.32	78.96	48.71	30.25
Mulao	2.77	1.20	1.57	2.07	0.88	1.19
Naxi	4.25	2.17	2.08	3.52	1.64	1.88
Nu	0.40	0.20	0.19	0.33	0.15	0.18
Oroqen	0.12	0.08	0.04	0.10	0.07	0.04
Pumi	0.46	0.23	0.23	0.38	0.18	0.20
Qiang	4.50	2.50	1.99	3.46	1.83	1.64
Russian	0.33	0.22	0.11	0.27	0.18	0.09
Salar	2.33	1.48	0.84	1.72	1.09	0.63
She	13.56	8.63	4.93	11.29	6.63	4.66
Shui	4.79	2.26	2.53	4.12	1.64	2.47
Tajik	0.94	0.62	0.32	0.75	0.52	0.24
Tatar	0.11	0.07	0.04	0.09	0.06	0.03
Tibetan	108.34	65.64	42.70	74.93	40.41	34.51
Tu	5.19	3.28	1.91	3.86	2.40	1.46
Tujia	108.53	57.93	50.60	93.43	47.51	45.92
Uygur	194.97	129.09	65.88	155.45	107.25	48.20
Uzbek	0.29	0.19	0.10	0.23	0.16	0.07
Va	5.42	2.75	2.67	4.50	2.09	2.42
Xibe	3.33	2.41	0.91	2.95	2.16	0.79
Yao	35.97	17.04	18.93	27.87	12.64	15.23
Yi	106.25	54.95	51.30	86.70	41.01	45.69
Yugur	0.16	0.08	0.08	0.15	0.07	0.08
Zhuang	220.31	95.93	124.38	162.87	70.73	92.14

8

Entertainment and Other Cultural Activity

Data on culture are estimated based on the data provided by the Ministry of Culture. Data on radio broadcasting, films and television are from State Administration of Radio, Film and Television. Data on number of books published for children and textbooks are from General Administration of Press and Publication. Data on sports are from General Administration of Sport.

For detailed information please refer to *Collection of China News and Publication Statistical Information* (Department of Publication Industrial Development, General Administration of Press and Publication), *Statistics on National Development Indicators of Radio, Film and Television* (Department of Arrangement and Finance, State Administration of Radio, Film and Television), and *Statistical Yearbook of Sports* (Finance Department, General Administration of Sport).

R. Guo, *China Ethnic Statistical Yearbook 2020*,
https://doi.org/10.1007/978-3-030-49024-9_8

Table 8.1 Population Coverage of Radio and TV Programs, and Radio and TV Programs Produced and Broadcasted

Region	Population Coverage Rate of Radio Programs (%)	Population Coverage Rate of TV Programs (%)	Number of Public Radio Programs (set)	Number of TV Programs (set)	Number of TV Plays Broadcasted (set)	Number of Cartoons Broadcasted (hour)
National Total	**98.94**	**99.25**	**2900**	**3559**	**217591**	**374485**
Achang	98.69	98.90	0	0	8	14
Bai	98.24	98.74	3	7	391	746
Baonan	98.44	98.78	0	0	5	9
Blang	98.70	98.91	0	0	21	39
Buyi	94.21	96.91	4	9	395	695
Dai	98.69	98.90	2	5	260	489
Daur	99.11	99.13	1	1	41	43
Deang	98.69	98.90	0	0	4	8
Derung	98.71	98.95	0	0	2	3
Dong	96.11	97.97	5	8	422	846
Dongxiang	98.38	98.73	2	3	171	306
Ewenki	99.22	99.21	0	0	11	10
Gaoshan	98.73	99.09	0	0	1	1
Gelao	94.10	96.85	1	2	76	134
Han	99.06	99.31	2536	3022	189366	321016
Hani	98.69	98.90	2	6	324	608
Hezhe	99.04	99.09	0	0	1	1
Hui	98.81	99.12	40	48	2894	5194
Jing	97.58	98.76	0	0	3	5
Jingpo	98.68	98.90	0	1	30	56
Jino	98.69	98.90	0	0	5	9
Kazak	97.83	98.07	11	15	1020	1610
Kirgiz	97.85	98.08	1	2	130	206
Korean	99.05	99.13	6	5	385	280
Lahu	98.70	98.91	1	2	102	191
Lhoba	97.19	98.24	0	0	1	4
Li	98.83	98.98	4	3	141	778
Lisu	98.67	98.90	1	3	142	265
Manchu	99.15	99.20	30	32	2106	1927
Maonan	96.54	98.21	0	0	15	24
Miao	96.47	98.09	14	25	1342	2700
Monba	97.23	98.26	0	0	3	14
Mongol	99.12	99.16	28	28	2002	1929
Mulao	97.15	98.54	0	1	30	46
Naxi	98.66	98.90	1	1	69	130
Nu	98.67	98.90	0	0	6	13
Oroqen	99.14	99.16	0	0	2	2
Pumi	98.69	98.91	0	0	8	14

(*continued*)

Table 8.1 (continued)

Region	Population Coverage Rate of Radio Programs (%)	Population Coverage Rate of TV Programs (%)	Number of Public Radio Programs (set)	Number of TV Programs (set)	Number of TV Plays Broadcasted (set)	Number of Cartoons Broadcasted (hour)
Qiang	97.84	98.79	1	1	61	79
Russian	98.42	98.57	0	0	10	14
Salar	98.58	98.66	1	1	42	80
She	98.87	99.21	2	2	95	263
Shui	94.33	96.97	1	1	55	95
Tajik	97.87	98.12	0	0	33	51
Tatar	97.91	98.15	0	0	4	6
Tibetan	97.77	98.51	42	93	1556	5285
Tu	98.58	98.70	2	2	90	173
Tujia	98.31	99.04	13	17	1259	2528
Uygur	97.84	98.08	77	99	6840	10795
Uzbek	97.86	98.10	0	0	10	16
Va	98.70	98.91	1	2	89	166
Xibe	98.86	98.97	1	1	60	73
Yao	98.17	99.08	5	7	397	786
Yi	97.94	98.64	13	28	1607	2754
Yugur	98.45	98.81	0	0	4	7
Zhuang	97.73	98.83	28	44	2420	3811

Table 8.2 Transmission Trunk and Users of Cable Radios and TVs

Region	Total Length of Transmission Trunk for Cable Radios and TVs (10 000 km)	Users of Cable Radios and TVs (10 000 households)	Users of Digital TV	Pay TV	Popularization Rate of Cable TV Programs (%)
National Total	**225.3**	**21832.4**	**20143.7**	**7729.9**	**49.01**
Achang	0.00	0.37	0.35	0.24	33.26
Bai	0.14	22.89	21.66	13.73	36.49
Baonan	0.00	0.14	0.11	0.06	24.78
Blang	0.01	1.01	0.95	0.66	33.31
Buyi	0.10	58.85	58.66	34.04	53.08
Dai	0.08	12.71	12.00	8.29	33.19
Daur	0.02	1.70	1.62	0.80	30.79
Deang	0.00	0.20	0.18	0.13	33.06

(*continued*)

Table 8.2 (continued)

Region	Total Length of Transmission Trunk for Cable Radios and TVs (10 000 km)	Users of Cable Radios and TVs (10 000 households)	Users of Digital TV	Pay TV	Popularization Rate of Cable TV Programs (%)
Derung	0.00	0.09	0.08	0.05	35.59
Dong	0.24	54.64	52.04	25.77	51.23
Dongxiang	0.05	4.55	3.66	1.78	25.27
Ewenki	0.00	0.34	0.32	0.20	26.71
Gaoshan	0.00	0.08	0.07	0.03	47.50
Gelao	0.02	11.55	11.52	6.70	53.37
Han	213.53	20138.18	18574.45	7048.01	49.85
Hani	0.10	15.78	14.89	10.31	33.18
Hezhe	0.00	0.08	0.08	0.03	40.84
Hui	1.68	159.95	149.93	58.60	43.57
Jing	0.00	0.36	0.32	0.15	44.46
Jingpo	0.01	1.45	1.37	0.95	33.26
Jino	0.00	0.23	0.22	0.15	33.16
Kazak	0.32	22.01	21.17	5.26	43.14
Kirgiz	0.04	2.83	2.72	0.68	43.13
Korean	0.21	33.17	31.81	14.05	44.52
Lahu	0.03	4.97	4.69	3.24	33.18
Lhoba	0.00	0.03	0.03	0.00	32.75
Li	0.04	36.66	25.05	5.30	83.77
Lisu	0.04	7.01	6.62	4.53	33.23
Manchu	1.48	175.01	161.62	49.75	43.65
Maonan	0.00	1.83	1.69	0.85	46.77
Miao	0.74	161.66	151.87	75.68	49.86
Monba	0.00	0.09	0.08	0.01	31.86
Mongol	0.74	70.36	66.12	35.19	30.39
Mulao	0.01	3.43	3.09	1.49	45.76
Naxi	0.02	3.42	3.23	2.20	33.35
Nu	0.00	0.32	0.30	0.20	33.40
Oroqen	0.00	0.11	0.11	0.05	33.40
Pumi	0.00	0.37	0.35	0.24	33.26
Qiang	0.01	4.42	4.20	1.97	36.79
Russian	0.00	0.24	0.23	0.08	38.30
Salar	0.02	1.93	1.88	0.73	50.13
She	0.27	16.15	15.91	7.86	67.55
Shui	0.01	7.95	7.91	4.59	52.45
Tajik	0.01	0.72	0.69	0.17	43.35

(*continued*)

Table 8.2 (continued)

Region	Total Length of Transmission Trunk for Cable Radios and TVs (10 000 km)	Users of Cable Radios and TVs (10 000 households)	Users of Digital TV	Pay TV	Popularization Rate of Cable TV Programs (%)
Tatar	0.00	0.09	0.08	0.02	43.12
Tibetan	0.72	68.13	63.58	20.47	36.33
Tu	0.03	4.39	4.27	1.70	49.95
Tujia	0.99	152.71	137.34	55.96	52.47
Uygur	2.18	147.98	142.38	35.40	43.21
Uzbek	0.00	0.22	0.21	0.05	43.52
Va	0.03	4.40	4.15	2.82	33.51
Xibe	0.02	3.32	3.07	0.81	46.70
Yao	0.26	42.33	37.57	15.82	46.39
Yi	0.43	100.14	95.64	57.75	36.36
Yugur	0.00	0.11	0.09	0.05	24.21
Zhuang	0.69	253.74	224.70	105.77	43.99

[a]Total length of transmission trunk for cable radios include 41 900 km directly under the State Administration of Radio, Film and Television

Table 8.3 Number of books published for children and textbooks

	Number of publications (kind)		Printed copies (10000 copies)		Printed sheets (1000 sheets)	
Ethnic group	Books for children	Textbooks	Books for children	Textbooks	Books for children	Textbooks
National total	**44196**	**82862**	**88858**	**348116**	**5412232**	**27458388**
Achang	0	0	0.60	6.31	30.14	435.04
Bai	24	10	36.42	354.02	2121.87	24250.15
Baonan	0	0	0.17	2.17	13.96	163.13
Blang	1	0	1.64	17.12	82.15	1179.90
Buyi	10	13	31.33	564.08	1777.41	39762.61
Dai	16	5	20.94	215.20	1049.32	14849.93
Daur	4	4	1.66	20.38	90.16	1496.14
Deang	0	0	0.31	3.33	15.69	229.84
Derung	0	0	0.17	1.40	8.90	96.96
Dong	33	27	83.28	628.89	6420.74	42173.58
Dongxiang	6	3	5.25	76.37	438.90	5658.19
Ewenki	1	1	0.30	4.99	15.99	366.97
Gaoshan	0	0	0.24	0.88	14.89	62.16

(continued)

Table 8.3 (continued)

Ethnic group	Number of publications (kind)		Printed copies (10000 copies)		Printed sheets (1000 sheets)	
	Books for children	Textbooks	Books for children	Textbooks	Books for children	Textbooks
Gelao	2	2	5.56	109.84	310.49	7748.97
Han	31670	32455	67093.69	235081.02	4002171.44	16436905.29
Hani	20	6	25.65	267.92	1281.10	18477.96
Hezhe	0	0	0.13	0.51	7.58	37.64
Hui	216	188	437.75	1867.58	25074.63	134755.69
Jing	1	0	1.47	5.31	95.16	358.04
Jingpo	2	1	2.34	24.56	117.38	1693.73
Jino	0	0	0.38	3.88	18.75	267.99
Kazak	17	41	11.77	478.81	942.08	33669.81
Kirgiz	2	5	1.52	61.21	121.10	4304.26
Korean	159	72	167.11	292.31	9263.55	20513.03
Lahu	6	2	8.05	84.41	402.42	5819.57
Lhoba	0	0	0.04	1.00	1.41	71.19
Li	14	4	20.14	234.85	1201.76	15509.30
Lisu	9	3	12.27	116.93	621.69	8082.65
Manchu	439	488	647.33	1634.40	40777.07	121675.49
Maonan	3	1	5.37	24.07	345.99	1637.76
Miao	93	104	217.82	1853.06	15951.40	125070.14
Monba	0	0	0.15	3.10	5.18	221.61
Mongol	124	224	118.68	996.36	6983.93	73282.75
Mulao	7	2	12.28	48.27	795.64	3261.44
Naxi	4	2	6.08	57.13	311.64	3952.03
Nu	0	0	0.53	5.43	26.55	374.50
Oroqen	0	0	0.14	1.11	7.95	82.09
Pumi	0	0	0.61	6.24	30.96	430.78
Qiang	9	8	22.59	38.74	1278.92	3012.09
Russian	0	1	0.30	4.59	20.10	327.00
Salar	0	3	0.40	19.78	32.19	1505.59
She	21	12	45.40	139.92	3101.41	9559.61
Shui	2	2	4.76	77.90	273.92	5481.15
Tajik	1	1	0.45	15.47	34.25	1087.80
Tatar	0	0	0.07	1.79	5.14	125.98
Tibetan	110	191	128.58	1304.20	6665.21	95220.92
Tu	1	6	1.27	44.74	86.57	3390.26
Tujia	95	225	221.00	1678.38	17883.19	112584.95
Uygur	112	273	81.31	3215.54	6451.93	226097.86
Uzbek	0	0	0.14	4.70	10.58	330.52
Va	5	2	7.30	73.94	367.33	5093.77
Xibe	6	11	10.05	35.22	640.88	2669.10
Yao	74	32	144.46	627.61	10215.89	41136.19
Yi	133	83	251.76	1317.66	13684.82	93542.08
Yugur	0	0	0.17	1.74	13.86	131.14
Zhuang	569	180	1014.03	3813.91	65394.85	256508.22

Table 8.4 Number of certified athletes at various technical grades (person)

Ethnic group	International master of sports	Female	Master of sports	Female	First grade	Female
National total	167	85	1820	864	9690	3396
Achang	0	0	0	0	0	0
Bai	0	0	0	0	2	1
Baonan	0	0	0	0	0	0
Blang	0	0	0	0	0	0
Buyi	0	0	3	1	16	5
Dai	0	0	0	0	0	0
Daur	0	0	0	0	1	0
Deang	0	0	0	0	0	0
Derung	0	0	0	0	0	0
Dong	0	0	2	1	15	5
Dongxiang	0	0	0	0	3	1
Ewenki	0	0	0	0	0	0
Gaoshan	0	0	0	0	0	0
Gelao	0	0	1	0	3	1
Han	144	74	1586	761	8922	3122
Hani	0	0	0	0	0	0
Hezhe	0	0	0	0	0	0
Hui	2	1	11	5	72	21
Jing	0	0	0	0	0	0
Jingpo	0	0	0	0	0	0
Jino	0	0	0	0	0	0
Kazak	0	0	1	1	5	2
Kirgiz	0	0	0	0	1	0
Korean	0	0	4	2	18	6
Lahu	0	0	0	0	0	0
Lhoba	0	0	0	0	0	0
Li	0	0	1	1	22	7
Lisu	0	0	0	0	0	0
Manchu	1	1	27	14	121	45
Maonan	0	0	0	0	0	0
Miao	1	0	8	3	45	16
Monba	0	0	0	0	1	0
Mongol	1	0	10	4	53	18
Mulao	0	0	0	0	1	0
Naxi	0	0	0	0	0	0
Nu	0	0	0	0	0	0
Oroqen	0	0	0	0	0	0
Pumi	0	0	0	0	0	0

(continued)

Table 8.4 (continued)

Ethnic group	International master of sports	Female	Master of sports	Female	First grade	Female
Qiang	0	0	0	0	0	0
Russian	0	0	0	0	0	0
Salar	0	0	0	0	0	0
She	0	0	1	1	7	3
Shui	0	0	0	0	2	1
Tajik	0	0	0	0	0	0
Tatar	0	0	0	0	0	0
Tibetan	3	1	11	4	157	60
Tu	0	0	0	0	1	1
Tujia	1	0	9	4	53	21
Uygur	0	0	8	4	36	11
Uzbek	0	0	0	0	0	0
Va	0	0	0	0	0	0
Xibe	0	0	1	0	2	1
Yao	0	0	1	0	12	5
Yi	0	0	1	0	8	3
Yugur	0	0	0	0	0	0
Zhuang	0	0	8	3	66	25

Note: All data are as of 2012

Appendix A: A Brief Description of China's 56 Ethnic Groups[1]

Throughout history, race, language and religion have divided China as much as physical terrain, political fiat and conquest. However, it is always a politically sensitive issue to identify those non-Han people as different ethnic groups. As a result, the total number of ethnic groups has never been fixed precisely in China. For example, in 1953, only 42 ethnic peoples were identified, while the number increased to 54 in 1964 and 56 in 1982. Of course, this does not include the unknown ethnic groups as well as foreigners with Chinese citizenship.[2]

Specifically, China's current 56 ethnic groups are, in alphabetical order, Achang, Bai, Baonan, Blang, Buyi, Dai, Daur, Deang, Derung, Dong, Dongxiang, Ewenki, Gaoshan, Gelao, Han, Hani, Hezhe, Hui, Jing, Jingpo, Jino, Kazak, Kirgiz, Korean, Lahu, Lhoba, Li, Lisu, Manchu, Maonan, Miao, Monba, Mongol, Mulao, Naxi, Nu, Oroqen, Pumi, Qiang, Russian, Salar, She, Shui, Tajik, Tatar, Tibetan, Tu, Tujia, Uygur, Uzbek, Va, Xibe, Yao, Yi, Yugur, and Zhuang. In the following, the general geographical and historical background of and the linguistic and religious features of each of them are briefly reported.

R. Guo, *China Ethnic Statistical Yearbook 2020*,
https://doi.org/10.1007/978-3-030-49024-9

Achang

The Achang ethnic minority lives mainly in the Dehong Dai-Jingpo autonomous prefecture of Yunnan province. They lived in the reaches of Nu river as long ago as the second century, and then migrated southwest to the present Longchuan and Lianghe counties. The Achang are mountain farmers. As one of the earliest people, they have their own language that belongs to the Tibetan-Burman family of the Sino-Tibetan phylum. However, the Achange language has no written form. Over time, they have accepted the language of the Dai ethnic minority as well as the written and spoken Mandarin of the Han people. In the past, some groups of the Achang believe in primitive spirits and practice ancestor worship, the others follow Theravada Buddhism, and they hold different religion festivals and activities to show their piety. Southern Buddhism is another popular religion among Achang people. Nearly in each of the villages, a Buddhist temple stands with various architecture styles. In addition, Taoism is also of great influences since the Ming dynasty (AD 1368–1644), which is reflected by the Imperial Pavilion Taoist Temple established by Achang people in Dehong of Yunnan.

Bai

The Bai people are mainly dominant in the Dali Bai autonomous county of Yunnan province, together with Lijiang, Kunming, Yuanjiang, Guizhou and so on. A Tibetan-Burman people, the Bai were a major ethnic group and cultural elite in the kingdom of Nanzhao (AD 738–937) that dominated the region to China's southwest. The Bai language derives from the Tibetan-Burman family of the Sino-Tibetan phylum. However, as a result of their close cultural ties with the Han people, the Bai have also applied Chinese characters as their written form of language. Although the Bai people believe in Buddhism, they also worship their village god ('Benzhu'), Nature god, the Prince of the Nanzhao regime, or even a hero of folklore.

Baonan

Located in the southwest of Gansu province, the area of Mt. Jishishan is home to the Baonan ethnic minority. It is thought that the Baonan ethnic minority developed over a long period of time formed largely by Mongolians. During the Yuan, the Ming and the Qing dynasties, some people of the Hui, the Tibetan, and the Tu ethnic minorities were assimilated into the group, often through marriage and in this way the groups influenced each other. The Baonan people did, however, retain most of their Moslem traditions and customs. The Baonan are culturally close to the Hui and, like them, are Muslims. They speak a unique Baonan language which is part of the 'Altai' language family descended from Mongolian. Most can also speak and write Mandarin Chinese like the majority Han people. They continue to follow Islam and are part of the Sunni branch.

Blang

The Blang ethnic minority is one of the oldest peoples in Yunnan province, living mainly in the mountain area of Menghai county of Dai autonomous prefecture in Xishuangbanna. Their earliest record can be traced back to the Han dynasty (BC 206–AD 220). The Blang speak a Mon-Khmer language (it belongs to the Austro-Asiatic phylum with an alveolar sound and pronunciation), and their culture is closely related to those of nearby Myanmer and Laos. As the Blang people live dispersedly, they speak different languages in separate regions. Without their own written characters, they use those of the Dai and the Han peoples. Like many other ethnic minorities, the Blang admire totems. However, the totems they admire are not fierce beasts like the tiger or lion, but the bamboo rat and toad. They believe that when they see those small animals, they must keep away from them, or their relatives will pass away. The Blang also believe in Theravada Buddhism, polytheism and ancestor worship.

Bouyei

The Bouyei ethnic minority have mainly inhabited Southwest China's Guizhou province. Their main living areas are now the Bouyei-Miao autonomous prefecture, Anshun and Guiyang cities. The Bouyei's way of life is quite similar to that of the Miao and their language is closely related to those of the Zhuang and the Dai. The Bouyei people speak their own language belonging to the Sino-Tibetan phylum; and some are able to read and write Mandarin and as well. The Bouyei people believe in many gods. There is a God for each Mountain; River, Lake or Pond; for each old and unusual tree, for megalith, caves, paddy field, and for when it rains or thunders, there are various gods. They also worship ancestors' supreme might with each family setting niches in their home.

Dai

The Dai ethnic minority is distributed throughout the Dai autonomous region and the Dehong Dai-Jingpo autonomous prefecture in Xishuangbanna in the southern part of Yunnan province. The Dai have two main branches—the Water Dai, who have a close affinity with the Thais; and the Han Dai, who are more or less identical with the Shan of the Myanmar. The Dai were one of the main ethnic groups dominating the kingdom of Nanzhao (AD 738–937). In the past, they were called 'baiyue', meaning a vast living area. Therefore, they have established a close relationship with ethnic groups like the Zhuang, the Dong, the Shui, the Bouyei and the Li, who are said to be the descendants of the Dai people. The Dai language belongs to the Zhuang-Dai branch of the Zhuang-Dong group of the Sino-Tibetan languages. The written language was derived from Devanagari and differs from region to region. The religion of the Dai people is Buddhism, which was adopted in the sixth to eighth century and had a profound influence on their politics, economy, culture and arts.

Daur

Daur is the title that the people of the Daur ethnic minority named themselves, meaning cultivator. With historical records dating back to the early seventeenth century, there are several stories about the origin of this minority. The most accepted is that they were descendants of the brave Khitan tribe (Qidan) in the Liao dynasty AD (916–1125). This minority helped guard the frontier during the Qing dynasty (AD 1644–1911) near Xinjiang. The population of the Daur ethnic minority is considerably smaller than many other minorities. They mainly inhabit Inner Mongolia autonomous region and Heilongjiang province, while some live in the Xinjiang Uyghur autonomous region. The Daur people have their own language, which has a strong affinity with that of the Mongolian dialect, both of which belong to the Altai phylum. As their land bordering upon the places where the Mongol, the Manchu, the Ewenki, the Han, and the Kazak minorities inhabited, they developed their vocabulary, benefiting from others. However, their language has no written form.

Deang

The Deang ethnic minority lives exclusively in Yunnan province and primarily in Luxi and Zhenkang counties, along with the Dai, the Jingpo, and the Va ethnic minorities. Their language belongs to the Mon-Khmer group of the Austro-Asiatic phylum, much close to that of the Va. They have no traditional written language, so some of people use the written Chinese language along with that of the Dai and the Jingpo languages. Influenced by the Dai ethnic minority, the Deang people are faithful to Theravada Buddhism. Boys of less than ten years old are sent to the temples to become monks, learning sutras. Most of them are secularized after several years, with only few promoted as Buddhists who are highly esteemed as both educated and knowledgeable. Meanwhile, they also worship the original gods, such as Dragon King, God of Mountain, God of Land, etc.

Derung

The Derung (also spelt Drung or Dulong) people are located in a canyon surrounded by the Tibetan plateau in the north, the Gaoligong Mountain in the east, and the Dandanglika Mountain in the west. The inhabitant area of the Derung ethnic minority is quite isolated. Their population is mainly found in the Nujiang autonomous prefecture of Yunnan province, in the Dulong valley, while a few others can be found east of the Dulong valley, living in the mountains above the Nujiang river near the village of Binzhongluo in northern Gongshan county. The Derung language, which is closely related to that of Jingpo, belongs to the Sino-Tibetan phylum and is without written form. The traditional religion of the Derung people is nature worship, with beliefs that there are spirits controlling their fortune and the change of nature, so they often worship and charm away those spirits. Recently, there are also some Christians.

Dong

The Dong ethnic minority lives primarily in the border regions between Guizhou, Hunan and Hubei provinces. The Dong people trace their origins back to about the third century BC and, during the Tang dynasty (AD 618–907), they separated from the mixed minority 'Baiyue', naming themselves Dong. The Dong are thought to be the modern-day descendants of the ancient Liao people. Dong legends generally maintain that the ancestors of the Dong migrated from the east. According to the legends of the Southern Dong people, the ancestors of the Southern Dong came from Guangzhou, Guangdong and Wuzhou, Guangxi. The Northern Dong maintain that their ancestors fled Zhejiang and Fujian because of locust swarms. The Dong people speak a Dai language—a branch of the Zhuang-Dong group of the Sino-Tibetan phylum though many of them also speak Chinese. The Dong's beliefs remain original, believing that all things have spirits and gods—of land, water, ox, and the spirit of ancestors, etc.

Dongxiang

The Dongxiang ethnic minority derived their name from their native region—Dongxiang. Today, the Dongxiang people mainly inhabit the Dongxiang autonomous county in Gansu province, with a small number in Xinjiang Uyghur and the Ningxia Hui autonomous regions. Historians are divided in their views about the origin of the Dongxiang ethnic minority. Some hold that they are descendants of Mongolian troops posted in the Hezhou area by Genghis Khan (AD 1162–1227) during his march to the west. Other historians say they are a mixture of many ethnic groups—Hui, Mongolian, Han and Tibetan. The Dongxiang language is similar to Mongolian, both of which belong to a branch of the Mongolian Austronesian of the Altaic phylum. Since the Dongxiang have no written language, literature developed orally. Huaer, a popular form can be sung in both daily life and at festivals, absorbing fully, the essence of their oratory creativity, though most can speak and write in Chinese. The Dongxiang ethnic minority holds firm faith in Islam.

Ewenki

The Ewenki ethnic minority treasures their name of nationality which means 'people living in the mountain forests'. This ethnic minority is distributed across seven banners (counties) in the Inner Mongolia autonomous region and in Nahe county of Heilongjiang province, where they live together with Mongolians, Daurs, Hans, and Oroqens. Nantunzhen, the seat of the banner government, is a rising city on the grassland. A communication hub, it is the political, economic and cultural center of the Ewenki autonomous banner (*Qi*). The Ewenki are a Tungus people and speak a Tungus language which belongs to the Tungus-Manchu branch of the Altaic phylum. Interestingly it has no written characters. In the Qing dynasty (1644–1911), the Ewenki group learned to write in the Manchu form whilst today they can master Mongolian and Chinese languages. Most of the Ewenki people are disciples of shamanism. Meanwhile, they also believe that there are gods controlling their life. The god of mountain, in their eyes, is a long bearded senior man.

Gaoshan

The Taiwanese aborigines in maninland China are collectively known as the "Gaoshan". They now mainly live in Henan, Fujian, Liaoning and Hebei provinces and Guangxi Zhuang autonomous region. It is said these Taiwanese aborigines originated from one branch of the ancient Yue people living along the coast of the mainland China during the Stone Age. They were later joined by immigrants from the Philippines, Borneo and Micronesia. The Gaoshan people do not have their own script, and their spoken language belongs to the Indonesian Austronesian branch of the Malay-Polynesian Phylum. They altogether have more than 20 languages, 13 of which are still in use. As they have lived with Han people for a long time, many of them can speak southern Min language. The Gaoshan people are animists who believe that everything in nature has a soul. They believe in strength of spirit, ancestors and totem. They think that after a person's death, his soul stays to protect his descendants.

Gelao

The Gelao are mountain subsistence farmers and hunters in Guizhou and Yunnan provinces and Guangxi autonomous region. They are an old ethnic minority. Over 2000 years ago, the Gelao people lived in many places in China. At present, some bridges, graves, wells, and even villages in Guizhou province still bear Gelao names. The ethnic minority's name dates back to the Ming dynasty (AD 1368–1644). Before then, they were called the "Liao". The Gelao people have their own language which belongs to the Zhuang-Dong Group of the Sino-Tibetan phylum. But their dialects are quite different from each other. Some cannot communicate with each other, although they live in the same county. Only one fourth Gelao people actually speak the Gelao language, while the other use Chinese language as well as those of the Miao, the Yi and the Bouyei ethnic minorities. They write in Chinese as they don't have their own written form of characters. The Gelao people believe in the blessing of many gods as well as their ancestors.

Han

Members of the ethnic majority in China have traditionally been referred to as the Han race. This may well be because of the relatively long period of social, political, economic, and military consolidation and stability enjoyed by the Chinese nation during the period of the Han dynasty (206 BC–AD 220). The term 'Han', however, does not offer a full account of the cultural and ethnic origins of the Chinese people. It was, instead, an inclusive name for the various tribes that lived together on the Central China Plains well before the time of Christ. The trend over the ages was for many ethnic groups living adjacent to the Hua-Xia people to be assimilated at different times and to different degrees into what the Chinese have ultimately termed the Han culture. The original ethnic stock for this amalgam seems to have primarily included the Hua-Xia, the Eastern Yi, the Chu-Wu, and the Baiyue groups. Other non-Han peoples were assimilated into the Han culture at different points in China's history. They are, for example, the Huns (Xiongnu) and Xianbei between the third and fifth century AD, the Eastern Hu and the Jurchens (ancestors of the Manchus) from the tenth through the early thirteenth century, and the Manchus through their conquest of China in the seventeenth century.

Hani

The Hani people mainly inhabit an area within the reaches of the Yuan and the Lantsang rivers. This is a branch of the ancient Qiang people who had been nomadic on the Tibetan plateau and then emigrated southward. Most of the Hani people live in the valleys between the Yuanjiang and Lancang (Mekong) rivers—a vast area between the Ailao and the Mengle mountains in southern Yunnan province. They are under the jurisdiction of Honghe Hani-Yi autonomous prefecture, which includes Honghe, Yuanyang, Luchun and Jinping counties. Others dwell in Simao prefecture, Xishuangbanna, etc. The Hani are subsistence farmers who speak a Tibetan-Burman language, which belongs to the Sino-Tibetan phylum. The language has no characters of its own, so in 1957 the Chinese government created a set of spelling characters based on Latin. The Hani people are convinced that everything has soul, so they worship many gods and their ancestors. Since the early twentieth century, Christianity and Buddhism have spread to them, but with little influence on the Hani society.

Hezhen

The Hezhen ethnic minority is one of the smallest minorities of China. From generation to generation, they lived in the reaches of the Amur river (Heilongjiang river), the Songhua river, and the Ussuri river (Wusuli river) and appropriately named themselves 'Hezhen', meaning people of the eastern lower reaches. They are descendants of Heshui Tribe which reigned during the Sui (AD 581–618) and the Tang (AD 618–907) dynasties. Among China's least populous ethnic group, the Hezhen people speak a Manchu-Tungus language. The Hezhen people speak a language that belongs to the Altaic phylum. But they do not have their own characters, so most of them write in Chinese. The Hezhen people are shamanists, believing all have spirits and worship as many gods are there as varieties of animals and plants.

Hui

One of China's largest ethnic minorities, the Hui people can be found in most of the counties and cities throughout China, especially in Ningxia Hui autonomous region and Gansu, Qinghai, Henan, Hebei, Shandong and Yunnan provinces and Xinjiang Uygur autonomous region. The name Hui is an abbreviation for "Huihui," which first appeared in the literature of the Northern Song dynasty (AD 960–1127). The Hui minority is descended from the Arabic and Persian merchants who came to China during the seventh century. During the early years of the thirteenth century when Mongolian troops were making their western expeditions, group after group of Islamic-oriented people from Middle Asia, as well as Persians and Arabs, either were forced to move or voluntarily migrated into China. Chinese is the native language. In addition, they retain some of the Arabic and Persian words. Islamism plays a vital role in the development of the Hui ethnic minority in China. There is typically a mosque in each community. In fact, the religious thought has influenced the Hui people in all walks of life.

Jing

The Jing ethnic minority has a small population. Most live on the three islands of Guangxi Zhuang autonomous region, and the rest live and mingle with the Han, Zhuang and Yao ethnic groups. The Jing cultivate rice and are good fishermen. The ancestors of the Jing emigrated from Vietnam to Southwest China in the early sixteenth century and settled on the uninhabited lands beyond the neighborhood which had been populated by people of the Han and the Zhuang ethnic groups. The Jing's spoken language is similar to Vietnamese while many now speak Cantonese. The Jing are descendants of Vietnamese migrants who arrived in China from the fifteenth century. The word 'jing' is an equivalent of the Vietnamese Kinh, a name given to the majority people of Vietnam. Most of the Jing people believe in Taoism together with some thoughts of Buddhism and wizardry. They believe there are many gods who control their life, which include the god who is said to have made manitou to pacify the sea.

Jingpo

The Jingpo ethnic minority lives mainly in the Dehong and the Dai-Jingpo autonomous prefectures with some in Nujiang Lisu autonomous prefecture of Yunnan province, as well as in Myanmar. According to local legends and historical records, Jingpo ancestors in ancient times inhabited the southern part of the Xikang-Tibetan plateau. They gradually migrated south to the northwestern part of Yunnan, west of the Nujiang river. The local people, together with the newly-arrived Jingpos, were called "Xunchuanman," who lived mainly on hunting. The Jingpo live in the mountain areas along the border with Myanmar and speak a language closely related to that of the Derung, both of which belong to the Tibetan-Burman group of the Sino-Tibetan phylum. They do, however, also use the Chinese language. The main traditional religion is polytheism. The Jingpo people think everything has a soul that can never die, so, if a Jingpo meets with misfortune, she or he will turn to worship the spirits. However, some Jingpo people are Christian as a result of missionaries who first came to these areas in the early twentieth century.

Jino

The Jino ethnic minority, which was not officially recognized as a nationality until 1979, lives mainly in Jino town of Jinghong county, Xishuangbanna Dai autonomous prefecture of Yunnan province. It is said that the Jinos migrated to Jinoluoke from Pu'er and Mojiang or places even farther north. Jinoluoke is a mountainous area stretching for 70 kilometers from east to west and 50 kilometers from north to south. The expression Jino refers to an ethnic group that respects the mother's brother as a prominent person in the family. The Jino people have their own language, which belongs to a Tibetan-Burman branch of the Sino-Tibetan phylum. However, they have no written characters. The Juno's religion is animism. It is said that their ancestors who were part of the troops of Zhuge Lian during the Three Kingdoms Period (AD 220–280) were dispersed from the main force. Therefore, they regard Zhuge Lian as a distinguished joss (god).

Kazak

The Kazaks (also spelled Kazakhs) are a Turkic people of Eastern Europe and the northern parts of Central Asia (largely Kazakhstan, but also found in parts of Uzbekistan, Russia, Mongolia, and China). Kazakh identity is of medieval origin and was strongly shaped by foundation of the Kazak Khanate in AD 1456–1465. In China, the Kazak ethnic minority is mainly in Ili Kazak autonomous prefecture, Mori and Barkol autonomous counties of Xinjiang Uyghur autonomous region, as well as in Qinghai and Gansu provinces. The Kazaks are Turkic people, speaking a language which belongs to the Turkic group of the Altaic phylum. The Kazak language has two scripts, one based on Arabic, the other on Latin letters. However, many Kazak people can use Chinese, Uyghur and Mongolian languages. In the past, they believed in the shamanism. In about the eleventh century, they began to turn to Islam while some continued to admire nature, soul and fire like the shamanists.

Kirgiz

The Kirgiz ethnic minority is named after a word meaning forty girls. Its population is mostly distributed throughout the Kirgiz autonomous prefecture, Ili, Dacheng, Aksu, Kashgar, the southwest of Xinjiang autonomous region, as well as in Heilongjiang province. The forefathers of the Kirgiz lived on the upper reaches of the Yenisey river. In the mid-sixth century the Kirgiz tribe was under the rule of the Turkic khanate. After the Tang dynasty (AD 618–907) defeated the Eastern Turkic khanate, the Kirgiz came into contact with the dynasty. Most of them speak the Kirgiz language, which belongs to the Turkic group of Altaic phylum, and has a written form based on Arabic letters. The Kirgiz people have used different spoken languages in Xinjiang. While those living in the south of Xinjiang speak Uyghur language, those in the north of Xinjiang speak Kazak. Most Kirgiz people believe in Islam, but a few of the other follow the Tibetan Buddhism.

Korean

The Korean (also called "Chaoxian" in China) ethnic group is scattered mainly in Heilongjiang, Jilin and Liaoning provinces. Smaller populations of Korean people live in other areas in the Inner Mongolian autonomous region, and Beijing, Xi'an and other cities. Members of this ethnic minority living in Yanbian Korean autonomous prefecture of Jilin province speak and write in Korean while those living in other parts of China usually speak Chinese. The ancestors of the present Korean people were immigrants from the Korea peninsula. When they settled in China they gradually formed unique customs and evolved into a Chinese ethnic group. The Korean ethnic group does not follow one particular religion. While most of them are atheists, some believe in Buddhism, a belief that has influenced Korean life in the past, and others follow Christianity which spread to them from South Korea.

Lahu

Most of the Lahu people are scattered around three autonomous counties of Lancangjiang Lahu, Menglian, and Shuangjiang, with the others living in Simao, Lincang and Xishuangbanna of Yunnan province. The forebears of the Lahu people, who were hunters, began migrating southward to lush grassland which they discovered while pursuing a red deer. In the eighth century, after the rise of the kingdom of Nanzhao in present Yunnan province, the Lahu people were compelled to move south. By no later than the beginning of the eighteenth century they already had settled in their present-day places. The Lahu ethnic minority have their own language, which belong to the Yi branch of the Tibetan-Burman group of the Sino-Tibetan phylum. Most Lahu people also speak Chinese or Dai, as a result of their close relations to the Han and the Dai peoples. Their written characters were not formed until 1957. Lahu, in their language, means to roast the meat of the tiger. It indicates that this ethnic group was quite good at hunting. Some Lahu people practice nature and ancestor worship, but still others believe in Mahayana Buddhism. In addition, a few of them are Christians.

Lhoba

Scattered primarily throughout the Luoyu region of southeast Tibet, the Lhoba is the smallest of China's 56 ethnic groups. The name "Lhoba" is derived from the Tibetan word for southerners. The majority of the Lhoba ethnic minority have their homes in Mainling, Medog, Lhunze and Nangxian counties in southeastern Tibet. Additionally, a small number of them live in Luoyu in southern Tibet. Living at the foot of Himalayas, almost completely isolated from the outside world, the Lhoba lagged behind the rest of the world. The Lhobas speak a distinctive language belonging to the Tibetan-Myanmese language family, a branch of the Sino-Tibetan phylum. Few of them know the Tibetan language. Having no written script, Lhoba people used to keep records by notching wood or tying knots. The Lhoba's traditional religion is nature worship, not Tibetan Buddhism. They pray to the spirits, seeking blessings, and believe that shamans have the power to control them.

Li

The Li ethnic minority live mainly in Li-Miao autonomous prefecture in the center and south of Hainan province, with a small number of the others being mixed with the Han people. As a branch of the ancient Baiyue groups, the Li people had a close relationship with such present ethnic minorities as the Buyi, the Dong, the Dai, the Shui, and the Zhuang. The name "Li" is derived from their pronunciation of 'mountains'. The Li's language, which has diverse dialects, belongs to the Zhuang-Dong group of the Sino-Tibetan phylum. Because of long association with the Han people, some of the Li can also speak Chinese. In 1957, they created the written form of their language based on Roman script. The Li people believe all things have spirits and in some places, there are still relics of totem adoration. Owing to the spread of Christianity, some of Li have taken to this religion.

Lisu

The Lisu ethnic minority mainly inhabit in Nujiang Lisu autonomous prefecture in Yunnan province, with a few others living in the other cities within Yunnan and Sichuan provinces. They can also be found in the mountain areas of Myanmar, Thailand, and the northeast Indian state of Arunachal Pradesh. According to their clan history, which is passed from one generation to the next in the form of songs, the Lisu originate from eastern Tibet. They had close ties with the Yi and the Naxi ethnic minorities. The Lisu's language belongs to the Tibetan-Burman branch of the Sino-Tibentan phylum. There have been three distinct forms of writing, with the last one, created in 1957 and based on the Latin alphabet, being widely used now. The Lisu people believe the existence of gods and totem; but in the late nineteenth century some of them began to turn to the Christian faiths as a result of the preaching of missionaries in China.

Manchu

Arising from the Jurchen tribes and establishing the Jin dynasty (AD 1115–1234) and the Qing dynasty (AD 1644–1911), the Manchu people have greatly influenced Chinese history. Today, the Manchu ethnic minority has a population mainly in Heilongjiang, Jilin and Liaoning provinces of northeast China although they can also be found in many other cities as well. In the sixteenth century, the written language of the Manchu people was created from characters based on the Mongolian language. The Manchu language is part of the Tungus-Manchu group, a branch of Altaic phylum. As the Manchu people migrated from the northern to the central China, they learned and adopted the language of the dominant Han Chinese. The ancient Manchu people believed in shamanism. Later, with the influence of Buddhism, Daoism and Confucianism, their beliefs took on a pluralistic quality.

Maonan

The Maonan ethnic minority lives mostly in Huanjiang county of Guangxi Zhuang autonomous region, especially in the three regions of Shangnan, Zhongnan, and Xianan. Interestingly, more than 80% of the Maonan share the same surname: Tan. Maonan with the surname "Tan" believe that they are descended from the old inhabitants of the province of Hunan that emigrated to Guangxi and married Maonan women. Their language belongs to the Zhuang-Dong group of the Sino-Tibetan phylum; nearly all of the Maonan people can speak Chinese and the Zhuang language. Traditional Maonan religion is both animistic and polytheistic, with heavy Taoist influences. Many deities and rituals are borrowed from Chinese folk religion. They think that there are many gods who can control their life and they must sacrifice during festive days.

Miao

The Miao ethnic minority is one of the largest minority groups in China. They live mainly in Guizhou, Yunnan, Hunan, Hubei, and Hainan provinces and in Guangxi Zhuang autonomous region. As early as the Qin and Han dynasties (2000 years ago), the ancestors of the Miao people lived in the western part of present-day Hunan province and the eastern part of present-day Guizhou province. As a result of large-scale migrations over many centuries the Miao became widely dispersed. The Miao are now divided into several branches, such as Black Hmong, White Hmong, Striped Hmong, etc. The Miao language, which belongs to the Miao-Yao group of the Sino-Tibetan phylum, has developed into three dialects: the dialect of western Hunan province, the one of eastern Guizhou province and the one of the border area of Sichuan, Guizhou and Yunnan provinces. As a result of the long time living with the Han and other people, the Miao can also speak Chinese and the Dong and Zhuang languages. They have been writing their own Miao language based on Latin since 1956. The Miao people believe that everything in nature has a spirit. They worship their ancestors. Some also believe in Catholicism or other forms of Christianity.

Monba

The Monba ethnic minority has a long history. Their name, 'Monba', pronounced 'Menba' in Chinese, derives from Tibetan, referring to the people living in Menyu in the lower reaches of the Yarlung Tsangpo (Brahmaputra) river. The area became the hereditary manor of Tibet during the mid fourteenth and early eighteenth centuries. In the mid-seventeenth century, the Fifth Dalai Lama sent two of his disciples to Menyu to set up an office there. As a result, the Tibetan rule of religion and politics over the area was integrated. The Monba now occupy Tsona, Metog, and Nyingchi counties in Tibet. Thanks to their proximity to the Zang people (Tibetan people), the Monba's customs, traditions and life styles appear very similar to those of the Tibetans. The Monba language is a member of the Tibetan-Burman group of the Sino-Tibetan phylum. The Monba are sub-divided into six sub-groups because of their variations in their language. There is no written language; instead Tibetan is used. The Monba are generally adherents of the Gelugpa sect of Tibetan Buddhism (Lamaism), which they adopted in the seventeenth century as a result of the evangelical influence of the Bhutanese-educated Mera Lama. In addition, some still follow traditional religions.

Mongol

The Mongol ethnic minority is distributed primarily in the Inner Mongolia autonomous region along with the other areas in Qinghai, Gansu, Liaoning, Jilin, and Heilongjiang provinces. They originated from a tribe in northern China and Mongolia during the seventh century. "Mongolian" originally was the name of one of the Mongolian tribes roaming along the Erguna river. At the beginning of the thirteenth century, a Mongolian tribe headed by Genghis Khan unified all the Mongolian tribes, giving birth to a new people—the Mongolian ethnic minority. In AD 1206, he was elected the Great Khan of all Mongols with the title of Genghis Khan. Kublai Khan, the grandson of Genghis Khan founded the Yuan dynasty (AD 1206–1368) in 1272, and subdued the Southern Song dynasty (AD 1127–1279) in 1279, bringing the whole of China under his centralized rule. The Mongol language belongs to the Mongolian group of the Altaic phylum and has three main dialects. The written form is derived from that of the thirteenth century and experienced many changes. They once believed in shamanism but have turned to Lamaism (Tibetan Buddhism) since the Yuan dynasty.

Mulao

The majority of the Mulao ethnic minority live in Luocheng county of Guangxi Zhuang autonomous region. Others are scattered in other, neighboring counties. In their own language, Mulao means mother. Historical records trace the Mulao ethnic minority back to the period of the Yuan dynasty (AD 1271–1368). The Mulaos lived in Luocheng city of present Guangxi autonomous region and called themselves Lings or Jins, but the neighboring Zhuang people called them Bujins and the Hans called them Mulao. The Mulaos were mostly inhabited by families sharing the same surname. The Mulao language is a member of the Zhuang-Dong branch of the Sino-Tibetan phylum. But because of their extensive contacts with the Han and local Zhuang peoples, many Mulaos speak one or both of these languages in addition to their own. The Mulaos have no written language of their own, and the Chinese characters are commonly used for communication. Although the religion no longer plays a main role in their daily life, traditionally the Mulao have been mostly animists. Some of them also practice Daoism and Buddhism.

Naxi

The Naxi are an ethnic group inhabiting the foothills of the Himalayas in the northwestern part of Yunnan province (mostly living in Naxi autonomous county in Lijiang), as well as the southwestern part of Sichuan province and Tibet autonomous region. The Naxi are thought to have come originally from Northwest China, migrating south toward Tibetan populated regions, and usually inhabiting the most fertile river-side land.

According to historical documents, the Naxi's forefathers were closely related to a tribe called "Maoniu Yi" in the Han dynasty (206 BC–AD 220), "Mosha Yi" in the Jin dynasty (AD 265–420) and "Moxie Yi" in the Tang dynasty (AD 618–907). In the name Naxi, Na means 'black' and Xi means people. The Naxi people speak a language belonging to the Yi branch of the Tibetan-Burman group of the Sino-Tibetan phylum. Before 1949, most of the Naxi people were Lamaists, with some also holding the faiths of Dongba (a form of shamanism), believing that all have spirits and those spirits could never die. Although there was Buddhism, Taoism and Christianity being taught there, few Naxi people turned to those religions.

Nu

The Nu people are divided into the Northern, Central and Southern groups. Their homeland is a country of high mountains and deep ravines crossed by the Lancang (Mekong), Dulong and Nujiang rivers. The name "Nu" comes from the fact that they were living near the Nujiang river, and the name of their ethnic group derives from there. There is also a sparse distribution of the Nu in Weixi county in Diqing Tibetan autonomous prefecture of Yunnan province and in Zayu county of Tibet autonomous region, particularly around the border between Yunnan and Tibet. In comparison to the other ethnic groups in China, the Nu population is relatively small. The Nu language belongs to the Tibetan-Burman subgroup of the Sino-Tibetan language family. The dialects within the Nu language, however differ so much that Nu people from different regions cannot communicate with each other. The language has no written characters, so most Nu people use written Chinese. The religious beliefs remain primitive and animistic, believing everything has spirits and admiring the power of nature. Some of them believe in Lamaism (Tibetan Buddhism) and Christianity.

Oroqen

The Oroqen mainly live in the Oroqen autonomous banner (*Qi*) of Hulunbuir League of Inner Mongolia autonomous region and in the Greater and Lesser Xing'an Mountains of Heilongjiang province, an area known for its abundant wild animal resources. A small number of others are scattered in the neighboring provinces. For generations the Oroqens had lived a life of hunting and fishing in the forests. The name Oroqen appeared as early as the Qing dynasty (AD 1644–1911). The Oroqen people speak a language that belongs to the Tungus-Manchu group of the Altaic phylum. Since there is no written form of the language they usually use Chinese whilst some use Mongolian. The Oroqen hold their faith in the power of nature, ancestors and totems. This is a kind of shamanism. There are many gods such as the god of the sun, moon, fire, wind, mountains, etc. To the Oroqen people, bears and tigers are known as god, lord, and governor.

Pumi

The Pumi ethnic minority is mainly distributed in Lanping, Lijiang, Weixi and Yongsheng counties of Yunnan province, as well as in the Yi autonomous county of Ninglang. Some live in Muli and Yanyuan counties of Sichuan province as well. According to Pumi legends and historical records, ancient Pumis were a nomadic tribe, roaming the Qinghai-Tibet plateau. Their descendents later moved south to warmer, more verdant areas along valleys within the Hengduan mountain range. By the seventh century, the Pumis were living in Sichuan's Yuexi, Mianning, Hanyuan, Jiulong and Shimian areas, constituting one of the major ethnic minorities in the Xichang prefecture. After the thirteenth century, the Pumis gradually settled down in their present places. The Pumi people speak a language that belongs to the Tibetan-Burman group of the Sino-Tibetan phylum. In the past, the Pumi used Tibetan characters, however, today, most write in Chinese. Though a few of the Pumi do follow Lamaism and Taoism, most believe that many gods and their ancestors influence their lives, They are led by wizards in their ceremonies for peace, happiness and harvest.

Qiang

This ethnic minority lives mainly in Aba Tibetan autonomous prefecture of Sichuan province. And Maowen Qiang autonomous county is the largest area that is home to the Qiang. They have a profound history as evidenced by inscriptions on oracle bones. "Qiang" was a name given by ancient Hans to the nomadic people living in western China. The Qiangs were not a single distinctive ethnic group then. According to historical records, a clan group made their homes in what is today's Sichuan province. The Han dynasty (206 BC–AD 220) court in the second century had set up an administrative prefecture for the area. During AD 600 to 900 when the Tibetans gradually expanded their rule over the region, some Qiangs were assimilated by the Tibetans. Closely related to the Tibetans, the Qiangs speak a similar language that belongs to the Tibetan-Burman group of the Sino-Tibetan phylum. The Qiang language is divided into two dialects. But the Qiangs do not have a written language; instead, most of them can write in Chinese. The Qiangs believe that everything in nature has a spirit. They especially consider white quartz stone as the symbol of rightness having the power of gods, while the black quartz represents evil.

Russian

The Russian ethnic minority descends from Russian immigrants to China in as early as the eighteenth century. The largest Russian population arrived in Northeast China and Xinjiang after the Russian Civil War of 1918–22. Most of the ethnic Russians now live in Ili, Tacheng, Altay and Urumqi of Xinjiang Uyghur autonomous region whilst a few live in the Heilongjiang province and Inner Mongolian autonomous region. These immigrants were called "Guihua people" and their villages "Guihua village". The Russians use their own language (Russian) and written script, which belongs to the Slavic group of the Indo-European language family, when they communicate with each other. They also use the Chinese language and script in their social or official activities. Culturally and linguistically, the Russians are the same as those in Russia. While the Russians speak and write Russian, most of them also use Chinese. The Russians believed in Eastern Orthodox, with fewer people believing in Christianity, but in the recent years, they are more and more tended to hold no religious thoughts.

Salar

The Salar people live mostly in the Qinghai-Gansu border region, on both sides of the Yellow river, namely in Xunhua Salar and Hualong Hui autonomous counties of Qinghai and the adjacent Jishishan Bonan, Dongxiang and Salar autonomous county of Gansu province. There are also Salars in Xinjiang (especially in the Ili Kazakh autonomous prefecture). Having arrived and settled in the Qinghai province 700 years ago, they originally made their living by hunting, forestry and livestock farming. More recently, they thrive on agriculture, handicrafts and horticulture. Living in a semi-desert area, the Salars are Muslims. The Salars' ancestors were migrating Oghuz Turks who intermarried with the Han, the Tibetans, and the Hui Chinese. They have their own Turkic language which is a subfamily of the Altaic language family that includes Turkish. Most Salar people can also speak Chinese and Tibetan and use Chinese script.

She

The She people live primarily in the mountain areas of Fujian and Zhejiang provinces, and to a lesser extent in Jiangxi, Guangdong, and Anhui provinces. They refer to themselves as 'Shanha' where Shan means mountain and Ha means customers, 'customers of the mountain'. Though scholars disagree about the true origins of the She, most believe that the She's ancestors originally lived in the Phoenix mountains in Chaozhou of Guangdong province. They left their native place to escape the oppression of their feudal rulers. That's why they called themselves "guests from the mountains." The only ethnic minority to live in the provinces of

Zhejiang and Jiangxi, the She are in many ways quite similar to the Han. Always most She nowadays speak Chinese, some use a language that belongs to the Miao branch of the Miao-Yao group of the Sino-Tibetan phylum. The She language is similar to the Hakka language, one of the seven dialects in China. Because they do not have their own written language, they choose to write in Chinese. Some She are Buddhists, while others are polytheists or ancestor worshippers.

Shui

Most of the Shui people dwell on the upper reaches of the Longjiang and Duliu rivers that meander across plains and rolling land interspersed with vast expanses of forests in southern Guizhou province. Some Shuis have their homes in the northwestern part of the Guangxi Zhuang autonomous region. The She live in villages of several dozen households or live along with Hans. Most reside in hilly country 500 to 1500 meters high. Rivers have carved out their valleys. The Shui people have a language that is closely related to that of the Dong, both of which belong to the Zhuang-Dong group of the Sino-Tibetan phylum. As no written form of the Shui language exists, they usually write using Chinese characters. Historically there was a written form of the Shui language whose characters were called 'Shui Shu', but it was used only for religious activities. The Shuis are believers of polytheism. In former days a shaman would be employed to say prayers and animals slaughtered to be offered to evil spirits when someone fell ill or died or when something bad happened. Catholicism that came to the area in the late Qing dynasty (AD 1644–1911) won very few converts.

Tajik

According to folklore, the word Tajik means crown and this is usually how they refer to themselves. The Tajik ethnic minority is mainly distributed across the Tashi Ku'ergan Tajik autonomous county in Xinjiang

Uyghur autonomous region. Although the Tajik is among the smaller ethnic groups of China, they boast a rich history. The origin of the Tajik ethnic group can be traced to tribes speaking eastern Iranian who had settled in the eastern part of the Pamirs more than twenty centuries ago. In the eleventh century, the nomadic Turkic tribes called those people "Tajiks" who lived in Central Asia. Of Iranian stock, the Tajiks speak an Iranian language that belongs to the Iranian group of the Indo-European language family. Some Tajik people can also speak the Uyghur language and most of them write in Uyghur since the Tajik language has no written form. The Tajik follow the faith of Islam but usually only go to mosque during major festivals.

Tatar

The Tatars were a native people of the Volga region of Russia, Tatarstan and Bashkortostan. Most Tatars live in Uzbekistan, Kazakhstan, Ukraine, and Russia. The Tatar ethnic minority live mainly in Yining, Tacheng and Urumqi of Xinjiang Uyghur autonomous region. Historically this minority was known as "Dada" in China. The name Tatar likely originated amongst the nomadic Tatar confederation in the north-eastern Gobi desert in the fifth century. Their history in China dates from the Tang dynasty (AD 618–907), when the Tatar tribe was ruled by the nomadic Turkic khanate in northern China. As this state fell into decline, the Tatars grew in strength, and their name was used to refer to several tribes in the north after the Tang dynasty. Their homeland was later annexed by the Mongols, and when the Mongols pushed west, many Central Asians and Europeans called them Tatars. The Tatars have their own language which is a member of the Turkic subgroup of the Altaic phylum. They also speak and write Uyghur and Kazak as a result of their proximity to these minorities. The Tatars now follow Islam.

Tibetan

The Tibetan ethnic people (also known as Zang in Chinese) mainly live in the Tibetan autonomous region on the Tibetan Plateau, with some groupings in Qinghai, Gansu, Sichuan and Yunnan provinces. According to archeological findings, their ancestors lived in the Yarlung Tsangpo (Brahmaputra) river delta. Historical records suggest that the Tibetans were part of the Xiqiang group during the Han dynasty (206 BC–AD 220). The Tibetans first settled along the middle reaches of the Yarlung Tsangpo river in Tibet. At the beginning of the seventh century, King Songzan Gambo began to rule the whole of Tibet and made Losha (today's Lhasa) the capital. He designated official posts, defined military and administrative areas, created the Tibetan script, formulated laws and unified weights and measures, thus establishing the slavery kingdom known as "Bo," which was called "Tubo" in Chinese historical documents. The Tibetan language that belongs to the Tibetan-Burman group of the Sino-Tibetan language family is divided into three dialects and has both spoken and written forms. The Tibetans believe in the Indian Mahayana form of Buddhism but have gradually developed a distinctive Tibetan Buddhism which is also called Lamaism.

Tu

The Tu (or Monguor) ethnic minority is located mainly in Huzhu, Minhe, and Datong counties of Qinghai province as well as in Gansu province. Chinese term "Tu" was derived from the name of Tuyühu Khan, who was the older son of the King of Murong Xianbei who migrated westward from the northeast in AD 284. The last character of Tuyühu, pronounced as "hun" today, may have been pronounced "hu" in some dialect of ancient Chinese language. The Tu people speak a language belongs to the Mongolian group of the Altaic phylum. However, no written form exists. They can write in Chinese and today they are also using the characters created in recent years. The Tu people practice the faith of animism and some are the followers of Daoism. After the Ming dynasty (AD 1368–1644), many turned to Lamaism. There are over 40 temples of that religion as the center of Buddhist activities where they live. Dignitaries had also edited many Buddhist sutras and spread widely. In most villages, a Buddhist temple and a Taoist shrine coexist. There have also been multiple Catholic churches constructed in the past.

Tujia

The Tujia are an ethnic minority found in the provinces of Hunan, Hubei, Sichuan, and Guizhou. The Tujia people have a long history, dating back more than 2000 years, when the Ba kingdom reached the zenith of its power between 600 BC and 400 BC but was destroyed by the Qin in 316 BC. Their ancestors first immigrated to the western parts of Hunan and Hubei provinces. After being referred to by a long succession of different names in ancient documents, the Tujia people appear in historical records as their present status from about fourteenth century onwards. The Tujia speak a language that is very similar to the one used in Tibet autonomous region and Myanmar. Because the Tujia language has no written form, many Tujia people use Chinese. The Tujia people believe in the power of ancestors and gods, and hold sacrificial ceremonies during festivals. White tigers are highly revered and are thought to prevent evil.

Uyghur

The Uyghur ethnic minority lives mainly in Xinjiang Uyghur autonomous regions, especially to the south of Mt. Tianshan. The name Uyghur, which they also use to refer to themselves, means alliance or assistance. The Uyghurs have a profound history. Historical records indicate that Uyghur people had strong trade and communication links with a variety of middle Asian countries and other ethnic groups of China. The origin of the ethnic group can be traced back to the Dingling nomads in northern and northwestern China and in areas south of Lake Baikal and between the Irtish river and Lake Balkhash in the third century BC. The Uyghurs have their own language and alphabet which belongs to the

Turkic group of the Altaic phylum. Much of the written Uygur literature has been passed down from the eleventh century. Originally the Uyghurs had believed in shamanism, Manicheanism, Jing, Zoroastrianism, and Buddhism. Since the eleventh century the Uyghur people have gradually turned to Islam. This has strongly influenced their way of life and most festivals celebrated today relate to this religion.

Uzbek

The Uzbek people live in Yining, Tacheng, Kashgar, Shache, Yecheng and Urumqi cities of Xinjiang Uyghur autonomous region. The name, Uzbek means 'leader of self'. It originated from the Uzbek Khan, one of the local rulers under the Mongol Empire in the fourteenth century. The ancestors of the Uzbek group moved to China's Xinjiang from Central Asia in ancient times. In the Yuan dynasty (AD 1271–1368), Uzbek merchants often traveled along "the Silk Road" through Xinjiang to do business in inland areas. Their language belongs to Turkic group of the Altaic phylum, and they write in Uyghur character. Living along the famous Silk Road, the Uzbek people were mainly involved in commerce and trade until the Qing dynasty (AD 1644–1911). The Uzbek people are Islamic, and their adherence to Islamic customs is reflected in their food, clothing and culture, which are similar to those of the Uyghur and Tatar people.

Va

The Va (or Wa) live mainly in northern Myanmar, especially in the northern part of Shan state and the eastern part of Kachin state, near and along the Sino-Myanmar border. In China, the Va ethnic minority lives primarily in Ximeng, Cangyuan and Menglian counties of Yunnan province. The Va were known as the "Wild Wa [Va]" by British administrators during Britain's colonial control of Myanmar due to their practice of headhunting. The Va speak a Mon-Khmer language that belongs to the

Austro-Asiatic phylum, and the Va people use three different dialects. In 1957 a written formal language was created for the Va, since there were no characters that had been widely used. Traditionally the Va believe in the power of natural things and believe that all things have their spirits, including for example water, mountain, and wood. In recent years, some of the Va have become followers of Buddhism and Christianity.

Xibe

The Xibe ethnic minority mainly inhabits Liaoning and Jilin provinces, and Xinjiang Uyghur autonomous region. The Xibes think they are descendants of the ancient Xianbei people—a branch of the ancient Donghu ethnic group in northern China. Between AD 158 and 167, the Xianbei people formed a powerful tribal alliance and, between the third and sixth centuries, established political regimes in central China, where they mixed with Han people. But a small number of the Xianbei people never strayed very far from their native land. They were probably the ancestors of the Xibe people. They traditionally lived in the northeast of Liaoning with the Manchus, but in AD 1764 many were sent to the west as guards on the border with Russian frontier. At present, the Xibe living in Xinjiang speak the Xibe language, part of the Tungus-Manchu group of the Altaic phylum; whereas those in Northeast China usually speak Chinese and Mongolian. The Xibe people once were animists, shamanists, Lamaists. More recently, as they assimilated other cultures, a few of them also observed Confucianism and Tibetan Buddhism.

Yao

The Yao ethnic minority is a typical nationality living in the mountain regions of the southern China. Their main habitats are Hunan, Yunnan, Guangdong, Guizhou, and Jiangxi provinces together with Guangxi Zhuang autonomous region. They are divided into several branches. Their language belongs to the Miao-Yao sub-group of the Sino-Tibetan language family. While most people speak the Yao language, some speak a language similar to the Miao language, and a few even use the Zhuang and Dong languages. They can also speak Han and Zhuang languages. As to the written characters, Nv Shu—a special written language in South China used only by women—is used. Han characters are widely used among Yao people, but written words were created in 1982. Traditional religions include nature worship, ancestor, and Daoism. However, the Yao people living in different regions have differing beliefs.

Yi

Although different groups of the Yi refer to themselves in different ways (including Nuosu, Nisu, Sani, Axi, Lolo, etc.), they have been grouped into a single ethnicity by the Chinese. The Yi minority lives mainly in the hillside and basin areas in Yunnan, Sichuan, and Guizhou provinces together with the northwestern part of Guangxi Zhuang autonomous region. Nearly all the Yi people live in mountain areas. The altitudinal differences of the Yi areas are the basis of the old saying that "weather is different a few miles away". This is the primary reason why the Yi in various areas are so different from one another in the ways they make a living. Divided into six mutually unintelligible dialects—Northern Yi (Nuosu), Western Yi (Lalo), Central Yi (Lolopo), Southern Yi (Nisu), Southeastern Yi (Sani), and Eastern Yi (Nasu), their language derives from the Tibetan-Burman family of the Sino-Tibetan phylum. With regard to its characters, the Yi ethnic minority created the earliest syllable letters in the thirteenth century. Various beliefs are treasured, such as the belief of the spirit, the worship of their ancestors, and the adoration of nature, along with the cherishing of Catholicism, Christianity, and Buddhism.

Yugur

In Chinese, 'Yugur' means 'wealth and solidity'. Most of the Yugur people live in the four areas of Sunan Yugur autonomous county, and the rest in the Yugur village of Huangnibao area in Jiuquan city (in western Gansu province). Though descended from the Uyghurs of the ninth century and originally speaking a Turkic language, three languages are being used by the Yugurs: the western Yuhur language, a Turkic branch of the Altaic language family, used by the Yugur people who live in the western part of Sunan Yugur autonomous county; the eastern Yuhur language, a Mongolian branch of the Altaic language family, used by the Yugur people living in the eastern part of the autonomous county; and Chinese language. However, they don't have their own written language. Chinese characters are widely used amongst all the Yugur people. The Yugur people believe in Tibetan Buddhism (Lamaism). Other forms of spirit worship, such as an original belief called the God Khan, are also cherished by them.

Zhuang

The Zhuang ethnic minority is the largest minority group in China. Over 90 percent of the population is dominant in Guangxi Zhuang autonomous region. The remaining Zhuang people reside in Yunnan, Guangdong, Guizhou and Hunan provinces. Thousands of years ago, ancestors of the Zhuang settled down in southern China. During the Spring and Autumn Period (770–221 BC), they were one branch of the Baiyue people. "Zhuang" was one of the names the ancestors of this ethnic minority gave to themselves. The Zhuang used to call themselves by at least a dozen other names, too. The Zhuang have a language of their own that belongs to the Zhuang-Dai branch of the Sino-Tibetan phylum. The language is divided into two dialects. Chinese characters were used before 1955 for writing. Since 1957, a writing system—which is based on the Latin alphabet—has been created. Since ancient times, the Zhuang have had numerous kinds of beliefs. They believe in the totem and their ancestors. Other religions include Buddhism, Daoism, and Christianity.

Appendix B: China's Ethnic Populations by Province

R. Guo, *China Ethnic Statistical Yearbook 2020*,
https://doi.org/10.1007/978-3-030-49024-9

Table B.1 China's total populations reported by the 2000 and 2010 national population censuses

	2000			2010		
Ethnic group	Population	Male	Female	Population	Male	Female
Total	1,242,612,226	640,275,969	602,336,257	1,332,810,869	682,329,104	650,481,765
Achang	33,936	17,189	16,747	39,555	19,751	19,804
Bai	1,858,063	947,019	911,044	1,933,510	978,998	954,512
Baonan	16,505	8416	8089	20,074	10,016	10,058
Blang	91,882	47,534	44,348	119,639	61,230	58,409
Buyi	2,971,460	1,530,887	1,440,573	2,870,034	1,455,720	1,414,314
Dai	1,158,989	578,938	580,051	1,261,311	625,176	636,135
Daur	132,394	65,699	66,695	131,992	64,866	67,126
Deang	17,935	9032	8903	20,556	10,039	10,517
Derung	7426	3649	3777	6930	3349	3581
Dong	2,960,293	1,566,575	1,393,718	2,879,974	1,511,959	1,368,015
Dongxiang	513,805	264,453	249,352	621,500	317,490	304,010
Ewenki	30,505	14,740	15,765	30,875	14,668	16,207
Gaoshan	4461	2418	2043	4009	2029	1980
Gelao	579,357	310,775	268,582	550,746	289,369	261,377
Han	1,137,386,112	586,159,888	551,226,224	1,220,844,520	625,032,848	595,811,672
Hani	1,439,673	751,899	687,774	1,660,932	863,370	797,562
Hezhe	4640	2289	2351	5354	2651	2703
Hui	9,816,805	5,002,072	4,814,733	10,586,087	5,373,741	5,212,346
Jing	22,517	11,328	11,189	28,199	14,416	13,783
Jingpo	132,143	65,291	66,852	147,828	71,318	76,510
Jino	20,899	10,596	10,303	23,143	11,744	11,399
Kazak	1,250,458	633,875	616,583	1,462,588	747,368	715,220
Kirgiz	160,823	81,695	79,128	186,708	94,645	92,063
Korean	1,923,842	956,946	966,896	1,830,929	910,535	920,394
Lahu	453,705	234,144	219,561	485,966	247,667	238,299
Lhoba	2965	1484	1481	3682	1803	1879
Li	1,247,814	647,547	600,267	1,463,064	756,992	706,072

Lisu	634,912	326,274	308,638	702,839	355,374	347,465
Manchu	10,682,262	5,547,750	5,134,512	10,387,958	5,401,812	4,986,146
Maonan	107,166	56,443	50,723	101,192	52,836	48,356
Miao	8,940,116	4,656,974	4,283,142	9,426,007	4,870,328	4,555,679
Monba	8923	4428	4495	10,561	5261	5300
Mongol	5,813,947	2,875,453	2,938,494	5,981,840	2,999,520	2,982,320
Mulao	207,352	107,154	100,198	216,257	110,516	105,741
Naxi	308,839	154,971	153,868	326,295	162,635	163,660
Nu	28,759	14,857	13,902	37,523	18,907	18,616
Oroqen	8196	3872	4324	8659	4033	4626
Pumi	33,600	17,043	16,557	42,861	21,433	21,428
Qiang	306,072	155,981	150,091	309,576	156,539	153,037
Russian	15,609	7365	8244	15,393	7284	8109
Salar	104,503	53,715	50,788	130,607	66,281	64,326
She	709,592	381,038	328,554	708,651	383,213	325,438
Shui	406,902	213,488	193,414	411,847	213,644	198,203
Tajik	41,028	20,954	20,074	51,069	26,112	24,957
Tatar	4890	2550	2340	3556	1899	1657
Tibetan	5,416,021	2,697,807	2,718,214	6,282,187	3,155,625	3,126,562
Tu	241,198	123,571	117,627	289,565	148,055	141,510
Tujia	8,028,133	4,196,469	3,831,664	8,353,912	4,307,260	4,046,652
Uygur	8,399,393	4,272,863	4,126,530	10,069,346	5,097,594	4,971,752
Uzbek	12,370	6498	5872	10,569	5673	4896
Va	396,610	202,626	193,984	429,709	216,439	213,270
Xibe	188,824	98,737	90,087	190,481	99,571	90,910
Yao	2,637,421	1,391,332	1,246,089	2,796,003	1,458,842	1,337,161
Yi	7,762,272	3,989,391	3,772,881	8,714,393	4,456,382	4,258,011
Yugur	13,719	6935	6784	14,378	7325	7053
Zhuang	16,178,811	8,376,754	7,802,057	16,926,381	8,689,488	8,236,893

Note: Total population includes servicemen (while ethnic breakdowns do not include them) as well as unknown ethnic groups and foreigners with Chinese citizenship

Table B.2 Anhui's populations reported by the 2000 and 2010 national population censuses

	2000			2010		
Ethnic group	Population	Male	Female	Population	Male	Female
Total	58,999,948	30,437,820	28,562,128	59,500,468	30,245,513	29,254,955
Achang	5	1	4	25	5	20
Bai	761	117	644	692	284	408
Baonan	1		1	15	5	10
Blang	33	7	26	78	13	65
Buyi	3103	970	2133	3413	845	2568
Dai	373	43	330	831	191	640
Daur	93	42	51	77	29	48
Deang	1		1	18	1	17
Derung	99	41	58	26	2	24
Dong	1917	423	1494	2147	571	1576
Dongxiang	9	3	6	112	83	29
Ewenki	17	4	13	11	5	6
Gaoshan	80	38	42	89	38	51
Gelao	199	73	126	448	196	252
Han	58,602,112	30,247,912	28,354,200	59,104,826	30,054,506	29,050,320
Hani	679	55	624	1138	166	972
Hezhe	8	2	6	23	8	15
Hui	337,521	169,697	167,824	328,062	165,284	162,778
Jing	28	15	13	92	39	53
Jingpo	20	2	18	166	27	139
Jino	3	1	2	8	4	4
Kazak	24	7	17	1203	603	600
Kirgiz	1	1		14	9	5
Korean	2660	1292	1368	1200	570	630
Lahu	219	29	190	347	45	302
Lhoba	8	3	5	2	1	1
Li	225	57	168	1610	672	938

Lisu	102	15	87	589	126	463
Manchu	8688	4204	4484	8516	4373	4143
Maonan	26	9	17	58	17	41
Miao	6995	1758	5237	13,856	4071	9785
Monba	4		4	65	29	36
Mongol	14,354	3730	10,624	2809	1260	1549
Mulao	47	14	33	123	41	82
Naxi	71	14	57	87	19	68
Nu	13	1	12	182	77	105
Oroqen	13	7	6	7	5	2
Pumi	36	8	28	20	8	12
Qiang	87	37	50	183	85	98
Russian	22	11	11	33	19	14
Salar	26	15	11	78	41	37
She	1563	848	715	1682	921	761
Shui	307	47	260	562	201	361
Tajik	98	46	52	3	2	1
Tatar	10	6	4	9	3	6
Tibetan	2263	935	1328	1279	511	768
Tu	223	59	164	493	219	274
Tujia	2196	766	1430	6185	2978	3207
Uygur	1733	912	821	710	409	301
Uzbek	4	2	2	4	3	1
Va	305	86	219	1019	354	665
Xibe	93	52	41	143	72	71
Yao	406	108	298	1171	390	781
Yi	5607	1683	3924	6667	2656	4011
Yugur	2	1	1	43	23	20
Zhuang	4331	1599	2732	6998	2298	4700

Note: Total population includes servicemen (while ethnic breakdowns do not include them) as well as unknown ethnic groups and foreigners with Chinese citizenship

Table B.3 Beijing's populations reported by the 2000 and 2010 national population censuses

	2000			2010		
Ethnic group	Population	Male	Female	Population	Male	Female
Total	13,569,194	7,074,518	6,494,676	19,612,368	10,126,430	9,485,938
Achang	6	4	2	28	14	14
Bai	1554	816	738	3493	1778	1715
Baonan	7	4	3	24	17	7
Blang	8	4	4	68	35	33
Buyi	1035	525	510	2768	1393	1375
Dai	265	105	160	1022	463	559
Daur	853	399	454	2043	868	1175
Deang	4	2	2	19	14	5
Derung	8	5	3	14	9	5
Dong	1616	825	791	3774	1865	1909
Dongxiang	101	65	36	484	345	139
Ewenki	164	74	90	433	182	251
Gaoshan	101	50	51	103	46	57
Gelao	272	169	103	1307	771	536
Han	12,983,696	6,779,560	6,204,136	18,811,154	9,729,984	9,081,170
Hani	164	78	86	680	329	351
Hezhe	84	38	46	201	81	120
Hui	235,837	117,222	118,615	249,223	122,993	126,230
Jing	22	8	14	56	22	34
Jingpo	37	13	24	112	48	64
Jino	6	4	2	20	9	11
Kazak	400	190	210	1602	685	917
Kirgiz	45	23	22	189	71	118
Korean	20,369	9416	10,953	37,380	17,437	19,943
Lahu	28	9	19	202	95	107
Lhoba	6	2	4	11	5	6

Li	343	176	167	1078	501	577
Lisu	48	23	25	264	142	122
Manchu	250,286	128,173	122,113	336,032	167,963	168,069
Maonan	31	20	11	124	51	73
Miao	5291	2835	2456	12,957	6698	6259
Monba	19	8	11	31	16	15
Mongol	37,464	18,247	19,217	76,736	36,758	39,978
Mulao	192	102	90	358	162	196
Naxi	246	130	116	554	282	272
Nu	7	5	2	50	22	28
Oroqen	78	33	45	165	77	88
Pumi	14	8	6	46	22	24
Qiang	177	95	82	661	308	353
Russian	216	78	138	343	124	219
Salar	413	305	108	644	399	245
She	629	399	230	1515	842	673
Shui	100	50	50	340	168	172
Tajik	22	13	9	21	12	9
Tatar	29	17	12	23	9	14
Tibetan	2920	1557	1363	5575	2746	2829
Tu	396	225	171	554	285	269
Tujia	8372	4579	3793	23,601	12,088	11,513
Uygur	3129	1798	1331	6975	3430	3545
Uzbek	23	9	14	51	25	26
Va	48	19	29	324	180	144
Xibe	1491	709	782	2569	1201	1368
Yao	1112	623	489	3213	1511	1702
Yi	1919	963	956	5849	3418	2431
Yugur	52	24	28	95	39	56
Zhuang	7322	3630	3692	14,994	7275	7719

Note: Total population includes servicemen (while ethnic breakdowns do not include them) as well as unknown ethnic groups and foreigners with Chinese citizenship

Table B.4 Chongqing's populations reported by the 2000 and 2010 national population censuses

Ethnic group	2000			2010		
	Population	Male	Female	Population	Male	Female
Total	30,512,763	15,841,429	14,671,334	28,846,170	14,608,870	14,237,300
Achang	12	3	9	19	6	13
Bai	1140	464	676	1569	712	857
Baonan	3	1	2	9	8	1
Blang	261	33	228	288	45	243
Buyi	2401	772	1629	3383	1310	2073
Dai	604	126	478	881	239	642
Daur	47	20	27	118	47	71
Deang	6	1	5	5	1	4
Derung	129	58	71	9	5	4
Dong	2585	1354	1231	3271	1724	1547
Dongxiang	25	13	12	102	56	46
Ewenki	22	9	13	25	12	13
Gaoshan	60	26	34	45	24	21
Gelao	1191	340	851	2808	1298	1510
Han	28,539,156	14,812,506	13,726,650	26,909,061	13,617,247	13,291,814
Hani	959	182	777	1398	365	1033
Hezhe	9	6	3	12	6	6
Hui	10,064	5019	5045	9056	4658	4398
Jing	27	13	14	25	14	11
Jingpo	16	5	11	82	21	61
Jino	31	6	25	27	9	18
Kazak	22	8	14	259	104	155
Kirgiz	2	1	1	28	11	17
Korean	1044	525	519	637	331	306
Lahu	459	51	408	479	82	397
Lhoba	17	6	11	2	2	

Li	228	108	120	587	277	310
Lisu	219	42	177	328	117	211
Manchu	3079	1620	1459	4571	2431	2140
Maonan	15	5	10	63	33	30
Miao	502,421	266,237	236,184	482,714	248,537	234,177
Monba	15	6	9	16	8	8
Mongol	7846	3228	4618	5688	2890	2798
Mulao	111	38	73	208	80	128
Naxi	217	80	137	421	171	250
Nu	10	3	7	28	11	17
Oroqen	5	2	3	3	3	
Pumi	11	3	8	51	28	23
Qiang	365	168	197	675	317	358
Russian	12	4	8	40	15	25
Salar	36	13	23	71	40	31
She	92	56	36	252	146	106
Shui	120	52	68	197	93	104
Tajik	177	121	56	2	1	1
Tatar	6	2	4	1		1
Tibetan	2292	931	1361	3086	1250	1836
Tu	220	81	139	715	351	364
Tujia	1,424,352	742,694	681,658	1,398,707	717,687	681,020
Uygur	1194	572	622	1162	605	557
Uzbek				4	2	2
Va	1445	770	675	577	112	465
Xibe	52	25	27	143	70	73
Yao	474	192	282	1045	455	590
Yi	4531	1397	3134	6336	2598	3738
Yugur	3		3	27	14	13
Zhuang	2764	1380	1384	4634	2066	2568

Note: Total population includes servicemen (while ethnic breakdowns do not include them) as well as unknown ethnic groups and foreigners with Chinese citizenship

Table B.5 Fujian's populations reported by the 2000 and 2010 national population censuses

	2000			2010		
Ethnic group	Population	Male	Female	Population	Male	Female
Total	34,097,947	17,568,535	16,529,412	36,894,217	18,981,054	17,913,163
Achang	3		3	62	29	33
Bai	608	302	306	4008	2127	1881
Baonan	3	2	1	5	2	3
Blang	10	4	6	226	117	109
Buyi	4206	2130	2076	22,172	12,141	10,031
Dai	169	56	113	2401	1230	1171
Daur	24	12	12	96	43	53
Deang	1		1	22	13	9
Derung	47	23	24	11	5	6
Dong	5768	3452	2316	15,608	9111	6497
Dongxiang	15	10	5	339	199	140
Ewenki	12	4	8	16	6	10
Gaoshan	416	218	198	423	224	199
Gelao	618	411	207	3249	1878	1371
Han	33,514,147	17,251,899	16,262,248	36,097,362	18,544,219	17,553,143
Hani	92	24	68	1373	749	624
Hezhe	1		1	43	22	21
Hui	109,880	61,664	48,216	115,978	65,663	50,315
Jing	67	18	49	260	120	140
Jingpo	31	4	27	295	137	158
Jino	4		4	16	5	11
Kazak	6	3	3	1492	709	783
Kirgiz	7	2	5	50	32	18
Korean	1785	895	890	2157	1088	1069
Lahu	26	4	22	375	203	172
Lhoba	26	12	14	16	10	6
Li	524	202	322	3551	1660	1891

Lisu	21	5	16	403	193	210
Manchu	7094	3716	3378	8372	4258	4114
Maonan	86	29	57	372	203	169
Miao	22,065	12,925	9140	88,017	50,024	37,993
Monba	24	10	14	23	9	14
Mongol	6114	2741	3373	5830	2948	2882
Mulao	131	69	62	527	245	282
Naxi	49	22	27	123	53	70
Nu	27	8	19	307	160	147
Oroqen	25	7	18	12	8	4
Pumi	7	2	5	47	28	19
Qiang	99	53	46	458	247	211
Russian	13	4	9	30	13	17
Salar	13	7	6	80	43	37
She	375,193	201,710	173,483	365,514	196,573	168,941
Shui	353	227	126	2433	1301	1132
Tajik	22	14	8	19	13	6
Tatar				17	11	6
Tibetan	1290	526	764	1739	711	1028
Tu	890	515	375	4000	2268	1732
Tujia	29,046	17,638	11,408	89,824	51,104	38,720
Uygur	1080	611	469	1159	632	527
Uzbek	8	3	5	9	4	5
Va	108	49	59	1325	723	602
Xibe	53	20	33	142	51	91
Yao	1226	560	666	5669	3163	2506
Yi	2615	1239	1376	13,536	7630	5906
Yugur	3	1	2	34	15	19
Zhuang	10,818	3909	6909	29,696	15,037	14,659

Note: Total population includes servicemen (while ethnic breakdowns do not include them) as well as unknown ethnic groups and foreigners with Chinese citizenship

Table B.6 Gansu's populations reported by the 2000 and 2010 national population censuses

	2000			2010		
Ethnic group	Population	Male	Female	Population	Male	Female
Total	25,124,282	13,021,654	12,102,628	25,575,263	13,064,193	12,511,070
Achang	1		1	1	1	
Bai	272	158	114	291	181	110
Baonan	15,170	7690	7480	18,170	8908	9262
Blang	9	3	6	12	5	7
Buyi	768	376	392	366	201	165
Dai	13	5	8	89	43	46
Daur	115	57	58	95	45	50
Deang	7	6	1	2	1	1
Derung	37	22	15	8	4	4
Dong	380	208	172	136	77	59
Dongxiang	451,622	231,589	220,033	546,255	276,107	270,148
Ewenki	16	9	7	13	7	6
Gaoshan	55	25	30	27	15	12
Gelao	18	7	11	98	64	34
Han	22,925,063	11,888,144	11,036,919	23,164,817	11,841,566	11,323,251
Hani	40	20	20	88	36	52
Hezhe	21	12	9	42	26	16
Hui	1,184,930	620,249	564,681	1,258,641	642,356	616,285
Jing	7	3	4	109	54	55
Jingpo	11	6	5	19	13	6
Jino	1		1	5	1	4
Kazak	2963	1453	1510	4444	2124	2320
Kirgiz	13	7	6	48	12	36
Korean	1565	804	761	559	273	286
Lahu	10	9	1	14	6	8
Lhoba				1		1
Li	58	32	26	517	250	267

Lisu	115	62	53	28	13	15
Manchu	17,285	8958	8327	14,206	7444	6762
Maonan	77	35	42	12	6	6
Miao	1509	721	788	1212	738	474
Monba	24	12	12	89	41	48
Mongol	15,774	6485	9289	10,935	5351	5584
Mulao	30	20	10	39	24	15
Naxi	28	9	19	53	26	27
Nu	7	4	3	101	44	57
Oroqen	10	7	3	10	5	5
Pumi	11	6	5	8	5	3
Qiang	64	29	35	115	62	53
Russian	55	22	33	48	16	32
Salar	11,784	6195	5589	13,517	6852	6665
She	201	132	69	245	154	91
Shui	88	36	52	50	31	19
Tajik	99	53	46	13	4	9
Tatar	186	90	96	18	10	8
Tibetan	443,228	222,362	220,866	488,359	245,262	243,097
Tu	30,338	15,410	14,928	30,781	15,154	15,627
Tujia	1341	754	587	2092	1269	823
Uygur	2131	987	1144	1937	853	1084
Uzbek	18	7	11	15	7	8
Va	143	75	68	97	50	47
Xibe	312	166	146	299	138	161
Yao	228	121	107	354	181	173
Yi	1722	772	950	870	493	377
Yugur	12,962	6567	6395	13,001	6640	6361
Zhuang	1308	642	666	1647	824	823

Note: Total population includes servicemen (while ethnic breakdowns do not include them) as well as unknown ethnic groups and foreigners with Chinese citizenship

Table B.7 Guangdong's populations reported by the 2000 and 2010 national population censuses

	2000			2010		
Ethnic group	Population	Male	Female	Population	Male	Female
Total	85,225,007	43,381,720	41,843,287	104,320,459	54,400,538	49,919,921
Achang	40	13	27	623	389	234
Bai	5905	2983	2922	16,692	9419	7273
Baonan	5	2	3	25	15	10
Blang	98	35	63	495	258	237
Buyi	23,237	11,089	12,148	64,253	35,809	28,444
Dai	1256	293	963	6675	3554	3121
Daur	158	72	86	411	208	203
Deang	7	1	6	62	38	24
Derung	64	34	30	51	27	24
Dong	55,870	25,767	30,103	83,574	46,825	36,749
Dongxiang	61	34	27	403	309	94
Ewenki	249	82	167	92	49	43
Gaoshan	142	71	71	161	81	80
Gelao	5782	2687	3095	10,897	5910	4987
Han	83,955,870	42,777,757	41,178,113	102,253,138	53,273,872	48,979,266
Hani	1061	425	636	5987	3585	2402
Hezhe	13	7	6	298	150	148
Hui	25,307	12,394	12,913	45,073	24,357	20,716
Jing	285	111	174	484	232	252
Jingpo	261	107	154	677	387	290
Jino	17	3	14	26	7	19
Kazak	46	22	24	4602	2504	2098
Kirgiz	15	7	8	577	314	263
Korean	10,463	5309	5154	17,615	9118	8497
Lahu	350	26	324	1335	723	612
Lhoba	8	4	4	8	5	3
Li	6550	2292	4258	19,579	9950	9629

Lisu	162	56	106	1693	1069	624
Manchu	17,972	9044	8928	29,557	15,200	14,357
Maonan	1263	502	761	5017	2866	2151
Miao	120,606	59,446	61,160	251,970	141,661	110,309
Monba	22	8	14	62	26	36
Mongol	20,669	8215	12,454	14,331	7495	6836
Mulao	4814	2089	2725	10,961	5918	5043
Naxi	144	79	65	499	277	222
Nu	38	15	23	584	277	307
Oroqen	26	12	14	52	24	28
Pumi	32	10	22	121	61	60
Qiang	340	164	176	1886	1058	828
Russian	50	21	29	125	38	87
Salar	89	46	43	823	508	315
She	28,053	15,322	12,731	29,549	16,743	12,806
Shui	1948	1028	920	6525	3675	2850
Tajik	95	41	54	165	98	67
Tatar	10	4	6	55	28	27
Tibetan	7020	2859	4161	5604	2723	2881
Tu	4500	2385	2115	10,161	5629	4532
Tujia	135,431	68,464	66,967	212,513	117,141	95,372
Uygur	3057	1682	1375	6438	2602	3836
Uzbek	42	22	20	73	41	32
Va	655	215	440	4718	2723	1995
Xibe	322	151	171	705	341	364
Yao	202,667	102,744	99,923	276,266	148,395	127,871
Yi	8700	4062	4638	36,264	20,632	15,632
Yugur	9		9	53	32	21
Zhuang	570,200	260,335	309,865	877,509	473,900	403,609

Note: Total population includes servicemen (while ethnic breakdowns do not include them) as well as unknown ethnic groups and foreigners with Chinese citizenship

Table B.8 Guangxi's populations reported by the 2000 and 2010 national population censuses

	2000			2010		
Ethnic group	Population	Male	Female	Population	Male	Female
Total	43,854,538	23,239,376	20,615,162	46,023,761	23,924,704	22,099,057
Achang	19	13	6	26	14	12
Bai	831	392	439	2489	1255	1234
Baonan	2	1	1	1		1
Blang	49	19	30	81	32	49
Buyi	20,826	9484	11,342	20,072	8094	11,978
Dai	847	339	508	796	276	520
Daur	60	23	37	83	37	46
Deang	2	2		7	2	5
Derung	28	15	13	21	9	12
Dong	303,139	156,153	146,986	305,565	153,819	151,746
Dongxiang	98	48	50	17	10	7
Ewenki	35	16	19	46	19	27
Gaoshan	409	228	181	278	159	119
Gelao	3820	1961	1859	3885	2048	1837
Han	27,024,974	14,471,260	12,553,714	28,916,096	15,156,624	13,759,472
Hani	214	90	124	474	222	252
Hezhe	13	10	3	63	34	29
Hui	32,512	16,433	16,079	32,319	16,420	15,899
Jing	20,123	10,256	9867	23,283	12,047	11,236
Jingpo	95	46	49	41	5	36
Jino	5	1	4	4	2	2
Kazak	49	27	22	1884	977	907
Kirgiz	9	5	4	28	16	12
Korean	2008	1055	953	2701	1417	1284
Lahu	65	38	27	111	42	69
Lhoba	1		1	3	3	
Li	2997	1535	1462	4542	2251	2291

Lisu	59	30	29	154	63	91
Manchu	9576	4842	4734	11,159	5695	5464
Maonan	73,578	39,083	34,495	65,587	34,112	31,475
Miao	462,956	237,672	225,284	475,492	241,305	234,187
Monba	3	2	1	77	27	50
Mongol	8651	2872	5779	3017	1485	1532
Mulao	170,225	87,729	82,496	172,305	87,513	84,792
Naxi	52	25	27	149	69	80
Nu	43	21	22	119	65	54
Oroqen	20	10	10	8	4	4
Pumi	21	5	16	25	18	7
Qiang	115	62	53	169	87	82
Russian	13	4	9	8	2	6
Salar	30	17	13	128	59	69
She	418	253	165	829	496	333
Shui	15,476	8332	7144	13,559	7025	6534
Tajik	135	71	64	2		2
Tatar	4	2	2	24	13	11
Tibetan	2194	998	1196	815	393	422
Tu	438	237	201	1501	665	836
Tujia	4630	2586	2044	9155	4830	4325
Uygur	1550	753	797	1795	930	865
Uzbek	47	22	25	13	8	5
Va	248	119	129	662	304	358
Xibe	118	56	62	146	79	67
Yao	1,471,946	775,032	696,914	1,493,530	772,111	721,419
Yi	9712	5033	4679	9700	5045	4655
Yugur	48	21	27	7	2	5
Zhuang	14,207,143	7,403,064	6,804,079	14,448,422	7,406,315	7,042,107

Note: Total population includes servicemen (while ethnic breakdowns do not include them) as well as unknown ethnic groups and foreigners with Chinese citizenship

Table B.9 Guizhou's populations reported by the 2000 and 2010 national population censuses

	2000			2010		
Ethnic group	Population	Male	Female	Population	Male	Female
Total	35,247,695	18,464,477	16,783,218	34,748,556	17,905,471	16,843,085
Achang	28	12	16	26	9	17
Bai	187,362	101,312	86,050	179,510	95,923	83,587
Baonan	3	2	1	8	4	4
Blang	30	14	16	49	16	33
Buyi	2,798,200	1,449,457	1,348,743	2,510,565	1,271,051	1,239,514
Dai	755	281	474	1217	488	729
Daur	120	58	62	32	11	21
Deang	2		2	16	6	10
Derung	82	43	39	87	44	43
Dong	1,628,568	869,205	759,363	1,431,928	750,208	681,720
Dongxiang	412	186	226	958	433	525
Ewenki	46	21	25	1	1	
Gaoshan	228	127	101	191	90	101
Gelao	559,041	300,372	258,669	495,182	258,935	236,247
Han	21,911,687	11,470,182	10,441,505	22,344,156	11,517,873	10,826,283
Hani	891	373	518	1092	403	689
Hezhe	13	3	10	8	4	4
Hui	168,734	87,683	81,051	184,788	95,009	89,779
Jing	641	340	301	1143	620	523
Jingpo	413	222	191	572	282	290
Jino	6	1	5	10	3	7
Kazak	226	98	128	2093	1072	1021
Kirgiz	17	8	9	2	1	1
Korean	1192	610	582	664	318	346
Lahu	82	29	53	182	53	129
Lhoba	70	41	29	85	49	36

Li	56,082	29,735	26,347	135,173	69,980	65,193
Lisu	120	45	75	337	150	187
Manchu	21,932	11,392	10,540	23,086	11,932	11,154
Maonan	31,240	16,426	14,814	27,332	14,243	13,089
Miao	4,299,954	2,247,415	2,052,539	3,968,400	2,040,932	1,927,468
Monba	5	2	3	9	6	3
Mongol	47,531	26,282	21,249	41,561	23,203	18,358
Mulao	28,435	15,500	12,935	24,956	13,293	11,663
Naxi	294	135	159	353	162	191
Nu	21	9	12	28	8	20
Oroqen	8	5	3	24	13	11
Pumi	4		4	16	8	8
Qiang	1431	826	605	1605	899	706
Russian	31	17	14	25	14	11
Salar	87	42	45	99	61	38
She	44,926	24,009	20,917	36,558	19,096	17,462
Shui	369,723	194,337	175,386	348,746	180,317	168,429
Tajik	16	5	11			
Tatar	2	1	1	3	1	2
Tibetan	1787	864	923	1281	585	696
Tu	2942	1531	1411	5154	2755	2399
Tujia	1,430,286	748,222	682,064	1,436,977	736,526	700,451
Uygur	1149	543	606	548	335	213
Uzbek	1	1				
Va	148	58	90	831	345	486
Xibe	171	85	86	185	89	96
Yao	44,392	23,912	20,480	40,879	21,428	19,451
Yi	843,554	441,058	402,496	834,461	429,553	404,908
Yugur	1	1		1	1	
Zhuang	52,065	27,061	25,004	52,577	26,500	26,077

Note: Total population includes servicemen (while ethnic breakdowns do not include them) as well as unknown ethnic groups and foreigners with Chinese citizenship

Table B.10 Hainan's populations reported by the 2000 and 2010 national population censuses

	2000			2010		
Ethnic group	Population	Male	Female	Population	Male	Female
Total	7,559,035	4,002,445	3,556,590	8,671,485	4,592,283	4,079,202
Achang	43	16	27			
Bai	222	101	121	305	150	155
Baonan						
Blang	23	16	7	120	65	55
Buyi	1544	900	644	1789	971	818
Dai	197	73	124	902	417	485
Daur	55	17	38	58	21	37
Deang				1		1
Derung	17	7	10			
Dong	1350	762	588	1819	1096	723
Dongxiang	11	4	7	19	9	10
Ewenki	67	37	30	14	2	12
Gaoshan	80	41	39	111	64	47
Gelao	89	52	37	406	246	160
Han	6,245,329	3,319,929	2,925,400	7,246,067	3,853,244	3,392,823
Hani	93	45	48	154	70	84
Hezhe	9	2	7	13	5	8
Hui	8372	4206	4166	10,670	5405	5265
Jing	123	39	84	189	92	97
Jingpo	37	20	17	15	5	10
Jino				1	1	
Kazak	36	15	21	1553	793	760
Kirgiz	16	8	8	1	1	
Korean	786	422	364	973	456	517
Lahu	3	2	1	48	24	24
Lhoba	1		1			
Li	1,172,181	609,534	562,647	1,262,262	655,504	606,758

Lisu	17	6	11	20	13	7
Manchu	1694	846	848	3750	1853	1897
Maonan	46	27	19	61	40	21
Miao	61,264	30,891	30,373	74,482	37,555	36,927
Monba	1		1	2		2
Mongol	1888	680	1208	3463	1679	1784
Mulao	151	75	76	168	97	71
Naxi	16	9	7	28	11	17
Nu	2	1	1	1385	713	672
Oroqen	1		1	4	1	3
Pumi	4	1	3	3	2	1
Qiang	62	33	29	104	56	48
Russian	14	4	10	17	4	13
Salar	49	42	7	21	12	9
She	274	144	130	403	227	176
Shui	72	41	31	130	67	63
Tajik	38	22	16			
Tatar	9	3	6			
Tibetan	450	202	248	248	111	137
Tu	250	157	93	399	220	179
Tujia	3321	1900	1421	4286	2289	1997
Uygur	354	175	179	393	211	182
Uzbek	29	17	12			
Va	37	16	21	154	85	69
Xibe	35	16	19	72	30	42
Yao	6984	3784	3200	7302	3833	3469
Yi	596	316	280	1086	564	522
Yugur	1		1	3	1	2
Zhuang	50,507	26,688	23,819	45,909	23,914	21,995

Note: Total population includes servicemen (while ethnic breakdowns do not include them) as well as unknown ethnic groups and foreigners with Chinese citizenship

Table B.11 Hebei's populations reported by the 2000 and 2010 national population censuses

	2000			2010		
Ethnic group	Population	Male	Female	Population	Male	Female
Total	66,684,419	33,936,333	32,748,086	71,854,210	36,430,286	35,423,924
Achang	8	5	3	15	5	10
Bai	946	197	749	859	380	479
Baonan				7	4	3
Blang	15	4	11	50	14	36
Buyi	4258	1073	3185	3630	1188	2442
Dai	229	49	180	447	134	313
Daur	705	273	432	962	398	564
Deang	6	1	5	7	2	5
Derung	36	15	21	21	7	14
Dong	2317	869	1448	1451	584	867
Dongxiang	37	12	25	78	52	26
Ewenki	127	42	85	172	63	109
Gaoshan	274	147	127	208	107	101
Gelao	161	68	93	425	247	178
Han	63,781,603	32,463,709	31,317,894	68,861,333	34,894,643	33,966,690
Hani	301	81	220	387	109	278
Hezhe	46	19	27	90	45	45
Hui	542,639	271,936	270,703	570,170	286,331	283,839
Jing	29	14	15	77	25	52
Jingpo	36	10	26	70	22	48
Jino	4	1	3	24	12	12
Kazak	29	12	17	320	163	157
Kirgiz	15	5	10	25	14	11
Korean	11,783	5301	6482	11,296	5358	5938
Lahu	89	13	76	175	50	125
Lhoba	5	1	4	6	2	4

Li	238	67	171	861	340	521
Lisu	1355	94	1261	1974	282	1692
Manchu	2,118,711	1,093,798	1,024,913	2,169,311	1,128,634	1,040,677
Maonan	76	20	56	76	23	53
Miao	8088	2756	5332	9703	3726	5977
Monba	10	1	9	17	9	8
Mongol	169,887	83,397	86,490	180,849	92,087	88,762
Mulao	344	102	242	291	90	201
Naxi	299	41	258	259	71	188
Nu	33	3	30	200	73	127
Oroqen	85	32	53	142	67	75
Pumi	15		15	14	4	10
Qiang	122	60	62	407	241	166
Russian	102	50	52	103	50	53
Salar	30	11	19	131	76	55
She	226	135	91	396	230	166
Shui	383	63	320	282	93	189
Tajik	35	14	21	8	6	2
Tatar	6	2	4	17	7	10
Tibetan	3096	1275	1821	1935	869	1066
Tu	341	117	224	598	259	339
Tujia	6354	2900	3454	8061	4071	3990
Uygur	1785	973	812	864	466	398
Uzbek	2	1	1	7	4	3
Va	148	48	100	674	355	319
Xibe	746	351	395	851	421	430
Yao	1491	400	1091	1776	692	1084
Yi	3721	1149	2572	4632	2207	2425
Yugur	13	6	7	33	20	13
Zhuang	20,832	4561	16,271	17,295	4780	12,515

Note: Total population includes servicemen (while ethnic breakdowns do not include them) as well as unknown ethnic groups and foreigners with Chinese citizenship

Table B.12 Heilongjiang's populations reported by the 2000 and 2010 national population censuses

	2000			2010		
Ethnic group	Population	Male	Female	Population	Male	Female
Total	36,237,576	18,520,747	17,716,829	38,313,991	19,426,106	18,887,885
Achang	3	2	1	3		3
Bai	278	142	136	149	83	66
Baonan	7	4	3	3	1	2
Blang	10	6	4	12	4	8
Buyi	856	413	443	425	220	205
Dai	23	15	8	76	29	47
Daur	43,608	21,670	21,938	40,277	19,985	20,292
Deang	3	1	2			
Derung	55	28	27	8	2	6
Dong	940	552	388	217	129	88
Dongxiang	64	42	22	19	11	8
Ewenki	2706	1263	1443	2648	1191	1457
Gaoshan	61	34	27	25	7	18
Gelao	51	31	20	90	54	36
Han	34,465,039	17,588,318	16,876,721	36,939,181	18,696,097	18,243,084
Hani	78	26	52	105	51	54
Hezhe	3910	1957	1953	3613	1803	1810
Hui	124,003	62,634	61,369	101,749	51,338	50,411
Jing	36	20	16	22	11	11
Jingpo	8	3	5	11	2	9
Jino	1		1	1		1
Kazak	48	19	29	165	106	59
Kirgiz	1473	727	746	1431	709	722
Korean	388,458	195,224	193,234	327,806	164,200	163,606
Lahu				11	1	10
Lhoba	7	2	5	4	3	1

Li	83	32	51	477	198	279
Lisu	18	8	10	39	16	23
Manchu	1,037,080	565,269	471,811	748,020	414,472	333,548
Maonan	7	4	3	5	1	4
Miao	3173	1655	1518	2575	1407	1168
Monba				2	1	1
Mongol	141,495	67,960	73,535	125,483	63,393	62,090
Mulao	52	34	18	46	22	24
Naxi	36	17	19	45	27	18
Nu	4	2	2	21	8	13
Oroqen	3871	1851	2020	3943	1872	2071
Pumi	17	10	7	4	2	2
Qiang	25	13	12	34	21	13
Russian	265	121	144	312	158	154
Salar	4	1	3	7	3	4
She	112	73	39	94	61	33
Shui	118	65	53	47	29	18
Tajik	73	40	33	9	5	4
Tatar	11	7	4	3	2	1
Tibetan	1655	766	889	589	312	277
Tu	113	62	51	101	60	41
Tujia	2217	1265	952	2175	1350	825
Uygur	1189	623	566	884	553	331
Uzbek	1	1		5	4	1
Va	73	42	31	64	26	38
Xibe	8886	5053	3833	7608	4294	3314
Yao	358	209	149	437	234	203
Yi	2060	935	1125	730	428	302
Yugur	28	16	12	28	14	14
Zhuang	2700	1432	1268	2070	1060	1010

Note: Total population includes servicemen (while ethnic breakdowns do not include them) as well as unknown ethnic groups and foreigners with Chinese citizenship

Table B.13 Henan's populations reported by the 2000 and 2010 national population censuses

	2000			2010		
Ethnic group	Population	Male	Female	Population	Male	Female
Total	91,236,854	47,046,599	44,190,255	94,029,939	47,493,063	46,536,876
Achang	15	3	12	148	67	81
Bai	946	225	721	581	245	336
Baonan	2		2	4	2	2
Blang	77	10	67	80	18	62
Buyi	2244	904	1340	5958	2604	3354
Dai	500	67	433	511	105	406
Daur	144	68	76	122	42	80
Deang	9	3	6	11		11
Derung	44	17	27	55	27	28
Dong	1314	633	681	558	254	304
Dongxiang	29	13	16	72	47	25
Ewenki	17	7	10	23	7	16
Gaoshan	946	626	320	780	397	383
Gelao	115	64	51	240	119	121
Han	90,093,286	46,468,976	43,624,310	92,908,354	46,924,281	45,984,073
Hani	425	44	381	373	83	290
Hezhe	17	7	10	30	13	17
Hui	953,531	478,488	475,043	957,964	479,252	478,712
Jing	17	7	10	120	51	69
Jingpo	85	6	79	130	12	118
Jino	1		1	7	1	6
Kazak	38	9	29	4805	2330	2475
Kirgiz	15	7	8	37	20	17
Korean	4312	2126	2186	1457	664	793
Lahu	1151	88	1063	700	51	649
Lhoba	8	3	5			

Li	241	79	162	1002	405	597
Lisu	212	28	184	167	25	142
Manchu	61,705	35,649	26,056	55,493	31,697	23,796
Maonan	19	4	15	23	6	17
Miao	5425	2180	3245	4321	1683	2638
Monba	10	4	6	45	16	29
Mongol	82,170	44,437	37,733	63,473	39,117	24,356
Mulao	41	15	26	72	30	42
Naxi	186	40	146	123	35	88
Nu	4	2	2	186	92	94
Oroqen	15	8	7	14	6	8
Pumi	29	8	21	9	2	7
Qiang	75	48	27	216	103	113
Russian	54	24	30	32	12	20
Salar	92	61	31	279	168	111
She	134	70	64	200	104	96
Shui	80	32	48	333	172	161
Tajik	73	32	41	23	8	15
Tatar	8	4	4	4	2	2
Tibetan	3953	1491	2462	1811	598	1213
Tu	419	175	244	576	236	340
Tujia	5122	2516	2606	5287	2642	2645
Uygur	4623	2542	2081	3035	1646	1389
Uzbek	10	2	8	16	13	3
Va	1715	145	1570	1572	337	1235
Xibe	292	142	150	273	123	150
Yao	408	183	225	763	276	487
Yi	5364	2026	3338	1764	672	1092
Yugur	6	3	3	52	21	31
Zhuang	4888	2185	2703	5361	2004	3357

Note: Total population includes servicemen (while ethnic breakdowns do not include them) as well as unknown ethnic groups and foreigners with Chinese citizenship

Table B.14 Hubei's populations reported by the 2000 and 2010 national population censuses

	2000			2010		
Ethnic group	Population	Male	Female	Population	Male	Female
Total	59,508,870	30,982,241	28,526,629	57,237,727	29,391,247	27,846,480
Achang	2	2		12	4	8
Bai	7173	3940	3233	6410	3288	3122
Baonan	3	1	2	6	4	2
Blang	9	4	5	36	10	26
Buyi	1214	683	531	2152	961	1191
Dai	141	62	79	353	162	191
Daur	37	22	15	92	41	51
Deang				20	9	11
Derung	21	7	14	18	8	10
Dong	69,947	38,418	31,529	52,121	27,604	24,517
Dongxiang	78	46	32	67	39	28
Ewenki	24	11	13	24	8	16
Gaoshan	63	38	25	162	88	74
Gelao	385	261	124	585	323	262
Han	56,911,968	29,614,784	27,297,184	54,769,192	28,128,850	26,640,342
Hani	151	63	88	314	117	197
Hezhe	9	3	6	16	10	6
Hui	77,759	40,114	37,645	67,185	34,858	32,327
Jing	42	29	13	93	54	39
Jingpo	15	5	10	38	11	27
Jino	1		1	10	4	6
Kazak	40	18	22	2191	1057	1134
Kirgiz	4	1	3	36	20	16
Korean	2949	1620	1329	1960	1025	935
Lahu	30	8	22	108	46	62
Lhoba	5	2	3	2		2

Li	706	390	316	2709	1327	1382
Lisu	50	26	24	138	59	79
Manchu	14,540	7581	6959	12,899	6762	6137
Maonan	50	30	20	151	62	89
Miao	214,266	117,904	96,362	177,490	94,179	83,311
Monba	4	2	2	25	10	15
Mongol	10,887	4935	5952	10,318	5415	4903
Mulao	177	102	75	276	88	188
Naxi	126	71	55	179	86	93
Nu	4	3	1	156	81	75
Oroqen	7	1	6	11	7	4
Pumi	12	6	6	26	12	14
Qiang	224	153	71	256	146	110
Russian	26	6	20	26	13	13
Salar	58	42	16	135	88	47
She	2523	1571	952	3058	1890	1168
Shui	94	54	40	577	309	268
Tajik	36	20	16	9	6	3
Tatar	2	1	1	10	4	6
Tibetan	1648	803	845	2175	974	1201
Tu	636	390	246	1963	958	1005
Tujia	2,177,409	1,140,541	1,036,868	2,100,052	1,069,839	1,030,213
Uygur	1457	813	644	2577	1457	1120
Uzbek				9	4	5
Va	66	28	38	532	255	277
Xibe	215	104	111	228	109	119
Yao	1569	856	713	2709	1242	1467
Yi	2117	1152	965	2748	1434	1314
Yugur	4	3	1	19	10	9
Zhuang	7824	4480	3344	12,240	5422	6818

Note: Total population includes servicemen (while ethnic breakdowns do not include them) as well as unknown ethnic groups and foreigners with Chinese citizenship

Table B.15 Hunan's populations reported by the 2000 and 2010 national population censuses

	2000			2010		
Ethnic group	Population	Male	Female	Population	Male	Female
Total	63,274,173	32,993,704	30,280,469	65,700,762	33,776,459	31,924,303
Achang	29	1	28	26	8	18
Bai	125,597	65,371	60,226	115,678	59,088	56,590
Baonan	6	4	2	13	7	6
Blang	100	9	91	138	9	129
Buyi	3173	1241	1932	4039	1463	2576
Dai	587	102	485	837	208	629
Daur	116	56	60	39	20	19
Deang	15	6	9	9		9
Derung	66	36	30	36	20	16
Dong	842,123	448,292	393,831	854,960	452,380	402,580
Dongxiang	28	13	15	62	41	21
Ewenki	34	17	17	4	2	2
Gaoshan	189	86	103	128	66	62
Gelao	397	241	156	911	430	481
Han	56,863,479	29,639,115	27,224,364	59,149,353	30,385,867	28,763,486
Hani	1337	285	1052	1055	182	873
Hezhe	5	3	2	36	15	21
Hui	97,368	50,412	46,956	94,705	49,291	45,414
Jing	46	25	21	86	34	52
Jingpo	136	18	118	135	21	114
Jino	13	2	11	17	2	15
Kazak	110	54	56	2775	1409	1366
Kirgiz	10	3	7	62	31	31
Korean	2693	1330	1363	1180	583	597
Lahu	480	27	453	383	38	345
Lhoba	15	9	6	3	2	1

Li	862	430	432	2350	1040	1310
Lisu	145	45	100	199	73	126
Manchu	8206	4112	4094	7566	3944	3622
Maonan	52	20	32	199	74	125
Miao	1,921,495	998,820	922,675	2,060,426	1,061,107	999,319
Monba	7	2	5	60	26	34
Mongol	15,869	5384	10,485	3693	1824	1869
Mulao	719	389	330	906	462	444
Naxi	113	60	53	126	56	70
Nu	29	18	11	210	103	107
Oroqen	8	4	4	5	2	3
Pumi	22	8	14	24	12	12
Qiang	73	34	39	180	88	92
Russian	25	7	18	24	7	17
Salar	272	126	146	79	39	40
She	2891	1736	1155	3059	1735	1324
Shui	270	91	179	598	283	315
Tajik	105	58	47	3	1	2
Tatar	16	8	8	15	8	7
Tibetan	2930	1339	1591	1622	758	864
Tu	1097	570	527	5137	2544	2593
Tujia	2,639,534	1,376,741	1,262,793	2,632,452	1,355,212	1,277,240
Uygur	7939	4148	3791	6716	3696	3020
Uzbek	22	8	14	33	15	18
Va	803	260	543	915	359	556
Xibe	93	44	49	136	71	65
Yao	704,564	378,435	326,129	713,191	377,080	336,111
Yi	4116	1793	2323	3183	1374	1809
Yugur	3	1	2	18	6	12
Zhuang	23,559	12,168	11,391	30,387	12,964	17,423

Note: Total population includes servicemen (while ethnic breakdowns do not include them) as well as unknown ethnic groups and foreigners with Chinese citizenship

Table B.16 Inner Mongolia's populations reported by the 2000 and 2010 national population censuses

	2000			2010		
Ethnic group	Population	Male	Female	Population	Male	Female
Total	23,323,347	12,061,615	11,261,732	24,706,291	12,838,243	11,868,048
Achang	6	2	4	16	11	5
Bai	248	108	140	443	194	249
Baonan	7	4	3	90	73	17
Blang	1		1	15	3	12
Buyi	822	409	413	537	260	277
Dai	96	34	62	179	74	105
Daur	77,188	38,535	38,653	76,255	37,684	38,571
Deang	1		1	5	2	3
Derung	190	91	99	7	3	4
Dong	540	257	283	438	246	192
Dongxiang	118	74	44	574	374	200
Ewenki	26,201	12,851	13,350	26,139	12,578	13,561
Gaoshan	144	69	75	120	62	58
Gelao	20	12	8	249	194	55
Han	18,465,586	9,630,944	8,834,642	19,650,665	10,306,496	9,344,169
Hani	92	30	62	320	106	214
Hezhe	54	24	30	50	23	27
Hui	209,850	106,491	103,359	221,483	113,289	108,194
Jing	13	4	9	25	10	15
Jingpo	28	10	18	39	7	32
Jino	1		1	11	4	7
Kazak	20	10	10	377	206	171
Kirgiz	153	84	69	141	79	62
Korean	21,859	10,726	11,133	18,464	9016	9448
Lahu	35	13	22	347	77	270
Lhoba						

Li	449	176	273	981	444	537
Lisu	145	42	103	443	109	334
Manchu	499,911	254,193	245,718	452,765	233,007	219,758
Maonan	15	6	9	14	9	5
Miao	2159	939	1220	3349	1953	1396
Monba	11	4	7	7	5	2
Mongol	3,995,349	1,994,916	2,000,433	4,226,090	2,108,197	2,117,893
Mulao	30	14	16	37	24	13
Naxi	31	17	14	60	29	31
Nu	9	2	7	18	3	15
Oroqen	3573	1702	1871	3632	1699	1933
Pumi	11	2	9	5	5	
Qiang	109	52	57	144	81	63
Russian	5020	2472	2548	4673	2276	2397
Salar	26	20	6	53	34	19
She	94	53	41	202	127	75
Shui	54	23	31	122	67	55
Tajik	29	11	18	6	3	3
Tatar	6	1	5	6	2	4
Tibetan	2062	906	1156	3259	1821	1438
Tu	437	211	226	557	297	260
Tujia	1678	823	855	3096	1822	1274
Uygur	1259	685	574	658	385	273
Uzbek	8	4	4	6	4	2
Va	206	82	124	519	130	389
Xibe	3023	1549	1474	3000	1555	1445
Yao	231	107	124	318	169	149
Yi	2089	813	1276	2854	1620	1234
Yugur	27	14	13	38	22	16
Zhuang	1895	929	966	2319	1239	1080

Note: Total population includes servicemen (while ethnic breakdowns do not include them) as well as unknown ethnic groups and foreigners with Chinese citizenship

Table B.17 Jiangsu's populations reported by the 2000 and 2010 national population censuses

	2000			2010		
Ethnic group	Population	Male	Female	Population	Male	Female
Total	73,043,577	36,982,038	36,061,539	78,660,941	39,626,707	39,034,234
Achang	42	5	37	98	44	54
Bai	2300	453	1847	4020	1723	2297
Baonan	3	1	2	32	16	16
Blang	180	10	170	265	67	198
Buyi	8229	2062	6167	16,689	7315	9374
Dai	1083	90	993	2189	693	1496
Daur	103	45	58	283	136	147
Deang	9		9	14	5	9
Derung	35	11	24	26	10	16
Dong	9528	2134	7394	12,280	4889	7391
Dongxiang	35	15	20	420	277	143
Ewenki	57	13	44	49	20	29
Gaoshan	120	47	73	120	54	66
Gelao	721	307	414	2488	1291	1197
Han	72,783,674	36,875,556	35,908,118	78,276,015	39,442,857	38,833,158
Hani	2049	123	1926	2916	953	1963
Hezhe	13	1	12	68	36	32
Hui	132,582	66,614	65,968	130,757	67,024	63,733
Jing	90	19	71	218	101	117
Jingpo	60	4	56	298	92	206
Jino	9	1	8	24	5	19
Kazak	73	33	40	2124	985	1139
Kirgiz	30	15	15	61	30	31
Korean	5048	2434	2614	9525	4920	4605
Lahu	610	29	581	1042	187	855
Lhoba	9	1	8	1	1	

Li	738	233	505	2447	974	1473
Lisu	842	53	789	1447	383	1064
Manchu	11,880	5699	6181	18,074	8865	9209
Maonan	54	19	35	184	94	90
Miao	22,246	5123	17,123	49,535	21,979	27,556
Monba	14	5	9	136	65	71
Mongol	14,167	4771	9396	10,691	5160	5531
Mulao	167	41	126	522	223	299
Naxi	256	61	195	329	123	206
Nu	66	5	61	356	158	198
Oroqen	25	9	16	43	16	27
Pumi	66	9	57	38	14	24
Qiang	215	82	133	954	486	468
Russian	67	30	37	109	48	61
Salar	51	18	33	353	187	166
She	742	401	341	1738	958	780
Shui	2775	1369	1406	13,089	7056	6033
Tajik	39	16	23	17	5	12
Tatar	10	5	5	19	11	8
Tibetan	2659	1073	1586	3358	1451	1907
Tu	706	237	469	2263	986	1277
Tujia	16,539	6112	10,427	41,258	20,177	21,081
Uygur	2213	1245	968	4367	2038	2329
Uzbek	5	1	4	15	6	9
Va	378	56	322	1481	701	780
Xibe	207	94	113	433	189	244
Yao	1159	315	844	3575	1644	1931
Yi	8244	1960	6284	18,896	8576	10,320
Yugur	7	2	5	41	25	16
Zhuang	8934	2419	6515	20,880	9272	11,608

Note: Total population includes servicemen (while ethnic breakdowns do not include them) as well as unknown ethnic groups and foreigners with Chinese citizenship

Table B.18 Jiangxi's populations reported by the 2000 and 2010 national population censuses

	2000			2010		
Ethnic group	Population	Male	Female	Population	Male	Female
Total	40,397,598	20,990,240	19,407,358	44,567,797	23,003,521	21,564,276
Achang	1		1	14	4	10
Bai	337	119	218	1621	815	806
Baonan						
Blang	13	6	7	31	16	15
Buyi	1762	680	1082	2156	838	1318
Dai	75	30	45	484	225	259
Daur	52	20	32	57	18	39
Deang	3		3	1		1
Derung	16	4	12	3	2	1
Dong	1564	797	767	2189	1170	1019
Dongxiang	8	3	5	49	31	18
Ewenki	5	2	3	19	6	13
Gaoshan	134	84	50	132	80	52
Gelao	122	52	70	336	156	180
Han	40,271,881	20,924,958	19,346,923	44,415,487	22,919,893	21,495,594
Hani	63	12	51	265	124	141
Hezhe				8	5	3
Hui	9972	5091	4881	8902	4679	4223
Jing	278	153	125	301	170	131
Jingpo	12	8	4	65	23	42
Jino	1	1		5	3	2
Kazak	9	3	6	1718	861	857
Kirgiz	8		8	46	24	22
Korean	1703	873	830	543	226	317
Lahu	12	1	11	140	33	107
Lhoba	1		1	1	1	

Li	301	98	203	1536	699	837
Lisu	21	11	10	96	34	62
Manchu	5075	2684	2391	4942	2638	2304
Maonan	35	17	18	86	41	45
Miao	5414	2533	2881	9125	4369	4756
Monba				78	30	48
Mongol	9010	2811	6199	3479	1770	1709
Mulao	72	35	37	181	81	100
Naxi	31	11	20	89	45	44
Nu	26	13	13	87	44	43
Oroqen	5	3	2	5	2	3
Pumi	5	4	1	6	4	2
Qiang	205	120	85	155	85	70
Russian	4	1	3	7	2	5
Salar	12	7	5	44	26	18
She	77,650	43,457	34,193	91,068	53,907	37,161
Shui	77	33	44	782	374	408
Tajik	57	24	33	33	15	18
Tatar				4	3	1
Tibetan	1649	760	889	1150	595	555
Tu	148	78	70	576	272	304
Tujia	1551	753	798	4815	2372	2443
Uygur	1142	591	551	852	420	432
Uzbek	6	3	3	9	2	7
Va	111	55	56	759	327	432
Xibe	82	42	40	81	35	46
Yao	1198	596	602	2599	1227	1372
Yi	2271	1013	1258	1850	946	904
Yugur	1	1		18	11	7
Zhuang	3046	1375	1671	7979	3363	4616

Note: Total population includes servicemen (while ethnic breakdowns do not include them) as well as unknown ethnic groups and foreigners with Chinese citizenship

Table B.19 Jilin's populations reported by the 2000 and 2010 national population censuses

	2000			2010		
Ethnic group	Population	Male	Female	Population	Male	Female
Total	26,802,191	13,720,747	13,081,444	27,452,815	13,907,218	13,545,597
Achang				22	1	21
Bai	298	161	137	276	148	128
Baonan	8	6	2	6	4	2
Blang				9	4	5
Buyi	1074	584	490	362	191	171
Dai	60	34	26	253	46	207
Daur	490	241	249	587	258	329
Deang				2		2
Derung				1		1
Dong	519	272	247	231	130	101
Dongxiang				32	17	15
Ewenki	75	32	43	104	46	58
Gaoshan	99	53	46	100	49	51
Gelao	90	51	39	71	48	23
Han	24,348,815	12,473,142	11,875,673	25,267,110	12,792,641	12,474,469
Hani	212	78	134	142	40	102
Hezhe	190	107	83	212	106	106
Hui	125,620	63,542	62,078	118,799	59,299	59,500
Jing	1		1	8	5	3
Jingpo	32	10	22	457	50	407
Jino	21	13	8	19	13	6
Kazak	89	46	43	467	209	258
Kirgiz	10	5	5	36	16	20
Korean	1,145,688	571,437	574,251	1,040,167	517,257	522,910
Lahu	12	5	7	33	8	25
Lhoba	5	1	4	3	1	2

Li	157	71	86	545	253	292
Lisu	30	13	17	100	22	78
Manchu	993,112	521,439	471,673	866,365	458,840	407,525
Maonan	3	2	1	6	2	4
Miao	1531	785	746	1446	749	697
Monba	11	6	5	18	8	10
Mongol	172,026	82,524	89,502	145,039	71,851	73,188
Mulao	28	12	16	30	11	19
Naxi	15	11	4	14	8	6
Nu				27	8	19
Oroqen	125	50	75	111	39	72
Pumi	19	7	12	4	2	2
Qiang	26	14	12	238	120	118
Russian	64	37	27	48	21	27
Salar	9	4	5	50	30	20
She	45	24	21	82	34	48
Shui	14	8	6	50	27	23
Tajik	3	2	1	2	1	1
Tatar	2	1	1	5	2	3
Tibetan	1615	721	894	652	264	388
Tu	49	28	21	128	60	68
Tujia	933	517	416	1523	864	659
Uygur	1500	868	632	1127	517	610
Uzbek	1		1	2	2	
Va	5	1	4	132	43	89
Xibe	3168	1649	1519	3113	1622	1491
Yao	220	127	93	308	148	160
Yi	2253	1068	1185	558	326	232
Yugur				8	4	4
Zhuang	1655	864	791	1547	738	809

Note: Total population includes servicemen (while ethnic breakdowns do not include them) as well as unknown ethnic groups and foreigners with Chinese citizenship

Table B.20 Liaoning's populations reported by the 2000 and 2010 national population censuses

	2000			2010		
Ethnic group	Population	Male	Female	Population	Male	Female
Total	41,824,412	21,323,383	20,501,029	43,746,323	22,147,745	21,598,578
Achang	2	1	1	10	7	3
Bai	449	223	226	559	292	267
Baonan				2	1	1
Blang	4	2	2	19	9	10
Buyi	1214	569	645	991	511	480
Dai	104	46	58	231	64	167
Daur	1282	558	724	1858	801	1057
Deang				5	2	3
Derung	169	80	89	6	2	4
Dong	799	430	369	821	454	367
Dongxiang	8	5	3	27	16	11
Ewenki	221	85	136	448	198	250
Gaoshan	305	143	162	211	96	115
Gelao	89	53	36	211	145	66
Han	35,105,991	17,873,551	17,232,440	37,103,174	18,737,977	18,365,197
Hani	157	83	74	304	131	173
Hezhe	82	33	49	154	72	82
Hui	264,407	133,155	131,252	245,798	123,200	122,598
Jing	6	3	3	15	10	5
Jingpo	24	18	6	80	26	54
Jino				10	6	4
Kazak	121	51	70	448	182	266
Kirgiz	45	22	23	125	62	63
Korean	241,052	118,885	122,167	239,537	118,896	120,641
Lahu	14	6	8	48	17	31
Lhoba	9	6	3	11	8	3

Li	615	304	311	1765	846	919
Lisu	152	20	132	646	96	550
Manchu	5,385,287	2,779,918	2,605,369	5,336,895	2,750,732	2,586,163
Maonan	20	8	12	19	12	7
Miao	3009	1626	1383	3952	2342	1610
Monba				9	5	4
Mongol	669,972	335,109	334,863	657,869	330,787	327,082
Mulao	53	34	19	71	28	43
Naxi	86	40	46	125	63	62
Nu	3	1	2	76	20	56
Oroqen	161	63	98	196	72	124
Pumi	16	9	7	14	4	10
Qiang	81	40	41	171	89	82
Russian	150	60	90	185	83	102
Salar	45	29	16	88	59	29
She	200	121	79	257	170	87
Shui	44	21	23	89	51	38
Tajik	46	15	31	10	7	3
Tatar	9	3	6	14	4	10
Tibetan	2017	953	1064	1881	890	991
Tu	171	102	69	264	135	129
Tujia	3757	2327	1430	5190	3185	2005
Uygur	2407	1302	1105	1917	1081	836
Uzbek	1	1		5		5
Va	129	60	69	220	99	121
Xibe	132,615	69,915	62,700	132,431	69,961	62,470
Yao	505	279	226	774	421	353
Yi	2641	1169	1472	1693	1088	605
Yugur	1		1	17	8	9
Zhuang	3576	1812	1764	4285	2160	2125

Note: Total population includes servicemen (while ethnic breakdowns do not include them) as well as unknown ethnic groups and foreigners with Chinese citizenship

Table B.21 Ningxia's populations reported by the 2000 and 2010 national population censuses

	2000			2010		
Ethnic group	Population	Male	Female	Population	Male	Female
Total	5,486,393	2,813,517	2,672,876	6,301,350	3,227,404	3,073,946
Achang				4	1	3
Bai	39	17	22	213	106	107
Baonan	14	10	4	21	12	9
Blang				2		2
Buyi	72	41	31	183	98	85
Dai	11	2	9	44	24	20
Daur	26	10	16	42	17	25
Deang				1		1
Derung				2	1	1
Dong	128	67	61	345	222	123
Dongxiang	2168	1191	977	1261	748	513
Ewenki	4	1	3	7	2	5
Gaoshan	15	10	5	10	8	2
Gelao	9	9		42	31	11
Han	3,590,563	1,850,231	1,740,332	4,086,367	2,103,760	1,982,607
Hani	12	8	4	52	29	23
Hezhe	3	2	1	4	1	3
Hui	1,862,474	947,187	915,287	2,173,820	1,102,835	1,070,985
Jing				5		5
Jingpo	1	1		6	2	4
Jino				2	1	1
Kazak	69	25	44	190	70	120
Kirgiz	5	2	3	12	6	6
Korean	472	227	245	403	207	196
Lahu				13	5	8
Lhoba				1		1

Li	24	13	11	146	69	77
Lisu	1		1	17	8	9
Manchu	21,962	10,723	11,239	24,902	12,287	12,615
Maonan	15	6	9	26	9	17
Miao	407	187	220	1113	732	381
Monba				2		2
Mongol	4898	2054	2844	6661	3174	3487
Mulao	2	2		10	4	6
Naxi	7	3	4	17	8	9
Nu				7	3	4
Oroqen	9	7	2	6	4	2
Pumi				6	3	3
Qiang	28	20	8	89	53	36
Russian	21	9	12	18	6	12
Salar	38	18	20	72	38	34
She	88	60	28	122	76	46
Shui	3		3	35	15	20
Tajik				1		1
Tatar	2	1	1	2		2
Tibetan	506	255	251	656	316	340
Tu	191	95	96	326	176	150
Tujia	758	362	396	1441	847	594
Uygur	312	165	147	613	272	341
Uzbek	2	1	1	3	2	1
Va				26	14	12
Xibe	216	94	122	184	88	96
Yao	63	38	25	197	108	89
Yi	137	57	80	530	359	171
Yugur	43	23	20	48	24	24
Zhuang	575	283	292	977	495	482

Note: Total population includes servicemen (while ethnic breakdowns do not include them) as well as unknown ethnic groups and foreigners with Chinese citizenship

Table B.22 Qinghai's populations reported by the 2000 and 2010 national population censuses

	2000			2010		
Ethnic group	Population	Male	Female	Population	Male	Female
Total	4,822,963	2,489,590	2,333,373	5,626,723	2,913,793	2,712,930
Achang	1		1	1		1
Bai	242	149	93	320	174	146
Baonan	635	337	298	904	477	427
Blang	22	6	16	2	2	
Buyi	170	86	84	251	185	66
Dai	4	2	2	31	13	18
Daur	47	17	30	26	15	11
Deang	9	5	4	1	1	
Derung	6	3	3	4	3	1
Dong	148	98	50	161	123	38
Dongxiang	2498	1564	934	6331	3976	2355
Ewenki	12	4	8	5	2	3
Gaoshan	22	9	13	20	8	12
Gelao	17	7	10	69	59	10
Han	2,606,050	1,364,527	1,241,523	2,983,521	1,574,280	1,409,241
Hani	3	1	2	17	8	9
Hezhe	15	7	8	11	9	2
Hui	753,378	388,789	364,589	834,298	423,527	410,771
Jing				10	6	4
Jingpo				5	3	2
Jino	3	1	2	1		1
Kazak	407	213	194	680	332	348
Kirgiz	8	3	5	4	1	3
Korean	453	230	223	312	152	160
Lahu	7	5	2	8	4	4
Lhoba	5	3	2			

Li	9	4	5	139	67	72
Lisu	58	39	19	21	13	8
Manchu	7788	4008	3780	8029	4172	3857
Maonan	23	11	12	8	6	2
Miao	436	209	227	911	576	335
Monba	11	6	5	4	1	3
Mongol	86,301	43,562	42,739	99,815	50,744	49,071
Mulao	23	7	16	15	7	8
Naxi	17	8	9	32	16	16
Nu	4	4		5	4	1
Oroqen	1	1		2	1	1
Pumi	12	6	6	3		3
Qiang	86	50	36	104	61	43
Russian	48	26	22	38	19	19
Salar	87,043	44,393	42,650	107,089	53,669	53,420
She	20	8	12	53	32	21
Shui	20	9	11	30	16	14
Tajik	15	7	8	3	1	2
Tatar	12	7	5	2		2
Tibetan	1,086,592	543,708	542,884	1,375,059	693,995	681,064
Tu	187,562	96,038	91,524	204,412	104,572	99,840
Tujia	978	534	444	1537	969	568
Uygur	431	216	215	209	124	85
Uzbek	1	1		2	1	1
Va	6	2	4	20	10	10
Xibe	142	77	65	128	52	76
Yao	105	55	50	209	115	94
Yi	274	133	141	683	550	133
Yugur	140	72	68	163	78	85
Zhuang	618	308	310	980	543	437

Note: Total population includes servicemen (while ethnic breakdowns do not include them) as well as unknown ethnic groups and foreigners with Chinese citizenship

Table B.23 Shaanxi's populations reported by the 2000 and 2010 national population censuses

	2000			2010		
Ethnic group	Population	Male	Female	Population	Male	Female
Total	35,365,072	18,378,759	16,986,313	37,327,379	19,287,575	18,039,804
Achang	4	4		2	1	1
Bai	338	193	145	486	276	210
Baonan	1		1	4	2	2
Blang	2	1	1	6	2	4
Buyi	450	267	183	727	371	356
Dai	68	44	24	117	31	86
Daur	75	28	47	93	42	51
Deang				1	1	
Derung	9	5	4			
Dong	509	310	199	731	413	318
Dongxiang	26	15	11	116	71	45
Ewenki	11	7	4	24	14	10
Gaoshan	27	14	13	15	7	8
Gelao	44	29	15	205	122	83
Han	35,188,651	18,289,425	16,899,226	37,137,743	19,191,534	17,946,209
Hani	40	17	23	99	42	57
Hezhe				4		4
Hui	139,232	70,003	69,229	138,716	69,739	68,977
Jing	9	7	2	28	11	17
Jingpo	19	16	3	22	7	15
Jino	1		1	9	3	6
Kazak	122	61	61	794	407	387
Kirgiz	19	11	8	23	6	17
Korean	1620	820	800	1129	534	595
Lahu	44	1	43	35	14	21
Lhoba	4	1	3	7	1	6

Li	161	88	73	441	199	242
Lisu	16	12	4	32	15	17
Manchu	15,801	7930	7871	16,291	8442	7849
Maonan	16	8	8	19	8	11
Miao	1388	798	590	2787	1659	1128
Monba	9	3	6	18	9	9
Mongol	6060	2913	3147	6976	3509	3467
Mulao	27	14	13	44	18	26
Naxi	69	34	35	101	48	53
Nu	1		1	31	13	18
Oroqen	6	1	5	8	3	5
Pumi	4	4		4	2	2
Qiang	54	27	27	182	80	102
Russian	69	28	41	73	35	38
Salar	22	15	7	156	95	61
She	104	66	38	212	132	80
Shui	17	10	7	83	50	33
Tajik	7	3	4	3	2	1
Tatar	1	1		1		1
Tibetan	3048	1407	1641	6345	2827	3518
Tu	290	180	110	499	265	234
Tujia	1721	1113	608	3876	2362	1514
Uygur	1187	661	526	1570	725	845
Uzbek	6	5	1	7	2	5
Va	44	22	22	160	86	74
Xibe	446	237	209	416	219	197
Yao	273	179	94	605	313	292
Yi	854	472	382	1644	988	656
Yugur	23	8	15	29	12	17
Zhuang	1987	1220	767	3555	1765	1790

Note: Total population includes servicemen (while ethnic breakdowns do not include them) as well as unknown ethnic groups and foreigners with Chinese citizenship

Table B.24 Shandong's populations reported by the 2000 and 2010 national population censuses

	2000			2010		
Ethnic group	Population	Male	Female	Population	Male	Female
Total	89,971,789	45,542,060	44,429,729	95,792,719	48,446,944	47,345,775
Achang	92	2	90	99	15	84
Bai	2405	220	2185	1247	411	836
Baonan	3		3	7	3	4
Blang	279	13	266	317	99	218
Buyi	2426	860	1566	1839	757	1082
Dai	1797	98	1699	2468	426	2042
Daur	541	224	317	960	432	528
Deang	18		18	50	10	40
Derung	100	30	70	30	5	25
Dong	1245	508	737	867	453	414
Dongxiang	28	10	18	126	77	49
Ewenki	107	34	73	220	95	125
Gaoshan	86	32	54	66	30	36
Gelao	97	52	45	597	364	233
Han	89,339,046	45,245,932	44,093,114	95,066,830	48,090,616	46,976,214
Hani	3041	103	2938	3023	345	2678
Hezhe	33	11	22	68	35	33
Hui	497,597	248,501	249,096	535,679	269,871	265,808
Jing	7		7	80	35	45
Jingpo	343	8	335	608	59	549
Jino	17	4	13	17	7	10
Kazak	49	22	27	1116	459	657
Kirgiz	16	6	10	90	35	55
Korean	27,795	13,032	14,763	61,556	31,229	30,327
Lahu	1403	69	1334	1880	237	1643
Lhoba	7	3	4	2	1	1
Li	297	55	242	1202	466	736

Lisu	1919	91	1828	1841	208	1633
Manchu	33,527	15,658	17,869	46,521	23,274	23,247
Maonan	35	9	26	50	25	25
Miao	6949	1813	5136	8414	3586	4828
Monba	5		5	20	10	10
Mongol	23,743	7104	16,639	17,669	8448	9221
Mulao	130	34	96	126	46	80
Naxi	249	24	225	256	69	187
Nu	97	10	87	373	161	212
Oroqen	60	28	32	98	33	65
Pumi	81	5	76	55	10	45
Qiang	41	13	28	243	121	122
Russian	68	24	44	128	58	70
Salar	21	8	13	609	354	255
She	330	210	120	363	226	137
Shui	95	20	75	191	85	106
Tajik	81	40	41	32	17	15
Tatar	9	4	5	11	4	7
Tibetan	2733	1045	1688	2146	875	1271
Tu	304	80	224	651	270	381
Tujia	2719	1262	1457	5730	3188	2542
Uygur	2386	1294	1092	4635	1551	3084
Uzbek	4	1	3	13	6	7
Va	4693	269	4424	5619	1315	4304
Xibe	356	158	198	661	291	370
Yao	468	109	359	878	353	525
Yi	6208	1366	4842	8298	3422	4876
Yugur	7		7	76	33	43
Zhuang	5444	1520	3924	5822	2273	3549

Note: Total population includes servicemen (while ethnic breakdowns do not include them) as well as unknown ethnic groups and foreigners with Chinese citizenship

Table B.25 Shanghai's populations reported by the 2000 and 2010 national population censuses

	2000			2010		
Ethnic group	Population	Male	Female	Population	Male	Female
Total	16,303,862	8,379,320	7,924,542	23,019,196	11,854,916	11,164,280
Achang	5	2	3	51	28	23
Bai	5296	2942	2354	3893	1979	1914
Baonan	6	3	3	16	11	5
Blang	15	9	6	133	80	53
Buyi	5120	2369	2751	5840	3043	2797
Dai	99	49	50	1289	540	749
Daur	89	36	53	449	186	263
Deang	1		1	15	10	5
Derung	18	6	12	8	5	3
Dong	798	410	388	7787	4156	3631
Dongxiang	77	44	33	362	282	80
Ewenki				63	30	33
Gaoshan	38	8	30	81	36	45
Gelao	212	97	115	2684	1496	1188
Han	6468	2654	3814	22,743,033	11,716,435	11,026,598
Hani	62	33	29	3185	1628	1557
Hezhe	86	40	46	40	20	20
Hui	1642	707	935	78,163	39,480	38,683
Jing	5	2	3	45	20	25
Jingpo	5	1	4	142	68	74
Jino				23	6	17
Kazak	246	73	173	639	274	365
Kirgiz	226	127	99	58	25	33
Korean	9087	4502	4585	22,257	10,292	11,965
Lahu	103	48	55	500	232	268
Lhoba	7	2	5	4	2	2

Li	27	9	18	1725	676	1049
Lisu	87	52	35	580	318	262
Manchu	1970	1011	959	25,165	11,892	13,273
Maonan	215	123	92	160	66	94
Miao	1443	634	809	31,351	16,418	14,933
Monba	4	2	2	3		3
Mongol	57,514	28,491	29,023	11,238	5295	5943
Mulao	54	23	31	441	180	261
Naxi	4	2	2	287	125	162
Nu	5	2	3	65	28	37
Oroqen	14	6	8	55	23	32
Pumi	24	11	13	38	14	24
Qiang	10	6	4	505	246	259
Russian	41	10	31	209	78	131
Salar	14	1	13	941	603	338
She	52	28	24	3020	1538	1482
Shui	20	17	3	745	375	370
Tajik	3	2	1	14	8	6
Tatar	19	11	8	12	4	8
Tibetan	1701	1052	649	2406	1031	1375
Tu	172	78	94	1009	545	464
Tujia	381	124	257	33,584	17,648	15,936
Uygur	4808	2566	2242	5254	2725	2529
Uzbek	76	31	45	14	4	10
Va	859	450	409	1353	807	546
Xibe				696	315	381
Yao	506	244	262	3627	1892	1735
Yi	2923	1138	1785	7113	3497	3616
Yugur	6	3	3	15	10	5
Zhuang	976	517	459	16,219	7894	8325

Note: Total population includes servicemen (while ethnic breakdowns do not include them) as well as unknown ethnic groups and foreigners with Chinese citizenship

Table B.26 Shanxi's populations reported by the 2000 and 2010 national population censuses

	2000			2010		
Ethnic group	Population	Male	Female	Population	Male	Female
Total	32,471,242	16,800,758	15,670,484	35,712,101	18,338,760	17,373,341
Achang	2		2	4		4
Bai	353	120	233	183	96	87
Baonan	2		2			
Blang	6	2	4	22	7	15
Buyi	912	375	537	373	134	239
Dai	68	15	53	187	58	129
Daur	92	39	53	85	43	42
Deang	2		2	6	3	3
Derung	127	67	60	1		1
Dong	632	318	314	280	194	86
Dongxiang	9	5	4	30	21	9
Ewenki	24	8	16	26	11	15
Gaoshan	7	3	4	9	4	5
Gelao	55	33	22	121	78	43
Han	32,368,083	16,751,349	15,616,734	35,618,454	18,290,925	17,327,529
Hani	55	10	45	214	34	180
Hezhe	2	2		12	4	8
Hui	61,690	31,152	30,538	59,709	30,210	29,499
Jing	4	1	3	29	13	16
Jingpo	52	1	51	108	9	99
Jino	4	1	3	1		1
Kazak	23	7	16	277	144	133
Kirgiz	1		1	6	2	4
Korean	1813	867	946	663	316	347
Lahu	35	7	28	136	14	122
Lhoba	2		2			

Li	92	47	45	521	266	255
Lisu	101	9	92	159	23	136
Manchu	13,665	7198	6467	11,741	6314	5427
Maonan	8		8	21	16	5
Miao	2805	1160	1645	2205	1124	1081
Monba	8		8	3	2	1
Mongol	9446	3399	6047	5070	2707	2363
Mulao	35	9	26	28	12	16
Naxi	57	17	40	42	17	25
Nu	9	2	7	88	40	48
Oroqen	1		1	3	2	1
Pumi	11	2	9	3	1	2
Qiang	159	109	50	286	214	72
Russian	8	1	7	5	2	3
Salar	8	4	4	43	26	17
She	251	156	95	171	117	54
Shui	20	2	18	30	15	15
Tajik	94	42	52	1	1	
Tatar				1		1
Tibetan	1544	678	866	1047	494	553
Tu	236	116	120	200	98	102
Tujia	2362	1301	1061	2936	1858	1078
Uygur	1084	566	518	670	414	256
Uzbek	3	1	2	3	1	2
Va	120	43	77	427	117	310
Xibe	152	79	73	158	93	65
Yao	202	88	114	325	164	161
Yi	2473	775	1698	2867	1426	1441
Yugur	8	3	5	7	3	4
Zhuang	2084	534	1550	2007	830	1177

Note: Total population includes servicemen (while ethnic breakdowns do not include them) as well as unknown ethnic groups and foreigners with Chinese citizenship

Table B.27 Sichuan's populations reported by the 2000 and 2010 national population censuses

	2000			2010		
Ethnic group	Population	Male	Female	Population	Male	Female
Total	82,348,296	42,561,620	39,786,676	80,417,528	40,827,834	39,589,694
Achang	26	11	15	54	17	37
Bai	7335	3441	3894	9449	4683	4766
Baonan	16	8	8	43	33	10
Blang	138	22	116	164	46	118
Buyi	8215	4063	4152	8756	4292	4464
Dai	6642	2956	3686	7652	3380	4272
Daur	73	38	35	124	57	67
Deang	11	1	10	24	8	16
Derung	51	22	29	47	20	27
Dong	1940	959	981	2376	1142	1234
Dongxiang	60	40	20	191	135	56
Ewenki	18	10	8	30	15	15
Gaoshan	101	47	54	100	42	58
Gelao	520	273	247	1235	630	605
Han	78,229,697	40,472,128	37,757,569	75,509,724	38,343,974	37,165,750
Hani	1104	290	814	1566	469	1097
Hezhe	14	5	9	84	38	46
Hui	109,960	55,504	54,456	104,544	52,797	51,747
Jing	38	20	18	264	126	138
Jingpo	79	10	69	173	51	122
Jino	48	4	44	54	12	42
Kazak	94	45	49	1882	927	955
Kirgiz	14	5	9	74	41	33
Korean	3137	1555	1582	1548	787	761
Lahu	512	59	453	521	104	417
Lhoba	5	1	4	8	2	6

Li	316	111	205	1688	744	944
Lisu	18,674	9294	9380	21,082	10,381	10,701
Manchu	13,849	7064	6785	15,920	8355	7565
Maonan	36	15	21	88	43	45
Miao	147,526	77,078	70,448	164,642	84,997	79,645
Monba	113	40	73	26	7	19
Mongol	42,316	19,719	22,597	36,646	18,350	18,296
Mulao	116	64	52	225	110	115
Naxi	8725	4448	4277	10,149	5098	5051
Nu	57	19	38	312	113	199
Oroqen	8	4	4	18	9	9
Pumi	166	61	105	137	55	82
Qiang	300,757	153,012	147,745	296,931	149,730	147,201
Russian	48	21	27	57	27	30
Salar	108	68	40	223	122	101
She	232	154	78	447	265	182
Shui	257	121	136	1178	537	641
Tajik	58	31	27	23	4	19
Tatar	7	4	3	15	6	9
Tibetan	1,269,120	631,389	637,731	1,496,524	747,138	749,386
Tu	646	350	296	1333	639	694
Tujia	41,246	22,358	18,888	59,231	31,106	28,125
Uygur	2158	1076	1082	1945	994	951
Uzbek	3		3	17	8	9
Va	1475	170	1305	1334	343	991
Xibe	216	96	120	381	187	194
Yao	742	362	380	1795	770	1025
Yi	2,122,389	1,089,245	1,033,144	2,643,953	1,348,832	1,295,121
Yugur	4	1	3	48	26	22
Zhuang	6905	3671	3234	10,050	4781	5269

Note: Total population includes servicemen (while ethnic breakdowns do not include them) as well as unknown ethnic groups and foreigners with Chinese citizenship

Table B.28 Tianjin's populations reported by the 2000 and 2010 national population censuses

	2000			2010		
Ethnic group	Population	Male	Female	Population	Male	Female
Total	9,848,731	5,016,375	4,832,356	12,938,693	6,907,091	6,031,602
Achang				9	7	2
Bai	184	94	90	686	374	312
Baonan	1	1		10	8	2
Blang	8	5	3	21	18	3
Buyi	507	217	290	839	437	402
Dai	24	8	16	184	100	84
Daur	353	157	196	629	300	329
Deang						
Derung	16	7	9	3	2	1
Dong	521	214	307	912	454	458
Dongxiang	51	29	22	121	95	26
Ewenki	84	35	49	130	59	71
Gaoshan	34	14	20	29	15	14
Gelao	63	36	27	374	260	114
Han	9,581,775	4,885,974	4,695,801	12,607,276	6,739,522	5,867,754
Hani	20	7	13	190	81	109
Hezhe	9	4	5	28	16	12
Hui	172,357	84,999	87,358	177,734	88,336	89,398
Jing	1		1	32	14	18
Jingpo	6	4	2	29	14	15
Jino	4		4	7	1	6
Kazak	34	19	15	476	212	264
Kirgiz	13	6	7	41	17	24
Korean	11,041	5030	6011	18,247	9303	8944
Lahu	7	2	5	44	27	17
Lhoba	4	2	2			

Li	54	25	29	564	304	260
Lisu	10	8	2	63	33	30
Manchu	56,548	28,548	28,000	83,624	43,293	40,331
Maonan	40	7	33	49	14	35
Miao	1582	767	815	3751	2354	1397
Monba				8	6	2
Mongol	11,331	4616	6715	20,328	9817	10,511
Mulao	47	20	27	116	59	57
Naxi	29	16	13	81	45	36
Nu	3	3		41	25	16
Oroqen	10	4	6	38	16	22
Pumi	1		1	16	15	1
Qiang	20	10	10	180	114	66
Russian	60	22	38	119	52	67
Salar	32	25	7	122	85	37
She	78	47	31	263	147	116
Shui	36	15	21	291	166	125
Tajik	30	15	15	11	9	2
Tatar	12	5	7	4	2	2
Tibetan	1271	600	671	1775	911	864
Tu	159	86	73	350	199	151
Tujia	3677	2097	1580	7052	4059	2993
Uygur	974	618	356	2170	970	1200
Uzbek	7	3	4	19	8	11
Va	42	21	21	209	133	76
Xibe	343	169	174	536	282	254
Yao	345	135	210	785	408	377
Yi	780	357	423	1825	1217	608
Yugur				39	20	19
Zhuang	4055	1256	2799	6123	2608	3515

Note: Total population includes servicemen (while ethnic breakdowns do not include them) as well as unknown ethnic groups and foreigners with Chinese citizenship

Table B.29 Tibet's populations reported by the 2000 and 2010 national population censuses

	2000			2010		
Ethnic group	Population	Male	Female	Population	Male	Female
Total	2,616,329	1,325,371	1,290,958	3,002,165	1,542,652	1,459,513
Achang						
Bai	722	505	217	395	247	148
Baonan	24	22	2	15	11	4
Blang	16	7	9	4	1	3
Buyi	437	192	245	81	61	20
Dai	14	10	4	35	17	18
Daur	3	2	1	5	3	2
Deang	1		1			
Derung	6	3	3	37	19	18
Dong	66	34	32	179	100	79
Dongxiang	111	91	20	757	523	234
Ewenki						
Gaoshan				2	1	1
Gelao	32	25	7	27	15	12
Han	158,570	98,589	59,981	245,263	151,158	94,105
Hani	24	19	5	23	16	7
Hezhe	1		1			
Hui	9031	6683	2348	12,630	8263	4367
Jing				5	2	3
Jingpo						
Jino				1	1	
Kazak	8	7	1	2143	1182	961
Kirgiz				2678	1338	1340
Korean	51	22	29	26	18	8
Lahu	19	13	6	4	3	1
Lhoba	2691	1353	1338	3489	1696	1793

Li	3	1	2	26	16	10
Lisu	17	9	8	25	10	15
Manchu	153	88	65	718	391	327
Maonan				1	1	
Miao	389	246	143	416	292	124
Monba	8481	4255	4226	9663	4876	4787
Mongol	690	341	349	307	187	120
Mulao	5	5		2	2	
Naxi	1223	603	620	1133	557	576
Nu	408	209	199	492	242	250
Oroqen						
Pumi	15	10	5	16	11	5
Qiang	20	15	5	94	59	35
Russian	20	9	11	3	1	2
Salar	228	157	71	255	163	92
She	6	2	4	8	8	
Shui				14	8	6
Tajik	4	4				
Tatar						
Tibetan	2,427,168	1,208,765	1,218,403	2,716,388	1,368,355	1,348,033
Tu	335	212	123	1068	634	434
Tujia	303	215	88	451	321	130
Uygur	701	394	307	205	138	67
Uzbek	1	1		4	2	2
Va	7	4	3	43	30	13
Xibe				6	3	3
Yao	26	20	6	137	85	52
Yi	287	199	88	396	293	103
Yugur	3	3		4	2	2
Zhuang	192	106	86	173	128	45

Note: Total population includes servicemen (while ethnic breakdowns do not include them) as well as unknown ethnic groups and foreigners with Chinese citizenship

Table B.30 Xinjiang's populations reported by the 2000 and 2010 national population censuses

	2000			2010		
Ethnic group	Population	Male	Female	Population	Male	Female
Total	18,459,511	9,552,181	8,907,330	21,815,815	11,270,147	10,545,668
Achang	2	1	1	5	3	2
Bai	409	216	193	407	216	191
Baonan	571	311	260	568	342	226
Blang	9	3	6	23	11	12
Buyi	977	555	422	797	516	281
Dai	59	23	36	121	42	79
Daur	5541	2813	2728	5536	2851	2685
Deang	14	9	5	3	1	2
Derung	51	26	25	11	5	6
Dong	946	560	386	753	501	252
Dongxiang	55,841	29,153	26,688	61,613	32,781	28,832
Ewenki	72	37	35	26	11	15
Gaoshan	41	18	23	44	15	29
Gelao	110	70	40	260	166	94
Han	7,489,919	3,972,142	3,517,777	8,829,994	4,674,383	4,155,611
Hani	62	25	37	190	79	111
Hezhe	22	6	16	33	20	13
Hui	839,837	431,196	408,641	983,015	506,076	476,939
Jing	12	4	8	69	40	29
Jingpo	27	15	12	33	13	20
Jino				3	3	
Kazak	1,245,023	631,268	613,755	1,418,278	725,515	692,763
Kirgiz	158,775	80,687	78,088	180,472	91,506	88,966
Korean	1463	745	718	1128	558	570
Lahu	28	13	15	73	41	32
Lhoba	33	20	13	4	2	2

Li	115	64	51	418	233	185
Lisu	34	13	21	104	53	51
Manchu	19,493	9910	9583	18,707	9786	8921
Maonan	9	3	6	28	21	7
Miao	7006	3749	3257	7626	4288	3338
Monba	11	7	4	4	1	3
Mongol	149,857	74,450	75,407	156,280	79,063	77,217
Mulao	29	19	10	77	50	27
Naxi	73	34	39	89	43	46
Nu	18	8	10	58	31	27
Oroqen	14	9	5	12	8	4
Pumi	10	6	4	12	5	7
Qiang	284	162	122	317	162	155
Russian	8935	4206	4729	8489	4067	4422
Salar	3762	1965	1797	3728	1998	1730
She	166	91	75	167	105	62
Shui	301	153	148	90	68	22
Tajik	39,493	20,170	19,323	47,261	24,000	23,261
Tatar	4501	2360	2141	3242	1757	1485
Tibetan	6153	3124	3029	8316	4346	3970
Tu	2837	1525	1312	3455	1777	1678
Tujia	15,787	8495	7292	17,850	9811	8039
Uygur	8,345,622	4,243,646	4,101,976	10,001,302	5,064,182	4,937,120
Uzbek	12,096	6371	5725	10,114	5444	4670
Va	68	32	36	142	60	82
Xibe	34,566	17,416	17,150	34,399	17,416	16,983
Yao	723	369	354	942	534	408
Yi	1593	892	701	2954	1756	1198
Yugur	302	153	149	391	198	193
Zhuang	5642	2780	2862	5646	3113	2533

Note: Total population includes servicemen (while ethnic breakdowns do not include them) as well as unknown ethnic groups and foreigners with Chinese citizenship

Table B.31 Yunnan's populations reported by the 2000 and 2010 national population censuses

	2000			2010		
Ethnic group	Population	Male	Female	Population	Male	Female
Total	42,360,089	22,194,343	20,165,746	45,966,766	23,856,696	22,110,070
Achang	33,519	17,083	16,436	38,059	19,017	19,042
Bai	1,505,644	763,316	742,328	1,564,901	786,370	778,531
Baonan	7	5	2	49	36	13
Blang	90,388	47,279	43,109	116,573	60,117	56,456
Buyi	54,695	29,667	25,028	58,790	31,341	27,449
Dai	1,142,139	573,780	568,359	1,222,836	609,021	613,815
Daur	152	84	68	294	135	159
Deang	17,804	8994	8810	20,186	9889	10,297
Derung	5884	2934	2950	6353	3096	3257
Dong	3498	2169	1329	4389	2505	1884
Dongxiang	179	135	44	181	123	58
Ewenki	16	7	9	23	10	13
Gaoshan	91	48	43	131	66	65
Gelao	2835	1637	1198	3461	2018	1443
Han	28,201,274	14,894,380	13,306,894	30,617,580	16,017,198	14,600,382
Hani	1,424,990	749,084	675,906	1,629,508	851,064	778,444
Hezhe	13	7	6	42	24	18
Hui	643,238	326,023	317,215	698,265	351,169	347,096
Jing	508	196	312	878	351	527
Jingpo	130,212	64,712	65,500	142,956	69,718	73,238
Jino	20,685	10,549	10,136	22,759	11,611	11,148
Kazak	199	91	108	896	456	440
Kirgiz	42	26	16	34	18	16
Korean	1693	884	809	1343	698	645
Lahu	447,631	233,563	214,068	475,011	244,774	230,237
Lhoba	5	4	1	7	5	2

Li	1426	759	667	3231	1622	1609
Lisu	609,768	316,149	293,619	668,336	340,729	327,607
Manchu	12,187	6537	5650	13,490	7161	6329
Maonan	99	57	42	154	93	61
Miao	1,043,535	547,298	496,237	1,202,705	621,721	580,984
Monba	7	2	5	18	3	15
Mongol	28,110	14,549	13,561	22,624	12,104	10,520
Mulao	244	150	94	304	164	140
Naxi	295,464	148,805	146,659	309,858	154,835	155,023
Nu	27,738	14,467	13,271	31,821	16,240	15,581
Oroqen	6	4	2	11	3	8
Pumi	32,923	16,838	16,085	42,043	21,055	20,988
Qiang	506	380	126	552	323	229
Russian	32	10	22	26	8	18
Salar	55	28	27	265	150	115
She	499	290	209	848	552	296
Shui	12,533	6742	5791	8834	4789	4045
Tajik	17	10	7	7	3	4
Tatar	12	8	4	10	6	4
Tibetan	128,432	64,352	64,080	142,257	71,239	71,018
Tu	3157	1712	1445	5632	2988	2644
Tujia	3907	2498	1409	5963	3694	2269
Uygur	1161	815	346	1282	773	509
Uzbek	6	2	4	11	6	5
Va	383,023	199,783	183,240	400,814	204,648	196,166
Xibe	130	65	65	158	69	89
Yao	190,610	100,176	90,434	219,914	113,812	106,102
Yi	4,705,658	2,423,233	2,282,425	5,041,210	2,576,570	2,464,640
Yugur	10	7	3	8	4	4
Zhuang	1,144,021	598,142	545,879	1,215,260	628,603	586,657

Note: Total population includes servicemen (while ethnic breakdowns do not include them) as well as unknown ethnic groups and foreigners with Chinese citizenship

Table B.32 Zhejiang's populations reported by the 2000 and 2010 national population censuses

	2000			2010		
Ethnic group	Population	Male	Female	Population	Male	Female
Total	45,930,651	23,581,512	22,349,139	54,426,891	27,965,641	26,461,250
Achang	25	5	20	93	44	49
Bai	2659	920	1739	11,685	5981	5704
Baonan				17	10	7
Blang	74	4	70	300	107	193
Buyi	21,457	9726	11,731	125,838	67,119	58,719
Dai	540	77	463	5973	2883	3090
Daur	69	21	48	204	93	111
Deang				43	20	23
Derung	14	4	10	26	7	19
Dong	17,906	9524	8382	88,106	48,560	39,546
Dongxiang	55	28	27	322	202	120
Ewenki	21	8	13	40	17	23
Gaoshan	79	44	35	88	50	38
Gelao	2179	1269	910	17,785	9777	8008
Han	45,535,266	23,383,689	22,151,577	53,212,194	27,320,326	25,891,868
Hani	883	94	789	4300	1754	2546
Hezhe	17	5	12	48	20	28
Hui	19,609	10,500	9109	38,192	20,732	17,460
Jing	51	20	31	148	87	61
Jingpo	43	5	38	444	183	261
Jino	5	1	4	21	8	13
Kazak	19	6	13	695	311	384
Kirgiz	37	17	20	279	178	101
Korean	1767	881	886	6496	3288	3208
Lahu	306	17	289	1661	431	1230
Lhoba	4	2	2	1	1	

Li	1640	780	860	9391	4759	4632
Lisu	454	17	437	1514	598	916
Manchu	5089	2447	2642	11,271	5705	5566
Maonan	178	60	118	1199	639	560
Miao	53,418	26,882	26,536	309,064	167,566	141,498
Monba	8	3	5	21	9	12
Mongol	3604	1368	2236	6872	3452	3420
Mulao	786	380	406	2792	1432	1360
Naxi	553	63	490	634	161	473
Nu	75	17	58	109	40	69
Oroqen	2	2		21	9	12
Pumi	20	3	17	47	21	26
Qiang	168	77	91	1482	797	685
Russian	21	5	16	40	16	24
Salar	45	24	21	424	253	171
She	170,993	88,990	82,003	166,276	85,601	80,675
Shui	1421	459	962	11,815	6181	5634
Tajik	7	3	4	3368	1880	1488
Tatar	3	1	2	9		9
Tibetan	1084	456	628	2850	1274	1576
Tu	941	480	461	4709	2539	2170
Tujia	55,310	31,194	24,116	227,012	123,951	103,061
Uygur	785	537	248	5377	2460	2917
Uzbek	8	6	2	86	45	41
Va	274	44	230	2987	1368	1619
Xibe	71	26	45	200	105	95
Yao	1928	808	1120	10,710	5688	5022
Yi	6344	2427	3917	49,243	26,212	23,031
Yugur	2	1	1	14	7	7
Zhuang	18,998	5263	13,735	72,820	35,324	37,496

Note: Total population includes servicemen (while ethnic breakdowns do not include them) as well as unknown ethnic groups and foreigners with Chinese citizenship

Appendix C: China's Ethnic Minority Autonomous Areas: General Background

R. Guo, *China Ethnic Statistical Yearbook 2020*,
https://doi.org/10.1007/978-3-030-49024-9

Provinces and autonomous regions	Number of regions at prefecture level (unit)	Cities at prefecture level	Autonomous prefecture	Number of regions at county level (unit)	Cities at county level	Autonomous counties (Qi)	Total population in minority areas (10,000 persons)	Ethnic minority population	Ethnic minority population as percentage to total population in minority areas (%)
National total	**77**	**38**	**30**	**711**	**78**	**120**	**19,141.30**	**9774.64**	**51.07**
Hebei				6		6	213.93	136.39	63.75
Inner Mongolia	12	9		103	11	3	2533.98	561.64	22.16
Liaoning				8		8	323.17	176.11	54.49
Jilin	1		1	11	6	3	318.56	109.86	34.49
Heilongjiang				1		1	23.53	5.15	21.87
Zhejiang				1		1	17.10	2.02	11.81
Hubei	1		1	10	2	2	460.64	261.53	56.78
Hunan	1		1	15	1	7	498.82	416.53	83.50
Guangdong				3		3	52.96	20.49	38.70
Guangxi	14	14		111	7	12	4926.00	2204.51	44.75
Hainan				6		6	176.36	91.16	51.69
Chongqing				4		4	277.23	206.22	74.39
Sichuan	3		3	51	3	4	790.78	498.42	63.03

Guizhou	3		3	46	5	11	1834.05	1102.95	60.14
Yunnan	8		8	78	12	29	2415.82	1422.29	58.87
Tibet	7	6		74			343.82	309.60	90.05
Gansu	2		2	21	2	7	376.52	236.03	62.69
Qinghai	6		6	35	3	7	382.91	258.72	67.57
Ningxia	5	5		22	2		688.11	257.29	37.39
Xinjiang	14	4	5	105	24	6	2487.00	1497.72	60.22

Notes: Ethnic minority autonomous areas refer to the areas of 5 ethnic minority autonomous regions, 30 ethnic minority autonomous prefectures and 120 ethnic minority autonomous counties. Data on the administrative divisions of the ethnic minority autonomous areas, shown below, are tabulated and prepared in accordance with *A Concise Book of the Administrative Divisions of the People's Republic of China* (in Chinese) (edited by the Ministry of Civil Affairs (MCA) of the People's Republic of China and published by SinoMaps Press, Beijing, China, 2019)

Appendix D: China's Ethnic Minority Autonomous Areas: Principal Statistical Indicators

R. Guo, *China Ethnic Statistical Yearbook 2020*,
https://doi.org/10.1007/978-3-030-49024-9

	Aggregate data							Indices and growth rates (%)								
								Indices (2018 as percentage)						Average growth rate		
Item	1990	1995	2000	2005	2010	2017	2018	1990	1995	2000	2005	2010	2017	1991–2018	1996–2018	2001–2018
Population and employment population (10,000 persons)																
Population at year-end	15,296	16,044	16,818	17,311	18,531	18,943	19,141	125.1	119.3	113.8	110.6	103.3	101.0	0.8	0.8	0.7
Ethnic minority population	6880	7232	7767	8239	8814	9680	9775	142.1	135.2	125.9	118.6	110.9	101.0	1.3	1.3	1.3
Employment																
Persons employed in various units (0000 persons)	1543	1672	1733	1202	1297	1580	1787	115.8	106.8	103.1	148.6	137.8	113.1	0.5	0.3	0.2
Macro economy																
Gross regional product (100 million yuan)		**4901**	**7486**	**15,706**	**38,989**	**72,046**	**77,722**		**1072.3**	**695.3**	**399.5**	**204.5**	**106.8**		**10.9**	**11.4**
Primary industry		1629	2022	3300	6198	10,737	11,274		340.3	259.0	196.5	148.7	105.1		5.5	5.4
Secondary industry		1747	2834	6419	18,809	28,152	30,036		1829.9	1086.8	521.4	222.1	106.0		13.5	14.2
Tertiary industry		1526	2629	5987	13,982	33,157	36,412		1110.7	690.7	402.4	215.7	107.9		11.0	11.3
Per capita gross regional product (yuan)		**3055**	**4451**	**8991**	**22,060**	**39,622**	**42,437**		**1389.2**	**953.4**	**472.0**	**192.4**	**107.1**		**12.1**	**13.3**
Government finance (100 million yuan)																
Public Budgetary Revenue	166.7	248	476	1026	3257	7262	7575	4544.2	3053.2	1592.9	738.1	232.6	104.3	14.6	16.0	16.6
Public Budgetary Expenditure	304.4	595	1173	3050	10,512	25,655	28,025	9206.7	4709.3	2389.4	918.7	266.6	109.2	17.5	18.2	19.3
Industry																
Agriculture																
Cultivated area (10,000 hectares)	1763	1508	2086	2033	2380	2793	2854	161.9	189.2	136.8	140.4	119.9	102.2	1.7	2.8	1.8

Irrigated areas (10,000 hectares)	764	838	936	1027	1156	1378	1394	182.4	166.3	148.9	135.6	120.5	101.1	2.2	2.2	2.2
Gross output value of agriculture, forestry, animal		2537	3200	5349	10,374	18,888	19,709	4404.6	315.9	240.7	176.6	112.2	105.3	14.5	5.1	5.0
Husbandry and fishery (100 million yuan)																
Output of major farm products																
Grain output (10,000 tons)	5373	5801	6381	7187	8308	10,118	10,362	192.9	178.6	162.4	144.2	124.7	102.4	2.4	2.6	2.7
Cotton output (10,000 tons)	47	95	146	188	248	457	511	1088.0	540.5	349.7	272.1	205.8	111.9	8.9	7.6	7.2
Oil-bearing crops output (10,000 tons)	208	264	353	372	422	576	533	256.1	201.8	150.8	143.2	126.1	92.5	3.4	3.1	2.3
Number of large domestic animals (year-end) (10,000 heads)	5286	5618	5566	6153	6068	5182	5135	97.1	91.4	92.3	83.5	84.6	99.1	−0.1	−0.4	−0.4
Goats and sheep (10,000 units)	11,362	11,906	13,076	16,391	14,885	16,751	16,144	142.1	135.6	123.5	98.5	108.5	96.4	1.3	1.3	1.2
Hogs (year-end) (10,000 heads)	5668	7240	8201	8526	8141	8312	7026	124.0	97.1	85.7	82.4	86.3	84.5	0.8	−0.1	−0.9
Industry																
Output of major industrial products																
Cloth (100 million m)	7.4	6.9	5.0	3.5	3.6	3.9	6.1	81.8	87.7	120.8	172.9	166.6	156.0	−0.7	−0.6	1.1
Machine-made paper and paperboard (10,000 tons)	94	191	175	273	385	470	446	474.1	233.3	254.3	163.5	115.8	94.9	5.7	3.8	5.3

(continued)

(continued)

Item	Aggregate data							Indices and growth rates (%)								
								Indices (2018 as percentage)						Average growth rate		
	1990	1995	2000	2005	2010	2017	2018	1990	1995	2000	2005	2010	2017	1991–2018	1996–2018	2001–2018
Refined sugar (10,000 tons)	223	240	498	678	907	1208	1287	578.1	537.3	258.3	189.8	141.9	106.5	6.5	7.6	5.4
Coal (100 million tons)	1.2	1.7	1.5	3.8	10.4	12.2	13.3	1099.4	801.4	909.7	350.1	128.0	108.7	8.9	9.5	13.1
Crude oil (10,000 tons)	1265	1610	2292	2833	3059	2889	2944	232.7	182.8	128.4	103.9	96.2	101.9	3.1	2.7	1.4
Electricity (100 million kwh)	739	1187	1712	3052	6730	15,764	19,249	2605.5	1622.4	1124.1	630.7	286.0	122.1	12.3	12.9	14.4
Crude steel (10,000 tons)	368	700	647	1846	4005	5659	5822	1580.9	832.2	899.8	315.4	145.4	102.9	10.4	9.7	13.0
Pig iron (10,000 tons)	417	555	725	2087	4447	5371	5929	1421.9	1068.9	818.0	284.1	133.3	110.4	9.9	10.9	12.4
Cement (10,000 tons)	1958	4296	5703	10,156	21,653	36,507	35,195	1797.7	819.3	617.1	346.5	162.5	96.4	10.9	9.6	10.6
Construction																
Number of employed persons (10,000 persons)			132	142	194	272	276			210.0	195.0	142.3	101.8			4.2
Gross output value of construction (100 million yuan)			754	1656	5203	11,097	12,037			1595.8	726.9	231.3	108.5			16.6
Floor space of buildings under construction (10,000 sq.m)			9232	15,964	35,052	57,713	54,985			595.6	344.4	156.9	95.3			10.4
Floor space of buildings completed (10,000 sq.m)			5326	8072	15,418	20,119	18,710			351.3	231.8	121.4	93.0			7.2
Transportation, postal and telecommunication services																
Length of railways in operation (10,000 km)	1.31	1.70	1.43	1.69	2.12	3.16	3.17			222.0	187.5	149.2	100.2			4.5
Highways (10,000 km)	29	33	42	59	91	124	126	429.7	380.0	297.9	214.0	138.4	102.1	5.3	6.0	6.3

Business volume of postal and telecommunication Services (100 million yuan)	9	78	297	892	2456	2382	5841			1967.4	655.0	237.8	245.2	26.2	20.6	18.0
Total length of postal routes and rural delivery routes (10,000 km)	88	107	110	110	127	244	203	230.7	190.1	185.4	185.1	160.3	83.3	3.0	2.8	3.5
Foreign trade																
Total value of imports and exports (100 million USD)						7099	7956						112.1			
Exports						3924	4308						109.8			
Imports						3181	3679						115.7			
International tourism																
Number of international tourists (10,000 person-times)			269	467	820	1936	2210			821.5	473.2	269.5	114.1			12.4
Foreign exchange earnings from international Tourism (100 million USD)			8	13	30	88	95			1261.7	744.1	317.5	108.8			15.1
Finance																
Deposits of national banking system (100 million yuan)			7906	16,324	46,622	113,907	118,138			1494.3	723.7	253.4	103.7			16.2
Loans of national banking system (100 million yuan)			6548	11,300	30,579	91,256	95,135			1452.9	841.9	311.1	104.3			16.0

(continued)

(continued)

Item	Aggregate data							Indices and growth rates (%)								
								Indices (2018 as percentage)						Average growth rate		
	1990	1995	2000	2005	2010	2017	2018	1990	1995	2000	2005	2010	2017	1991–2018	1996–2018	2001–2018
Education, culture and public health																
education																
Total enrollment (10,000 persons)																
Regular institutions of higher education	13.6	18.6	34.2	100.0	161.9	223.4	231.1	1699.2	1242.4	675.7	231.1	142.8	103.4	10.6	11.6	11.2
Regular secondary schools	610	632	873	1082	1050	1031	1072	175.9	169.7	122.8	99.1	102.1	104.0	2.0	2.3	1.1
Regular primary schools	1853	1889	1886	1668	1536	1539	1573	84.9	83.2	83.4	94.3	102.4	102.2	–0.6	–0.8	–1.0
Full-time teachers (10,000 persons)																
Regular institutions of higher education	2.8	3.7	3.6	6.3	9.5	11.9	12.2	434.8	329.0	334.5	193.2	128.6	102.4	5.4	5.3	6.9
Regular secondary schools	41.5	41.5	47.9	61.1	67.4	76.3	78.2	188.4	188.6	163.3	128.0	116.0	102.5	2.3	2.8	2.8
Regular primary schools	84.8	85.8	89.9	88.1	90.7	91.0	94.7	111.6	110.3	105.3	107.5	104.3	104.0	0.4	0.4	0.3
Culture																
Publications																
Books (10,000 volumes)	30,166	42,275	42,310	41,958	43,099	68,020	71,371	236.6	168.8	168.7	170.1	165.6	104.9	3.1	2.3	2.9
Number of magazines issued (10,000 volumes)	7866	7881	8332	10,280	8276	9886	9298	118.2	118.0	111.6	90.4	112.3	94.0	0.6	0.7	0.6
Newspapers (10,000 copies)	79,120	94,985	123,277	169,518	174,848	172,137	170,706	215.8	179.7	138.5	100.7	97.6	99.2	2.8	2.6	1.8

Public health																
Number of hospitals (10,000 units)	1.06	1.23	1.25	1.18	1.20	5.33	5.45	515.5	442.1	436.4	460.2	455.8	102.3	6.0	6.7	8.5
Number of beds in health care institutions (10,000 beds)	33.2	35.7	36.1	38.4	55.7	99.0	104.8	315.7	293.5	290.1	272.6	188.0	105.9	4.2	4.8	6.1
Social services																
Beds on social welfare institutions (10,000 beds)					27.3	35.5	34.7					127.2	97.9			
Number of persons receiving minimum living allowance in urban and rural areas (10,000 persons)					1907.4	1639.5	1366					71.6	83.3			

Notes: Data on the social and economic development in ethnic minority autonomous areas, shown below, are collected from the surveys conducted by areas. A statistical reporting form system on the economic and social development in the ethnic minority autonomous areas has been established jointly by the State Ethnic Affairs Commission (SEAC) and the National Bureau of Statistics (NBS) and implemented by the provincial and local ethnic affairs commissions and statistical bureaus. The reporting form system covers all units under the jurisdiction of the 5 ethnic minority autonomous regions, 30 autonomous prefectures and 120 autonomous counties. In addition, data on the public health are provided by the Ministry of Health (MOH)

Appendix E: China's Spatial (Dis) integration as a Multiethnic Paradox[3]

Abstract Using China's interprovincial panel data, this paper shows that the negative effect of distance-related transactions costs on trade tends to rise from 2000 to 2010. After constructing China's 56 ethnic groups into a single, interprovincial similarity index, we cannot find any evidence that supports the view that ethnic links should serve as a factor promoting bilateral trade. However, our estimated coefficients on 37 major ethnic groups show that both positive and negative ethnic influences on trade exist in China. Specifically, 14 ethnic groups (Lahu, Qiang, Jingpo, Tu, Mongol, Manchu, Hui, Zhuang, Dongxiang, Daur, Kirgiz, She, Maonan, and Tibetan) are found to contribute to China's interprovincial trade, while five ethnic groups (Han, Va, Kazak, Dai, and Blang) tend to retard China's interprovincial trade and the remaining ethnic groups do not have any influences.

Keywords Trade; Spatial (dis)integration; Interprovincial relation; Ethnic linkage; Province; China

R. Guo, *China Ethnic Statistical Yearbook 2020*,
https://doi.org/10.1007/978-3-030-49024-9

Introduction

The first decade of the twenty-first century was unusual to China. Promoted by its entry into the World Trade Organization (WTO) on December 11, 2001, China's economic growth has significantly driven by its remarkable performance in foreign trade. WTO data shows that China's exports and imports enjoyed an average annual growth rate of 18% and 16% from 2000 to 2010, respectively, much higher than the average annual growth rate of the global trade volume in the same period, which was only 3%.[4] In 2000, for example, China was the 7th leading exporter and 8th largest importer of merchandise trade. Since 2001, China has steadily increased its share of global manufactured exports. Notwithstanding the global reductions in trade, which resulted from the US financial crisis in 2008, China replaced Germany as the world's largest exporting nation in 2009. In 2010, China continued to be the leading merchandise exporter (US$1.58 trillion, or 10.4 percent of world exports), followed by the United States (8.4 percent of world exports), Germany (8.3 percent of world exports), and Japan (5.1 percent of world exports).[5]

When looking inside China, however, one can only find less encouraging news. For example, compared with its surging foreign trade as mentioned above, which has increased by more than four (for exports) or three (for imports) times from 2000 to 2010, China's domestic trade has only achieved a growth of 86.26% during the same period (see Table E.1). This means that China's domestic trade—both intra-provincial and interprovincial—has only had an average annual growth rate of about 6 percent from 2000 to 2010. Frankly speaking, this may not have been treated as a low figure in many other countries during that period of time. However, compared with its 16–18 percent of annual foreign trade growth rate and 10 percent of annual gross domestic product (GDP) growth rate from 2000 to 2010, China's domestic trade performance can only but be labeled as "poor".

Even worse news comes from China's interprovincial trade performance. China's official statistics on interprovincial trade (in terms of freight exchange via national railways) are puzzling. For example, except for China's two peripheral territories (i.e., Hainan and Tibet) whose data

Table E.1 Changes of China's domestic and interprovincial trade from 2000 to 2010

	Domestic trade (thousand tons)			Ratio of interprovincial trade (%)		
Provincial economy	2000	2010	Change (%)	2000	2010	Change (%)
Anhui	6087	12,092	98.65	56.84	47.93	−8.91
Beijing	2612	1571	−39.85	72.21	95.23	23.02
Chongqing	1613	2197	36.21	56.79	65.95	9.16
Fujian	2475	3704	49.66	46.22	53.48	7.26
Gansu	3236	6186	91.16	52.10	61.27	9.17
Guangdong	4521	7505	66.00	74.70	79.72	5.02
Guangxi	2815	6109	117.02	67.10	75.82	8.72
Guizhou	3585	7991	122.90	69.29	82.98	13.69
Hainan	311	542	74.28	NA	10.89	NA
Hebei	11,399	16,481	44.58	60.61	56.09	−4.52
Heilongjiang	12,701	16,888	32.97	54.47	49.19	−5.28
Henan	9655	13,374	38.52	78.92	71.53	−7.39
Hubei	3937	5698	44.73	62.81	66.57	3.75
Hunan	4668	5783	23.89	65.62	61.27	−4.35
Inner Mongolia	9171	37,698	311.06	69.55	77.00	7.46
Jiangsu	4076	6372	56.33	63.67	85.75	22.08
Jiangxi	2959	5376	81.68	57.92	51.95	−5.97
Jilin	5630	7674	36.31	60.55	69.53	8.98
Liaoning	12,520	18,118	44.71	34.03	29.94	−4.09
Ningxia	1782	4414	147.70	73.12	86.45	13.33
Qinghai	647	3096	378.52	81.14	61.66	−19.48
Shaanxi	3280	8836	169.39	65.95	69.09	3.15
Shandong	10,585	18,285	72.74	52.24	62.67	10.43
Shanghai	1054	959	−9.01	89.56	93.53	3.97
Shanxi	28,469	60,812	113.61	91.96	92.76	0.80
Sichuan	5516	7389	33.96	46.79	51.59	4.80
Tianjin	2004	7240	261.28	81.64	54.46	−27.18
Tibet		30	NA		100.00	NA
Xinjiang	3353	6775	102.06	73.67	74.05	0.39
Yunnan	2882	5209	80.74	59.51	67.92	8.41
Zhejiang	1929	3806	97.30	62.10	41.59	−20.51
All	165,472	308,210	86.26	65.53	69.06	5.39

Notes: (1) "Trade" only includes freight exchange via national railways. (2) NA = data are not available

Source: Calculated by the author based on China Association of Communications and Transportation and the National Development and Reform Commission of the PRC

are not available in 2000, the proportions of interprovincial trade to total domestic trade have risen in only 17 provincial economies (i.e., Beijing, Jiangsu, Guizhou, Ningxia, Shandong, Gansu, Chongqing, Jilin, Guangxi, Yunnan, Inner Mongolia, Fujian, Guangdong, Sichuan, Shanghai, Hubei, and Shaanxi) from 2000 to 2010. By way of contrast, the proportions for the remaining provincial economies have either decreased (i.e., in Tianjin, Zhejiang, Qinghai, Anhui, Henan, Jiangxi, Heilongjiang, Hebei, Hunan, and Liaoning) or been kept almost unchanged (i.e., in Shanxi and Xinjiang) during the same period (see Table E.1 for more details).[6]

Indeed, the above phenomenon is unusual, especially after the following facts are taken into account:

1. Since the 1990s, there has been a significant improvement of transport infrastructures (including, inter alia, the completion of various expressways and high-speed railways across the nation) in China;
2. Since 1999, the "Western Regional Development Policy" has been implemented by the Chinese central government in order speed up the development of the western and central provinces by encouraging the economic cooperation between the East-West provinces; and
3. Since 2008, and as a result of the global reductions in trade, which resulted from the US financial crisis, the Chinese government has made various efforts in order to stimulate China's domestic consumption.

Then, what are the driving forces behind the dynamic patterns of China's domestic trade and how to explain its interprovincial trade puzzle?

Analytical Framework

Literature Review

Past studies of the determinants of spatial economic interdependence seem controversial, or at least incomplete. According to the Heckscher-Ohlin theorem, if the two factors of production are capital and labor, countries with dissimilar levels of per capita income (or, more precisely, dissimilar capital/labor ratios) will trade more than countries with similar levels.[7] However, a number of empirical results indicate that the inclusion of income level as a determinant of trade contradicts the assumptions of traditional Heckscher-Ohlin theory.[8] In order to fill up this gap, economists have put forward new theories that base international trade on, among others, economies of scale, market imperfections, and cross-national differences in technology.[9]

However, past studies have raised more questions than they have answered. For example, the effects of geographical proximity on trade have not been shown to fall over time. Rather, these effects have been shown to strengthen over time for 1950–1988 and 1965–1992.[10] Similarly, Rauch provides no evidence that, as a result of technological innovation, declining distance-related transactions costs should have led to increased trade flows.[11] One possibility is that these analyses exclude important explanatory variables, thereby biasing the estimates.[12] To clarify related issues, it is necessary to isolate the influences of all distance-related variables on trade. In particular, the inclusion of some relevant cultural variables might allow us to gain a better understanding of the black box containing the distance-related transactions costs that affect spatial economic activities.

China has officially identified, except other unknown ethnic groups and foreigners with Chinese citizenship, 56 ethnic groups. Although the majority of China's population is of the Han nationality (which accounts for more than 90% of China's total population), the non-Han ethnic groups have a population of more than 100 million. Thanks to the easing migration policy that has been implemented since the 1980s, China's interprovincial labor flows have increased dramatically. It is noteworthy that these flows have also been conducted by people coming from the inland, ethnic-minority, areas and moving into the coastal, Han-majority areas. Consequently, China's interprovincial ethnic networks have been enhanced. As of 2010 when the Sixth National Population Census of the PRC was conducted, each of China's 31 provinces has become home to almost all ethnic groups. How have these growing ethnic networks contributed to (or impeded) China's interprovincial economic cooperation and integration?

There is a widely held view that easily observable impediments, such as transportation costs, do not adequately capture transactions costs in international trade. Trade is also reduced by hidden transaction costs associated with unobserved trade barriers.[13] In addition, some studies use international panel data and find that cultural distance or dissimilarity—as proxied by, among other things, the ethnic/linguistic and religious differences across national populations—is a robust determinant of the volume of international trade.[14]

Since the 1990s, numerous quantitative studies have examined the role that cultural factors play in international trade.[15] These studies used linguistic or/and religious links as one or more explanatory variables. The estimated results suggest that countries which are similar to one another have been more likely to trade with each other in the postwar period. In other words, there is evidence of cultural barriers to trade.

Indeed, trade and economic cooperation may be affected by cultural dissimilarities, as it is easier and more efficient for people with the same cultural identity (ethnicity, language, religion, or any other cultural element) to trust and communicate each other than for those with different cultural identities. In this paper, our particular interest is to test how ethnic differences have influenced China's interprovincial trade and economic cooperation. Even though language is an effective tool of communication and that religion can provide insights into the characteristics of a culture, we would rather select ethnicity as the explanatory variable. The rationale is that most, if not all, of China's ethnic groups are identified in terms of either linguistic or religious traditions. Another reason lies in the fact that, in China, it is more difficult, if not impossible, to collect interprovincial panel data on linguistic and religious groups than those on ethnic groups.

The gravity model is most commonly used by international and regional economists to study trade. The classic early application of the model was by Linnemann, who continued work first reported in Tinbergen and then in Pöyhönen.[16] Generally, a gravity model assumes that the volume of trade between any two economies will be directly proportional to the product of their economic masses (measured by GDP or GNP) and inversely proportional to the distance between them. Per capita incomes (measured by product of per capita GDPs or GNPs) have become a standard covariate in the gravity models.[17]

The Model

In this paper, our particular interest is to test how various ethnic groups have influenced China's interprovincial trade and economic cooperation. Recent gravity equations, compared to the earlier ones, have included multilateral trade resistance (MTR) terms.[18] The MTR terms arise because in a general equilibrium model, trade flows between any two provinces not only depend on trade costs between the two provinces under consideration, but also on trade costs between all other trading pairs. However, in this paper, we intend to simplify the MTR terms. The rationale is that China's domestic MTR terms, if they do exist, are much weaker than international ones. To this end, we only add country fixed effects to the gravity models. As noted by Adam and Cobham, these effects can be thought of theoretically as approximations to MTR terms.[19] The basic form of the gravity model to be used in our empirical analysis of interprovincial trade is as the following:[20]

$$\begin{aligned}\ln\left(\text{TRADE}_{ij}\right) = \alpha_0 + \alpha_1 \ln\left(\text{GDP}_i\text{GDP}_j\right) + \alpha_2 \ln\text{DISTANCE}_{ij} \\ + \alpha_3 \text{ADJACENT}_{ij} + \alpha_4 \ln\left(\text{GDPPC}_i\text{GDPPC}_j\right) \\ + \alpha_5 \text{PD} + \beta \text{ETHNIC56}_{ij}\end{aligned} \tag{E.1}$$

In Eq. (E.1), 'ln' represents natural logarithm; TRADE*ij*, measured in thousand tons, is the total freight exchange between provinces *i* and *j*. GDP*i*GDP*j* is the product of GDP (in Chinese currency) of the *i*th and *j*th provinces. DISTANCE*ij* represents the distance between the geographical centers of gravity of the *i*th and *j*th provinces (in kilometers).[21] ADJACENT*ij* is a dummy variable, which takes the values of '1' for provinces *i* and *j* to have a common border and of "0" otherwise. GDPPC*i*GDPPC*j* is the product of GDP per capita (in Chinese currency) of the *i*th and *j*th provinces. PD denotes a province dummy, which takes the values of "1" for provinces to be either a mountain-dominated or an island province (Chongqing, Guizhou, Hainan, Qinghai, Sichuan, Tibet, or Yunnan—we include these provinces since they have China's most complicated geographical conditions and therefore have the most difficulties in transportation) and of "0" otherwise.

ETHNIC56*ij* represents the extent to which the *i*th and *j*th provinces are ethnically linked each other (details about the measurement will be discussed in Eq. (E.6) in section "The Data"). Note that since ETHNIC56 is a comprehensive index for all of China's 56 ethnic groups, it can only be used to derive a general pattern of correlation between interprovincial trade and ethnic linkage. If one wants to examine the role that each ethnic group plays, the gravity model can be now written as the following:

$$\begin{aligned}\ln\left(\text{TRADE}_{ij}\right) = \alpha_0 + \alpha_1 \ln\left(\text{GDP}_i\text{GDP}_j\right) + \alpha_2 \ln\text{DISTANCE}_{ij} \\ + \alpha_3\text{ADJACENT}_{ij} + \alpha_4 \ln\left(\text{GDPPC}_i\text{GDPPC}_j\right) \\ + \alpha_5\text{PD} + \sum_{k=1}^{37}\beta\text{ETHNIC}_{ijk}\end{aligned} \tag{E.2}$$

In Eq. (E.2), ETHNIC*ijk* represents the extent to which the *k*th ethnic group is linked between the *i*th and *j*th provinces (details about the measurement will be discussed in Eq. (E.5) in section "The Data"). Only 37 ethnic groups—each with a population of less than 100,000 persons (see Annex for more detailed information)—are included in this equation.

Theoretically, cultural dissimilarity can result in both social transactions costs (a factor directly impeding trade) and 'economic complementarity' (an important factor directly facilitating trade) simultaneously. As a result, the relationship between trade and cultural similarity may follow a non-linear pattern.[22] Our interest now goes to the clarification of specific cultural groups which may have different types of influences on trade with provinces differing in income levels. To go further, this paper employ a new explanatory variable: ln(GDPPC*i*GDPPC*j*)ETHNIC56*ij*. Consequently, a modified form of gravity model is written as:

$$\begin{aligned}\ln\left(\text{TRADE}_{ij}\right) = \alpha_0 + \alpha_1 \ln\left(\text{GDP}_i\text{GDP}_j\right) + \alpha_2 \ln\text{DISTANCE}_{ij} \\ + \alpha_3\text{ADJACENT}_{ij} + \alpha_4 \ln\left(\text{GDPPC}_i\text{GDPPC}_j\right) \\ \text{ETHNIC56}_{ij} + \alpha_5\text{PD} + \sum_{k=1}^{37}\beta_k\text{ETHNIC}_{ijk}\end{aligned} \tag{E.3}$$

In Eq. (E.3), ethnicity variable is now entered into the gravity model linearly and also as a product with the natural log of per capita GDPs. Thus, the effect of an ethnic group on interprovincial trade is now allowed to exist separately and to depend on the income levels of trading partners, measured by the natural log of their per capita GDPs. As a matter of fact, since ETHNIC56*ij* can be written as Ethnicij_1+Ethnicij_2+ …+ Ethnic*ijk* +…+Ethnicij_{56}, the non-linear effects of some, if not all ethnic variables on interprovincial trade may be derived from Eq. (E.3).

Specifically, as for the *k*th ethnic group (*k* = 1, 2, …, 37), if the estimated coefficients on Ethnic*ijk* (that is, βk) and on ln(GDPPC*i*GDPPC*j*) ETHNIC56*ij* (that is, α_4) have different signs (such as $\alpha_4 < 0$ and $\beta k > 0$; or $\alpha_4 > 0$ and $\beta k < 0$) and are statistically significant in Eq. (E.3), one obtains a threshold value (ln(GDPPC*i*GDPPC*j*)**k*) by letting the first-order differential of the dependent variable (ln(TRADE*ij*) with respect to Ethnic*ijk* be zero, that is:

$$\ln\left(\text{GDPPC}_i\text{GDPPC}_j\right)^*_k = -\beta_k / \alpha_4 > 0\left(\text{with}\alpha_4 \langle 0\text{and}\beta_k \rangle 0;\right. \\ \left.\text{or}\ \alpha_4 > 0\text{and}\beta_k < 0\right). \tag{E.4}$$

As for the case of $\alpha_4 < 0$ and $\beta k > 0$:

1. If ln(GDPPC*i*GDPPC*j*)*k* is smaller than ln(GDPPC*i*GDPPC*j*)**k*, the *k*th ethnic group has a positive effect on the trade between the *i*th and *j*th provinces;
2. If ln(GDPPC*i*GDPPC*j*)*k* is larger than ln(GDPPC*i*GDPPC*j*)**k*, the *k*th ethnic group has a negative effect on the trade between the *i*th and *j*th provinces.

The Data

The major task of this paper is to quantitatively investigate the sources for changes in China's spatial economic integration over time. Thus, the use of the cross-sectional data from China' s provincial economies in different years enables that the estimated results are not artifact of any particular time period and to allow for changes in coefficients. Generally, a decade-long period is appropriate for this kind of research because analysis for a shorter period would not reflect relevant social and economic changes, while significant changes in transportation and communication technologies would have to be accounted for if a longer one is used. Of course, a longer period is still more helpful if three or more sets of cross-sectional data are available. However, this would increase inevitably the costs in data collection. In this paper, after taking into account data availability, we select two years—2000 and 2010.

The data on interprovincial trade are cited from *China Communications Yearbooks* (2000 and 2010).[23] China's 2000 and 2010 provincial GDP and per capita GDP data are from *China Statistical Yearbooks*. Unlike those of many Western democratic economies, China's provincial capitals usually are also the economic centers of their respective provinces. To this end, the following terms are used to express China's interprovincial geographical proximity: "distance between capitals" and "interprovincial adjacency". "Distance between capitals" is represented by the distance (in kilometers) between two provinces' capitals via national railway. The data on "distance between capitals" are calculated by the author based on the data released by the Ministry of Railways of the PRC).

In this paper, a comprehensive method is used to construct interprovincial ethnic linkages. Suppose that there are *k* ethnic groups in both provinces *i* and *j*. If the *i*th and *j*th provinces' population shares for the *k*th ethnic group are expressed by *xk* (it ranges between 0 and 1) and *yk* (it ranges between 0 and 1), respectively, the *k*th ethnic group's linkage index between provinces *i* and *j* can be measured by the following formula:

$$\text{ETHNIC}_{ijk} = \min\left(x_k, y_k\right), \text{where}\, x_k \in \left(0,1\right) \text{and}\, y_k \in \left(0,1\right). \quad \text{(E.5)}$$

In Eq. (E.5), min (•) denotes the minimization of the variables within parentheses. The data on the population shares (*xk* and *yk*) are calculated by the author based on the data released by the Fifth and Sixth National Population Census of the PRC (conducted at 0:00 a.m. on November 1 of 2000 and 2010, respectively).

Since there are 56 ethnic groups in China, the overall ethnic linkage between provinces *i* and *j* can be measured by the following formula:

$$\begin{aligned}\text{ETHNIC56}_{ij} &= \text{ETHNIC}_{ij1} + \text{ETHNIC}_{ij2} + \ldots + \text{ETHNIC}_{ij56} \\ &= \sum_{k=1}^{56} \min\left(x_k, y_k\right)\end{aligned} \tag{E.6}$$

In Eq. (E.6), min (•) denotes the minimization of the variables within parentheses. For all *k*, $xk \in (0,\ 1)$, $yk \in (0,\ 1)$, and $\sum xk = \sum yk = 1$. Consequently, ETHNIC56*ij* ranges between 0 and 1. In the extreme cases, when ETHNIC56*ij* = 1, provinces *i* and *j* have a common ethnic structure (i.e., for all *k*, *xk* = *yk*); when ETHNIC56*ij* = 0, the two provinces do not have any ethnic linkage with each other (i.e., for all *k*, *xk* (or *yk*) = 0). In other words, greater values of ETHNIC56*ij* indicate greater degrees of ethnic linkages between the two provinces.[24]

A brief statistical description of selected variables included in Eqs. (E.1), (E.2) and (E.3) is given in Table E.2a (for 2000) and Table E.2b (for 2010). The largest numbers of observations (i.e., interprovincial samples) are 465 for both 2000 and 2010. However, because the data on interprovincial trade are unavailable for the two provinces of Hainan and Tibet (including 59 province pairs) from 2000 as well as for 13 province pairs (i.e., Beijing-Hainan, Guizhou-Tibet, Hainan-Heilongjiang, Hainan-Jilin, Hainan-Liaoning, Hainan-Ningxia, Hainan-Shanghai, Hainan-Tianjin, Hainan-Tibet, Hainan-Xinjiang, Jilin-Tibet, Ningxia-Tibet, and Tibet-Yunnan) from 2010, the total numbers of observations that can be actually used for our regressions are reduced to 406 (i.e., 465–59 = 406) for 2000 and 452 (i.e., 465–13 = 452) for 2010 accordingly.

The Estimation Results

The gravity models constructed in section "Analytical Framework" can be tested by using the data described in section "The Data". We first run Eq. (E.1) by using both the data of 2000 and 2010 (the estimated results are

Table E.2a Descriptive statistics for the data on selected variables, 2000

Variable	*N*	Minimum	Maximum	Mean	SD
ln(TRADE*ij*)	406	2.99573	11.59910	6.84499	1.36932
ln(GDP*i*GDP*j*)	465	5.73532	13.62832	10.70744	1.43231
ln(GDPPC*i*GDPPC*j*)	465	16.19674	20.00507	17.70224	0.69716
ln(DISTANCE*ij*)	465	4.91998	8.75037	7.47203	0.64053
ETHNIC56*ij*	465	0.06160	0.99930	0.75563	0.24827
k = 1. Bai	465	0.00001	0.00532	0.00004	0.00028
k = 2. Blang	465	0.00000	0.00001	0.00000	0.00000
k = 3. Buyi	465	0.00001	0.00129	0.00005	0.00008
k = 4. Dai	465	0.00000	0.00008	0.00000	0.00001
k = 5. Daur	465	0.00000	0.00120	0.00001	0.00006
k = 6. Dong	465	0.00001	0.01331	0.00011	0.00077
k = 7. Dongxiang	465	0.00000	0.00303	0.00001	0.00015
k = 8. Gelao	465	0.00000	0.00009	0.00001	0.00001
k = 9. Han	465	0.06061	0.99682	0.74690	0.25065
k = 10. Hani	465	0.00000	0.00003	0.00001	0.00001
k = 11. Hui	465	0.00025	0.15621	0.00371	0.00904
k = 12. Jingpo	465	0.00000	0.00001	0.00000	0.00000
k = 13. Kazak	465	0.00000	0.00012	0.00000	0.00001
k = 14. Kirgiz	465	0.00000	0.00004	0.00000	0.00000
k = 15. Korean	465	0.00002	0.01072	0.00013	0.00064
k = 16. Lahu	465	0.00000	0.00002	0.00000	0.00000
k = 17. Li	465	0.00000	0.00159	0.00001	0.00007
k = 18. Lisu	465	0.00000	0.00023	0.00000	0.00001
k = 19. Manchu	465	0.00006	0.03705	0.00118	0.00443
k = 20. Maonan	465	0.00000	0.00089	0.00000	0.00004
k = 21. Miao	465	0.00004	0.03037	0.00069	0.00280
k = 22. Mongol	465	0.00008	0.01789	0.00064	0.00164
k = 23. Mulao	465	0.00000	0.00081	0.00000	0.00004
k = 24. Naxi	465	0.00000	0.00047	0.00000	0.00002
k = 25. Qiang	465	0.00000	0.00004	0.00000	0.00000
k = 26. Salar	465	0.00000	0.00047	0.00000	0.00003
k = 27. She	465	0.00000	0.00372	0.00004	0.00024
k = 28. Shui	465	0.00000	0.00035	0.00001	0.00003
k = 29. Tibetan	465	0.00002	0.22530	0.00074	0.01057
k = 30. Tu	465	0.00000	0.00121	0.00002	0.00006
k = 31. Tujia	465	0.00003	0.04172	0.00066	0.00438
k = 32. Uygur	465	0.00002	0.00027	0.00004	0.00002
k = 33. Va	465	0.00000	0.00005	0.00000	0.00000
k = 34. Xibe	465	0.00000	0.00187	0.00001	0.00009
k = 35. Yao	465	0.00000	0.01114	0.00009	0.00064
k = 36. Yi	465	0.00002	0.02577	0.00022	0.00196
k = 37. Zhuang	465	0.00005	0.02701	0.00025	0.00142

Notes: *N* = number of observations; and SD = standard deviation. Definitions of the variables shown in this Table E.are given in section "The Model"

Table E.2b Descriptive statistics for the data on selected variables, 2010

Variable	*N*	Minimum	Maximum	Mean	SD
ln(TRADE*ij*)	452	2.30259	12.62984	6.95446	1.76181
ln(GDP*i*GDP*j*)	465	8.83243	16.76316	13.75672	1.38476
ln(GDPPC*i*GDPPC*j*)	465	19.15152	22.40275	20.60043	0.62203
ln(DISTANCE*ij*)	465	4.91998	8.75037	7.47203	0.64053
ETHNIC56*ij*	465	0.08280	0.99870	0.75979	0.24414
$k = 1$. Bai	465	0.00000	0.00526	0.00005	0.00027
$k = 2$. Blang	465	0.00000	0.00016	0.00000	0.00001
$k = 3$. Buyi	465	0.00001	0.00231	0.00007	0.00016
$k = 4$. Dai	465	0.00000	0.00011	0.00001	0.00002
$k = 5$. Daur	465	0.00000	0.00105	0.00001	0.00005
$k = 6$. Dong	465	0.00001	0.01301	0.00013	0.00076
$k = 7$. Dongxiang	465	0.00000	0.00282	0.00002	0.00015
$k = 8$. Gelao	465	0.00000	0.00033	0.00001	0.00003
$k = 9$. Han	465	0.08176	0.99660	0.75070	0.24660
$k = 10$. Hani	465	0.00000	0.00014	0.00001	0.00001
$k = 11$. Hui	465	0.00020	0.14827	0.00356	0.00865
$k = 12$. Jingpo	465	0.00000	0.00002	0.00000	0.00000
$k = 13$. Kazak	465	0.00000	0.00071	0.00002	0.00004
$k = 14$. Kirgiz	465	0.00000	0.00089	0.00000	0.00004
$k = 15$. Korean	465	0.00001	0.00856	0.00013	0.00058
$k = 16$. Lahu	465	0.00000	0.00003	0.00000	0.00000
$k = 17$. Li	465	0.00001	0.00396	0.00003	0.00018
$k = 18$. Lisu	465	0.00000	0.00026	0.00001	0.00001
$k = 19$. Manchu	465	0.00011	0.03156	0.00111	0.00378
$k = 20$. Maonan	465	0.00000	0.00080	0.00000	0.00004
$k = 21$. Miao	465	0.00005	0.03136	0.00088	0.00296
$k = 22$. Mongol	465	0.00005	0.01774	0.00056	0.00157
$k = 23$. Mulao	465	0.00000	0.00073	0.00001	0.00003
$k = 24$. Naxi	465	0.00000	0.00038	0.00000	0.00002
$k = 25$. Qiang	465	0.00000	0.00005	0.00001	0.00001
$k = 26$. Salar	465	0.00000	0.00053	0.00001	0.00003
$k = 27$. She	465	0.00000	0.00306	0.00004	0.00021
$k = 28$. Shui	465	0.00000	0.00029	0.00001	0.00003
$k = 29$. Tibetan	465	0.00002	0.24438	0.00080	0.01149
$k = 30$. Tu	465	0.00000	0.00120	0.00003	0.00007
$k = 31$. Tujia	465	0.00006	0.04210	0.00079	0.00438
$k = 32$. Uygur	465	0.00001	0.00036	0.00004	0.00003
$k = 33$. Va	465	0.00000	0.00006	0.00001	0.00001
$k = 34$. Xibe	465	0.00000	0.00158	0.00001	0.00008
$k = 35$. Yao	465	0.00001	0.01086	0.00011	0.00064
$k = 36$. Yi	465	0.00002	0.03288	0.00027	0.00220
$k = 37$. Zhuang	465	0.00005	0.02644	0.00031	0.00141

Notes: *N* = number of observations; and SD = standard deviation. Definitions of the variables shown in this Table E.are given in section "The Model"

Table E.3 Basic regressions—56 ethnic groups as a single variable, 2000 and 2010

Explanatory variable	Coefficient in 2000	Coefficient in 2010
Constant	14.461[a] (1.462)	29.057[a] (2.447)
ln(GDP*i*GDP*j*)	0.647[a] (0.046)	0.759[a] (0.063)
ln(GDPPC*i*GDPPC*j*)	−0.253[a] (0.072)	−1.041[a] (0.108)
ln(DISTANCE*ij*)	−1.212[a] (0.097)	−1.377[a] (0.127)
ADJACENT*ij*	0.504[a] (0.149)	0.579[a] (0.196)
ETHNIC56*ij*	−1.560[a] (0.324)	−1.393[a] (0.367)
PD	−0.350[a] (0.099)	−0.521[a] (0.134)
Coefficient of correlation (R^2)	0.644	0.586
Standard error of regression	0.823	1.141
F-statistic	120.556	104.786
Sig. of regression	0.000	0.000
Number of observations	405	451

Notes: Dependent variable is the natural log of interprovincial trade. Figures within parentheses are standard errors. "a" denotes statistically significant at greater than the 1% level

shown in the second and third columns of Table E.3, respectively) and the pooled data (the estimated results are shown in Table E.4 in which the year-fixed effects on trade are also included in regression shown in the third column).

Early comparative studies, using the international panel data of China and East Asia, show that geographical influence on international trade was reduced from the 1980s to 1990s.[25] One of the major driving forces contributing to this tendency might be technological advance in transportation and communications. Intuitively, wide application of E-commerce and the declining of distance-related transactions costs have increasingly contributed to the growth of international trade. However, in this paper, the negative effect of "distance" on interprovincial trade is found to rise from 2000 to 2010. Obviously, this doesn't reflect China's improvement of transport infrastructures; neither does it conform to the general pattern of international trade. The main cause of China's interprovincial trade barriers may be the market-segmenting behavior that the Chinese provinces carry on in order to maintain social stability and maximize fiscal incomes.[26] Undoubtedly, our finding shows a sign of China's spatial economic disintegration during the first decade of the twenty-first century.

Table E.4 Regressions based on pooled data—56 ethnic groups as a single variable

Explanatory variable	Coefficient (excl. year-fixed effects)	Coefficient (incl. year-fixed effects)
Constant	30.733[a] (1.840)	30.764[a] (1.839)
ln(GDP*i*GDP*j*)	0.865[a] (0.047)	0.862[a] (0.047)
ln(GDPPC*i*GDPPC*j*)	−1.131[a] (0.081)	−1.129[a] (0.081)
ln(DISTANCE*ij*)	−1.486[a] (0.095)	−1.450[a] (0.097)
ln(DISTANCE*ij*) in 2010	–	−0.064[b] (0.031)
ADJACENT*ij*	0.429[a] (0.148)	0.466[a] (0.190)
ADJACENT*ij* in 2010	–	−0.065 (0.236)
ETHNIC56*ij*	−1.694[a] (0.274)	−1.939[a] (0.313)
ETHNIC56*ij* in 2010	–	0.487[c] (0.298)
PD	−0.587[a] (0.102)	−0.587[a] (0.101)
Coefficient of correlation (R^2)	0.598	0.600
Standard error of regression	1.229	1.228
F-statistic	225.620	151.267
Sig. of regression	0.000	0.000
Number of observations	856	856

Notes: Dependent variable is the natural log of interprovincial trade. Figures within parentheses are standard errors. "[a]", "[b]" and "[c]" denotes statistically significant at greater than the 1%, 5% and 10% levels, respectively

The estimated coefficients on "ADJACENT", which are statistically significant, slightly increase from 2000 to 2010 (see Table E.3). However, the year-fixed effect derived from the regression based on the pooled data (see the third column of Table E.4) does not show any statistical significance for this kind of increase.

The estimated coefficients on "ETHNIC56" are statistically significant for 2000 and 2010. However, they are negative, suggesting that the interprovincial links of 56 ethnic groups as a whole have only but impeded China's interprovincial economic activities. Obviously, this provides no evidence that supports the widely recognizable view that ethnic linkage index tends to encourage trade between provinces that are multi-ethnically linked. In fact, since the partial correlation between the natural log of TRADE and the ETHNIC56 scores yields an inverted-U shape curve for 2010 (see Fig. E.1), the above estimated coefficients on ETHNIC56 may be misleading (at least for 2010).

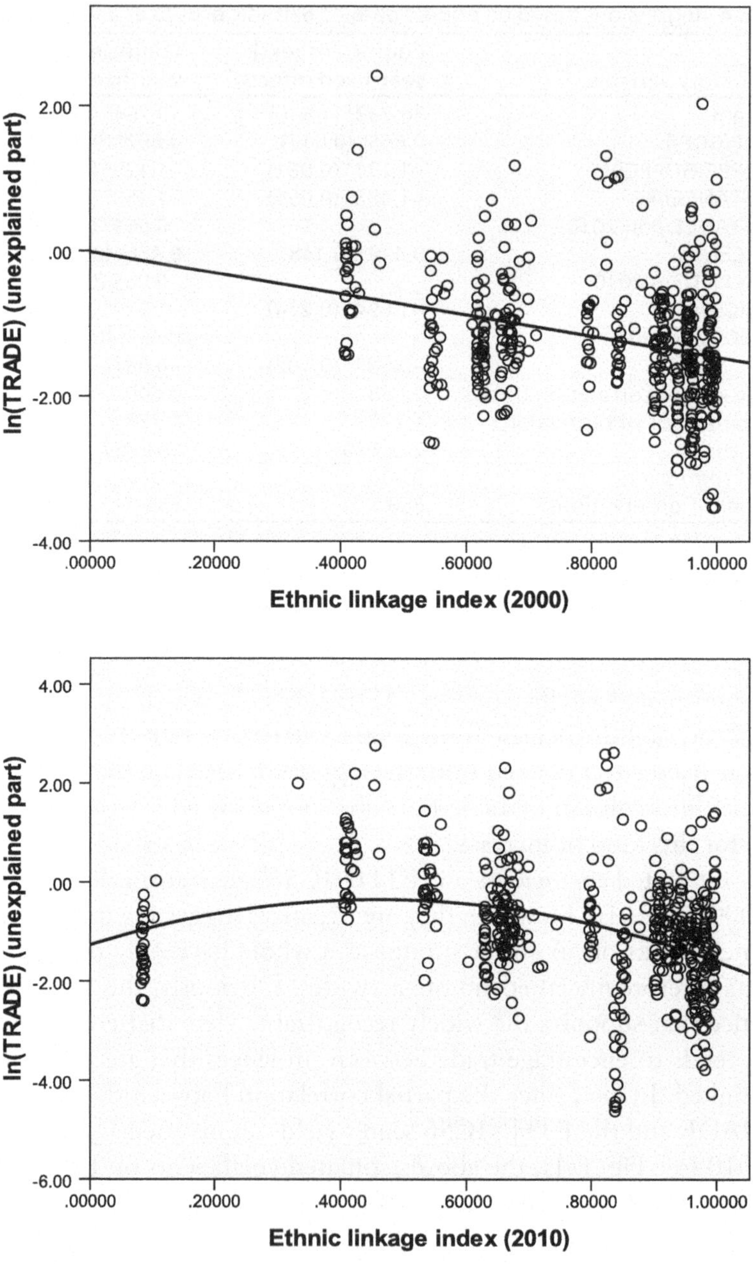

Fig. E.1 Partial correlations between trade and ethnic linkage, 2000 and 2010. (Sources: Table E.5 for the estimated coefficients (2010) and Annex for ethnic population)

Let us now run Eq. (E.2) constructed in section "Analytical Framework". In China's Fifth National Population Census conducted in November 2000, only permanent populations were counted (whereas in 2010, those who had stayed at their current residences for six months or longer were also counted). This could affect the final estimated coefficients in 2000 (remember that the "floating" populations may sometimes play more important roles in interprovincial marketing and trade than permanent residents). To this end, we will not use the pooled data of 2000 and 2010; instead, we will only run regressions based on the data of 2000 and 2010, respectively. The estimated results shown in Table E.5 are derived by excluding the variables whose VIFs (variance inflation factors) exceed 10 (a value that is often regarded as indicating multicollinearity). These results, compared with those shown in Tables E.3 and E.4, can help us to better explain the diverse ethnic influences on interprovincial trade:

Table E.5 The estimated coefficients on the ethnic variables defined in Eq. (E.2)

	2000		2010	
Explanatory variable	Coefficient	Standard error	Coefficient	Standard error
1. Bai			−192.637	341.756
2. Blang	−114,466.708	83,123.810	−36,909.300[b]	17,153.46
3. Buyi	−1989.870[c]	1044.715	767.807	753.124
4. Dai	−17,883.500	14,948.590	−16,349.312[a]	5046.068
5. Daur	1432.134[b]	656.009	2586.816[a]	951.629
6. Dong	48.212	69.223	68.102	91.598
7. Dongxiang	1284.739[a]	488.076	1515.314[a]	433.379
8. Gelao	27,798.940[a]	9578.905	−4593.947	4339.398
9. Han	−1.350[a]	0.319	−1.421[a]	0.359
10. Hani	−24,297.300[b]	11,902.110	−1843.340	8839.561
11. Hui	10.359[b]	4.765	13.374[b]	6.508
12. Jingpo	245,643.800[a]	75,461.210	60,181.957[a]	33,170.5
13. Kazak	-9719.600	11,494.670	−10,010.414[a]	3264.211
14. Kirgiz	−17,486.600	19,645.340	5896.574[b]	2606.726
15. Korean	-44.290	70.080	-91.085	103.646
16. Lahu	1913.425	34,644.910	69,627.249[a]	27,110.080
17. Li	−25,132.900[a]	9002.619	−249.689	262.76
18. Lisu	8126.747	6308.788	7117.415	7282.878
19. Manchu	52.555[a]	11.183	48.142[a]	17.541
20. Maonan	2042.121[c]	1088.550	4115.362[b]	1693.773
21. Miao	2.001	23.957	-7.926	34.356

(continued)

Table E.5 (continued)

	2000		2010	
Explanatory variable	Coefficient	Standard error	Coefficient	Standard error
22. Mongol	35.200	26.217	132.086[a]	36.313
23. Mulao				
24. Naxi			−2385.250	8354.333
25. Qiang	4665.429	16,645.120	35,288.611[a]	12,540.510
26. Salar				
27. She	58.482	152.286	452.580[c]	245.120
28. Shui			−4178.755	2932.771
29. Tibetan	45.738	35.168	9.441[b]	4.825
30. Tu	−415.235	1047.778	3469.553[c]	2133.557
30. Tujia	−8.852	11.024	−8.700	14.283
31. Uygur	1081.944	2407.569	1386.841	1977.202
32. Va	12,915.170	13,274.480	−42,682.902[a]	11,427.990
33. Xibe	−65.376	411.421	−194.667	660.486
34. Yao	21.566	75.760	80.423	101.235
35. Yi	9.209	36.782	−4.697	40.519
36. Zhuang	45.252	33.230	98.107[b]	42.746
Coefficient of correlation (R^2)	0.745		0.645	
Standard error of regression	0.725		1.095	
F-statistic	29.877		20.337	
Sig. of regression	0.000		0.000	
Number of observations	405		451	

Notes: Only the coefficients on ethnic variables are included in this table. The ethnic variables whose variance inflation factors (VIFs) are larger than 10 are omitted from regressions. "a", "b" and "c" denote statistically significant at greater than the 1%, 5% and 10% levels, respectively

- As for 2000, seven ethnic groups (Jingpo, Gelao, Manchu, Hui, Dongxiang, Daur, and Maonan) have positive effects; four ethnic groups (Han, Li, Hani, and Buyi) have negative effects on interprovincial trade; and 26 ethnic variables (Bai, Blang, Dai, Dong, Kazak, Kirgiz, Korean, Lahu, Lisu, Miao, Mongol, Mulao, Naxi, Qiang, Salar, She, Shui, Tibetan, Tu, Tujia, Uygur, Va, Xibe, Yao, Yi, and Zhuang) are not found to have any significant influences on trade.

- As for 2010, 14 ethnic groups (Lahu, Qiang, Jingpo, Tu, Mongol, Manchu, Hui, Zhuang, Dongxiang, Daur, Kirgiz, She, Maonan, and Tibetan) have positive effects on interprovincial trade; five ethnic groups (Han, Va, Kazak, Dai, and Blang) have negative effects; and 18 ethnic variables (Bai, Buyi, Dong, Gelao, Hani, Korean, Li, Lisu, Miao, Mulao, Naxi, Salar, Shui, Tujia, Uygur, Xibe, Yao, and Yi) are not found to have any significant influences on trade.

Remember that there is a negative relationship between China's interprovincial ethnic links and trade, which can be witnessed by the negative coefficients on ETHNIC56 in Tables E.3 and E.4. Then why there are fewer ethnic groups with negative influences on interprovincial trade than those with positive influences? This may plausibly stem from the very fact that the Han majority whose estimated coefficients are negative for both 2000 and 2010 (see Table E.5) has a much larger weight than any other ethnic minorities.

Using the estimated coefficients reported in Table E.5, one may calculate each ethnic group's contribution to interprovincial trade (the results are reported in Table E.6). Here take the Hui ethnic group as an example. As shown in Table E.2b, the minimum, maximum and mean values of interprovincial ethnic links—represented by $\text{ETHNIC}ij_{11}$ in Eq. (E.2)—are 0.00020 (i.e., the one for Jiangxi and Zhejiang), 0.14827 (i.e., the one for Ningxia and Qinghai) and 0.00356, respectively, in 2010. Given that the estimated coefficient on $\text{ETHNIC}ij_{11}$ is 13.374 (shown in Table E.5), the Hui's contribution to interprovincial trade in 2010 ranges from 0.268 (that is, exp.(0.00020 × 13.374) × 100–100) percent to 626.423 (that is, exp.(0.14827 × 13.374) × 100–100) percent, with the mean value being 4.876 (that is, exp.(0.00356 × 13.374) × 100–100) percent.

It must be noted that the estimated coefficients on some important ethnic minorities—such as Miao, Tibet, Uygur, Xibe, Yao, Yi and Zhuang—are statistically insignificant in either 2000 or 2010 (see Table E.5). Technically, if an ethnic group is not found to exert any significant influences on China's interprovincial trade, it may have, subject to different economic conditions, both positive and negative effects on the trade of different groups of provinces. In order to test this kind of non-linear

Table E.6 Quantifying the ethnic groups' contributions to interprovincial trade (%)

	2000			2010		
Ethnic group	Minimum value	Maximum value	Mean value	Minimum value	Maximum value	Mean value
1. Bai						
2. Blang				0.000	−99.734	−2.643
3. Buyi	−2.057	−98.996	−12.583			
4. Dai				−3.191	−83.380	−18.414
5. Daur	0.085	350.646	1.170	0.154	1417.056	2.123
6. Dong						
7. Dongxiang	0.047	3668.286	2.256	0.056	7127.996	2.666
8. Gelao	6.748	882,465.122	51.102			
9. Han	−10.450	−73.957	−63.703	−10.968	−75.736	−65.587
10. Hani	−6.241	−96.533	−22.619			
11. Hui	0.207	364.588	3.762	0.268	626.423	4.876
12. Jingpo	0.000	6032.297	53.249	0.000	174.133	11.025
13. Kazak				−4.219	−99.922	−22.057
14. Kirgiz				0.035	19,224.296	1.813
15. Korean						
16. Lahu				2.019	737.508	28.358
17. Li	−19.574	−10.000	−57.647			
18. Lisu						
19. Manchu	0.584	425.169	5.992	0.535	356.895	5.475
20. Maonan	0.027	412.995	0.697	0.054	2598.034	1.410
21. Miao						
22. Mongol				0.626	941.393	7.657
23. Mulao						
24. Naxi						

25. Qiang	3.181	425.512	28.270
26. Salar			
27. She	0.096	298.641	1.680
28. Shui			
29. Tibetan	0.015	904.629	0.759
30. Tu	0.919	6409.243	10.314
30. Tujia			
31. Uygur			
32. Va	−6.882	−91.864	−37.559
33. Xibe			
34. Yao			
35. Yi			
36. Zhuang	0.531	1238.236	3.037

Notes: Figures in each row, which are calculated based on Tables E.2 and E.5, represent percentages by which provinces that are linked by the left-side ethnic group would increase (or decrease if the figures are negative) bilateral trade as opposed to those that are not linked by the same ethnic group. Blank denotes unavailability since either the ethnic variables are omitted from the regressions or the estimated coefficients are statistically insignificant in Table E.5

effects, let us run Eq. (E.3). Since, as mentioned earlier, the quality of 2000s ethnic data is less reliable than that of 2010s, we only test the regression by using 2010s data. Unfortunately, we cannot derive more encouraging results (the estimated coefficients are not reported here).

Nevertheless, we do find that some ethnic groups (such as the Hui, the Mancu, the Mongol and the Zhuang) have some non-linear influences on interprovincial trade. Specifically, the above regression yields not only positive coefficients on these ethnic minorities (i.e., $\beta k > 0$) but also a negative coefficient (i.e., $\alpha_4 < 0$) on the interaction of ETHNIC56 and the income levels of trading partners (measured by the natural log of their per capita GDPs). However, since the threshold value—i.e., ln(GDPPC*i* GDPPC*j*)$^*k$ defined in Eq. (E.4)—is extremely large, the fundamental changes of these ethnic groups' positive effects on interprovincial trade will not occur in the near future.

Policy and Analytical Implications

During the past decades, along with the gradual reform in the decentralization of authority (that is, transferring economic management and decision making from the central government to provincial and local governments), China's interprovincial relations have been transformed accordingly. Naturally, the examination of the driving forces to the causes and consequences of interprovincial economic (dis)integration in China is an important taskforce not only to economists but also to policymakers who have concerns about their internal spatial economic efficiencies.

It has been found that ethnic Chinese (mainly encompassing the Han ethnic Chinese) networks play an important role in international trade. Rauch and Trindade, for example, find that ethnic Chinese networks have a quantitatively important impact on bilateral trade through the mechanisms of market information and matching and referral services, in addition to their effect through community enforcement of sanctions that deter opportunistic behavior. Their estimated results show that for trade between countries with ethnic Chinese population shares at the levels prevailing in Southeast Asia, the smallest estimated average increase in bilateral trade in differentiated products attribuTable E.to ethnic Chinese networks is nearly 60 percent.[27]

However, in this paper, we have not found any evidence that supports that the Han majority has played positive roles in China's interprovincial trade. Although it seems that more in-depth investigation is still needed, we believe that our small and negative coefficients on the Han (see Table E.5) stem from the very fact that the Han majority accounts for more than 90% of China's total population (more than 1.3 billion). A large population per se also implies a great degree of diversity or dissimilarity of its members (Alesina and Spolarore 1997, p. 1029). As a result, a common standard cannot be fully realized among different provinces' Han people in China.

To develop this argument further, let us assume that China's domestic trade can be divided into interprovincial and intra-provincial trade, on the one hand, and interethnic and intra-ethnic trade, on the other hand. Obviously, according to the cost of transactions, intra-provincial trade is always preferable to interprovincial trade and intra-ethnic trade is preferable to interethnic trade. Therefore, ceteris paribus, the intra-provincial and intra-ethnic trade is always more profiTable E.than the interprovincial and interethnic trade. If the population of an ethnic group is very small, then the intra-provincial and intra-ethnic trade is not able meet the demand of economic growth. As a result, the interprovincial and intra-ethnic and intra-provincial and interethnic trade may still be needed. In this case, the interprovincial and intra-ethnic trade is preferable to the intra-provincial and interethnic trade if interprovincial transactions cost is lower than interethnic transactions cost, and vice versa. Fig. E.2, in which smaller ethnic groups have greater (in both positive and negative directions) effects on interprovincial trade, has provided evidence that small ethnic groups are always more important in promoting interprovincial trade than large ethnic groups.

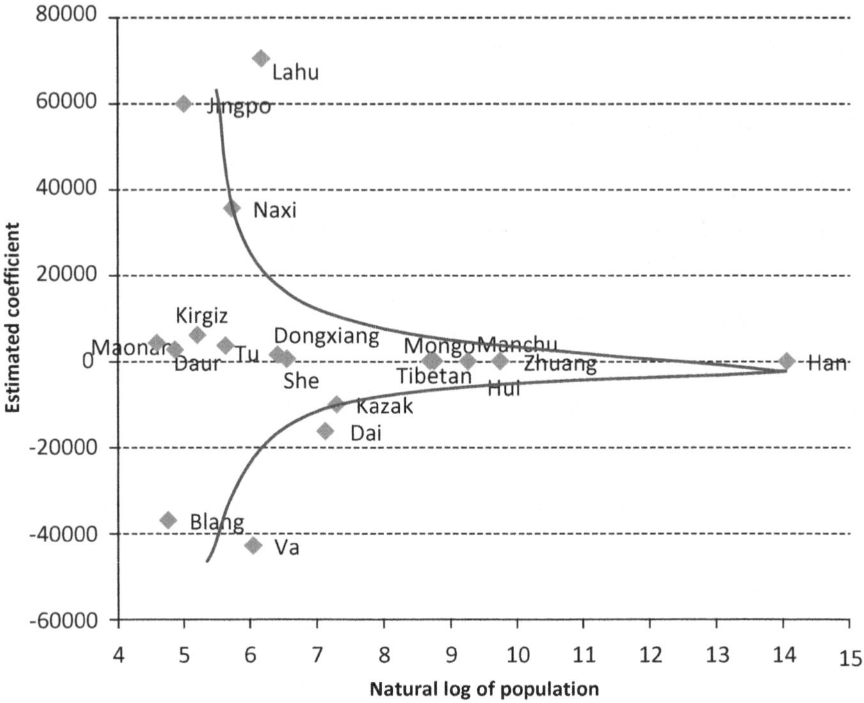

Fig. E.2 Ethnic influence on interprovincial trade decreases with the size of ethnic population

We need to clarify the inherent forces behind the differing influences of all the ethnic minorities on China's spatial economic (dis)integration. The Han-Uyghur unrest in and outside Xinjiang would have been responsible for the Uyghurs' insignificant effects on interprovincial trade. In addition, Tibetans' positive influences on interprovincial trade in 2010 has benefited from the Qinghai-Tibet Railway which went into operation in 2006. With the operation of the Qinghai–Tibet railway, the costs of transportation of both passengers and goods should be greatly reduced, allowing for an increase in volume—the costs per ton-kilometer will be reduced from 0.38 yuan to 0.12 yuan.[28] As a result, more commodities will be carried to and from Tibet by the railway.

Since China adopted different approaches when conducting the population census in 2000 and 2010, our ethnic data may not be comparable from 2000 to 2010. Therefore, cares should be taken when the changes of ethnic influences on interprovincial trade from 2000 to 2010 are to be clarified. But our estimated coefficients for 2010 seem to be more reliable than those for 2000 (shown in Table E.5). If the 2010s results shown in Table E.6 are correct, we may conclude that 14 ethnic groups (Lahu, Qiang, Jingpo, Tu, Mongol, Manchu, Hui, Zhuang, Dongxiang, Daur, Kirgiz, She, Maonan, and Tibetan) tend to contribute to China's interprovincial trade, that five ethnic groups (Han, Va, Kazak, Dai, and Blang) tend to retard China's interprovincial trade. These findings will be useful for policy-makers to reappraise which of China's ethnic groups are playing the most (least) important roles in, and to introduce the optimal informal institutions into, the promotion of interprovincial economic cooperation in China.

It must be noted that interprovincial trade may also foster the interprovincial migration of ethnic groups in China, raising an issue of potential endogeneity in the analysis of ethnic influences on interprovincial trade in this paper. However, since our ethnic data only include permanent populations and that most, if not all, seasonable, short-stay migrants have only been officially defined as the "floating populations" (liudong renkou), this kind of potential endogeneity problem does not render the estimated results biased and inconsistent.

In order to overcome the problems with multicollinearity, we have omitted a number of ethnic groups from our regressions. The general rule of thumb is that VIF (variance inflation factor) exceeding 4 warrant further investigation, while those exceeding 10 are signs of serious multicollinearity requiring correction.[29] In weaker models, especially in those that are not supported by large sets of data, VIF above 2.5 may also merit further investigation.[30] In this paper, we have re-run all the regressions in Table E.5 by omitting the explanatory variables with VIF exceeding 4 (the estimated results are not reported here). But we have found that the estimated results are quite sTable E.after the variables with the VIF exceeding 10 are omitted from the regressions. Thus, even though the variables with VIF exceeding 4 are included, the estimated coefficients reported in this paper are not affected by multicollinearity.

Annex: Names and Demographic Distributions of China's 56 Ethnic Groups

Name	Population (thousand persons)	Five major host provinces
Achang[a]	39.56	Yunnan, Guangdong, Henan, Shandong, Jiangsu
Bai	1933.51	Yunnan, Guizhou, Hunan, Guangdong, Zhejiang
Baonan[a]	20.07	Gansu, Qinghai, Xinjiang, Inner Mongolia, Yunnan
Blang	119.64	Yunnan, Guangdong, Shandong, Zhejiang, Chongqing
Buyi	2870.03	Guizhou, Zhejiang, Guangdong, Yunnan, Fujian
Dai	1261.31	Yunnan, Sichuan, Guangdong, Zhejiang, Shandong
Daur	131.99	Inner Mongolia, Heilongjiang, Xinjiang, Beijing, Liaoning
Deang[a]	20.56	Yunnan, Guangdong, Shandong, Zhejiang, Sichuan
Derung[a]	6.93	Yunnan, Guizhou, Henan, Guangdong, Sichuan
Dong	2879.97	Guizhou, Hunan, Guangxi, Zhejiang, Guangdong
Dongxiang	621.50	Gansu, Xinjiang, Qinghai, Ningxia, Guizhou
Ewenki[a]	30.88	Inner Mongolia, Heilongjiang, Liaoning, Beijing, Shandong
Gaoshan[a]	4.01	Henan, Fujian, Guangxi, Liaoning, Hebei
Gelao	550.75	Guizhou, Zhejiang, Guangdong, Guangxi, Yunnan
Han	1,220,844.52	Guangdong, Shandong, Henan, Jiangsu, Sichuan
Hani	1660.93	Yunnan, Guangdong, Zhejiang, Shanghai, Shandong
Hezhe[a]	5.35	Heilongjiang, Guangdong, Jilin, Beijing, Liaoning
Hui	10,586.09	Ningxia, Gansu, Xinjiang, Henan, Qinghai
Jing[a]	28.20	Guangxi, Guizhou, Yunnan, Guangdong, Jiangxi
Jingpo	147.83	Yunnan, Guangdong, Shandong, Guizhou, Jilin
Jino[a]	23.14	Yunnan, Sichuan, Chongqing, Guangdong, Jiangsu
Kazak	1462.59	Xinjiang, Henan, Guangdong, Gansu, Hunan
Kirgiz	186.71	Xinjiang, Tibet, Heilongjiang, Guangdong, Zhejiang
Korean	1830.93	Jilin, Heilongjiang, Liaoning, Shandong, Beijing
Lahu	485.97	Yunnan, Shandong, Zhejiang, Guangdong, Jiangsu
Lhoba[a]	3.68	Tibet, Guizhou, Fujian, Beijing, Liaoning
Li	1463.06	Hainan, Guizhou, Guangdong, Zhejiang, Guangxi
Lisu	702.84	Yunnan, Sichuan, Hebei, Shandong, Guangdong
Manchu	10,387.96	Liaoning, Hebei, Jilin, Heilongjiang, Inner Mongolia

(*continued*)

Name	Population (thousand persons)	Five major host provinces
Maonan	101.19	Guangxi, Guizhou, Guangdong, Zhejiang, Fujian
Miao	9426.01	Guizhou, Hunan, Yunnan, Chongqing, Guangxi
Monba[a]	10.56	Tibet, Jiangsu, Gansu, Jiangxi, Guangxi
Mongol	5981.84	Inner Mongolia, Liaoning, Hebei, Xinjiang, Jilin
Mulam	216.26	Guangxi, Guizhou, Guangdong, Zhejiang, Hunan
Naxi	326.30	Yunnan, Sichuan, Tibet, Zhejiang, Beijing
Nu[a]	37.52	Yunnan, Hainan, Guangdong, Tibet, Shandong
Oroqen[a]	8.66	Heilongjiang, Inner Mongolia, Liaoning, Beijing, Hebei
Pumi[a]	42.86	Yunnan, Sichuan, Guangdong, Shandong, Chongqing
Qiang	309.58	Sichuan, Guangdong, Guizhou, Zhejiang, Jiangsu
Russian[a]	15.39	Xinjiang, Inner Mongolia, Beijing, Heilongjiang, Shanghai
Salar	130.61	Qinghai, Gansu, Xinjiang, Shanghai, Guangdong
She	708.65	Fujian, Zhejiang, Jiangxi, Guizhou, Guangdong
Shui	411.85	Guizhou, Guangxi, Jiangsu, Zhejiang, Yunnan
Tajik[a]	51.07	Xinjiang, Zhejiang, Guangdong, Jiangxi, Shandong
Tatar[a]	3.56	Xinjiang, Guangdong, Guangxi, Beijing, Jiangsu
Tibetan	6282.19	Tibet, Sichuan, Qinghai, Gansu, Yunnan
Tu	289.57	Qinghai, Gansu, Guangdong, Yunnan, Guizhou
Tujia	8353.91	Hunan, Hubei, Guizhou, Chongqing, Zhejiang
Uygur	10,069.35	Xinjiang, Beijing, Hunan, Guangdong, Zhejiang
Uzbek[a]	5.67	Xinjiang, Zhejiang, Guangdong, Beijing, Hunan
Va	429.71	Yunnan, Shandong, Guangdong, Zhejiang, Henan
Xibe	190.48	Liaoning, Xinjiang, Heilongjiang, Jilin, Inner Mongolia
Yao	2796.00	Guangxi, Hunan, Guangdong, Yunnan, Guizhou
Yi	8714.39	Yunnan, Sichuan, Guizhou, Zhejiang, Guangdong
Yugur[a]	14.38	Gansu, Xinjiang, Qinghai, Beijing, Shandong
Zhuang	16,926.38	Guangxi, Yunnan, Guangdong, Zhejiang, Guizhou

Source: The Sixth National Population Census of the PRC (conducted at 0:00 a.m. on November 1, 2010)

Note: "[a]" denotes that ethnic groups are not analyzed as individual variables in this paper

Notes

1. The text is prepared by Rongxing Guo based on the following sources: (1) *The Ethnic Minorities in China* (title in Chinese: "zhongguo shaoshu minzu", edited by the State Ethnic Affairs Commission (SEAC) of the People's Republic of China and published in 2010 by the Central Nationality University Press, Beijing) and (2) the introductory text of China's 56 ethnic groups (in Chinese, available at http://www.seac.gov.cn/col/col107/index.html, accessed on 2016-06-20).
2. As of 2010, when the Sixth National Population Census of the People's Republic of China was conducted, the populations of the unknown ethnic groups and foreigners with Chinese citizenship were 640,101 and 1448, respectively.
3. This appendix draws heavily on the following paper: Guo, R. (2015). China's spatial (dis)integration as a multiethnic paradox: what do the interprovincial data say? China Financ. and Econ. Rev. 4, 1. https://doi.org/10.1186/s40589-015-0025-4.
4. Calculated by author based on the data released by the World Trade Organization (Available at http://www.wto.org/english/thewto_e/countries_e/china_e.htm. Accessed 2013-5-20).
5. Data sources: Rumbaugh and Blancher, China: International trade and WTO accession; and WTO, World Trade 2010, 7.
6. Note that Beijing and Shanghai's reductions of domestic trade from 2000 to 2010 are mainly due to their removals of large industrial, pollution-making plants during the above period.
7. Heckscher, The effect of foreign trade on the distribution of income, pp. 497–512; Ohlin, *Interregional and International Trade.*
8. E.g., Linder, *An Essay on Trade and Transformation*; Deardorff, Determinants of bilateral trade, p. 15.
9. E.g., Markusen, Explaining the volume of trade, pp. 1002–11; Helpman, Imperfect competition and international trade, pp. 62–81; Krugman, Growing world trade, pp. 327–62.
10. See Boisso and Ferrantino, Economic distance, cultural distance and openness in international trade, pp. 456–484; Frankel and Wei, *Regional Trading Blocs in the World Economic System.*
11. Rauch, Networks versus markets in international trade, pp. 7–35.
12. For a more detailed analysis of the distance puzzle, see Head and Disdier, The puzzling persistence of the distance effect on bilateral trade, pp. 37–48.

13. These trade barriers take a number of forms including legal and institutional differences (Anderson and Marcouiller 2002; Linders et al. 2005; Combes et al. 2005; Guiso et al. 2006), ethnic/linguistic fractionalization (Rauch 2001; Rauch and Trindade 2002; Melitz 2008; Felbermayr et al. 2010), and linguistic and religious dissimilarities (Guo 2004, 2007).
14. See, for example, Rauch and Trindade (2002); Noland (2005); Guiso et al. (2006); and Guo (2009, pp. 77–102).
15. E.g., Havrylyshyn and Pritchett (1991); Foroutan and Pritchett (1993); Frankel and Wei (1995); Frankel et al. (1997a); Rauch (1999); Guo (2007); Melitz (2008); Felbermayr et al. (2010).
16. See Linnemann, *An Econometric Study of International Trade Theory*; Tinbergen, An analysis of world trade flows; and Pöyhönen, A tentative model for the volume of trade, pp. 93–99. The earliest application of the gravity model can be traced back to the 1940s (see, e.g., Zipf, The P^1P^2/D hypothesis, pp. 677–686; Stewart, Demographic gravitation, pp. 31–58). More recent summaries can be found in Baldwin and Taglioni, Gravity for dummies and dummies for gravity equations, 1251; and Head and Mayer, Gravity equations, 9322.
17. See, e.g., of, for example, Eaton and Tamura, Bilateralism and regionalism in Japanese and U.S. trade, pp. 478–510; Frankel, Stein and Wei, Regional Trading Blocs in the World Economic System; Trading blocs and the Americas, pp. 61–69; and Rauch, ibid.
18. E.g., Feenstra, *Advanced International Trade*; Baldwin and Taglioni, ibid.; Head and Mayer, ibid.
19. Adam and Cobham, Modeling multilateral resistance in a gravity model, 12.
20. Since GDPPC equals GDP/POP (where POP is population), Eq. (E.1) can be written as $\ln(\text{TRADE}ij) = \alpha_0 + (\alpha_1 + \alpha_4)\ln(\text{GDP}i\text{GDP}j) + \alpha_2\ln\text{D ISTANCE}ij + \alpha_3\text{ADJACENT}ij - \alpha_4\ln(\text{POP}i\text{POP}j) + \alpha_5\text{PD} + \beta\text{ETHN IC56}ij$. However, we will not use this equation since the inclusion of GDP and POP—unlike that of GDP and GDPPC—can easily result in multicollinearity problems.
21. A direct measure of transport costs (instead of distance) has been suggested as a proxy for trade costs, especially for within-country studies (Combes et al. 2005). However, since we only consider the trade via national railways in our research and that the per-kilometer costs of transportation via national railways are almost fixed throughout China, these two measures are not different from each other.

22. See Guo, How culture influences foreign trade, pp. 785–812; *Intercultural Economic Analysis*, pp. 96–101.
23. They are compiled by China Association of Communications and Transportation and the National Development and Reform Commission of the PRC and published by China Communications Yearbook Press in 2001 and 2011, respectively.
24. This formula has been used in Guo, *intercultural economic analysis*, p. 89; and Noland, Affinity and international trade. Several other methods can also be used. Boisso and Ferrantino Economic distance, cultural distance and openness in international trade, pp. 456–484, for example, use $\sum xkyk$ as the construct of similarity index. However, Eq. (E.6) can prevent the index of interprovincial ethnic linkages from further reduction when the values of xk and yk are small.
25. Guo, *Linguistic and religious influences on foreign trade*, pp. 100–121; *Understanding the Chinese Economies*, p. 210.
26. Poncet, A fragmented China, pp. 409–430.
27. See Rauch and Trindade, Ethnic Chinese networks in international trade, pp. 116–130. More recently, there is an empirical work in which the Chinese network is found to lead to a modest amount of trade creation of only about 15% (see Felbermayr, Jung and Toubal, Ethnic networks, information, and international trade, pp. 41–47).
28. Cnradio, Qingzang railway transported 0.73M passengers.
29. Simon, Detecting multicollinearity, 23.
30. See Berry and Feldman, *Multiple Regression in Practice*, p. 49; Arceneaux and Huber, What to do (and not to do) with multicollinearity, pp. 81–101.

References

Adam, C. and D. Cobham (2007). Modeling multilateral resistance in a gravity model with exchange rate regimes. The Centre for Dynamic Macroeconomic Analysis, University of St Andrews. Available at www.st-andrews.ac.uk/cdma. Accessed on 2014-4-8.

Alesina, A. and E. Spolaore, 1997. On the number and size of nations. The Quarterly Journal of Economics, 112 (Nov.), pp. 1027–56.

Anderson J.E. and D. Marcouiller, 2002, Insecurity and the pattern of trade: empirical investigation. The Review of Economics and Statistics, 84, pp. 342–352.

Arceneaux, K. and G.A. Huber, 2007, What to do (and not to do) with multicollinearity in state politics research. State Politics and Policy Quarterly, 7(1), pp. 81–101.

Baldwin, R. and D. Taglioni, 2006, Gravity for dummies and dummies for gravity equations. NBER Working Paper No. 12516.

Berry, W.D. and S. Feldman, 1985, Multiple Regression in Practice. Sage Publications, London.

Bikker, J., 1987, An international trade flow model with substitution: An extension of the gravity model. Kyklos, 40, pp. 315–37.

Boisso, D. and M. Ferrantino, 1997, Economic distance, cultural distance and openness in international trade: Empirical puzzles. Journal of Economic Integration, 12, pp. 456–84.

R. Guo, *China Ethnic Statistical Yearbook 2020*,
https://doi.org/10.1007/978-3-030-49024-9

China Association of Communications and Transportation and the National Development and Reform Commission of the PRC, 2001, China Communications Yearbook 2000. China Communications Yearbook Press, Beijing.

China Association of Communications and Transportation and the National Development and Reform Commission of the PRC, 2011, China Communications Yearbook 2010. China Communications Yearbook Press, Beijing.

Cnradio, 10 November 2006, Qingzang railway transported 0.73M passengers, boosts Tibet economy (in Chinese). China National Radio (Cnradio), Beijing. Available at www.cnradio.com.cn/2004news/internal/200611/t20061110_504324840.html. Accessed 2013/4/15.

Combes, P.-P., M. Lafourcade and T. Mayer, 2005, The trade-creating effects of business and social networks: Evidence from France. Journal of International Economics, 66(1), pp. 1–29.

Deardorff, A.V., 1998, Determinants of bilateral trade: Does gravity work in a neoclassical world? In: *The Regionalization of the World Economy* (ed. Frankel J.A.), pp. 7–22. University of Chicago Press, Chicago.

Eaton, J. and A. Tamura, 1994, Bilateralism and regionalism in Japanese and U.S. trade and direct foreign investment patterns. Journal of the Japanese and International Economics, 8, pp. 478–510.

Eichengreen, B., and D. Irwin, 1995, Trade blocs, currency blocs and the reorientation of trade in the 1930s. Journal of International Economics, 38(2), pp. 89–106.

Feenstra, R.C., 2004, Advanced International Trade: Theory and Evidence. Princeton University Press, Princeton, NJ.

Feenstra, R.C., R.E. Lipsey, H. Deng, A. C. Ma and H. Mo, 2005, World trade flows: 1962–2000. NBER Working Paper No. 11040. National Bureau of Economic Research, Cambridge, MA.

Felbermayr, G., B. Jung and F. Toubal, 2010, Ethnic networks, information, and international trade: revisiting the evidence. *Annales d'Economie et de Statistique*, Issue 97–98, pp. 41–70.

Foroutan, F. and L. Pritchett, 1993, Intra-Sub-Saharan African trade: Is it too little? Journal of African Economics, 2(May), pp. 74–105.

Frankel, J.A. and S.-J. Wei, 1995, European integration and the regionalization of world trade and currencies: The economics and the politics. In: *Monetary and Fiscal Policy in an Integrated Europe* (eds Eichengreen B., Frieden F. and von Hagen J.), pp. 23–51. Springer, New York.

Frankel, J.A., E. Stein and S.-J. Wei, 1997a, Regional Trading Blocs in the World Economic System. Institute for International Economics, Washington, DC.

Frankel, J.A, E. Stein and S.-J. Wei, 1997b, Trading blocs and the Americas: The natural, the unnatural, and the super-natural. Journal of Development Economics, 47(1), pp. 61–95.

Greene, W.H., 2002, Econometric Analysis, 5th edition. Prentice-Hall, Upper Saddle River, NJ.

Guiso, L., P. Sapienza and L. Zingales (2006), Does culture affect economic outcomes? The Journal of Economic Perspectives, 20, pp. 23–48.

Guo, R., 2004, How culture influences foreign trade: Evidence from the U.S. and China. The Journal of Socio-Economics, 33, pp. 785–812.

Guo, R., 2007, Linguistic and religious influences on foreign trade: Evidence from East Asia. Asian Economic Journal, 21(1), pp. 100–21.

Guo, R., 2009, Inter*cultural Economic Analysis: Theory and Method.* Springer, New York.

Guo, R., 2013, Understanding the Chinese Economies. Academic Press/ Elsevier, Oxford.

Havrylyshyn, O. and L. Pritchett, 1991, European trade patterns after the transition. Policy, Research and External Affairs Working Paper No. 74. The World Bank, Washington, DC.

Head, K. and A. Disdier, 2008, The puzzling persistence of the distance effect on bilateral trade, Review of Economics and Statistics, 90(1), pp. 37–48.

Head, K. and T. Mayer, 2013, Gravity equations: workhorse, toolkit, and cookbook. CEPR Discussion Paper 9322.

Heckscher, E.F., 1919, The effect of foreign trade on the distribution of income. Ekonomisk Tidskrift, 21, pp. 497–512.

Helpman, E., 1987, Imperfect competition and international trade: Evidence from fourteen industrial countries. Journal of the Japanese and International Economies, 1(Mar.), pp. 62–81.

Krugman, P.R., 1995, Growing world trade: Causes and consequences. Brookings Papers on Economic Activity, 1, pp. 327–62.

Linder, S.B., 1961, An Essay on Trade and Transformation. John Wiley and Sons, New York.

Linders, G.-J.M., A. Slangen, H. de Groot, and S. Beugelsdijk (2005), Cultural and institutional determinants of bilateral trade flows, Tinbergen Institute Discussion Paper No. 074/3.

Linnemann, H., 1966, An Econometric Study of International Trade Theory. North-Holland, Amsterdam.

Markusen, J., 1986, Explaining the volume of trade: An eclectic approach. American Economic Review, 76, pp. 1002–11.
Melitz, J., 2008, Language and foreign trade. European Economic Review, 52(4), pp. 667–699.
NBS (National Bureau of Statistics), 2001, China Statistical Yearbook 2000. China Statistics Publishing House, Beijing.
NBS (National Bureau of Statistics), 2011, China Statistical Yearbook 2010. China Statistics Publishing House, Beijing.
Noland, M., 2005, Affinity and international trade. Working Paper Series WP 05-3. Institute for International Economics, Washington, DC.
Ohlin, B., 1933, Interregional and International Trade. Harvard University Press, Cambridge, MA.
Poncet, S., 2005, A fragmented China: Measure and determinants of Chinese domestic market disintegration. Review of International Economics, 13(3), pp. 409–430.
Pöyhönen, P., 1963, A tentative model for the volume of trade between countries. *Weltwir*tschaftliches Archiv, 90(1), pp. 93–9.
Rauch, J.E. and V. Trindade, 2002, Ethnic Chinese networks in international trade. Review of Economics and Statistics, 84(1), pp. 116–30.
Rauch, J.E., 1999, Networks versus markets in international trade. Journal of International Economics, 48(1), pp. 7–35.
Rauch, J.E., 2001, Business and social networks in international trade. Journal of Economic Literature, 39(4), pp. 1177–203.
Rumbaugh, T., and N. Blancher, 2004, China: International trade and WTO accession. IMF Working Paper WP/04/36, Washington, DC: International Monetary Fund (IMF).
Simon, L.J., 2004, Detecting multicollinearity using variance inflation factors. Penn State Department of Statistics, The Pennsylvania State University.
Stewart, J.Q., 1948, Demographic gravitation: Evidence and applications. Sociometry, 2, pp. 31–58.
Tinbergen, J., 1962, An analysis of world trade flows, the Linder hypothesis, and exchange risk. In: *Shaping the World Economy* (ed. Tinbergen J.). The Twentieth Century Fund, New York.
WTO, 2011, World Trade 2010, prospects for 2011 (Trade growth to ease in 2011 but despite 2010 record surge, crisis hangover persists), World Trade Organization (WTO) Press/628, 7 April. Available at: http://www.wto.org/english/news_e/pres11_e/pr628_e.htm. Accessed 2013/4/5.
Zipf, G.K., 1946, The P^1P^2/D hypothesis: On the intercity movement of persons. American Sociological Review, 11(6), pp. 677–86.

The manufacturer's authorised representative in the EU is Springer Nature Customer Service Centre GmbH, Europaplatz 3, 69115 Heidelberg, Germany. If you have any concerns regarding our products, please contact ProductSafety@springernature.com

Printed and bound by CPI Group (UK) Ltd, Croydon, CR0 4YY
25/09/2026
02222886-0002